THE
GOOD
CHURCH
GUIDE

THE
GOOD
CHURCH
GUIDE

Over 1,000 of the best churches to visit in Britain

by
David N. Durant

Illustrations by Charles Avery

VERMILION
LONDON

To Kyle, Scott, Mason and Sam

Copyright © David N. Durant 1995
Illustrations © Charles Avery 1995

David N. Durant has asserted his right to be identified as the author of this work.

Designed by Clive Dorman
Jacket designed by Patrick McCreeth

First published in the United Kingdom in 1995 by Vermilion,
an imprint of Ebury Press Limited
Random House, 20 Vauxhall Bridge Road, London SW1V 2SA

Random House Australia (Pty) Limited
20 Alfred Street, Milsons Point, Sydney
New South Wales 2061, Australia

Random House New Zealand Limited
18 Poland Road, Glenfield, Auckland 10, New Zealand

Random House South Africa (Pty) Limited
PO Box 337, Bergvlei, South Africa

Random House UK Limited Reg. No 954009

A CIP catalogue record for this book is available from the British Library

ISBN 0 09 177214 1

Typeset from author's disks by Clive Dorman & Co.

Printed in Great Britain by Clays Ltd., St Ives plc

CONTENTS

PREFACE

This is a guide book to churches and chapels, their interiors and fittings. It does not include ruined churches nor anything about the magnificence of cathedrals. The treasures of the latter are already well known and written about, and the former are omitted because they are empty and would only merit an architectural description; also, we are recommending only 1,000 churches and space is limited. We are concerned with the little known and often surprising treasures to be found in village and town churches throughout Britain. They are all worth visiting, but items of particular interest are shown in italics. Not mentioned, because they are too frequent, are the fascinating scratch dials on the south outside walls of many churches. These consist of a drilled hole for a stick and lines radiating downwards like part of a sun-dial – for that it what it is – to tell the times of Mass. These are more interesting when discovered for oneself.

Although this book is about churches, it also extends to the churchyard. Where someone well-known is buried there, he or she will be mentioned. It would be irritating, for example, to visit St Mary's church at Cholsey in Berkshire, without knowing that Agatha Christie is buried beneath a large grey stone in the west part of the graveyard.

Finally, there can be a problem of access to churches. Some churches are opened in the morning and locked at sunset. Others, due to fear of vandalism and theft, are kept locked. However, it is not difficult for the resolute visitor to make enquiries at nearby houses. Here, I make a plea that the name and address of the key holder should be displayed in the church porch – the revenue in the collection box for the church fabric will increase surprisingly.

INTRODUCTION

Astonishment would be our reaction if we could see the church interiors of the fifteenth century. They were a riot of colour: walls were covered with overall patterns; capitals, cornices and window plays were all painted, and large areas of wall depicted biblical scenes. There were screens in the chapels as well as the transepts, and there were many altars with candles burning where private masses were said for the souls of the dead. We would recognise the brightly painted rood screen but not the rood above it, for the carved figure of crucified Christ, gilded and painted, above the screen disappeared with the Reformation. The interiors of our medieval churches were suffused with what Pugin called 'a dim religious glow'.

The first violations made on church interiors came in the late fourteenth century by the anti-clerical Lollard followers of John Wycliff who attacked the authority of the papacy. The peak of destruction came in the reign of Edward VI. Images were smashed, wooden roods and statues of saints were burnt along with clerical vestments. This was the effect of early Calvinism and Puritanism after the final break with Rome by Henry VIII. His death in 1547 allowed more radical reformers, led by Archbishop Cranmer, to introduce Protestantism to England under Edward VI, resulting in the destruction of anything suggestive of Popery. In contrast to the iconoclasm of her brother's reign, Elizabeth I passed an Act to prevent the demolition of monuments and even ordered their restoration.

Another less violent influence was the change in liturgy introduced by the new prayer book of 1549. Pre-Reformation services were conducted very much for the clergy with the congregation as spectator and, except for the sermon, the service was entirely in Latin. Moreover the laity was discouraged from entering the chancel. On the other hand the nave, when not used during services, became a public hall for many secular activities. In fact the nave belonged to the congregation and the chancel to the clergy.

The new prayer book required the congregation to take a more active part in services and the chancel became less a place of religious mysteries. Archbishop Cranmer and Bishop Ridley, two of the Protestant martyrs, campaigned for the replacement of stone altars with wooden tables. By 1550 this became mandatory and communion was taken almost informally, by comparison with earlier days, around wooden tables in the chancels. This innovation had a brief set-back in

Catholic Mary's reign when the old ritual returned.

In Scotland, Protestantism was strengthened in the 1540s by a visit from Geneva of the militant Calvinist, John Knox, and reinforced on his return in 1559. In 1560 a Reformation parliament abolished papal jurisdiction and adopted a Calvinist profession of faith.

In England in that year of 1560, Elizabeth I ordered that the ten Commandments, the Creed and the Lord's Prayer should be set up on boards in the east end of every church. The following year she decreed that screens be retained but that the loft above, from where part of the service of Easter mass was conducted, be removed. The Royal Arms, signifying that the monarch was head of the church, should also be placed over the screen or elsewhere. The communion table was to be covered, but no directions were given as to where it should be placed. In some churches the table was put in the nave for the celebration of Holy Communion. Puritans recommended that its place was in the centre of the chancel where it still is at Hailes, Gloucestershire. The importance of the chancel declined and the nave and crossing were used for services.

A reaction set in during the 1630s when the high-church Archbishop Laud attempted to return ritual to services. The chancel came back into its own again when the altar was removed to the east end. To protect the altar from roaming dogs, he introduced altar rails and a number still exist. If one wishes to see a Laudian interior at its most original, the church at Staunton Harold, Leicestershire, has remained unchanged since it was built, surprisingly, during the Commonwealth (1649-60).

The new prayer book required that congregations be seated during part of the service. As most pre-Reformation churches had no seating, except in the remote South-West and East Anglia, simple benches were provided. By the mid-seventeenth century, plain benches had evolved into fixed box pews centred on the pulpit that now became the focus of services.

More iconoclasm followed the establishment of the Commonwealth. This brief interlude is too often blamed for much of the obvious damage done to our churches; in fact the worst was done in the mid-sixteenth century. By the 1640s there was little else left to smash except the glass of medieval windows.

After the Great Fire of London in 1666 and the rebuilding of City churches, supervised by Sir Christopher Wren, a form of lay-out, called by Wren 'convenient auditory', evolved. In this the seating was centred on the pulpit and, where practical, view-blocking pillars were kept out of the way. The chancel was relegated to the background.

More recently, the Oxford Movement, led by the high church John Newman (who became a Catholic in 1845), had a dramatic effect on church interiors. Between 1833 and 1845, the Tractarians (the alternative name for members of the Oxford Movement) favoured a return to pre-Reformation Catholic tradition. Cambridge, not to be left out of the excitement, founded the Camden Society in 1839. Its publication, *The Ecclesiologist,* gave Anglican clergy directions on how to 'improve' their churches by sweeping away the furnishings of the previous 300 years and focusing the service once more on chancel and altar.

The Ecclesiologists considered that the ideal style was late-thirteenth, or early-fourteenth, Gothic, with nave, aisles, chancel and porch. This would be complete with a tower or spire at the west end. Box pews were anathema – they prevented a view of the altar – and the font was placed preferably in the south-west by the south door. Chancels were raised from the nave by a step and the altar, the focus of ritual, raised from the chancel by two steps.

Few parishes were able to resist the pressure and influence of the Ecclesiologists and it is to them that we owe the interiors of the great majority of our 8,000 churches.

The reaction against this religious frenzy came with the Arts & Crafts movement in the 1860s when William Morris's glass, needlework and church furnishings were made and designed in the original medieval fashion. Morris and his followers brought back the colour to church interiors that had been stripped out over the centuries.

Modern church interiors tend to be somewhat stark due, in the main, to lack of funds to pay for decoration and to the modern trend. However, there is more to it than this. Two influences are at work: the liturgical movement begun in the 1950s and associated with the ecumenical ideal of many beliefs using the same church, and greater informality. The former usually draws the line at having the Stations of the Cross on the aisle walls and goes the other way in having nothing to offend other denominations. The latter point is respected by diocesan authorities who in general do not allow fixtures to be moved but, provided the parochial council agree, almost anything else may be done. Movable altars, rather like tea trolleys, that can be put anywhere, and movable fonts, are recent features of church fittings. The pulpit becomes superfluous in churches of vicars, unrobed, who give rousing homilies from the chancel steps. Who can say where this informality will lead?

Finally, in some churches you will see Lily Crucifixions, in glass or painted. Slender stems of the pure lily bend to support the sagging weight of the crucified Christ. This symbolism is unique to England and arises from the belief that Christ was crucified on the same day, 24 March, as the date of the Virgin's Annunciation. To give two examples where this is to be found: in glass (c.1450) in the Clopton Chapel at Long Melford, Suffolk; and painted on the ceiling (c.1390s) of the Lady Chapel of St Helen's church in Abingdon Oxfordshire.

WHAT TO LOOK FOR
IN CHURCHES

Box Pews. Boxed-in-pews with a door, to keep dogs in, sometimes with a farm name painted on the door. These date from the time when seating in churches was by subscription and most were swept away by the C19 Tractarians.

Brasses. About 8,000 monumental brasses, made between c.1250 and 1650, survive in churches in the British Isles. Brass memorials had the advantage of being less costly than stone and more endurable. They vary from representations of the full figure set in a Gothic frame to a simple chalice or heart. Monumental brasses originated from incised slabs of stone but once it was realised that more detail could be included in a brass memorial they quickly became popular from c.1200. The oldest are the thickest and most deeply engraved, and the earliest is to Sir John D'Abernon (d.1277) at Stoke d'Abernon, Surrey. The best designs came between 1330 and 1400, after which time they became smaller and had lost much of their art by 1490. Between 1500 and 1560 they are at their most numerous but are shallowly cut on thin sheets of brass and English took the place of Latin in inscriptions.

Chests. Originally used to contain the church valuables and there are quite a number of undatable medieval chests made from a dug-out log with a lid strengthened with iron bands. Chests of the C14 and C15 are usually made of planks and strengthened with iron bands. The C15 saw decoration being carved on the outside of chests, and by the C15 they were heavily reinforced with iron bands and painted.

Effigies. Portrait likenesses unlikely before C16, many alabaster figures were ready-made. Pre-Reformation effigies are shown lying with hands in prayer attitude; in C16 a kneeling position was fashionable; more relaxed after C17.

Glass, Medieval. If clean, medieval glass glows with deep colours. Unfortunately most was smashed in Edward VI's reign and during the Commonwealth. The art of creating jewel-like colours was only rediscovered in the 1860s by William Morris whose coloured glass is always worth seeking. Coloured glass is often called stained glass, a misleading term; it should be coloured glass for only yellow can be stained in glass.

Hatchments. Usually lozenge-shaped boards or canvas with arms painted on them. Originally carried at the funeral of an arms-bearing deceased replacing the more ancient practice of putting armour and arms on the coffin. After the funeral the hatchment was hung on the front of the deceased's house. Last used in the 1920s.

Helms and armour. These are found hanging high up above a tomb and were carried on the coffin at a funeral. Those placed lower have long since vanished. The practice was established in the period of medieval knighthood and only applied to males. The coffins of deceased females carried hatchments. Undertakers provided the arms and armour and most often were created for the funeral. A genuine helmet, for example, will have a mark on the back.

Maidens' Garlands. A garland carried at the funeral of a virgin and hung in the church after the service. As these are fragile and perishable it is surprising that any have survived. The best are at St Mary's, Abbotts Ann, Hampshire.

Misericords. A shelf on the underside of a hinged seat in a choir stall, giving support to a standing person when the seat is turned up. They are often deeply carved with delightful examples of contemporary life and mainly date from the C14. Usually found in cathedral and minster choirs and in formerly collegiate parish churches.

Royal Arms. In 1534 Parliament confirmed Henry VIII (1509-47) as head of the Church of England and Royal Arms appeared in churches after that date in place of the rood; many were later removed by Mary (1553-8). From 1660 it was compulsory for churches to display Royal Arms to remind the congregation that the monarch was head of the church. Some are painted boards or canvas, others are modelled in plaster, carved on wood or painted on the wall. A good carved wood arms of Charles II, for example, is at St Cuthbert's, Norham, Northumberland.

Three-Decker Pulpit. Now quite a rarity, for many were cut down by the C19 Tractarians. They comprise the pulpit with, below it, a built-in lectern, or reader's desk, and the clerk's desk

Wall paintings. Almost all medieval churches had painted interiors. There is a deplorable modern practice of stripping plaster from church walls, leaving exposed stonework never intended to be seen – it was plastered. The plaster was often painted to imitate ashlar stonework with red or black joints and each rectangular stone painted in the centre with a rose or other flower. Some of these masonry patterns dated from c.1100. It was probably the case that most medieval churches had a depiction of St Christopher credited with the power of protecting those who saw it from infection and sudden death. At Woodeaton, Oxfordshire, a text on a St Christopher explains this in Norman French. In the frequent plagues this must have given some hope to parishioners.

THE WEST COUNTRY

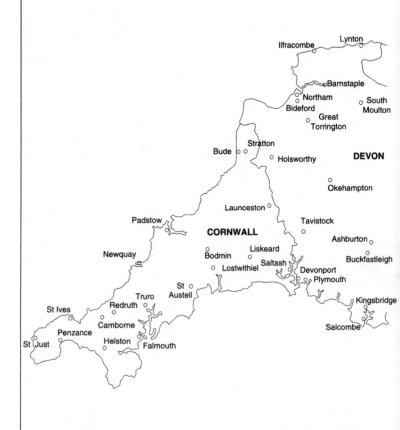

THE WEST COUNTRY

Avon

Avon is a new county created in the 1970s out of parts of Somerset and Gloucestershire. It is not really a county in the true sense but an alien conglomerate owing nothing to history; no one will ever refer to an 'Avon type of church tower'. However, whatever one's view of Avon, there is no lack of good quality stone for building and Bath and Cotswold stones with their distinctive golden colour lend a mellowness to many villages and towns. In Bristol merchant wealth was spent on churches, but there is not one left with an original interior although memorials, fittings and ironwork were left intact. In the nineteenth century many churches were rebuilt, restored and altered, generally sympathetically.

BACKWELL. 6m SW of Bristol off A370. *St Andrew*
The church has a complicated architectural history and consists of all periods from the C12 to the C17 with an impressive C15 tower with C17 top put on after damage in 1603. Inside there is a circular Norman *font*, a two-tier brass candelabra dated 1786, a *brass* of two, male and female, kneeling figures dated 1604. There are good *monuments* in the C16 Rodney Chapel north of the chancel.

BATH. *Abbey of SS. Peter & Paul.*
Begun in 1499 by Bishop King, and almost the last of the monastic churches to be built. Incomplete at the Dissolution, it was roofed in 1612-16 and became the parish church for Bath. The vaulting in the nave was only put in during Sir George Gilbert Scott's restoration of 1864-73. The exterior is a perfect example of late-Perpendicular. The west front shows angels climbing up and down ladders based on a dream of Bishop King. The interior has lost the mystery of the east end owing to the removal of the screen and organ loft. There is some heraldic *glass* of c.1604-20 in the north aisle and many wall plaques of the C18 and the C19 including one in the south aisle to *Beau Nash*, who is buried under pew 33.

BRISTOL. *St Mary Redcliffe.* Redcliffe Way.

Queen Elizabeth called this 'the fairest, goodliest, and most famous parish church in England'. Large as a cathedral and built on the profits of prosperous merchants – many voyages began and ended in Bristol. Note the amazing north *doorway* c.1325. This is one of only two parish churches in the country to have stone vaulting – see also Steeple Ashton, Wiltshire. Inside there are: a C18 mace-shaped *sword rest*, an almost complete set of *armour* of Admiral Sir William Penn (d.1670) and a C17 embroidered Italian *cope*. Under the tower is a wooden statue of Queen Elizabeth I, probably made for her

Bristol, St Mary Redcliffe.
The stone-vaulted nave looking west.

visit in 1574. Finally there are over 1100 roof *bosses*, some indecent!

John Wesley's New Room, The Horsefair.

Built in 1739 by Wesley and enlarged in 1748, this is the oldest *Methodist chapel* in the world. It is rectangular in shape with galleries down the long sides meeting at an attractive stair down to the pulpit. The green wall colour is matched with the original, discovered from scrapes.

CAMELEY. 9m S of Bristol off A37. *St James.*

In the care of the Redundant Churches Fund. One of John Betjeman's favourite churches. An C11 church rebuilt in the C15 and consisting of an aisleless nave, chancel and west tower. Enter by the C12 south door into a gratifying and intimate atmosphere created by the mix of fittings and decoration of all ages. The white painted interior has a chancel arch, with an interlaced rope decoration, of the C12, the *pulpit* with an octagonal tester, is early-C17, the same date as the rector's and clerk's *pews*. Overhead is a fine waggon-roof, and of particular interest are the many fragments of *wall paintings*, some as old as the C12; note the Commandments over the chancel arch.

YATTON. 13m SW of Bristol on B3133. *St Mary.*
An impressive cruciform church begun in the 1320s with lofty nave and aisles of the C15. The Newton Chapel on north side of the chancel has a *monument* to Sir John Newton (d.1488) and his wife, Isobel of Cheddar, (d.1498). The treasure of the church is displayed in a glass case, a C15 blue velvet *dalmatic* converted to a funeral pall in the C16.

Other Churches

ALMONDSBURY. 7m N of Bristol on A38. *St Mary.*
Norman and Early English with central tower and cruciform plan, Norman *font*, a *hatchment* of 1779 and Royal Arms.
COMPTON MARTIN. 12m S of Bristol on A368. *St Michael.*
Norman and C12, with C15 tower.
GREAT BADMINTON. 12m N of Bath off B4040. *St Michael.*
Built by Charles Evans in 1785 in the style of St Martin-in-the-Fields. Contains many Beaufort monuments including a vast one to the 1st Duke, by *Grinling Gibbons.*
WELLOW. 4m S of Bath off A367. *St Julian.*
Almost all of the late-C14, with a chancel rebuilt in 1890 by George Frederick Bodley. There is a *wall painting* in north chapel.
WESTBURY-ON-TRYM. 2.5m NW of Bristol centre. *Holy Trinity.*
Mainly C13 with chancel built in 1460s. Once collegiate and now parochial, it has many good monuments to wealthy Bristol merchants.

Cornwall

Cornwall is a Duchy and has more sea coast than any other county. Slate and granite are the main building materials and both present problems. Granite is hard and therefore unsuitable for carved decoration. Slate, on the other hand, is easily cut and used for grave stones; it also splits, so making an ideal roofing stone. There are many attractive waggon-roofs, a form common to most Cornish churches. Similarly most have three east-end gables. The majority of Cornish churches were altered, added to, or rebuilt, in the C15. A surprising number of Norman fonts have survived, perhaps more than in any other county.

Inland Cornwall is generally considered less attractive than the coast. However, the best churches are inland, such as those at Altarnum, Blisland and Bodmin.

Cornwall is also unique in the strange names of its Celtic saints. Many of these go back to C6 and C7 and are associated with Brittany, Wales and Ireland.

ALTARNUN. 7m W of Launceston off A30. *St Nonna.*
This is a church built in the C15 with one of the tallest towers in Cornwall. Note seventy-nine *bench ends* made after 1525 – look for

the bagpiper. Notice the magnificent Norman *font* and the early-C17 *panels* on east wall showing Holy Communion and the Crucifixion.

BLISLAND. 4m N of Bodmin off A30. *SS Protus & Hyacinth.*

Essentially Norman with a C15 tower. The inside is waggon-roofed throughout and there are: a circular Norman *font*, a *Royal Arms* of 1604, a *brass* to John Balsam, Rector of Blisland (d.1410), a late-C17 pulpit and nearly 200 roof *bosses.*

Altarnun, St Nonna. Built in the C15 with one of the tallest towers in Cornwall.

BODMIN. 28m W of Plymouth on A38. *St Petrock.*
Rebuilt 1469-72 and the largest church in Cornwall. Three times restored in the C19 but retaining the original waggon-roof, it contains the best Norman *font* in Cornwall. There is also an incised slate slab to Richard Durant (d.1632), his wives and twenty children! In the south aisle see the C12 Spanish, ivory, *Bodmin Casket.*

COTEHELE HOUSE. (NT). 8m NE of Plymouth off A390. *Chapel.*
The chapel dates from late-C15, with restorations of the C19. The *screen* is original, as also is the oldest unaltered *clock* in England, made of wrought-iron in the 1480s. The Flemish *triptych* on the altar depicting The Adoration is dated 1589, to its left and right are two German paintings of c.1500 representing Our Lady and the Angel of the Annunciation.

LAUNCESTON. 20m NW of Plymouth off A30. *St Mary Magdalene.*
With an unspectacular C14 tower, the rest of the church is 1511-24 and shows what can be carved on unyielding granite given determination. The waggon-roof is new. After the exterior the interior is an anti-climax: there is a carved *Royal Arms*, an early-C18 organ front and nearly 400 roof *bosses.*

MORWENSTOW. 6m N of Bude off A39. *SS Morwenna & John Baptist.*

A part Norman church and, unusually for Cornwall, part C13 and part C16. The waggon-roofs of nave and aisles are of c.1564 with a few bosses. Notice the early Norman *font*, the early Renaissance *bench ends*, the faint *painting* of St Morwenna on the north wall. The church is famous for its vicar, Robert Stephen Hawker, a character of the C19 church who claimed to have been the first to introduce the Harvest Festival in 1843. (See East Brent, Soms.)

MULLION. 5m S of Helston on B3296. *St Mellanus.*

A church mainly of 1500 with earlier C13 work in the tower and chancel. Both north and south *doors* are original and that on the south has a small dog door – to send dogs out? Inside there is a plaster *Royal Arms* of Charles II. The rood screen was put in in 1925, but gives a good impression of how a rood (Christ on the Cross, with St Mary and St John Evangelist on each side) dominated the interior.

PROBUS. 5m NE of Truro on A390. *SS Probus & Grace.*

This church boasts the tallest tower in Cornwall, built in the 1520s. Inside the space is beautifully managed. There is no clerestory and so the tall aisles give a lofty feeling to the whole, set off by the slender, graceful columns of the arcades. The church was over-restored by G.E. Street in 1851.

ST ENDELLION. 4m N of Wadebridge on B3314. *St Endellienta.*

A standard C15 Cornish church. The altar in the south aisle is a c.1440 *tomb chest* of brilliant quality and may be the shrine of St Endellienta. The *stoup* inside the south door is by the same 'Master of St Endellion'. There is a Norman *font*, plain and simple, the waggon-roof was restored in 1938, when it was found to have been restored earlier in 1675. There is a Georgian bell ringers' *rhyme* painted on a board in the tower.

St Germans, St Germans. The monastic Norman west front.

ST GERMANS. 10m W of Plymouth on B3249. *St Germans.*

The magnificence of this

church makes one suspect a glorious past. In fact it was the seat of the Saxon, Cornish Bishops, and attached to a C12 Augustinian priory. The wide west front with a heavy portal and two towers, one octagonal and the other rectangular, is impressively C12 Norman. Before going in, notice the Arts and Crafts decoration of the west door. Go down six steps and into the vast nave. The north aisle, the aisles' roofs and the north transept with the Port Eliot pew are all of 1803, and the waggon-vault roof nave is 1888. In the south aisle the first three bays are Norman and the rest a rebuild of c.1592. There is little of the original furnishings: in 1358 they were taken to St Ives, near Liskeard – only one choir stall with a *misericord*, a battered font of c.1200 and fragments of a rood screen of c.1500 from Port Eliot remain. In the chancel the east *window* is Morris & Co designed by Sir Edward Burne-Jones in 1896. Another Burne-Jones window of 1902 is in the south wall of the Lady Chapel.

ST NEOT. 5m NW of Liskeard off A38. *St Neot* or *St Anietus*.
An attractively situated village on a bend of the river Glynn and dominated by the church. The tower is early-C14, the rest is C15 and C16. The church is renowned for its C15 and C16 *glass*. There are fifteen windows with more than 350 figures, all carefully restored in c.1830.

ST WINNOW. 3m S of Lostwithiel off B3296. *St Winnow.*
The church has an alluring setting on the Fowey river. There is Norman detail on north side and a Norman transept arch, reconstructed in the C13. Note the barrel-vault roof with carvings, the C16 rood screen, restored in 1907, and the C16 and C17 bench ends. The important feature is the east window in the south aisle filled with C15 and C16 *glass* in the original arrangement.

Other Churches

LAUNCESTON. 20m NW of Plymouth off A30. *St Thomas.*
Originally a chapel of ease. Note the Norman *tympanum* in the south porch. Inside is the largest Norman *font* in Cornwall and two *wall paintings* at the east end of the south aisle.
MAWGAN-IN-MENEAGE. 4m NE of Newquay off B3276. *St Mawgan.*
A church of the C13-C15 in a spectacular setting, with a good three-storey tower, and a north aisle rebuilt in the C19. Note the knight and his lady's *tomb* of c.1300. The C10 Mawgan Cross is by the cross-roads.
ST ENODOC. 7m NW of Wadebridge off A3314. *St Enodoc.*
A C13 chapel with spire, buried in sand until 1863, in a romantic site on a golf course. Sir John Betjeman, Poet Laureate, (d.1984), is buried near the south side of the church.
ST KEVERNE. 9m SE of Helston on B3293. *St Akeveranus.*
A church rebuilt in the C15, with tower of 1770. The spacious interior

has a C15 *wall painting* of St Christopher on north wall.
ST KEW. 4m NE of Wadebridge off A39. *St James.*
A large church next to a large vicarage in a wooded valley. There is a
good C15 *waggon-roof* supported by angels, and 193 roof *bosses*. The
north-east window has *glass* dated 1469. Notice the *Royal Arms* of 1661
in coloured plaster, and the original *stocks* in the porch.

Devon

The county has a very wide variety of building stone but not of the
quality of the Jurassic limestone of neighbouring Dorset and Somerset.
The variety ranges from red sandstone on the south coast through
many colours to the dull carboniferous sandstones in central Devon,
and the upper greensand stone, called chert, of the east coast. Then
there is the granite of Dartmoor and, like Cornwall, slate. As in
Cornwall there was a great rebuilding of churches in the C15.

ASHTON. 7m SW of Exeter off B3193. *St John Baptist.*
An attractive church in a beautiful setting and well worth visiting.
Rebuilt and refitted between 1400 and 1485, it was perceptively
restored in 1881-3 and 1899-1901. The *rood screen* was restored in
1908, when a new rood loft was built. The rest, however, is C15 and,
with the *parclose screen*, offers some of the best figure painting in
Devon. On the north wall of the north chapel is a faint C15 *wall painting* of Christ with the Emblems of the Passion. There are also: a good
Jacobean *pulpit* with sounding board, the *Royal Arms* of George II,
1735 and a wooden *monument* to George Chudleigh (d.1657).

BRANSCOMBE. 5m E of Sidmouth off A3052. *St Winifred.*
An early church and an interesting delight to visit, from the late
Norman central tower and nave to the early-C14 chancel, all carefully
restored in 1911 by W.D. Caroë. The interior has a good selection of
C17-C18 furnishings: a three-decker *pulpit*, a rarity in Devon, a plain
screen of c.1660, a three-sided altar rail of the same date, *box pews* in the
north transept, a west gallery of the late-C17 and a *hatchment*. On the
north wall there are fragments of a C15 *wall painting* of the seven
deadly sins: lust is certainly recognisable!

CHITTLEHAMPTON. 6m SE of Barnstaple off B3227. *St Urith.*
This church has the finest tower in the county and was the shrine for
the C6 St Hieritha foully murdered by scythes. The nave, chancel
and chapels are all C15 and an arched recess in the chancel north
wall formerly contained the saint's shrine. The early-C16 stone *pulpit*
has her portrait showing her carrying a palm. Note the small *brass*
near the pulpit to John Cobleigh (d.1480) and his two wives, and the
two C17 Giffard monuments.

CREDITON. 8m NW of Exeter on A377. *Holy Cross.*
A large red sandstone collegiate church, sunk in a low churchyard.
Originally a C12 cruciform plan, remodelled in the C14 and C15 with
a C16 south transept, all restored from 1848 to 1877. Praised for the
beauty of its clerestory windows and the elegance of the stumpy central
tower, it was all but in ruins in 1413 when the nave and chancel north
wall were rebuilt. Inside the greater part of the fittings are of the 1880s
with glass of the same date, in the south transept is armorial *glass* of
1926. Of particular note is the *muniment chest* thought to be Flemish of
c.1450. W.D. Caroë was responsible for the font cover and the
mismatched tower screen of 1904. Note the *wall-monument* to Sir
William Piariam (d.1605), one of twenty judges who sentenced to
death Mary Queen of Scots, his helmet may be a 1910 fake and the
original sold to the USA. There are other items of funeral armour.

CULLOMPTON. 12m NE of Exeter on B3181. *St Andrew.*
A town church of the C15 and C16 with a massive tower in red sandstone completed in 1549. Notice the carved decoration of ships and
sheep-shearers on the
buttresses between the
windows. Entering under
the west tower one is met
by the sight of a magnificent C15 boarded
waggon-vault *ceiling* with
bosses, angels and carved
decoration picked out in
gold on a blue ground.
The colour scheme is
carried into the flat roofs
of the north and south
aisles. The Lane aisle, a
second south aisle built in
1526, is gorgeously fan-
vaulted. A splendid but
many times restored *rood
screen* reaches right across
the church. A squire's pew,
box pews and west gallery
are all early-C19, while
the pulpit reader's desk
and and reredos are of
1849. Note the iron-
bound chest and the late
Morris & Co glass in the
south aisle.

Collumpton, St Andrew. The splendid
barrel-vaulted roof.

MOLLAND. 7m E of South Molton off A361. *St Mary.*

Mainly C15 with east and south chancel walls rebuilt in C19. A memorable C17 to early-C19 *interior* preserved complete and untouched by the Camdenians. There are: a three-decker pulpit, an C18 screen with solid plaster tympanum with a Royal Arms, a commandment board painted in 1808, a three-sided communion rail of c.1700, box pews, baptismal pew, a *children's pew* and the splendid Courtenay *monuments* of the C17 and the C18.

NEWTON ABBOT. 16m S of Exeter on A381. *St Luke.*

This church is strictly for those who enjoy eccentricity. It was begun in 1931, completed only in 1963 and built of rendered concrete with a central tower topped by a copper pyramid dome. The plan came to the vicar, Keble Martin, in a dream and the result is extraordinary. A St Andrew's cross is imposed on a long nave giving, in effect, three naves at different angles focused on the altar, in an apsed chancel. There are no aisles. Inside there is a splendid feeling of space.

OTTERY ST MARY. 11m E of Exeter on B3177. *St Mary.*

A large low church built by Bishop Grandison in the mid-C14 and restored by William Butterfield in the mid-C19. The church has one of the earliest (mid-C14) eagle *lecterns* in England and an interesting *clock* showing the phases of the moon, probably C14 with a C15 face. Contemporary with the building are some fine roof *bosses* including one of Bishop Grandison, also twenty *misericords* of c.1430 in the choir. The south transept wall decoration was done in 1878 by William Butterfield; also his is the 1850 dazzling polychrome *font* inlaid with local marbles. Particularly notable is the late-C14 *tomb* to Ortho Grandison (d.1358) and his wife (d.1374), one of the best in the west country.

SIDBURY. 6m S of Honiton on A375. *St Giles.*

A noteworthy and pleasing church of many medieval periods: a Norman tower and chancel with earlier *crypt* beneath, an early-C13 nave and transepts, all restored in 1898-9. The choir stalls, altar and reredos date from c.1900. Many fragments of a C13 *wall painting* remain, giving a good idea of the background decoration to the main subjects. St Christopher survives on the tower arch. Additionally there are three C19 windows by Kempe.

TAVISTOCK. 12m N of Plymouth on A386. *St Eustace.*

A large early-C16 church with central tower, restored in 1844-5. Much to see inside: the fine Elizabethan *altar table* in St George's Chapel, two iron-bound *chests*, perhaps C14, and very good C19 *glass* in the east window of the north aisle by Morris & Co; also in the north aisle a window by Kempe, and another, by Clayton & Bell, in the south aisle. The roof has 210 *bosses*, mostly foliage, but include an odd one, signifying the Trinity, of three rabbits with only three ears between them! Forty-four angels support the roof of the south aisle.

TAWSTOCK. 2m S of Barnstaple off A377. *St Peter.*
The tall C15 spire over the crossing makes this an unusual church for Devon. The rest is C14, and it stands in the grounds of Tawstock Court. There are noteworthy *waggon-roofs* in nave and chancel; noteworthy too is the pre-1550 *manorial pew* of the Earls of Bath and the early-Renaissance *bench ends*, one with arms of Henry VIII. There is an amusing *hourglass stand* in the form of an arm, and an embroidered *altar cloth* of 1697. Above all there is the finest collection in any Devon church of *monuments* to the Earls of Bath, their countesses and families, and a wooden C14 *effigy.*

TORBRYAN. 4m SW of Newton Abbot off A381. *Holy Trinity.*
In the care of the Redundant Churches Fund. A church entirely of the C15, with notable medieval window tracery. A large white interior shows off the C15 *rood screen* with vividly painted decoration, including saints in the wainscot panels. There are *box pews* with candleholders, a colourful pulpit made up from parts of a C15 screen and an equally colourful altar made from the original C15 pulpit.

WIDECOMBE-IN-THE-MOOR. 5m NW of Ashburton off B3357. *St Pancras.*
The church in this small over-visited village is well worth a detour. The tower is early-C16 with the rest mainly from the C14. Inside there is the remains of an early-C16 *rood screen* with painted panels of saints and martyrs. Notice also the remains of a *reredos* at the west end with large paintings of Abraham sacrificing Isaac, and Moses and Aaron. Look up at the ceiling *bosses* and notice a pelican, a stag, an antelope and three rabbits sharing three ears as at Tavistock. Lightning struck on Sunday 21 October 1638 killing and injuring many of the congregation. This is remembered on four *painted boards* in the tower, dated 1786.

Other Churches

CRUWYS MORCHARD. 5m W of Tiverton on A3137. *Holy Cross.*
The old house of the Cruwys family stands alone beside the medieval church, burnt out in 1689. The C18 restoration remains almost unaltered. Here is the finest C18 Classical *rood screen* in the county together with *box pews, family pew, pulpit,* communion rails and plaster panelling, all of C18.

PARRACOMBE. 4m SW of Lynton off A39. *St Petrock.*
In the care of the Redundant Churches Fund. Saved from the Camdenians when a dull new church was built in 1878. The interior is unrestored Georgian and includes *box pews, family pew, hat pegs,* text boards and Royal Arms of George III.

SALCOMBE REGIS. 2m NE of Sidmouth off B3175. *SS. Mary & Peter.*

The tower is C15, the rest of the church is mainly C13 with re-used Norman decoration, all restored in 1924. The chancel was restored in 1869. Note the C15 oak *lectern* and a slate *tablet* with inscription in Hebrew, Greek, Latin and English.

SAMPFORD COURTNEY. 5m NE of Okehampton on A3072. *St Andrew.*

Mainly early-C16, the church was carefully restored in 1889. Inside are: waggon-roofs with many good *bosses*, a Norman *font* and some late-medieval *glass* in the north aisle. The village is famous for the Prayer Book Rebellion of 1549.

SUTCOMBE. 5m N of Holsworthy off A388. *St Andrew.*

Mostly a late-C15 church with some Norman parts, all restored 1876. There are a good number of early-C16 decorated *bench ends.*

UPTON HELLIONS. 2m N of Crediton off A3072. *St Mary.*

A part Norman church with a C15 aisle and waggon-roof. Peaceful and truly rural. Inside are: a Norman *font*, carved bench ends, a *Royal Arms* in plaster and a rustic monument to the local squire.

WEST OGWELL. 1m SW of Newton Abbot off A381.

In the care of the Redundant Churches Fund. The north and south transepts are of c.1300, the rest with the west tower is of c.1400. The interior has box pews, pulpit and wall panelling, all of the C17, and a *fireplace* in the south transept!

Dorset

The county is blessed with the best of building materials: Portland stone and the black Purbeck marble, which is not marble but limestone. In fact limestone is the principal stone, ranging in colour from the white of Portland, used by Wren for St Paul's Cathedral, to the golden stone of Sherborne. Flint is found in the centre of the county but when used for building it is combined with limestone bands. The majority of Dorset churches were rebuilt in the C15 and are noted for their stumpy towers.

However, Dorset has some of the best church architecture from the C14 to early-C16. The choir of Sherborne has the earliest fan-vaulting in England, built in c.1450, and while waggon-roofs in wood are common, St Catherine's Chapel, Abbotsbury, has late C14 wagon-vaulting in stone. Dorset is a county of surprises.

BLANDFORD FORUM. 16m NW of Bournemouth on A354/350. *SS Peter & Paul.*

The church was rebuilt in 1733-9 after a disastrous fire in the town; it remains unaltered except for the chancel of 1896. The interior is noble, spacious and light with contemporary *font* and *cover*, *box pews*, *Benefaction boards*, *Commandment boards*, and west gallery. The *pulpit* is from Wren's St Antholin, London. A nice touch is the Bastard family monument to John and William who built the church, and much of the town.

CERNE ABBAS. 7m N of Dorchester on A352. *St Mary.*
Built in flint and stone in the late-C13, and once a Benedictine Abbey, it was extensively rebuilt in the C15 and C16, when the west tower was put up, and reconstructed in the C17. The interior is as gratifying as the outside. Note the very unusual stone *rood screen*, the *pulpit* of 1640, the C15 *glass* in the east window and the C14 *wall paintings* in the chancel.

EASTON. 4m S of Weymouth on A354. *St George Reforne.*
An impressive Classical church built 1754-66 in Portland stone and standing on top of Portland surrounded by old quarries. The interior is majestically formal with contemporary, numbered, west facing *box pews*, baptismal pew, squire's and rector's pews, three galleries, an early-C18 pulpit and reader's desk.

LEWESTON. 2.5m S of Sherborne off A352. *Holy Trinity.*
A neat example of a squire's chapel built in 1616 for his household, and now a chapel of the Roman Catholic St Anthony's College. Apart from the mass-produced angels and electricity, the *interior* is all of 1616, from the two-decker pulpit to the round-headed benches and the wall panelling.

MILTON ABBAS. 5m SW of Blandford Forum off A354. *SS Mary & Michael.*
As a Benedictine abbey this was built comparatively late and begun in 1309. The original east end has gone – the east wall shows five blocked arches – leaving us with the original choir, crossing and tower. The high, blocked central arch on the west front shows where the unbuilt nave would have been. It was all restored in 1789 by James Wyatt and again in 1865 by Sir George Gilbert Scott. A surprising quantity of original furnishings have survived; the stalls with twelve uninteresting misericords, the c.1500 *reredos*, the sedilia and the early-C14 *Pulpitum*. A.W.N. Pugin designed the *glass* in the south transept in 1847 and the touching marble monument to Lady Milton (d.1775) is by Robert Adam.

SHERBORNE. 15m SW of Shaftesbury on A30. *St Mary.*
A cathedral until 1075 and a Benedictine monastery from 998 until the Dissolution, when it became the parish church of the town. Cruciform in plan with Norman crossing and transepts, the chancel is c.1420-30 with the earliest *fan-vaulting* of c.1450, while the nave is late-C15. J.G. Grace is responsible for the mid-C19 painted decoration in the choir.

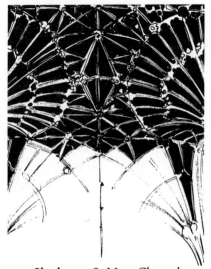

Sherborne, St Mary. Chancel fan-vaulting of c.1450.

Notice the many amusing ceiling *bosses* and the ten mid-C15 *misericords.* Purbeck marble is used in many of the early *monuments,* of later examples the finest is to John Digby, Earl of Bristol (d.1698), and signed by John Nost. The earliest brass *chandelier* of its kind in England, dated 1657, is in the Lady Chapel. Finally there is much good C19 and C20 *glass* and many fragments of C15 glass in St Katherine's Chapel.

STUDLAND. 3m N of Swanage on B3351. *St Nicholas.*

One of the most complete Norman churches in Britain. Norman interiors were intended to be dark and mysterious; this was mainly dispelled by inserting the C13 east window and when other windows were enlarged in the C18. The glass is all C19 and includes a window by Willement. Notice the two *hatchments* to the Bankes family and the C17 Psalm LXXXIV painted above the nave arch.

WHITCHURCH CANONICORUM. 4m NE of Lyme Regis off A35. *SS Candida & Holy Cross.*

The south door is Norman but the rest of the church is C13, with a C15 west tower. What is remarkable is the survival of the bones and *shrine* of St Wite, the original patroness. Otherwise note the small Norman *font,* the Jacobean pulpit and the *Roman tiles* re-used in the external north wall.

Whitchurch Canonicorum, St Candida. The C13 shrine of St Wite in the chancel.

WIMBORNE MINSTER. 7m NW of Bournemouth on A341. *St Cuthberga.*

From the outside this grey church is not impressive. Cruciform in plan with a Norman central tower, arcades and transepts, and a C13 choir, the rest is of the C14, with a C15 west tower. There is good C19 *glass* and a noteworthy early C16 Flemish *Tree of Jesse* in the choir. Fragments of *wall paintings* cover other paintings of the C13, C14 and C15 in the north transept. Other interesting items include a *clock* said to date from c.1320, a *Saxon chest* thought to be 1,100 years old and thirteen *misericords* of 1608 in the choir. The 1st Duke of Somerset (d.1444) and his Duchess, the grandparents of Henry VII, have a large, fine *tomb* in the presbytery. Notice the monument to Sir Edmund Uvedale (d.1606), his recumbent figure has two left feet, the result of a long-forgotten restoration.

WIMBORNE ST GILES. 12m NE of Blandford off A354. *St Giles.*

Built in 1732 of flint and greensand stone, the church was burnt out in 1908 and rebuilt in the early Georgian style by Sir Ninian Comper, long enough ago for the detail to seem authentic. Inside it is Comper at his best. His Gothic screen dominates the church and the alabaster reredos in white and gold is typical of his work. The pulpit, seating and ornate west gallery are likewise all his. The Ashley *monuments* (including three Earls of Shaftesbury) alone are worth a visit; these were rescued from the fire, but it is a pity that Comper didn't allow them sufficient space.

Other Churches

ABBOTSBURY. 8m SW of Dorchester on B3152. *St Nicholas.*

Mainly c.1500 with earlier decorative detail and a C18 chancel plaster waggon-vault. Note the good C15 *glass* – a half-figure of the Virgin – the Jacobean pulpit and the early C13 *effigy* of an abbot in Purbeck marble in the porch.

BOURNEMOUTH. 100m SW of London. *St Peter.*

The church was built piecemeal from 1854-79 by G.E. Street. The interior is rich Victorian, with one window by *William Morris*, painted decoration by Clayton & Bell and G.F.Bodley. The *pulpit* was exhibited at the 1851 Crystal Palace Exhibition. For romantics, the poet Shelley's heart (d.1822), Mary Shelley (d.1851), William Godwin (d.1836) and Mary Godwin (d.1797) are all buried in the churchyard.

CHARMINSTER. 1m N of Dorchester on A37. *St Mary.*

A C12 church rebuilt in the early-C16, with a chancel of 1838 in which the east window tracery is inside out! The interior is essentially Norman. Note the fragments of original all-over painted *decoration* on nave north wall, the *pulpit* dated 1635, and the C16 Purbeck marble *monuments.*

CRANBORNE. 15m N of Bournemouth on B3078. *SS Mary & Bartholomew.*

A large church and once monastic, it is basically Norman, overlaid in C13 and C15, with a heavy C15 tower and boring C19 chancel. Note the fragments of C15 *glass* in the south window, and particularly the early-C14 *wall paintings* over the south arcade.

W I N T E R B O R N TOMSON. 6m W of Wimborne Minster off A31. *St Andrew.*

In the care of the Redundant Churches Fund. A small Norman church with nave and chancel in one and an apsed east end. The fittings are of 1716-37 and include a two-decker *pulpit, box pews,* and *communion rail.* The *west gallery* is C16 and may be made from the old rood loft. Restored by A.R. Powys for the SPAB in 1931. His memorial tablet is in the church.

Winterborn Tomson, St Andrew. The nave looking east with C18 furnishings.

WORTH MATRAVERS. 4m W of Swanage off B3069. *St Nicholas.* After Studland the most complete Norman church in Dorset, restored 1869. Note the Norman *tympanum* and the C14 east window. The actor Leslie Banks (d.1952) is buried in the churchyard.

Gloucestershire

This is one county that never had any problem in finding good building stone. In the west of the county in the Forest of Dean is found the Old Red Sandstone, as good a building stone as any; Hereford Cathedral is built of it. In the east is the well-known Cotswold limestone used not only for walls but, until recently, split for slates as well. With such a long tradition of stone-working it is no surprise to find superb workmanship everywhere.

As if nature's gifts were not enough, this is a county with a wide offering of churches from pre-Conquest and Norman times through to the sublime examples of the fifteenth-century 'wool' churches at Cirencester and Northleach and later. Many of its churches have fragments of earlier details overlaid by fifteenth-century restorations, or entirely rebuilt in the fifteenth-century.

At Deerhurst is the famous tenth-century St Mary's church with nearby the equally famous eleventh-century St Odda's Chapel. Bibury has St Mary's, a large pre-Conquest church rebuilt after 1130. There are pre-Conquest Crucifixes at Holy Rood, Daglingworth, and St Catherine's, Wormington, while at St Mary's, Beverstone, is a pre-Conquest Resurrection.

Tewkesbury Abbey is a major Norman church on the grandest scale but it is for the 'wool' churches that the county is justly famous. Fairford's Mary, Cirencester's St John and Chipping Campden's St James, are only three built out of the enormous profits of the fifteenth-century wool trade that made English cloth famous throughout Europe. It was an opportunity for church building that did not come again until the nineteenth century, only represented here by St Matthew, built by Ewan Christian in 1878-9, in Clarence Street, Cheltenham, and the exciting Holy Innocents, Highnam, by Henry Woodyer, built 1849-51. Others, not mentioned here, are worth seeing such as St Gregory, the R.C church with the tallest spire in Cheltenham, built 1854-7 by R.C. Hansom, the inventor of the Hansom cab, and the gloriously lavish St John at Huntley built in the 1860s by S.S. Teulon. For more a modern example of church architecture there is St Barnabas at Tuffley, Cheltenham, built 1939-40, in reinforced concrete, an uncompromising material which nevertheless achieves a calm and dignified interior in this case.

AMPNEY ST MARY. 4m E of Cirencester off A417. St Mary.
The church has a Norman nave with a C13 chancel and a unique carved *lintel* to the north door. This small church has several noteworthy details; a rare original stone *rood screen*, a *holy table* and, the chief attraction, C12-C15 wall paintings. St Christopher is inevitably on the north wall, with St George and the Dragon, and on the south wall a naked Christ with tradesmen's tools – a warning to Sabbath breakers.

BIBURY. 5m NE of Cirencester on A4425. *St Mary.*
For William Morris Bibury was the most beautiful village in England, and few would dispute his claim. Additionally it has a pre-Conquest church. Almost completely rebuilt in the C12, it was added to in the C13, C14 and C15. Both north and south doorways are late-Norman, with a slightly later south porch. Oddly set in the north wall of the chancel is part of the sculptured cross shaft of a Saxon cross much earlier than the church itself. The tower attached to the C12 west wall of the north aisle is C13. Inside the overall flavour is of c.1200, or the change from Norman to the early-Gothic, with chubby Norman piers supporting a slightly pointed arcade. In the C13 the chancel arch was rebuilt leaving it resting on the old Saxon jambs and imposts; at the same time the nave was heightened and given a clerestory. The nave *roof* with its magnificent carved timber is C15. Notice in the chancel the ten *aumbries* or cupboards. Also do not miss the C17 Spanish needleworks. In the trim churchyard there are examples of the local table-tombs, some with cherub heads.

BUCKLAND. 5m SE of Evesham off B4632. *St Michael.*
A small church, mainly C15 with C13 nave, restored in 1885 when the walls were stripped of their plaster and wall paintings! The C15 *glass* in the east window was restored by William Morris at his own cost. There are: some original C15 benches (others are copies), C17 panelled seating with shallow canopies and a C17 Communion rail. Note the C15 blue velvet embroidered *cope*, and the early-C15 carved and coloured stone *panels* in the north aisle.

CHIPPING CAMPDEN. 7m SE of Evesham on B4035. *St James.*
This is another of the fine 'wool' churches, modernised in the C15 and so similar to Northleach that the same mason must have been involved. The church was completely restored in 1875-6. In the magnificent interior are six C15 *brasses* to wool merchants, a late-C15 falcon *lectern,* some medieval glass fragments in the east windows and a curious *monument* to Viscount Campden (d.1642) on which two shrouded corpses are revealed through double doors. Displayed in a glass case are two *copes,* one of c.1440, the other C15, and a C15 embroidered *altar frontal.* Note the pulpit of 1612 and the C15 triple sedilia in the chancel.

CIRENCESTER. 11m NE of Tetbury on A433. *St John Baptist.*
Not only is this the largest and most splendid of all the 'wool' churches it is one of the largest parish churches in Britain. Seeing the church from the busy market place one cannot help remarking on the magnificence of the three-storey porch built c.1490 and which served as the Town Hall until the 1890s. Behind rises the nave rebuilt 1516-30, with the great west tower of c.1400-60. Although appearing to be C15 it is older and basically of the C12, and originally attached to the Augustinian Abbey. The chancel was rebuilt in 1180 and the nave and Lady Chapel in 1235-50, followed by the outer walls of the chancel aisles in 1250-60. The whole was restored by Sir George Gilbert Scott

Chipping Campden, St James. The C15 nave of a great 'wool' church.

in 1865-7. On entering, the high arcades give the grandest impression of height and space. To the east, the chancel of c.1180 was extended and both the Lady and St Catherine's Chapels built by c.1250. Henry Tapper left £20 in 1532 for completion of the *rood screen*, barely time before the loft was torn down, leaving only the lower sections.

Of the original glass there is little, it had been neglected and in 1642 glass was broken to pass food to Prince Rupert's prisoners held inside. What survived is collected in various windows; the medieval *glass* in the lower half of the east window was brought from *St Peter*, Siddington, in c.1800. A rarity for the county, for being in stone, is the C15

Cirencester, St John. The west tower and three-storey porch built in 1490.

pulpit, gilded and painted, on a wine-glass pedestal. No less that fifteen mainly C15 *brasses* can be found in the church, of which only five have emblems of wool merchants; one, however, with casks was a wine merchant, and another to William Prelatte (d.1462) and his two wives show three very surprised expressions on identical faces. At the east end of the south aisle the silver-gilt Boleyn Cup made in 1535 for Anne Boleyn's family is displayed. Notice the C15 *wall paintings* of SS Catherine and Nicholas in the chantry and the *Royal Arms* of Henry VIII over the chancel arch, Also note the fine pair of brass *chandeliers* of 1701.

DEERHURST. 2m SW of Tewkesbury off A38. *St Mary.*
This is one of the two finest and loveliest Saxon churches in Britain, the other being at Brixworth in Northamptonshire, which is more complete. A monastery was here in 804 and the nave is of that date. Slighter later, in c.1030, was a two-storey west porch, now the lower stage of the tall tower. Curious pieces of Saxon stone project above the west door and over a higher window. Viking raids destroyed both church and monastery and the church was rebuilt in c.930. One enters by the west door, noting the beautiful C8 relief of the Virgin and Child, which was certainly originally painted and explains the unfinished appearance. The unusual height of the narrow nave, with north and south arcades of c.1200, the date of the aisles, is highlighted by the two small windows in the west end, opening from what was once a

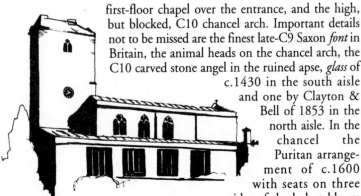

first-floor chapel over the entrance, and the high, but blocked, C10 chancel arch. Important details not to be missed are the finest late-C9 Saxon *font* in Britain, the animal heads on the chancel arch, the C10 carved stone angel in the ruined apse, *glass* of c.1430 in the south aisle and one by Clayton & Bell of 1853 in the north aisle. In the chancel the Puritan arrangement of c.1600 with seats on three sides of the holy table, as at Hailes, is a surprise. In the south aisle the pews are C15 and there is medieval *glass* in the west window.

Deerhurst, St Mary. Rebuilt in the C10 with later windows.

Three *brasses* in the north porticus include a large and unusual one of c.1400 to Sir John Cassey (Baron of Exchequer to Richard II) and his wife Alice, with her dog 'Terri' at her feet. It is the only example in Britain of a 'dog brass'. The church was restored in 1861-3 when the nave roof was replaced.

St Odda's Chapel.

Some 200 yards south-west of *St Mary's* lies this small chapel attached to the half-timbered Abbot's Court. Only discovered in 1885, the nave had served as a kitchen! Restored in 1965, it is one of the most complete of pre-Conquest churches. The dedication stone, now in the Ashmolean Museum, Oxford, of which there is an exact replica in the church, was found in 1675 and tells us that Earl Odda built and dedicated it to the Holy Trinity on 12 April 1056. Two pre-Conquest windows survive, that in the south wall has part of a wooden frame; is this the earliest surviving wood window-frame? The plain simplicity of the interior of this small church has enormous charm.

DUNTISBOURNE ROUS. 3m NW of Cirencester off A417.
St Michael.

This fascinating little pre-Conquest church stands on a steep bank above a stream. Taking advantage of the sloping site to the east a tiny crypt chapel, entered from the churchyard, was put beneath the Norman chancel. To the west end is attached a small C15 tower with an upper stage of 1587 and saddle-back roof. A triangular-headed south door leads into a simple Saxon nave unspoilt by C19 'improvements'. Fine C17/18 box pews and panelling survive giving a timeless feeling to the interior. In the chancel the C15 stalls have five late-C13 to early-C14 *misericords* all with the same bearded grotesque head. On the north wall of the chancel are the remnants of a C15 *wall painting* and a mutilated C14 cross is preserved in the churchyard.

ELKESTONE. 6m S of Cheltenham off A417. *St John Evangelist.*
Of the many Norman churches in the county this, built of rubble stone and dating from c.1160 is one of the most fascinating. A central tower collapsed in the mid-C14 and a more substantial west tower of free-stone blocks was built in c.1370. Just under the eaves on the south side notice the typical Norman detail on the carved corbel-table of birds, animal heads and signs of the Zodiac. The porch of a church marks the entrance to the Kingdom of Christ and the Norman *tympa-num* of Christ in Majesty over the south door makes this point. The east end of the high nave is marked by a splendid low Norman arch, decorated with chevrons, leading into a dark low-vaulted, tunnel-like, chancel, which once supported the central tower. This gives an air of mystery to the small Norman sanctuary glowing with light at the far end. In the south window the sill holds the *piscina* and the jamb a *credence recess.* Other details are easily listed; the 1609 pulpit, the reader's desk of 1604, a fragment of *wall painting* on the inside north doorway and the modern glass. However, this is an interior to be enjoyed for its Norman subtlety and decoration, other details are a distraction. Finally, the churchyard has some good C17 table-tombs typical of the county.

FAIRFORD. 6m E of Cirencester on A417. *St Mary.*
This glorious church built c.1491-7, is a perfect example of the Perpendicular style and a wool church in the truest sense in that it was built by one rich family of wool merchants, John Tame and his son Sir

Fairford, St Mary.
A 'wool' church rebuilt in c.1500.

Edmund. With a squat west tower, the low nave, chancel and aisles seem to spread out and hug the churchyard. Armorial shields on the tower refer to the Earls of Warwick who built the earlier lower stage. Tame was not ashamed of his trade and his own arms, together with those of Warwick, appear on the parapet. He retained some of the grotesque sculptures from the earlier building and be sure to find the amusing carved stone figures just below the parapets. St Christopher *painted* on the north wall welcomes us in the nave, large windows flood the interior with light. The church is famed for its c.1500 *glass;* every window is filled with coloured panes of outstanding quality made by Barnard Flower, glazier to Henry VII. Beginning in the north aisle we can follow the whole and complete religious scheme concluding with the great west window, showing the Last Judgement with all its horrors and glories. Another survival from the earlier church is the C15 *font*, one side showing the badge of Edward IV, a rose on a sun. The chancel fittings all date from after 1500 and were provided by Sir Edmund. It is rare in Gloucestershire for screens to survive but here are both *rood* and *parclose* screens. Also there are richly carved stalls and fourteen *misericords* of c.1490, all carved with amusing details of everyday life. Do not overlook the chained *Bible* of 1551, a holy table of 1626 and an Elizabethan *chest* with three locks in the south chapel. The founder's tomb deserved a place close to the altar and John Tame's (d.1500) is in the chancel with a brass showing him in full armour. The altar was designed by Sir Ninian Comper in 1920. Finally, on the way out do not miss the *wall paintings* in the tower.

HAILES. 9m NE of Cheltenham off A4632. Dedication unknown.
This small and simple church near to the abbey ruins may be the least altered in the county. Built in c.1130 with C14 windows it consists only of a nave and a small chancel, with a short timber belfrey and sanctus bellcote on the nave roof, and a south porch of 1905. It was sympathetically restored in 1961. Inside nothing has changed since the pulpit and tester were renewed in the C18. Beyond the chancel arch of c.1200 the floor of the chancel is paved with C13 red and yellow *tiles* from the abbey. It is impossible to miss the faded *wall paintings* St Christopher on the north wall and in the window splays are two early-C14 female saints with monks at their feet. Strange mythical beasts cavort above the windows. In the chancel the paintings are of elaborate heraldry. A C17 *holy table* stands in the middle of the chancel in the Puritan manner surrounded by C17 stalls and panelling. The simple C15 screen, the benches and the mid-C14 font, all add to the peaceful rural atmosphere giving an impression of timelessness; one might be in almost any century.

KEMPLEY. 13m NW of Gloucester off B4215. *St Mary.*
An early Norman church with very rare *'fresco'* paintings (that is,

painted on wet plaster) of c.1130-40 in the tunnel-vaulted chancel. Previously whitewashed, they were discovered in 1871 and cleaned in 1956; they include a Wheel of Life, a Doom, assorted saints, and Balaam with his Ass, a cycle unique in Britain. The nave ceiling is dated 1670, the south door is medieval with original *iron-work* and above it is a stone tympanum showing a carved Tree of Life. The *Royal Arms* are of George III and the *chest* is C14.

LITTLE WASHBOURNE. 6m NE of Cheltenham on B4077. *St Mary.*

In the care of the Redundant Churches Fund. Small churches have a certain charm for us that the larger ones never achieve and this small lonely Norman church, untouched for centuries, is a good example. From the outside we see a nave and smaller chancel with a bellcote on the gable between. Heavy buttresses support the already substantial walls giving an impression of independent strength. It is at once obvious that the windows are later, in fact late-C18, inserted to give more light to the dark Norman interior. The interior is welcoming and still without electric light, tall candelabra line the chancel and nave. Narrow as it is the nave is made more narrow by the C18 box pews. At the west end open pews are dramatically raised. The surprising marble-topped *holy table* is C18, as is the pulpit with an inlaid tester, only the font may be C19. In the north window splay of the chancel is *painted* the remnants of a once all-over pattern of red rectangles, simulating stonework, each filled with a rosette. One leaves with a feeling of lingering nostalgia.

NORTH CERNEY. 4m N of Cirencester on A435. *All Saints.*

A mainly C12 church; the two lower stages of the west tower are Norman, with a C13 bell stage, and Norman also are the south wall of the nave and the south porch. Notice the late-C16 graffito of a leopard on the west face of the tower and the scratch dial on the door jamb. Beneath the south transept window is another late-C16 graffito of a mythical creature. The chancel is C18 and C19. A serious fire in the 1460s caused the rebuilding of the rest. Inside is a feast of beauty, mainly due to the work of the Arts and Crafts F.C. Eden who contributed the painted *rood* in 1925 with an Italian Christ of c.1600 over the c.1180 chancel arch, the parclose screen to the Lady Chapel, the *reredos* in the chancel and much else. The three wood figures of the reredos are C15; the delicate Virgin is French and the two bishops German. Of particular note is the pre-1485 *glass* in the east window in the Lady Chapel and the *pulpit* of c.1480 cut from a single block of stone. There is much else here to admire and one should allow time for a visit.

NORTHLEACH. 9m NE of Cirencester on A429. *SS Peter & Paul.*

The church has a strong claim to being the most beautiful in the county and the south porch with its upper chamber and soaring crockets can claim to be the most perfect in Britain. Although traces of Norman masonry from the earlier church are in the Lady Chapel, it was entirely rebuilt from wool wealth in the first half of the C15. Nave and north chapel roofs are C15, but the chancel was re-roofed in 1960. A re-organisation of the interior took place in the 1960s, but some original fittings remain; the *font* is C14, the stone pulpit C15 and there are no less than eight *brasses* four of which show a woolsack and one the shears of wool merchants. One other is to a clothier, Thomas Fortey (d.1447), who may have had a considerable part in the rebuilding. Notice the carved heads on the south chapel corbels, the demons on the base of the C14 font, the

Northleach, SS Peter & Paul.
A double brass of 1400
of a wool merchant
and his wife.

framed *painting* of St Peter by Ribera (1588-1656) in the north aisle and the original *holy table* in the chancel. The carillon plays 'O worship the King' every three hours.

STOKE ORCHARD. 4m NW of Cheltenham off A38. *St James the Great.*
A small, interesting Norman chapel-of-ease of c.1170 originally attached to St Michael's church at Bishop's Cleeve, with an aisleless nave, chancel and single bell turret. Inside is a Norman *font*, and in the nave, unique to Britain, faded *wall paintings* of the life of St James of Compostela dated as c.1180-1200 – Bristol was a pilgrim port of embarkation for Compostela. The borders with fantastical creatures are reminiscent of the carvings at Kilpeck, Hereford. These were discovered in the 1880s and restored in 1953-5.

TETBURY. 11m SW of Cirencester on A433. *St Mary.*
Francis Hiorne was both the architect and builder of the main body of the church in 1777-81. One hundred and ten years later the spire took a serious lean and was rebuilt in 1890. The parish specified 'elegant ... Gothic' and what they got is enthusiastic early Gothic Revival with amazingly large windows filling the interior with light. The exterior is all one could wish for in Gothic; castellated parapets, slender flying buttresses, some narrow lancet windows and crocketted pinnacles. The parish must have been completely satisfied. The interior is even better; the amazing height of the plaster-vaulted ceiling is supported on the

slenderest of columns. Original linenfold box pews luckily survived a restoration in 1900, likewise two magnificent brass chandeliers of 1781. Circulation must have exercised Hiorne's mind because polite access to the box pews is gained from the passage-aisles; no late stumping down the nave and banging of pew doors. The reredos has a painting of The Holy Family by Benjamin West. There is a good collection of monuments from an Elizabethan couple in armour and ruffs (d.1586) to the inevitable Classical draped urns.

TEWKESBURY. 9m N of Gloucester on A38. *St Mary.*
This is Norman architecture in the grandest manner. Once the church of a great C12 Benedictine Abbey, it has the finest Norman tower in the country and a soaring, inspired Norman nave. With a simple west front consisting mainly of a huge recessed window replaced in 1686, it is built on the breathtaking scale of a cathedral. To the south are the foundations of the destroyed cloisters. At the Dissolution in 1539 the town bought the church for £453 on the grounds that the nave was theirs anyway. The price reflected the value of the lead and bells. Earlier, in May 1471, the Battle of Tewkesbury was fought out on Bloody Meadow. Defeated Lancastrians took refuge in the church, believing they had sanctuary. However, victorious Yorkists led by Edward VI and his two brothers, burst into the church and slaughtered them. It took all of a month to purge the building of this disaster and reconsecrate the church. Inside the church the thirty-feet high nave, with its fourteen massive columns, has a wooden vaulted *ceiling* of the C14 with a magnificent collection of fifteen *bosses* telling the story of the Life of Christ. Beneath the crossing the tower above was designed as an impressive lantern but was covered by another wooden

Tewkesbury, St Mary.
West front of the abbey church.

vaulted *ceiling* in the C14. The ambulatory, with five radiating chapels, was remodelled in the C14. The sacristry, on the south side, has another memory of the bitter battle of 1471; the inside of the door is covered with iron plates made from armour found on the battlefield. The *presbytery*, the last and best part of the church, was taken down to the lower part of the Norman piers in the C14 and rebuilt in the Decorated style with a glorious lierne-vaulted *roof*, this also has exceptional *bosses*. The black Purbeck marble *altar* was consecrated in 1239. There is no space here to detail all the many monuments, the best of which are in the chapels off the ambulatory; the Beauchamp chapel is the most rewarding. Next, in the Wakeman Cenotaph, is the C15 *tomb* of John Wakeman (d.1549), the last Abbot. On it is a cadaverous effigy crawling with putrefaction, with worms, frogs, snails and mice! Behind the high altar is the vault of the Duke of Clarence, brother of Edward IV, said to have been drowned in a butt of Malmsey wine, and buried here in 1478. Do not overlook the Milton organ made in c.1580 still with the original case and tin pipes.

Old Baptist Chapel. Church Street.

Here is one of the oldest Nonconformist chapels in the county. A C15 timber-framed hall house was converted to a chapel in 1623 and restored to its early-C18 appearance in 1976. Extensive alterations were made in c.1720, the sunken baptistery, ceiling and the tall windows are all of this date, while the panelled pulpit and galleries are late-C17.

Other Churches

BEVERSTON. 2m W of Tetbury on A4135. *St Mary.*
The lower part of the tower is early-Norman, the chancel is also Norman with a fine C14 east window. All restored in 1844. Famed for the C11 sculpture of the Resurrection on the south wall of the tower. There is a particularly fine C13 south arcade and the restored C15 rood screen is well worth seeing. Note the local wrought-iron light hangings.

COLN ROGERS. 5m SW of Northleach off A429. *St Andrew.*
A small Saxon church preserving its nave and chancel almost intact, apart from later windows and a C19 restoration.

COLN ST DENNIS. 4m SW of Northleach off A429. *St James.*
This small Norman parish church, with central tower and some C14 windows was restored twice; in 1890 and 1904. Nevertheless, it retains many Norman details; priest's door, bell-stage, north door and font.

DUNTISBOURNE ROUS. 4m NW of Cirencester off A417. *St Michael.*
Small and remote, with a Saxon nave and a Norman chancel with crypt. Notice the five C13 *misericords* with identical bearded heads, the C17 *box pews* and panelling, and the C15 *painted masonry pattern* on chancel north wall.

HIGHNAM. 3m W of Gloucester on A40. *Holy Innocents.*
An exciting Gothic Revival of 1850 built by Henry Woodyer for
Gambier Parry as a memorial to his wife. Religiously dim interior lit by
coloured glass, very rich decoration with wall paintings by Parry
himself.

SHORNCOTE. 5m S of Cirencester off B4696. *All Saints.*
Basically a Norman church, with a double bellcote on the east gable, a
C14 north chapel and waggon-roofs in both nave and chapel. In the
chancel there is a rare C15 *Easter Sepulchre*, also a C17 *Holy Table*,
unused, and *wall paintings* over the chancel arch and in the chancel,
where there is an overpainted C12 consecration cross.

Somerset

This county is unrivalled for the perfection of its Perpendicular
(c.1350-1540) towers, some sixty in all. Like its neighbouring county,
Wiltshire, it possesses very good varieties of building stone. As in
Wiltshire the prosperity of wool in the C15 provided the wealth for the
building of so many fine medieval churches begun at the end of the
C14 after the Black Death. The most common form of plan is a west
tower, vaulted aisles and nave attached to an earlier chancel. Somerset is
also a county that largely escaped the attentions of Victorian restorers.

BRENT KNOLL. 7m S of Weston-super-Mare on B3140. *St Michael.*
Rebuilt in the C15 this church has a Norman south door, a C14 south
porch and south transept. The aisles have fine panelled ceilings and
the nave, a notable *waggon-roof.* The church is well known for its amusing bench ends; look for the preaching fox dressed as an abbot while,
below, two apes roast a pig. Note the pulpit of 1637 and the monument to J. Somerset (d.1663) on the south wall; now re-coloured, it
gives a good idea of the lost brightness of church interiors.

CROSCOMBE. 3m E of Wells on A371. *St Mary.*
A church mostly of the C15 and early-C16 with one of the most
complete set of Jacobean *furnishings.* The pulpit is dated 1616 and the
reader's desk, the rood screen, parclose screens, box pews and the stalls
are all of the same date. High on the chancel wall is a plaque where the
Fortescue arms denote this generosity. Notice the carved wood roof
bosses: one is a mermaid with mirror and another is a rare one of a bat.
The chancel roof is dated 1664 and the brass chandelier 1707. Notice,
too, the Royal Arms and the waggon-roof.

EAST BRENT. 6m S of Weston-super-Mare on A370. *St Mary.*
A mainly C15 church, with one of only eighteen stone spires in the
county. The chancel was rebuilt 1840-50. The unusual plaster nave
ceiling, an early example of Gothic Revival, is dated 1637. The C15

wood eagle *lectern* is one of only twenty-one medieval survivors in the country. There is good medieval *glass* in the north aisle east window, restored in 1852. The pulpit and west gallery, made up of parts of the original rood screen, are of the 1630s. Notice the Royal Arms of 1825, the C15 *bench ends*, and the bier in the south chapel dated 1734. There is a painting of c.1873 in the porch, that is only interesting because it is by the then Rector, Archdeacon Denison, a high churchman, who claimed to have introduced the first Harvest Festival in 1857. (See Morwenstow, Cornwall.)

PILTON. 3m SW of Shepton Mallet on A361. *St John Baptist.*
The south door and north arcade of the church are Norman, the west tower is C13, and the chancel C15. There are some magnificent C15 *roofs* supported on angel busts. Note the Easter *sepulchre*, the parclose *screens* in the north chapel, and the fragments of medieval glass in the chancel. Particularly noteworthy are the fragments of a C15 *cope* once used as an altar frontal.

STOGURSEY. 7m NW of Bridgwater off A39. *St Andrew.*
A late-Norman cruciform church with central tower, the chancel formed the choir of a vanished Benedictine Priory. Restored in 1865, the east end is of that date, as are the roofs. The nave was remodelled in the C15. Inside, the slender late-Norman pillars are a contrast to the usual massive columns. The pulpit is a made-up piece but the *benches* are genuine c.1530-40. There are also many good-quality monuments.

STOKE-SUB-HAMDON. 5m W of Yeovil off A3088. *St Mary.*
A church with a Norman nave and chancel, and a C12 tower base on the north side topped by a C15 timber spire, all well restored in 1862. The north doorway *tympanum* is particularly interesting in that it incorporates, unusually, Sagittarius and Leo with the Tree of Life. Inside, note the fine Norman detail, the circular Norman *font*, the C15 *bench ends* and the fine nave *roof* of the C15.

Stoke-sub-Hamdon,
St Mary. Unusual tympanum over north door showing Sagittarius, the Tree of Life. Leo and the Lamb of God.

SUTTON BINGHAM. 3m S of Yeovil off A37. *All Saints.*
A remote small Norman church with C13 alterations. Inside the c.1300 *wall paintings* are the main feature: a large Coronation of the Virgin, bishops and saints in the chancel, with a splendid Death of the Virgin

in the nave. There is also a circular Norman *font.*

TAUNTON. 30m NE of Exeter off M5. *St Mary Magdalene.*
A large church rebuilt c.1500 with the highest and finest tower in
Somerset. The tower was exactly rebuilt in 1862. Inside, the double
aisles are a peculiarity, and the only clue to an earlier church is the late-
C13 arcade between the north aisles. The C15 roof has gilded (1968)
angels, with red and blue painted tiebeams. The reredos is 1872 by
G.E. Street, there are pieces of C17 and C18 glass in the south chapel
and the east window commemorates Queen Victoria's Golden Jubilee
of 1887.

TRULL. A suburb of Taunton. *All Saints.*
The church was rebuilt, save for the C13 tower, in c.1500, and has a
surprising amount of C17 and C18 interior fittings. Unique to the
county is the wood *pulpit* of c.1500 with undamaged saints. The
benches with good carved ends are of c.1520 with an unusual religious
procession extending over five bench ends. Against the back wall is a
bench dated 1560 and signed by the maker, Simon Warman. Notice
the substantial remains of what must have been a fine *rood screen* with a
rare tympanum of plaster. The chancel has considerable pieces of C15
glass, while the rest is C19 with the west window by C. E Kempe of
1913.

Other Churches

AXBRIDGE. 2m W of Cheddar off A371, *St John Baptist.*
The church was rebuilt in the C15, the Gothic revival plaster ceiling is
of 1636, and there are: a mid-C15 *wall painting* in the south transept of
Christ showing his wounds, a needlework *altar frontal* of 1720, a chan-
delier of 1730, and a brass of 1493.
BROCKLEY. 10m SW of Bristol on A370. *St Nicholas.*
A part Norman church, well restored in 1820-30. The interior has a
Norman *font,* and good Pigott *monuments.* Note the fireplace in the
family chapel and the copy of Volterra's Deposition.
DOWNSIDE ABBEY CHURCH. 6m NE of Wells off A37.
The church is early C20 by T. Garner and Sir George Gilbert Scott,
with an east window by Sir Ninian Comper. Note the Flemish *triptych*
of c.1525, the altar *painting* by F. Botticini (1446-97), and the
outstanding mid-C15 wood *sculpture* of Virgin and Child by N. von
Leiden.
HARDINGTON. 6m NW of Frome off A362. *St Mary.*
In the care of the Redundant Churches Fund. A small church of the
early-C14 with small west tower and no aisles. The interior is one of the
most alluring in the West Country and it is unaltered since the late-
C18 to early-C19.
NUNNEY. 4m SW of Frome on B3090. *All Saints.*

A C14 church, with a C13 chancel rebuilt in 1874, the waggon-roof is late-C15. Note the *wall painting* of St George, a fragment of Saxon cross, and two C15 *monuments* to knights.

WELLOW. 4m S of Bath off A367. *St Julian.*
The church is C14, with chancel by Bodley & Garner, 1890. The rood screen is C14 with loft by W.D. Caroë. Note the twelve *carved* heads in the chancel, the recently discovered c.1500 *wall paintings* of Christ and Twelve Apostles in the north chapel, and the c.1400 *effigy* of a priest in north aisle.

Weston Zoyland, St Mary. The C15 nave roof.

WESTON ZOYLAND. 5m E of Bridgewater on A372. *St Mary.* *(15)
A magnificent C15 church with a C14 chancel and one of the highest towers in Somerset. The C15 nave *roof* is a gem, with carved tie-beams, angels and bosses. Note *pulpit.* Restored by W.D. Caroë.

Wiltshire

The greater part of Wiltshire lies on chalk and it is no surprise to find that flint is a common building material. Chalk is a comparatively recent deposit which, if compressed for a few million years, becomes limestone. Beneath the chalk is good limestone of many colours and this surfaces in the Vales of Pewsey and Warminster.

Apart from a few notable exceptions such as Edington and Steeple Aston, which has no steeple (it collapsed in 1670), the church architecture is unremarkable and we have to look at the interiors for excitement. Like Gloucestershire in the C15 and C16, Wiltshire owed its prosperity to wool and this is expressed in church furnishings and monuments.

BISHOPSTONE. 4.5m SW of Salisbury off A354. *St John Baptist.*
The place owes its name and the large size of its church to the fact that it was a living of the bishops of Winchester. Cruciform with central tower and with no aisles, it was remodelled in the C14 and, because of the bishop's patronage, the interior is unusually sumptuous. The south transept and chancel are rib-vaulted with interesting stone *bosses* – look for the Coronation of the Virgin – notice, too, the ornate, gabled and crocketted *sedilia.* However, the elaborate woodwork of the stalls and

pulpit is European Renaissance, put in by a C19 rector whose ornate memorial of 1844 in the south transept is by A.W.N. Pugin, who also designed the three-light window. On the west wall are monuments to the Throope family, with coloured crests; also in the north transept is an anonymous pilastered Jacobean monument of c.1630. The *altar frontal* was used at Westminster Abbey at the coronation of Queen Elizabeth II in 1953.

BRADFORD-ON-AVON. 3m NW of Trowbridge on A363. *St Lawrence.*

This small pre-Conquest church is almost unaltered owing to the fortunate fact that it was put to other uses after the building of the larger Holy Trinity in the C11. It was discovered in 1856 and restored in the 1870s. Notice high up on the nave east wall two hovering *angels*, part of a long vanished rood, the contemporary *floor* of the chancel and the *cross* above the altar. The altar itself was recently made up from fragments of stone.

Bradford-on-Avon, St Mary.
Exterior of the almost unaltered Saxon church.

CRICKLADE. 6m NW of Swindon on A419. *St Sampson.*

The unusual crossing tower was built at the expense of the Duke of Northumberland, beheaded in 1553. From the heraldry it can be dated to the late-1550s. Over the Norman south arcade is evidence of Saxon work, a remaining pilaster. The south aisle, however, is 1864 by Ewan Christian, as are the nave and aisle roofs. Inside, notice the Saxon *carving* over the north door and two Norman *carvings* of animals set in the north wall of the south aisle. The reredos is of the 1930s by Martin Travers, also three windows in the north aisle and the east window are by him. In a recess in the north wall is a well worn female figure now identified as Agnes Lushill, d.1442.

DAUNTSEY. 5m SE of Malmesbury off B4069. *St James.*

A stone-built church with Norman north and south doorways, a C14 chancel and C15 nave, with a tower built by the Earl of Danby in 1632. Inside, the *screen* is C14 with a C17 lower stage, the *stalls* are part C15 and part C17, with a C16 *pulpit*, and early C17 *box pews*. Note the painted *glass* dated 1525, the wood *tympanum* painted with an early C16 Last Judgement. In 1993 a painting of The Massacre of the Innocents, bizarrely hanging in the children's corner, was discovered to be by a C17 Neapolitan artist, Pacecco. Its sale went a long way to paying for the new roof.

EDINGTON. 4m E of Westbury on B3098. *All Saints.*

A priory church built all at one time in 1352-61 by William Edington, Bishop of Winchester, one of the first parish churches to be built in the Perpendicular style, and one of the outstanding churches in England. Outstanding because it is architecturally unaltered except for a pretty plaster

Edington, SS.Mary, Katherine & All Saints.
Built in 1352-61; the exterior, east end.

ceiling of c.1789 in the chancel. From outside it is low and squat with a stumpy central tower. The clue to its collegiate origins lies in the fact that the parishioners' west end and nave have simple windows whereas the transepts and chancel, the monastic end, have finer decoration.

INGLESHAM. 9m N of Swindon on A361. *St John Baptist.*
In the care of the Redundant Churches Fund. A small aisled church with a C13 double bellcote. The C13 nave is flanked by aisles rebuilt in the C15, all carefully restored in 1888-9 by the Society for the Preservation of Ancient Buildings, as the inscription tells us '...through the energy and with the help of William Morris, who loved it'. The fascinating interior jumble resembles nothing so much as a good antique shop. The walls have painted fragments of texts over C13 wall paintings and decorative patterns. In the south aisle is a notable C11 *sculpture* of the Virgin and Child. The reredos is re-assembled from c.1330 fragments, while other notable features are the Elizabethan *pulpit* with tester, three C15 *screens*, C18 *box pews* and the *Royal Arms* of William IV.

LYDIARD TREGOZE. 3m W of Swindon off B4534. *St Mary.*
A small, late-C15 church behind Lydiard Park, notable for the contents

that include extensive *wall paintings* of the C15 comprising St Thomas Becket, St Christopher, the Risen Christ and Christ Crowned with Thorns. The chancel ceiling is charmingly covered with stars in a blue sky of c.1700, the pulpit and screen with Royal Arms are Jacobean and the box pews partly so. Notice in the south chapel particularly the remarkable St John *monument* of 1594 with triptych of 1615, the important monument to Sir John St John said to be by Nicholas Stone and the famous *'Conversation Piece'* to Lady Mompesson, d.1633, over the chapel door. There are remains of C15 *glass* in nearly all the windows.

MALMESBURY. 14m W of Swindon on A429. *St Mary.*

The south porch of the abbey church is renowned for having the best Norman sculpture in Britain: it is an astonishingly rich carving of c.1160 illustrating biblical scenes. Of the rest of the abbey the crossing, nave arcades, aisle walls and the south part of the west front are all of 1160, the nave clerestory and the windows are c.1350. Inside massive Norman pillars support the triforium on shallow pointed arches. Above is a C14 vaulted roof and clerestory windows of similar date. Of the original furnishings there is nothing left. The two C15 stone screens in the east ends of the two aisles are said to be from St Paul's church in the town. In the south aisle is *glass* of 1901 by Morris & Co designed by Edward Burne-Jones. Note the C15 tomb chest of King Athelstan (d.940) who was certainly buried in an earlier abbey church.

MERE. 7m NW of Shaftesbury on B3095. *St Michael.*

An exceptional church for Wiltshire. Of all dates from the C12 to the C15 and mainly rebuilt in the C15, the interest lies inside. The nave pews date from 1640, the *rood screen* is C15 with the gallery above restored in the C19, and the *Royal Arms* are dated 1684. In the chancel are ten *misericords;* those on the north side are medieval but inserted in 1949; notice the fox beneath the vicar's stall. In the south chapel is funerary *armour*, now becoming a rarity. In the Bettesthorne chapel is a 4' 3" *brass* to Sir John Bettesthorne, d.1398, one of the finest in the county.

MILDENHALL. 1m E of Marlborough off A4. *St John Baptist.*

Small church of many dates in flint and stone, with a Norman tower on a Saxon base, the north aisle and chancel are c.1200, clerestory is C15, the nave and chancel roofs are c.1610. The Gothic *furnishings*: pulpit, reader's desk, pews, box pews, Royal Arms and west gallery are unchanged since 1815-16.

OLD DILTON. 2.5m NW of Warminster on B3099. *St Mary.*

In the care of the Redundant Churches Fund. A small church with stone bellcote and nothing earlier than the C14 porch. The *interior* has not changed since the C18. The three-decker pulpit with tester, the family pews, box pews, the painted text of the Lord's Prayer, the Benefaction Board, the Royal Arms of George III and a splendid octagonal faced clock by Cook of Warminster are all C18. Of earlier date are C15 *benches* and octagonal font. Do not overlook the north gallery with *fireplace*.

SALISBURY. 18m NW of Southampton on A36. *St Thomas of Canterbury.*
The church was rebuilt in 1224 when the town moved from Old Sarum. The south tower was built c.1400, the north and south chapels and chancel in c.1450, after a collapse, and the nave aisles in c.1465. Justly famous for the Doom *painting* over the chancel arch dating from c.1475. Overpainted in C16, and restored in C19, this is the largest and best preserved in Britain. Other treasures include the remnants of a C15 *altar frontal* in the north aisle, a medieval *chest* in the west end of the south aisle, the *Royal Arms* of Elizabeth I over the tower door, four C15 *misericords* and a robustly carved wooden memorial tablet dated 1671 on the south wall. Notice in the north chancel aisle a large pyramidical *monument* to Sir Alexander Powell, d.1786. Apart from a few medieval fragments in the south chapel the glass is mid-C19.

STEEPLE ASHTON. 3m E of Trowbridge off A350. *St Mary.*
A remarkable church in an attractive market town, begun in 1480 at the height of the Wiltshire cloth-weaving prosperity. Impressive as the tower is today, its steeple fell down during a storm in 1670. The chancel was rebuilt, lengthened and heightened in 1853. This is one of only two parish churches in the country intended to be stone vaulted throughout; the other example is St Mary Redcliffe, Bristol. The nave, however, is vaulted by an impressive C17 wood roof and it is suggested that the original vaulting was destroyed when the steeple fell. The south aisle has many fragments of late-medieval *glass*, including the white rose of York which must pre-date Richard III's death at Bosworth in 1485. Note the interesting *palimpsest* on the wall of the Lady Chapel. Otherwise there are many C18 and C19 memorials. Over the south porch is the Samuel Hay library.

Other Churches

AVEBURY. 6m W of Marlborough on A361. *St James.*
The church has Saxon work and two Saxon windows in the nave, C12 aisles, and a chancel rebuilt 1879. It also has a brilliantly painted C15 *rood screen*, restored in the C19, with C20 coving, a Norman *font*, and a *brass* of 1427 from Berwick Bassett.

DEVIZES. 10m SE of Chippenham on A342. *St John.*
A large Norman church built c.1130, altered in the C15, C16 and C19, with a Norman three-stage crossing tower. Inside is a large display of mainly C18 and C19 monuments. Notice the many carved Norman

heads, and visit the ornate *Beauchamp Chapel* of c.1490.

DURNFORD. 5m N of Salisbury off A345. *St Andrew.*
The church has Norman north and south doors and a Norman nave; the chancel was rebuilt in 1880 and the C13 west tower restored in 1903. Inside are many fragments of *wall paintings* including a Doom and a St Christopher, a Jacobean *lectern* (with chained book) and family pew, a Norman *font*, and pulpit of 1619.

EAST KNOYLE. 9m S of Warminster on A350. *St Mary.*
The chancel has Norman fabric, the rest of the church is of all dates. Inside is remarkable *plasterwork* by the father of Christopher Wren, who was born here.

FARLEY. 5m E of Salisbury off A36. *All Saints.*
A church built in 1688-9 in brick, possibly to designs by Wren. There are good contemporary interior fittings, and splendid *monuments.*

GREAT CHALFIELD. 1.5m NE of Bradford-on-Avon off B3107. *All Saints.*
This small church, C13 with bellcote and with Tudor renovations, has a C17 three-decker *pulpit,* and C15 *glass* in the west window. See the Tropenhall Chapel of c.1480 with *wall paintings* of six panels from the Life of St Katharine.

LAYCOCK. 4m S of Chippenham off A350. *St Cyriac.*
A cruciform plan church of mainly the C14 and C15, with a C15 west tower, the chancel was rebuilt 1902-3. The Lady Chapel of c.1430 has remarkable stone *vaulting* and a noteworthy *monument* to Sir William Sharrington (d.1553). Fox Talbot (d.1877), pioneer of photography is buried in the town cemetery

WARDOUR CASTLE. 4m NE of Shaftesbury off A30. *Chapel.*
Administered by a charitable trust. The house, begun by James Paine in 1770 and completed by Sir John Soane in 1789-90, incorporates the most splendid C18 Catholic chapel in Britain. It opened in 1776 and is completely Classical on a very grand scale, enriched with Italian marble, silver and gilt bought in Rome. The altar was built there, designed by Giacomo Quaragenghi and shipped over in 1776. The fittings and decoration are of the highest C18 quality. Additionally the vestments ranging from C15 orphreys to C18 copes can only be described as breathtaking. There is too much to describe in this splendid chapel and one should allow plenty of time for a visit.

WINTERBOURNE BASSETT. 7m S of Swindon off A4361. *SS Katharine & Peter.*
A church with nave, north aisle, chapel and chancel all of c.1320, the west tower is C15. Inside there are: a Jacobean pulpit and reader's desk, some C14 *glass* in the chancel north window, and a charming C13 *tomb* slab with man and wife holding hands. Late Norman *font* and C18 brass *candle brackets.*

SOUTHERN ENGLAND

Bedford

Newport
Pagnell

BEDFORDSHIRE

Banbury

Milton
Keynes   Ampthill

Buckingham

Letchworth

Chipping
Norton

Stevenage

Bicester   Luton   **HERTS**   Bishop's
Stortford

Woodstock   **BUCKINGHAM-
SHIRE**   Hertford

Witney   Aylesbury   Hemel   Welwyn
Hempstead

Oxford   Chesham   St Albans

OXFORDSHIRE   Thame   High   Watford
Wycombe

Abingdon   Wallingford

Wantage   Slough

Henley   Maidenhead

BERKSHIRE   Windsor
Bracknell

Reading

Newbury   Wokingham

Basingstoke   Aldershot

Andover   Alton

HAMPSHIRE

Winchester

Romsey   Petersfield

Eastleigh

Southampton   Fareham   Havant

Lymington   Gosport   Portsmouth
Ryde

Newport

Sandown

48

SOUTHERN ENGLAND

Bedfordshire

A county deprived of quality building stone, but possessing varied building materials from the brown limestone in the north, where it joins Northamptonshire, through the flat eastern claylands and the sandstone country between Luton and Bedford to the chalk in the south. As varied as the building materials are the varied dates: there are four Saxon churches in the north-west of the county; the Norman church at Dunstable Priory; there is the highest quality of C13 work at Felmersham and the C14 is represented by Wymington and Swineshead.

CHALGRAVE. 4m N of Dunstable on A5120. *All Saints.*
Stumpy tower due to collapse in 1889. Consecrated in 1213, with rich C13 decoration in the unspoilt interior. Exceptional wall paintings: c.1300 twelve life-sized apostles in niches in the aisles; C14 armorial shields hanging by painted ropes, and scrolls over nave arcades; c.1400 St Martin of Tours dividing his cloak over south door; C15 St Christopher in the north aisle, c.1300 St Thomas of Canterbury in the south aisle and part of an Annunciation in the north aisle. Two C14 knights monuments in north and south aisles.

DUNSTABLE. 5m W of Luton on A5. *St Peter.*
All that remains of the once important Augustinian Priory founded by Henry I in 1131 is the gatehouse and a substantial part of the church, one of the best examples of Norman architecture in Britain. The east end has gone and the impressive west front is a mix of Norman and C13, restored in 1900 by G.F .Bodley. Inside, the nave roof is 1871 and the south aisle vaulting is 1852. The rich c.1400 screen is remarkable in having its original colours. Note the early C16 brocade Fayray pall and the magnificent Norman *font*, restored in the C19, and the four C16 brasses, one with an Agnus Dei and golden lion that only appears on two others in Britain. On leaving by the new west door notice the old doors pockmarked by Civil War shot.

EATON BRAY. 3m W of Dunstable off A4146. *St Mary.*
Built in c.1200 and unremarkably remodelled in the C15. Inside is C13 magnificence in the two nave arcades, matched by a C13 font. Notice the high quality of the C13 scrolley *ironwork* of the south door, the huge *thatching hooks* in the north aisle used to tear off thatch from burning cottages and a brass to Lady Bray (d.1539) is a palimpsest of C.1450.

FELMERSHAM. 6m NW of Bedford off A6. *St Mary.*
A rare example of a magnificent church built c.1240 in one piece and practically unaltered save for the clerestory and a heightened central tower, restored 1848, 1854 and 1869. The remarkable west front has upper windows of the C14, while the crossing is the climax of a glorious interior which includes a fine C15 *painted screen*, Jacobean chairs and oak table in the sanctuary and a chest dated 1628. The mystery is why so rich a village church was built when it belonged to Lenton Priory in far-away Nottinghamshire.

HOUGHTON CONQUEST. 5m S of Bedford off A6. *All Saints.*
A church built in the C14 and C15 of ironstone and ashlar with C19 chancel roof. Over the chancel arch is a large C14 *Doom*, above the north door a 16ft high *St Christopher* and a faint Instruments of the Passion in the south aisle, both C15. Note the brass to Isabel Conquest (d.1493) with two identical husbands.

SHELTON. 5m SW of Bedford off A421. *St Mary.*
Isolated and rural with a delightfully unrestored interior, part Norman and part C12 and C13. On the north wall are a St Christopher and a Weighing of Souls by St Michael, both C15. Many fragments of medieval *glass* and a C16 pulpit.

TURVEY. 7m W of Bedford on A428. *All Saints.*
A large church extended in 1854, with pre-Conquest stonework in the nave and tower, C13 arcades and C19 chancel. In the south aisle is a gorgeous early C14 *Crucifixion* on a Tau Cross set against a dark green background picked out with tiny flowers. In the south wall of the chan-

Turvey, All Saints. The C13 south door exuberant iron scroll work.

cel is an important *monument* to Lord Mordaunt (d.1560), other Mordaunt monuments worth attention and three brasses, two of them to Mordaunts

WYMINGTON. 11m NW of Bedford off A6. *St Lawrence.*
A church built from 1350 all in one style. There is a fine nave roof, but aisles re-roofed 1923. Some original colour is still on arches and capitals and a large but faded C15 Doom painted over the chancel arch. Note a faint C15 Trinity high up in the south aisle and four good *brasses*, one outstanding to John Curteys (d.1391) who built the church.

Other Churches

BARTON-LE-CLAY. 11m S of Bedford on A6. *St Nicholas.*
Marooned in a housing estate, significant C15 tower, C14 chancel, C13 Easter Sepulchre, Norman font, a good early C16 *wall painting* of St Nicholas and two brasses.
FLITTON. 9m S of Bedford off A507. *St John Baptist.*
Built of ironstone in the C15 by the de Greys, Earls of Kent. Notable for their monuments in the rooms of the vast, and amazing, de Grey mausoleum in the east end. Four brasses.
SWINESHEAD. 10m N of Bedford off B660. *St Nicholas.*
Almost all built in the C14. Splendid chancel with, in the north wall, an ornate *Easter Sepulchre*, and eight late C15 misericords. In the south aisle is an unrecognisable wall painting.
WOBURN. 12m SW of Bedford on A4012. *St Mary.*
Built in 1865-8 in early French Gothic style for the 8th Duke of Bedford at a cost of £35,000. Very grand, stone vaulted interior, east window by C.E. Kempe, 1894, reredos by W.D. Caroë, painting by Carlo Maratta (1625-1713), brass of 1394.

Berkshire

The county lies mainly on chalk with flint deposits and consequently flint plays a major part in church building. There is no building stone in the county though Bath and Portland stone are conveniently near. The eastern part of Berkshire has long been a dormitory for London commuters and most of the churches in the area have been wrecked by C19 restorations. The western part belongs to the West Country and here there are some gems to be enjoyed.

There is almost nothing of the pre-Conquest; the tower of St Swithin's at Wickham is the only substantial survival. The Norman period is equally bleak; SS Mark & Luke at Avingdon and St John, Padworth, being the only complete examples, otherwise there are a few Norman features, such as the door at St Laurence, Tidmarsh.

Gothic examples are far more numerous; the C13 polygonal apse at Tidmarsh again; and St John's at Shottesbrooke is unforgettable and almost entirely of the C14. Later, there is the rarity of a mid-C17 church, St Andrew's at Shrivenham, and from the C19 the amazing interior of St Swithin's, Wickham.

ASHAMPSTEAD. 10m NW of Reading off B4009. *St Clement.*
An interesting early-C13 church with weatherboarded bell-turret. The roof is worth examining for its tie-beams, arched braces and wind-braces. However, the important part of any visit here is to see the many C13 *wall paintings* in the nave and chancel. The subjects include Christ in Majesty above the chancel tie-beam, a Visitation, a Nativity and an Annunciation.

HAMPSTEAD MARSHALL. 4m SW of Newbury off A4. *St Mary.*
This church was once the ancillary of a long vanished house. It has a simple late-Norman south door in what is basically a C12 building, a C18 brick west tower, and a north aisle of c.1350. All sympathetically restored in 1929. The interior escaped C19 vandalism; the two-decker *pulpit* with tester is of 1622, the communion table C17 and the communion rail c.1700. All the C18 *box pews* remain, together with an C18 west gallery. Out of context is the late-C18 reredos with a later roundel of the Virgin and Child. Gaining entrance needs determination and money for the public phone box, persistance brings a reward.

LANGLEY MARISH. 2m SE of Slough on B470. *St Mary.*

Langley Marish, St Mary.
The Kedderminster Library of c.1620.

The church is a mixture of all dates and materials from flint and stone rubble to brick of the C17 tower. The interior is no less of a fascinating jumble. The north arcade of 1630 is surprisingly built of timber with Tuscan columns, while the rest of the church is in the Gothic of c.1340. Unique is the *Kedderminster pew* at the back of the Bateson Harvey mortuary chapel. Decorated with marble and panelling of c.1630 the family must have prayed here very comfort-ably. West of the chapel is the *Kedderminster Library* of c.1620, again panelled but the panelling opens to reveal nearly 300 books. Note the *hatchments,* the carved *Royal Arms* and the many *monuments.*

PADWORTH. 8m SW of Reading off A4. *St John Baptist.*
An aisleless church and completely Norman except for five windows of C15. Impressive within, the half-domed apse has glass of 1891 by C.E. Kemp, a C17 communion rail and *painted* consecration crosses. On the east wall is *painted* a large St Nicholas with a *miracle of the three boys* beneath (St Nicholas is said to have raised the three boys from the dead after they were murdered in a brine-tub by a butcher).

SHOTTESBROOKE. 3m SW of Maidenhead on B3024. *St John Baptist.*
This is an unforgettable church almost completely of the mid-C14. Cruciform in plan, built of flint with a slender spire, and unusually the work of one architect. It was originally collegiate and was founded by Sir William Trussell in 1337. Inside, all is whiteness and space. In the north transept is what must be the founder's tomb. There are many pieces of original *glass*, but the east window is C19 by J. Hardman & Co; the pulpit is 1854 by G.E. Street. Note partic-ularly the *brasses*; an outstanding double one of c.1370 shows, unusu-ally, a priest and his yeoman brother.

SHRIVENHAM. 6m NE of Swindon off A420. *St Andrew.*
Of the original church only the central tower of c.1400 remains. The rest was unusually built, at a time when little was done, in 1638 at the expense of Lord Craven. The round-headed arches supported on Tuscan columns in the nave are unconventional. Note the unusual C17 *pulpit* with tester, the C17 panelling and the C12 *font* of Purbeck marble. In the east window is heraldic *glass* of an Abbot of Cirencester, and throughout, many C18 monuments.

WICKHAM. 5m NW of Newbury on B4000. *St Swithin.*
To the flint Saxon tower of long-and-short work was added a nave and chancel by Benjamin Ferrey in 1845-9. The interior, created by Ferrey, is richly luxuriant with tracery, canopies and foliate capitals, all lit by purple and red stained glass. The nave roof is supported by angels and the aisle roofs by life-sized papier-mâché *elephants' heads* shown at the Paris Exhibition of 1862! This is a memorable interior.

WINDSOR CASTLE. 25m W of London off M4. *St George's Chapel.*

Windsor Castle, St George's Chapel.
Princess Charlotte's Memorial 1824 by
Matthew Cotes Wyatt.

Begun in 1475 by Edward IV and completed fifty years later by Henry VIII, it was built to accommodate members of the Order of the Garter, and has been a Royal burial place since Henry VII (d.1509). The chapel is a glory of fan-vaulting. The remains of earlier monarchs were transferred here from earlier chapels. Quite simply there is too much here to list and only the principal or curious points of interest can be mentioned. Ninety-six *misericords;* of 1475-85; 700 Garter *stall plates,* an iron almsbox marked with 'H', probably for offerings at Henry VI's tomb (d.1461); his *helmet* above the tomb;

an unusual *brass* of c.1630 of a child in a cradle and a painting of the Last Supper by Benjamin West in the vestry. Fortunately the fire of 1992 was prevented from spreading to the chapel.

Other Churches

AVINGTON. 6m W of Newbury on A4. *SS Mark & Luke.*
A small, completely Norman church sheltered by a vast cedar. The chancel arch is richly decorated with Norman beakheads, zigzags and pelletts. The tub-shaped *font,* decorated with assorted bishops and devils, is also Norman.

ENBORNE. 3m SW of Newbury off A343. *St Michael.*
A small church, originally early-Norman, with mid-C12 aisles, a chancel of the C13 and a timber bell-turret. The north transept was added in 1893. Some Norman detail is re-set in the south side. Inside, a Norman font and on the chancel north wall a glorious early-C14 *wall painting* of the Annunciation.

TIDMARSH. 4m W of Reading on A340. *St Laurence.*
For the magnificent Norman south door and unusual C13 poly-gonal apse alone, this church is worth seeking out. But there is more: faded C13 *painted* figures on the jambs of two lancet windows, two brasses of c.1500 and a re-cut C12 font.

Buckinghamshire

The county incorporates a wide range of poor building materials. In the extreme south, where there is no stone, brick is commonly used, as at Penn where it is mixed with flint. In the Chilterns, flint and clunch is used, until one reaches the north of the county where the only good building stone is found, although there is little enough of it, in a limestone belt at Westbury and Thornborough. Owing to the lack of good stone and the wide variety of alternatives there is no 'Buckinghamshire type' of church.

Few would dispute that All Saints at Wing is an outstanding example of Saxon architecture, but it is the only one. At Stewkley, St Michael & All Angels provides a harvest of Norman beakheads, lozenges and zigzag decoration and St Laurence at Upton would be entirely Norman had not a south aisle been added in 1851. St Bartholomew's at Fingest has a famous and massive Norman tower which, it has been suggested, once served as the nave, as in some pre-Conquest churches. Apart from isolated Norman detail, like the beautiful font in St Mary's, Aylesbury, from which similar fonts in the region take their name, that is the extent of Norman work in the county. The early-Gothic is represented by SS Mary & Nicholas at Chetwode. All that remains of an Augustinian Priory of 1245 is this church, once the priory chancel and containing the best work of the time in the county. The glass in the chancel makes a rewarding visit. Eton College chapel is internationally admired for its C15 church architecture. Thereafter there is little of note; St Peter's at Gayhurst, built in 1728, reveals interesting if fumbling architecture, but worth a visit if only for the unaltered interior.

CHENIES. 3m E of Amersham on A404. *St Michael.*
Completely rebuilt in the C15 and almost as completely again in 1861 and 1881, in the name of restoration. The point of any visit is the locked Bedford Chapel, added in 1556. Unless one is to gaze at the many recumbent figures of the Dukes of Bedford through the glazed screen it is necessary to make written application to the Bedford Estate Office. Perseverance brings its own reward. The *monuments* in alabaster and marble are remarkable, ranging from the first Earl (d.1555) to the late-C19.

Edlesborough, St Mary. Brass of John de Swynstede, 1394.

EDLESBOROUGH. 5m NE of Tring off A4146. *St Mary.*

In the care of the Redundant Churches Fund. Superbly sited on a lonely hilltop and of two period: the nave arcades and chancel are C13, and the rest mid-C13, with a C14 tower. All was over-restored in the C19. Its treasures lie within; there is much rich C15 woodwork, heavily restored in the C19, from the splendid 'wine-glass' *pulpit* with a tall Gothic four-tier canopy, a very good *screen*, to the six *misericords* in the stalls each showing some animal, bird or dragon. The low-pitched roofs are also C15. The red painted decoration of the nave is of 1867 and the glass is of the same date except for the chancel south window by C.E. Kempe of 1901. Note the four interesting *brasses*.

ETON COLLEGE. 20m W of London off M4 (exit 4). *St Mary's Chapel.*

Founded by Henry VI in 1440, the original chapel was demolished and rebuilt in 1449. Raised up to first-floor level the plan is of chancel and nave as one with an ante-chapel entrance. One of the rewards of a visit is to see the remarkable *wall paintings* of scenes from the Miracles of the Virgin, which are virtually in their original colours and glow with a master's touch; another is the C20 *glass*, of which two windows are by John Piper.

GAYHURST. 2m NW of Newport Pagnell off B526. *St Peter.*

Completed in 1728, the architect of this charming church in the Classical style is unknown. From the outside the nave walls present the façade of a minor country house. Inside, the *original fittings* are all but complete and one steps back to the style of Wren. The two-decker pulpit (cut down from three decks) and tester are beautifully inlaid, the portable pillar *font*, *communion table* and *rail*, together with the massive *reredos* with Creed board and Lord's Prayer, are all of 1728. The organ case is not original. A *monument* to Sir Nathan Wrighte (d.1728), Keeper of the Privy Seal, tends to dominate. Note the four *hatchments* and the round *Royal Arms* of George II.

LITTLE MISSENDEN. 4m NW of Amersham on A413. *St John Baptist.*

The heart of the modest church is pre-Conquest. The nave was altered in the C12, and the north chapel and chancel are early-C14, the porch and west tower C15. The church is famous for its *wall paintings* discovered in 1931, some almost complete. Like many other churches it once had an all-over scheme of the C12 of which the dado in the nave survives. Later this was overpainted; St Christopher on the north wall is C13. Also overpainted is the C15 Seven Deadly Sins on the south wall. There is a splendid late-C13 *Crucifixion* on the first west pier of the north arcade.

NORTH MARSTON. 8m N of Aylesbury off A413. *St Mary.*

A church mostly of c.1400 with a stumpy west tower, and a superb chancel and south chapel restored by Digby Wyatt in 1855 for Queen Victoria in memory of J.C. Neild, who left the Queen £250,000. In 1947-8 some bones were disinterred, supposedly those of John Schorne, the vicar in the late-C13 and early-C14, who triumphantly imprisoned the devil in a boot! This miracle-worker was accorded a shrine in the south aisle; the relics were later appropriated by Windsor Chapel. The reredos and glass are all C19. The stalls, with six *misericords*, are C15. Notice the angels supporting the roof.

PENN. 5m NE of High Wycombe off A404. *Holy Trinity.*

With a squat early-C14 west tower and built of brick and flint this church has an attractive charm. The C15 nave roof, with arched wind-braces and queen posts, rests on stone heads and figures. It covers an interior best described as a intriguing jumble. Box pews, *Royal Arms*, hatchments, wall tablets and five late brasses, all compete for attention. A rarity was discovered in the roof here in 1938; one of only five Dooms in the country painted on oak boards. This is now replaced over the chancel arch where it once hung. Note the rare Norman lead *font* and, in the south aisle, the tombstone of a descendant of William Penn of Pennsylvania. The ashes of Donald Maclean (d.1983), the spy, are in the churchyard in an urn decorated with the hammer and sickle.

QUAINTON. 5m NW of Aylesbury off A41. *St Mary & The Holy Cross.*

The church tower is C15; the proportions of the C14 nave and aisles were spoilt in the C15 when the arcade piers were heightened and, at the same time, the clerestory inserted. As if that were not enough, the whole church was virtually rebuilt in 1877, and the chancel entirely rebuilt. However, the saving grace of this church is the remarkable collection of, mostly signed, Renaissance *monuments*, by, amongst others, Leone Leoni (c.1509-90), an Italian sculptor, and the

Quainton, St Mary & The Holy Cross. Monument to Sir Richard and Ann Winwood by Thomas Staynon, 1689.

Frenchman, François Roubiliac (c.1705-62). In the north aisle four *panels* depicting saints from a painted C15 rood screen survive. Note particularly the *brass* of c.1360 in Norman French. One of the translators of the 1611 Authorised Version of the Bible was Rector here, his monument is in the south aisle.

STEWKLEY. 6m S of Milton Keynes on B4032. *St Michael & All Angels.*
A church for devotees of Norman architecture. It was built c.1140 and comprises nave and chancel with a massive central tower. The interior was made bland by G.E. Street's restoration of 1862. There is rich Norman decoration everywhere, particularly on the west front. The chancel vault, mostly rebuilt in 1844, has a C19 design painted between fine carved ribs. Set in the north wall of the chancel are C15 alabasters which were possibly a reredos. The one piece of good *glass* is the east window of 1844.

WEST WYCOMBE. 1m NW of High Wycombe on A40. *St Laurence.*
This is an old site, for the church, rebuilt between 1751 and 1762, with a C13 chancel, is inside an iron-age earthwork. The church is inalienably associated with Sir Francis Dashwood (d.1781) and the Hell Fire Club. This is perhaps unfortunate because Dashwood was a man of fine taste as well as Chancellor of the Exchequer, and it is to him that we owe most of the interior fittings: the unique C18 *font* combining one serpent and five doves in its decoration; the C18 *lectern* with a splendid armchair *pulpit* and two *stalls*, are no less unique and all of the finest workmanship. All this is contained in a nave likened to the Egyptian Hall of Vitruvius. On the chancel ceiling is a Last Supper by Giovanni Borgnis, who painted so many of the Dashwood ceilings. Note the Creed and Lord's Prayer boards.

WING. 6m NE of Aylesbury on A418. *All Saints.*
This is one of the most outstanding and interesting pre-Conquest

Wing, All Saints. The east end, showing the late C10 Anglo-Saxon apse.

churches in Britain. Built in the late-C10, it uniquely incorporates a polygonal apse, a crypt and aisles in the same building. The west tower, ground-floor and clerestory windows are all C15, as are the remarkably fine *roofs* and the high tower arch. The south aisle was rebuilt in the early-C14. Inside, there are the largest Saxon chancel and the largest Saxon arch in Britain. These, together with the astonishing height of the nave, give an impression of a surprisingly spacious church. There is also an amazingly good selection of *monuments*: that of Sir Robert Dormer (d.1552), has a surprisingly early use of Renaissance elements and is the best example of its date in Britain. A restored rood screen and south-east chapel screen are early-C16 and the pulpit is Jacobean. Notice, in the porch, the base of a Norman font.

Other churches

AYLESBURY. 40m NW of London on the A41. *St Mary.*
A large cruciform church of the C13 and early-C14, so wrecked by Sir George Gilbert Scott's restoration in 1850-69 that it looks C19. Notable for its late-C12 circular and finely carved *font* from which other similar fonts in the county take their name. Note, too, the four late-C15 *misericords*, one unfinished, the very rare C15 *vestment chest*, and the *glass* of 1855-60 by Thomas Willement in the east lancets.
CHETWODE. 5m SW of Buckingham off A421. *SS Mary & Nicholas.*
All that remains of an Augustinian Priory founded in 1245 is this church, once the priory chancel, with a slim tower added in C.1480. It contains some of the best C13 work in the county. Note the painted *triptych* dated 1696, the magical *glass* of c.1250 and the C14, the joined *piscina* and *sedilia*, the north chapel converted to manor pew complete with a fireplace.

***West Wycombe,** St Laurence.* The fine plasterwork
of the 1762 nave.

CLIFTON REYNES. 5m N of Newport Pagnall off A509. *St Mary.*
What is visible is C13 and C14. There are good *monuments* with the
rarity of four remarkable oak *effigies* of two knights and their ladies
(c.1300). The C14 tomb of Sir John and Lady Reynes should not be
overlooked; the dog at his feet has a collar with B O' on it. The collar
suggests that the animal was a pet.

FINGEST. 5m W of High Wycombe off B482. *St Bartholomew.*
A Norman church with a famous and massive Norman tower wider
than the nave, capped by a C17 double saddleback roof, which may
be a copy of the original. The chancel is C13.

HEDGERLEY. 3m SE of Beaconsfield off A355. *St Mary.*
Built mainly in flint in 1852 by Benjamin Ferrey in the Gothic style
and containing items from two earlier churches; a C15 cylindrical
font, a painting of the Ten Commandments showing the fate of the
wicked, a piece of red cloth said to be a cloak belonging to Charles I
and given as an altar frontal, and two brasses.

HILLESDON. 3m S of Buckingham off A421. *All Saints.*
A church unusual for being all of one date, c.1493 with a west tower
of c.1430, and restored by Sir George Gilbert Scott in 1875. Inside,
the chancel, the *glass*, roof, screen and benches are all contemporary,
and the woodwork mainly C16. The Denton family *pew* is of 1660
and there are stone angels beneath the chancel roof. A drawing of the
church by Scott, aged fifteen, is in the vestry. There are interesting
monuments.

LATHBURY. 1m N of Newport Pagnell on B526. *All Saints.*
Its Norman past is obvious from the *tympanum* re-set in the south
aisle and a window in the south wall. The west tower is C13, the
arcading C12. Do not miss the C15 *wall paintings* over the chancel
arch and on the nave north and south walls.

LITTLE KIMBLE. 5m S of Aylesbury on A4010. *All Saints.*

A small basically C13 church built of flint and 'modernised' in the early-C14, the date of the doors and windows. The only reason for a visit is to examine the important series of early-C14 *wall paintings*, fragmentary but mostly identifiable. Note the Jacobean pulpit, and the *tiles* in the chancel depicting scenes from the Arthurian legends.

UPTON. 1m SE of Slough centre. *St Laurence.*

Dismiss the south aisle of 1851 by Benjamin Ferrey and what remains, the nave, central tower, and chancel are pure Norman. Note the cylindrical Norman font. In the vaulting, the painting of the ribs may represent the original. The south window is by Thomas Willement of 1857.

Hampshire
& Isle of Wight

Hampshire lies mainly on chalk and the chief building material is flint. The county has none of the best building stone such as is found in Dorset and Wiltshire, although there is good limestone on the Isle of Wight. Its churches are mainly of flint, with wooden belfries.

There is an abundance of Saxon examples and two are of national interest: St Mary at Braemore and St Nicholas at Boarhunt. At St Cross, Winchester one can see the transition from Norman to early-Gothic, while the C14 is well represented by Winchester College Chapel and the Tudor period cannot be bettered in Britain than by the Vyne Chapel, built 1518-27. Of all the Hampshire churches, St Mary's at Avington is worth a major diversion. It has an interior unaltered since built in 1768-71. Finally, the county is unique in having no less than four Norman Tournai black marble fonts. There are only ten in Britain.

Abbotts Ann, St Mary.
A comparatively modern Maiden's Garland dated 1952.

ABBOTTS ANN. 3m SW of Andover off A343. *St Mary.*

Thomas 'Diamond' Pitt, East India merchant and Lord Chatham's grandfather, built the church, of brick with stone dressings, in 1716. The interior has a coved ceiling, and many original fittings: pulpit, box pews and a west gallery supported on Tuscan columns. What makes the church remarkable is that it has more *Maiden Garlands* (see Introduction) than any other church in Britain.

ALTON. 10m SE of Basingstoke on A339/A31. *St Laurence.*
Except for the Victorian spire the exterior is all C15. A memorial tablet recalls a bitter defence of the church by eighty Royalists against a superior Parliamentary force. Bullet marks on the door and nave piers are reminders of this bitter episode when the Royalists, taking cover behind barricades made from pews, were finally overcome and slaughtered on the chancel steps.

AVINGTON. 4m NE of Winchester off B3047. *St Mary.*
Built in 1768-71 for Margaret, Marchioness of Caernarvon, of brick with stone dressings, it has one of the finest parish church interiors in Britain. Luckily it survived the 'improving' of the Camdenians (see Introduction) in the early-Victorian years. The three-decker pulpit, a luxurious squire's pew, the box pews, and two sets of hat pegs on the north wall are all *original fittings*, made of Spanish mahogany. As for metal work, the brass chandelier of two tiers of branches and the *altar rail*, which may be of lead, are all as original as the rest of the fittings. Note the Commandment and Creed boards beside the altar, the single *hatchment* of the Brydges family, the *Royal Arms* of 1771 and a barrel organ of 1830. The rare 'Vinegar Bible' is alas, displayed in full daylight and is deteriorating badly.

BOARHUNT. 4m NW of Portsmouth on B2177. *St Nicholas.*
A Saxon church of c.1064, refitted in the mid-C19 and surprisingly

Avington, St Mary. Built in 1768-71 and one of the finest unaltered church interiors.

unaffected by the Camdenians (see Introduction). It is a very satisfy-ing interior. The squire's pew, the three-decker pulpit, west gallery and communion rail are all in modest pitch pine blending subtly with the simple Saxon architecture. In the south door arch there is scroll *painting* of the C15.

BRAMLEY. 4m N of Basingstoke off A33. *St James.*
The church is of all periods, from a Norman window to Sir John Soane's Gothick chapel of 1801. Nevertheless, the interior is quite plain apart from its *wall paintings*. The best is in the nave, the Murder of Becket of the C13, showing him realistically, and unusu-ally, kneeling at an altar wearing a cassock. Facing the visitor on the north wall is a very large St Christopher of the C15. In the chancel are remains of the original all-over C13 masonry design centred with flowers. North of the altar is *painted* a large and over-restored St James, with a faded Virgin south of the altar. In the south transept are two C16 brasses. In the north window are fragments of original C14 *glass*, with some *Flemish glass* in Soane's chapel.

BREAMORE. 8m S of Salisbury on A338. *St Mary.*
This is one of the best late-Saxon churches in the country. Originally cruciform with a central tower it has lost the north transept. Over the south transept arch is an Anglo-Saxon inscription 'Here the covenant is revealed to thee'. Over the south door is a mutilated *Saxon rood* in relief with the body of Christ bent in agony. Behind the rood are *wall paintings* of rolling hills with a church and other buildings, once the background to figures of Christ, the Virgin and St John.

BURGHCLERE. 5m S of Newbury off A34. *Sandham Memorial Chapel.*
In the care of the National Trust. The chapel, commissioned by Mr & Mrs J.L. Behrend, is a war memorial dedicated to the memory of Lt. H.W. Sandham who died in 1919 from malaria caught in Macedonia. From 1927-32 Sir Stanley Spencer painted nineteen scenes showing soldiers occupied with the ordinariness of war, from a dugout in Salonika to sorting laundry. A Resurrection of Dead Soldiers covers the east wall. Spencer painted the series when he was thirty-six and at the height of his skill.

CARISBROOKE. 1m SW of Newport I.o.W. on B3401. *St Mary.*
Claimed to be the 'most important ecclesiastical building on the island', the church is all that remains of a former Benedictine Priory suppressed as early as 1414. The nave is firmly Norman with a south aisle of c.1200 framed by a fine arcade. The chancel was demolished in c.1565 leaving an arch of c.1200. For those who relish architec-tural problems the purpose of the C13 arch across the south aisle remains unresolved. The impressive five-stage west tower is C15.

Inside, the font is 1602 and the pulpit 1658. Note the two *monuments* of the C16 and C17.

CHRISTCHURCH.
6m E of Bournemouth off A35. *Holy Trinity.*
This is the longest church in Britain and once an Augustinian priory which became the parish church at the Dissolution. The nave, with ribbed plaster vault of 1819, and transepts date from 1091 to 1190. The choir and the great Tree of Jesse *screen* contain the most interesting features: a full set of C14 and C15 *misericords*, late-C15 and early-C16 bosses, the c.1350 *reredos*, the altar table of 1831 by A.W.N. Pugin, whose wife is buried here, and the Salisbury chapel containing the body of the Countess of Salisbury, beheaded in 1541.

CORHAMPTON. 9m N of Fareham on A32.
This stands, like the church at Sopley, on an artificial mound and is therefore a very old site. It is a perfect small Saxon church of c.1030, only spoilt by an unfeeling C19 brick east end. Inside, the Saxon chancel arch matches in style the former north doorway. The familiar Norman rope design decorates a circular Norman *font.* In the chancel are C13 *wall paintings* of stylised draperies consisting of circles surrounded by squares, with birds, and scenes above.

EAST MEON. 4m W of Petersfield off A272. *All Saints.*
This is one of the most exciting churches in the county. The gem of the interior is the black Tournai Norman *font* of c.1135, one of only ten in Britain. Its sides are carved with scenes representing the Creation of Adam, Creation of Eve, Temptation, Expulsion, and an Angel teaching Adam to dig. The pulpit of 1706 is from *Holy Trinity* in Minories, London. Sir Ninian Comper carried out extensive restoration in 1907; the *glass* of the east window, the *reredos* of the Lady Chapel and the Chapel *screen* are his.

GODSHILL. 3m from Shanklin I.o.W. on A3020. *St Lawrence.*
Nothing in this church is older than C14. However, it is worth visiting if only to see the very rare, faded, but recognisable *wall painting* of Christ hanging, not from the usual cross, but from three leafy thorn branches. The painting of the late C15 to early-C16, although touched up, has lost little of its beauty. There is also a big Rubens (1577-1640), or 'school of', painting of Daniel in the Lions' Den. This came from Mapledurham House, I.o.W.; if it is a copy, the original is lost, but at least two replicas are known.

IDSWORTH. 9m NE of Portsmouth off A3. *St Hubert.*
A small isolated and delightful Norman church with an C18 bell-turret. The interior, although mainly C18, was skilfully restored in 1912. The box pews, communion rail, pulpit and west gallery are genuine. Notice the Royal Arms. The C14 *wall painting* of the legend

of St Hubert is outstanding, and the hunting scene and the history of St John Baptist are particularly vivid.

LYNDHURST. 9m SW of Southampton on A35. *St Michael.*
William White built the church in 1858-70, a time to benefit from the early *Arts & Crafts* movement. It has a very large interior, with walls consisting of bricks in two shades of red, yellow and white, with a nave roof supported by human-sized angels. Filling the south windows (1862-3) of the south transept with his remarkable colours is some of the best *glass* by William Morris. It puts the west window (1903) by C.E. Kempe in second place. Morris's close friend, Sir E. Burne-Jones, designed the east window. As if all this colour was not enough, Lord Leighton painted the *reredos* fresco of the Wise and Foolish Virgins. Alice Liddell (1852-1934), the Alice of *Alice in Wonderland*, is buried in the churchyard.

NORTH BADDESLEY. 3m E of Romsey off A27. *St John.*
The church is built on lands granted to the Knights Hospitallers, which explains the extravagant C15 *tomb-chest* in the chancel marked with the Hospitallers' cross. In the nave is an open timber roof, and a waggon-roof in the chancel. The screen, marked 'T.F.1602' and claimed to have come from North Stonham, looks all of a piece with the pulpit. A temporary removal of a monument in the chancel in the 1960s revealed a simple pattern of wall painting that must have covered all the chancel walls.

PORTCHESTER. 3m NW of Portsmouth off A27. *St Mary.*
Standing in the south-east corner of the remarkably preserved Roman fort the church is all that remains of an Augustinian Priory founded in 1133. It is built of stone, apart from the C19 flint vestry, with a low crossing tower. The south transept has gone and the chancel was ruthlessly shortened in c.1600. A particularly insensitive parish room is hitched on to the south of the nave and built of breeze blocks! The *west front* is the prize; relatively simple with restrained Norman decoration it is one of the finest surviving Norman west fronts. The interior is also simple until one comes to the north transept, now the Lady Chapel, where the C19 restoration has replaced the lost rich foliate capitals. The *font*, apart from the base of 1888, is a good C12 piece. It is impossible to miss the *arms* of Queen Anne on the north wall recording a royal grant for restoration after a fire in 1705. Before leaving see the *monument* by Nicholas Stone to Sir Thomas Cornwallis (d.1618) and note the arms of Elizabeth I.

ROMSEY. 6m NE of Southampton on A3057. *SS Mary & Ethelfreda.*
The chancel and crossing are distinctly Norman C12 and the west end C13. The south-east apse has a sculptured Anglo-Saxon *rood*.

Romsey Abbey, St Mary & Ethelfreda.
The C13 nave of the abbey church.

This is a Crucifixion of C10-C11 with two angels on the arms of the cross. Beneath are St John and the Virgin and further away Longinus and the Soldier with the sponge soaked in vinegar. In 993 Abbess Elwina had a vision that invading Danes would attack the Abbey. She had the forethought to pack books and silver away. The vision was fulfilled, and is commemorated in a medieval *wall painting* in the retrochoir. In the north transept is a rare survivor, a *reredos* of c.1525. It depicts nine standing saints on the top row, above Christ rising from his tomb on the bottom row. Earl Mountbatten of Burma (1900-79) is buried in the south transept.

SELBORNE. 4m SE of Alton on B3006. *St Mary.*
Another manor that belonged to the Knights Hospitallers; a coffin lid marked with their cross, like that at North Baddesley, is in the church. Gilbert White (1720-93), the author of *The Natural History of Selborne*, is buried in the churchyard and is Selborne's claim to fame. It is fitting that his great-nephew restored the church in 1856. A St Francis window commemorates his life. Additionally there is an outstanding Flemish *triptych* of c.1520 attributed to Jan Mostert (1470-1560). The centre panel shows the Adoration of the Magi and the two wings show the donor and SS Andrew and George.

SHALFLEET. 3m E of Yarmouth I.o.W. on A3054. *St Michael.*
Basically a Norman church with a stumpy fat Norman west tower, a C13 chancel and a south arcade that is late-C13 with C17 windows. Above the north doorway is a Saxon *tympanum* of a bearded saint throttling two lions with his bare hands. The north windows of the nave are 1812. Note the *reredos* dated 1630 in the south aisle and the early-C17 pulpit with bookrest and the box pews.

SHORWELL. 4m SW of Newport, I. o W. on B3323. *St Peter.*

The west tower with recessed stone spire has a weather cock dated 1617 when the spire was built. The oldest part of the church is the north wall, which has two features: a lancet window and a blocked door, both c.1200. The plan is oddly rectangular because originally the north aisle and chancel belonged to Carisbrooke Priory and the nave and south aisle to the parish. A polygonal stone pulpit is mid-C15, with a very decorated tester dated 1620. Note the iron *hour-glass* and stand. In place of a rood beam is a beam carrying the figure of Christ in Majesty flanked by SS Michael and Gabriel. This is supported by two carved corbels representing Sin and Death. A curiosity is the vestry which was originally a gunroom and one of the last to survive. *Wall paintings* show St Christopher on the nave north wall; on the right is St Christopher's martyrdom, while above these are a king and an executioner. Note also the copy of a C16 Icelandic altar-piece of The Last Supper. There are interesting early-C17 monuments to the Leigh family. A rarity is a 1541 Cranmer Bible.

SILCHESTER. 6m N of Basingstoke off A340. *St Mary.*
The church, probably built over the site of a Roman temple, is the only unquestionably Christian church site remaining from Roman Britain. The present church is mercifully not over-restored, but the Victorian passion for removing box-pews went unchecked. Fortunately they left the C15 *screen* with a frieze of wing-spread angels, and the Jacobean pulpit with domed tester, dated 1639. In the splays of the chancel south lancet windows is the now familiar painted masonry patterning with floral centres, of c.1300.

SOPLEY. 3m N of Christchurch on B3347. *St Michael & All Angels.*
The church stands on an artificial mound suggesting an early prehistoric site. There is C16 linenfold panelling in the screen beneath the central tower and more in the choir stalls. The large Crucifixion painting above the chancel arch is by J. Emms, 1869. A good example of Eric Gill's *lettering* is on the War Memorial of 1927.

SOUTHAMPTON. *St Michael.*
This is the only medieval church left in the city. Inside is one of the ten black Tournai Norman *fonts* remaining in Britain, of c.1170. There is also a most beautiful early-C15 Flemish, brass eagle *lectern* which was rescued, very damaged, from the blitzed wreckage of *Holy Rood* church. The other *lectern* is English of the C15 and similar in design to those at Southwell, Newcastle, Coventry and Urbino. Here too is the oldest pre-Reformation piece of plate in Britain: a silver-gilt *chalice* of 1551.

SOUTHWICK. 6m NW of Portsmouth on B2177. *St James.*
Built in 1566 in Gothic revival style, it had an unaltered interior until the 1950s, when decayed nave pews were insensitively and

incongruously replaced by polished open pews. The gallery, three-decker pulpit and two family pews in the chancel remain untouched. A light grey is used to good effect on the walls instead of the usual whitewash. The *reredos* is the gem of the church; a central C18 panel of doves and cherubs circling in the sky surrounded by an architectural frame. Brasses to John Whyte (d.1567), who rebuilt the church in 1566, his wife (d.1548) and children are on the *tomb-chest* in the north chapel arch.

STOKE CHARITY. 5m N of Winchester between A33 & A34. *SS Mary & Michael.*
The seemingly uninteresting exterior of this isolated church with west bell-turret conceals some remarkable treasures. To begin with the oldest, the north aisle is Saxon, the south porch and the chancel arch are both Norman, and the two-bay north arcade early-Norman, while the North Chapel is of c.1250. On the south wall of the chapel are unrestored fragments of a mid-C13 *wall painting*, and medieval tiles on the floor. The glory of the church, the untidy mass of *monuments* and *brasses* that tumble out of the chapel, date from 1448 to 1780. Note the *sculptured* Mass of St Gregory in the North Chapel, it is a unique undamaged survivor of c.1500, and the two squints.

THE VYNE. 4m N of Basingstoke off A340. *Chapel.*
Maintained by the National Trust. Built in 1518-27, this is one of the best medieval chapels in Britain and substantially unaltered. The interior is simple with a three-sided apse and a wood ribbed roof. The exceptional Flemish *glass* of c.1520 in the east window is unri-

valled for its time. Note the thirty-two carved *heraldic badges* on the underside of the canopies above the stalls which, like all the other carving, were done in c.1527. Set in the borders of the stone floor are Flemish tiles of c.1512. Preceding the chapel is an ante-chapel with a family gallery above. On the gallery walls is a *trompel'oeil* of fan-vaulting by Spiridone Roma done in 1771. In the south wall a screen door leads to the Strawberry Hill Gothic *Tomb Chamber* made in

The Vyne, The Chapel. The reclining figure of Challoner Chute (d.1659), made in 1775-6 by Thomas Carter.

c.1757 in which is a contrasting Classical marble *tomb* with the fully dressed semi-reclining figure of Chaloner Chute (d.1659), Speaker of the House of Commons, who is actually buried at Chiswick. There are two windows with good *glass* by John Rowel done in 1730-1 and a Holy Family attributed to Girolamo Siciolante (1504-50).

WARNFORD. 9m W of Petersfield on A32. *Our Lady.*
The C13 Latin inscription over the south porch tells us that St Wilfred built this church during his exile in Wessex in 675 and Adam de Port rebuilt it in the C12. Of St Wilfred's church nothing remains, but the Norman tower could be Adam's. The *rood screen* is partly of c.1630, the *benches* with moulded ends are early- C16, while in the choir there are C15 *stalls.*

WINCHESTER. 10m N of Southampton on A33. *St Cross.*
Of the St Cross hospital, founded in 1136, nothing survives. The present Norman church, built 1160-1225, with tower and clerestory of 1335, is one of the most perfect in Hampshire. Inside there is much to enjoy; the C15 *lectern* with parrot's head, eagle's body and webbed feet, and late-C15 *glass* in four of the east windows. The south transept has the remains of faded painted masonry pattern of the C13 with more in the north chancel aisle. In the chancel are early-C16 fragments of Renaissance woodwork. Many medieval floor *tiles* throughout, but particularly of interest is the Flemish *triptych* in the south chapel painted c. 1520. In the chancel are three *brasses,* two to Masters of the hospital: John de Campedon (1410), 6ft long, and one of his successors Richard Harward (1493), only 2ft long.
St John Baptist. St John's Street.
This is the most rewarding of the city's churches. A C14 *screen* set between chancel and chapel and two poppy-head bench ends are just some of the early-Renaissance woodwork. In the splays of two lancet windows in the north wall are *wall paintings*; in one St John Evangelist, St Christopher with a Bishop in the other.
St Swithun-Upon-Kingsgate, Kingsgate.
Few churches over town gates survive but this is one, and obviously loved by the congregation. Built of stone and entered by timber covered stairs the small church is difficult to date because there is little decorative detail. The windows date from c.1500 and the timber roof from the 1660s. There are small remnants of medieval glass set in the east window.
Winchester College Chapel.
Consecrated in 1395, it contains fittings and glass which, though restored and altered in the late-C19 and early-C20, are of the highest order. One enters at the west end beneath a gallery of 1908 by W.D. Caroë, who also designed the stalls, pews and panelling in 1913-21; the eighteen *misericords* are C14. The *reredos* dating from c.1470 was

restored in the 1870s and altered by Caroë in 1920. The east window has a Tree of Jesse of the 1820s. Some of the original *glass* sections, dated 1393, have been reassembled, with one panel lent by the V & A Museum, in the west window of the Thurbern Chantry Chapel (begun 1473) on the south side. Note the two large Flemish tapestries of c.1500.

WHIPPINGHAM. 2m SE of Cowes I.o.W. off B3021. *St Mildred.* The Osborne estate church built 1854-5 for Prince Albert by A.J. Humbert in an incongruous North German style with English detail of c.1200. But whatever one thinks about the curious mix of styles, including an Italian Romanesque porch to the Royal pew, the inside does have considerable Royalist interest. Princess Louise designed the carpet surrounding the font and the marble figure on the altar of Christ on the Cross. Edward VII gave the elaborate alabaster *reredos* as a memorial to his mother. Queen Victoria gave the screens in 1897 as a memorial to Prince Henry of Battenburg and she also crocheted a hassock. Other Royal mementos clutter the interior as do the many monuments. One wall of the north porch has a Roman tympanum set in it and another fragments of Norman decoration. Uffa Fox (d.1972), the yachtsman, is buried in the churchyard near to the Royal tomb of Earl Mountbatten's parents.

Other Churches.

ANDOVER. 20m W of Basingstoke on A303. *St Mary.*
Built 1840-6 with soaring interior influenced by Salisbury Cathedral.

ASHMONDSWORTH. 7m SW of Newbury off A343. *St James.*
A small Norman and C13 church with unrestored interior and late C13 and C15 wall paintings.

BASING. 2m E of Basingstoke off A30. *St Mary.*
Damaged in the siege of Basing House in 1645. Painted floor, *helms* and *Royal Arms* of 1660.

BRAMSHOTT. 1m N of Liphook off A3. *St Mary.*
There is medieval glass in the chancel north window, Arts and Crafts glass in the north aisle west window, and a C15 monument to John Weston and his wife.

CHILCOMB. 2m SE of Winchester off A31. *St Andrew.*
Small Norman church with Norman piscina and medieval tiles in the chancel.

ELLINGHAM. 2m N of Ringwood off A338. *St Mary.*
Although the brick porch is dated 1720 and the west end 1747 this stone-built church of aisleless nave and chancel is C13. Inside, the splendid *reredos* is c.1700. Over the screen is a *tympanum* with texts. A Jacobean *pulpit* with an *hourglass, family pew*, a C15 barrel *roof* and *Royal Arms* of 1671, were spared the restoration of 1869 into the 1880s.

HALE. 7m SE of Salisbury off B3080. *St Mary.*
A small rural church incompletely restored by the Baroque architect Thomas Archer in 1717, who rebuilt the chancel and transepts at his own expense. His own pompous monument, surely not by him, is in Roman dress.

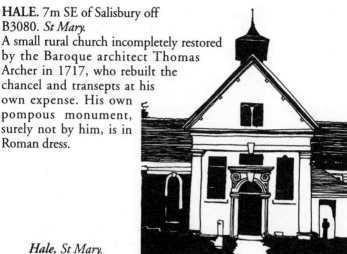

Hale, St Mary.
Rebuilt in 1717 in a classical style.

Hertfordshire

A county of undulating chalklands and glacial clays in river valleys provides almost nothing in the way of building materials except flint and brick. Where stone is employed it has been expensively transported and consequently is used sparingly. An alternative was chalk clunch which weathers badly on exteriors. In many cases weathered clunch was replaced with stone in the nineteenth century. Wood, of which there was plenty, inspired much work of high standard. A local feature crowning the towers of many churches are the thin lead spires known as 'spikes' or 'snuffers' dating from the middle ages.

There are no complete pre-Conquest churches in the county, although St Mary at Westmill comes near to it with a pre-Conquest nave. St Mary at Walkern has a partly mid-C10 nave, with a pre-Conquest rood near the south porch, and St Michael at St Albans has a nave and chancel with pre-Conquest walls. Norman churches are more plentiful; the two important ones being St Leonard at Bengoe and St Stephen at St Albans. Early Gothic is represented by St George at Anstey and St Etheldreda at Hatfield. Later wool churches are those of St Mary at Watford and St Mary at Ware. Of the seventeenth century, St Peter at Buntingford, based on a Greek cross plan, is noteworthy. The nineteenth century is well represented; J.P. Seddon designed the early Arts and Crafts St Peter at Ayot St Peter in 1874-5, and J.F. Bentley, the magnificent Holy Rood at Watford in

1883-90, both well worth a detour. Finally there is Sir Ninian Comper's All Saints Chapel at London Colney, begun in 1927.

ANSTEY. 6m SE of Royston off B1368. *St George.*
This cruciform church with central tower of c.1200 has a nave of the early-C14 with chancel and transepts of the late-C13. Unusually for the county it is built in stone which, it has been suggested, came from the nearby castle, now only a mound to the north. Inside, the nave roof is C15 and do not overlook the Norman *font* decorated with four mermen, one of only two in Britain; the other is at *St Peter*, Cambridge. The chancel, the finest of its date in the county, has twelve c.1300 stalls with seven *misericords.* An unusual feature is the *sedilia* and *piscina* combined with a doorway and windows. Very interesting *graffiti* is to be seen in the chancel, some heraldic, the earliest of which may have been on the castle walls, while the later efforts are Elizabethan. The south transept was once used as a chantry chapel which explains the squint directed at the chancel altar. Sadly it is now dominated by a gloomy organ. Notice the C15 *glass* of an angel in the north wall of the nave, and the c.1300 tomb-chest.

ASHWELL. 3m NE of Baldock off A505. *St Mary.*
This large, low C14 church of flint and chalk is surprisingly dominated by a magnificent three-stage west tower built of clunch and capped with the inevitable 'spike'. The whitewashed aisleless interior is unexpectedly plain. The *sedilia* and Lady Chapel *screen* are all C15, while the pulpit is C16. There are also some late-C14 fragments of glass in the clerestory windows. Very moving and interesting *graffiti* are scratched on the interior of the tower: one retails the horror of the Black Death in the mid-C14, another shows the pre-Wren St Paul's, London, and yet another records a devastating storm in 1361. Other scratchings are on the nave arcades.

AYOT ST LAWRENCE. 3m W of Welwyn off B651. *New St Lawrence.*
Built in 1778-9 to replace the old church and to fill a picturesque view from Ayot House. Nicholas Revett was one of the very few architects to visit Greece, consequently the church has a Greek façade based on the Temple of Apollo at Delos, and is one of the first of the Greek Revival buildings. However, it is Greek detail grafted on to a Palladian composition. One enters by a vestibule and, under a two-columned screen, into a nave with a coffered tunnel-vault ceiling. To each side are tunnel-vaulted transepts. The east end is a coffered apse. All very Classical. G.B. Shaw (1856-1950), being an atheist, was not buried here but his ashes were scattered in his garden at Shaw's Corner.

BENGOE. 1m N of Hertford on B158. *St Leonard.*

One of the rare Hertfordshire complete Norman churches with an even rarer apse. Windows in the south wall are C14 and C15, the brick porch C18 and the bellcote C19. Inside, are fragments of a *painted* overall pattern; in the chancel ashlar with a later lozenge design, while on the nave east wall is the remains of a C13 Deposition. Some C14 *tiles* remain in the sanctuary. Notice the two C17 monuments.

BISHOP'S STORTFORD. 8m N of Harlow on A1184. *St Michael.* This big low C15 church built in flint has a west tower of which the upper stage of the tall slim spire was added in brick in 1812. The C15 chancel was lengthened and re-roofed in 1660. When the north chapel was added in the C19, the roof was lifted to insert a clerestory. A restoration was completed in 1868. The nave roof is C15 and rests on twelve corbels of the apostles; note the coloured heraldic *bosses*. Do not miss the C15 choirstalls and screen. The eighteen stalls have C15 *misericords* reputed to be from old St Paul's, London. The *font* of Purbeck marble is C12 and from the earlier church. In the south aisle is a curious C17 *monument* recording the deaths from smallpox of an entire family.

FLAMSTEAD. 5m N of Hemel Hempstead off A5. *St Leonard.* The nave is Norman, as is the stumpy west tower with 'spike' spire. The short chancel is C13, the same date as the two aisles. Built of flint and in some places, Roman brick, this is one of the few Norman churches in the county. It was restored in 1898. Inside, the nave arcades have C13 capitals carved with typical stiff-leaf decoration. Notice the inlaid *pulpit* of 1698 and the C15 screen. On no account miss the C14 *wall paintings*, only uncovered in the 1930s and the

Ayot St Lawrence, St Lawrence. Rebuilt in 1778-9 in a Classical style.

best in this county other than those in St Alban's Cathedral. The paintings show eight subjects in all, together with twelve apostles above the nave arcades. Note the *brass* to John Oudeby (d.1414), and the several good monuments.

HATFIELD. 20m N of London on A1. *St Etheldreda.*
The impression is that of a C19 church with a flint C15 tower. This is partially correct because the nave was rebuilt in 1871 when all the good box pews and three-decker pulpit were thrown out. The chancel, transepts and chapels are C13. One reason for a visit must be to see the *monuments* in the Salisbury Chapel, extravagantly refurbished in 1871 by the 3rd Marquess. The striking white monument to the 1st Earl (d.1612), supported by four virtues, is by Maximillian Colt. The C13 armoured knight with shield is unidentified but he is not a Salisbury. Also another intruder is William Curll (d.1617) whose *effigy* is by Nicholas Stone. In the north transept is some C17 armorial *glass*, the rest is C19, and outstanding is the south transept *window* by Morris & Co and designed in 1894 by Sir E. Burne-Jones. The chancel east window of c.1870 is by Clayton & Bell. Note the 1760 memorial busts by Rysbrack of Sir James Read and his son Sir John.

Hatfield, St Etheldreda. 1st Earl of Salisbury's (d.1612) tomb by Maximillian Colt.

ST ALBANS. 20m NW of London on A6. *St Michael.*
The tower and west end are of 1898 by Lord Grimthorpe and are of no interest, for the nave and chancel are late-C10 and far more rewarding. Built of flint with stone dressings and in places re-used Roman brick, it is the most interesting parish church in the county. Aisles were added in the early-C12, when the massive Saxon walls were pierced by Roman arches, and the nave heightened in the C13. The interior fittings are mostly C19; however, the oak pulpit is late-

C16 and the hourglass C17. Do not miss the alabaster seated and sleeping figure of Sir Francis Bacon (d.1626) on the north side of the chancel, nor the fine *brass* to Thomas Peacock (d.1380) and his wife in the south chapel.

St Stephen.

Like St Michael's, this has Saxon and early-Norman origins. Built of flint with stone dressings and Roman brick, it has a complicated evolution. The north wall of the nave is Saxon with an inserted wide Norman arch. The chancel is also Norman, but the north wall was rebuilt in the C15, and a south chapel was added in the early-C13. One can spend a great deal of time here disentangling the confusing architectural history. The brass *lectern* was looted from Holyrood in the Scottish campaign of 1544. All the glass is C19 and the south aisle windows are 1862-4 by Clayton & Bell.

STANSTEAD ABBOTS. 2m SE of Ware on A414. *St James.*

In the care of the Redundant Churches Fund. The broad C15 west tower is completed with a 'spike', and adjoins a C12 nave with C13 chancel, all in flint with stone dressings. An open C15 timber porch distinguishes the south door, and a north chapel was added in brick in 1577. All pretty average, but the interest lies in the unaltered C18 'prayer book' whitewashed *interior* which remains complete with box pews, communion rail and table, three-decker pulpit, royal arms, textboards, four hatchments and tower screen. Note also the C15, C16 *brasses*, and the texts on the walls of the C16 Baesche chapel. Above the plastered ceiling is a medieval king-post roof.

WALKERN. 4m E of Stevenage on B1037. *St Mary.*

The C14 exterior covers a much earlier church. One enters through a Norman south door into a Norman south aisle and arcade, with the remnants of a late-Saxon Rood set in the south wall. This south aisle was once the nave of an earlier church. Across the nave, the north aisle is C14. At the east end the chancel was badly restored in 1878 and 1880, but fortunately a C13 *sedilia* and *piscina* were left untouched. There are several good monuments including a fine *effigy* of a knight in Purbeck marble, and some late brasses.

Other Churches

AYOT ST PETER. 1m SW of Welwyn off B656. *St Peter.*

Built 1874-5 in blue, white and red brick by J.P. Seddon with an unusually complete and exceptional early Arts and Crafts interior. Worth a detour.

BUNTINGFORD. 8m S of Royston on A10. *St Peter.*

A small brick church built 1614-26 on a Greek-cross plan, the apse is 1899 when the church suffered a restoration. See the C17 brass plate showing the interior.

FURNEUX PELHAM. 5m NW of Bishop's Stortford off B1038. *St Mary.*

A large church with tall west tower with a Herts spike, aisled nave, with a south chapel of c.1518, and chancel. Good angel *roof,* mid-C13 *sedilia* and *piscina,* brilliant, early William Morris *glass* designed by Sir E. Burne-Jones in 1867 in the south chapel, south wall; that in the east wall was designed by Morris and Burne-Jones in 1876.

HITCHIN. 3m NW of Stevenage on A602. *St Mary.*

The largest church in the county, built of flint rubble with stone dressings with, in places, Roman brick. The tower and lower part of the nave are C12, the rest of the nave is C14. Both aisles are also C14 and the clerestory early-C16, while the roofs are C14 and C15. High quality workmanship marks the screens and fittings. The many monuments and twelve *brasses* in the south chancel chapel are worth looking for.

LONDON COLNEY. 3m SE of St Albans on B5378. *All Saints Chapel.*

Begun in 1927 by Sir Ninian Comper and extended in 1964 by Sebastian Comper. High, narrow and long, built in the style of c.1300. The extremely successful all white interior with large baldicchino was designed to the last detail by Comper. Well worth a visit.

WARE. 3m NE of Hertford on A10. *St Mary.*

A very large church of the C14 and C15, the exterior over-restored in 1847-50. There are many C14 and C15 decorative details in the chancel and transepts. The late C14 *font* is heavily decorated. The pulpit, communion rails and panelling are mid-C17, and there are three pretty average C15 brasses.

WATFORD. 17m NW of London off M1 exits 5 & 6. *Holy Rood.*

Built 1883-90 by J.F. Bentley and the finest Gothic Revival church of its time. Much detail is influenced by the Arts and Crafts movement. Art Nouveau light fittings of 1890s. Worth visiting for the detail. *St Mary.*

A large C13 church with clerestory, arcades and south chapel added in C15. All over-restored in 1871. Note the C18 pulpit, a Flemish vestment *cupboard,* and two *monuments* by Nicholas Stone. Of the three *brasses* that of 1415 is particularly fine.

Oxfordshire

As a county Oxfordshire has diverse sources of building stone, reaching from Banbury in the north, where lies brown ironstone, to Henley-on-Thames and the Chilterns in the south-east, which is chalk land and where flint is the principal building material. In the middle is the Cotswold limestone used in the city of Oxford, while the best, a grey limestone, is found round Burford in the west. Understandably the best churches are found where the quarries are, in the north and west. With so much diversity of building material there is, therefore, clearly no typical 'Oxfordshire' church style.

The county has little Saxon work but the tower of Langford and its carvings is the best, followed by the tower of St Michael-at-the-Northgate, Oxford. Norman architecture is better represented by Swyncombe and Checkendon. Childrey and Dorchester are the best of the C13. Thereafter one looks to Oxford: Merton chapel is early-C14, while from the C15 are All Souls, New College and Magdalen which all built new chapels. Outside the city many wool churches were being built and altered in the C14 and C15; Abingdon, Dorchester, Witney and Burford are but a few of them.

ABINGDON. 6m S of Oxford off A34. *St Helen.*
With a tall C13 steeple, the church is mainly C15 and C16; it was restored in 1873. The interior gives an impression of space and it is the second widest church in Britain: Go straight to the Lady Chapel for here are the rarest *painted panels* in Britain, they are also unique. In the 1390s Pope Boniface XI offered reduced sessions in purgatory for donations towards the erection of the chapel. Originally there were fifty-two ceiling panels, depicting the Tree of Jesse, but restorations and age have reduced these to thirty-eight. A full restoration begun in 1990 and costing £240,000 has brought out the original colours on a background of vermilion. Gold, reds, greens, purples and yellow now shine out nearly as new. The nave roof is painted with a huge Tree of Jesse. Notice particularly the *Lily Crucifix* [see Introduction], at the apex of the whole scheme. What follows can only be an anticlimax, but is nevertheless worth seeking: two good, but small, *brasses*, the Mayor's seat of 1706, with sword rest, a very good *pulpit* dated 1636, a *font* shown in the 1851 Exhibition, the reredos of 1879 by G.F .Bodley and *glass* of 1889, 1893 and 1914 by C.E .Kempe.

ADDERBURY. 3m S of Banbury on A41. *St Mary.*
This is a C13 church enlarged in the C14, with a tall early-C14 spire similar to that of its contemporary neighbour, *Our Lady*, at Bloxham – a grander building. Another similarity is that an anonymous sculptor worked at both, producing *carvings* for which these two churches are well known. The chancel was restored in 1831-4 and Sir George Gilbert Scott restored the nave and aisles in 1866-70, but the full restoration was only completed in 1888. Before entering, notice the original C14 *ironwork* on the west door. In the chancel, the C15 *rood screen* remains, with a loft by Scott. Further east, in the chancel, the reredos was restored in 1831. The misericords are C19 except for one in the south-east of the choir.

BLOXHAM. 3m SW of Banbury on A361. *Our Lady of Bloxham.*

A C12 church with nave rebuilt in C13, the chancel, north and south aisles in the C14, and the south chapel in the C15. It is presumed that the anonymous C14 sculptor also worked at St Mary, Adderbury. Both churches are well known for their similar *carvings*. A restoration by G.E. Street in 1864-6 dates from the time that William Morris, who had been in Street's Oxford office, founded his own company, Morris & Co. The *east window* is by William Morris, Philip Webb and Sir E. Burne-Jones, and the north aisle *east window* by J.H. Dearle who worked for Morris. Note the remnants of a Doom over the chancel arch, the fragmentary St Christopher over the north door, the C15 rood *screen* with painted panels and the large *monument* to Sir John Thorneycroft (d.1725). The choir stalls, pulpit and reredos are all Street's.

Bloxham, Our Lady. The superb C14 spire can be seen for miles.

BURFORD. 15m W of Oxford on A40. *St John Baptist.*
One of the Cotswolds' grandest wool churches. With a fine Norman *tower* and Norman nave west wall, the rest is of all dates: a C12 south transept, a C13 north transept, and C15 south and north chapels. All drastically restored by Street the in 1870s, provoking William Morris to found the Society for the Protection of Ancient Buildings. The then Vicar rebuked Morris: 'The church is mine, and if I choose I shall stand on my head in it'.

CHILDREY. 2m NW of Wantage off B4507. *St Mary.*
A large church with nave basically of c.1300 and a chancel of the late C13. The gem of this church is the Norman lead *font* decorated with twelve bishops, many of them cast from the same mould. There is a C14 *Easter sepulchre*. Note the nine *brasses* including an excellent

large one of a knight and his lady, dated 1444.

CHISLEHAMPTON. 6m SE of Oxford on B4015. *St Katherine.*
In the care of the Redundant Churches Fund. A small, stuccoed church with bellcote and clock. Built in 1762 for Charles Peers, a London porcelain merchant, this must be the best preserved C18 church in Britain and worth a long detour. Inside, nothing has changed and one sees the church as it was planned. Except for a Jacobean *pulpit*, all is of the 1760s. The altar rails are the then old-fashioned Puritan three-sided model, around the sanctuary. Behind the altar is a high, garlanded, *reredos* with commandment boards. Inevitably there are fine *box pews* with clerk's desk, reader's desk and a west gallery. Three splendid brass *chandeliers* hang in the centre line, with candle brackets on the pulpit and walls. Charmingly, children's *pews* flank the pulpit where the Vicar could keep an eye on discipline.

DORCHESTER. 9m SE of Oxford off A423. *SS Peter & Paul.*
An abbey and one of the early shrines of Britain. However the oldest part of the building is the C12 north wall of the nave. Alterations and rebuilding on a grand scale in the C13 and extension of the choir in 1340 resulted in the abbey as it is today. The whole was restored in the 1840s, and again by Sir George Gilbert Scott from 1859-74. The glory of the abbey is the *Jesse window* of c.1340 in the choir. It is of striking originality. The carved stone tree grows from the navel of the sleeping Jesse, who is lying on the sill, the branches forming the panes for the *glass* showing Christ's ancestors. Only slightly less dramatic is the *east window*, also of c.1340. The *piscina* and *sedilia* are equally inspired and are of the same date. The lead *font* is of c.1170 and the chancel stalls are early-C16 with the crozier of Abbot Beauforest, the donor, on the ends. At the east end of the south aisle is a C14 *wall painting*, a crucifixion on a diapered background. Amongst other *paintings* there is a John Piper of the abbey. Notice the C17 embroidered *cope* in the crossing, the re-assembled C14 shrine of St Birinius in the south choir aisle, and the numerous early stone effigies, particularly an inspired one of a C13 knight. The remaining *glass* is almost all of c.1290-1320.

EWELME. 13m SE of Oxford off B4009. *St Mary.*
A very attractive church completed in 1450 with a C14 west tower. Built in a chequerboard pattern of flint and stone, with a brick battlemented parapet, and consisting of a nave and south aisle, it has been spared the Tractarians' attention. The *font*, with its amazing Gothic cover, is contemporary but the pulpit and pews are of the 1830s. In the chancel the east wall is covered with IHS initials in red and green. Note the C17 wall monument of a dead man emerging from an urn. The south chapel is a gem: the roof is painted and IHS is repeated;

here is one of the best C15 tombs in Britain, of the Duchess of Suffolk (d.1475) – Chaucer's granddaughter Alice. Her alabaster effigy lies on a tomb-chest beneath a painted alabaster canopy guarded by knights, and below is the figure of death. Jerome K. Jerome (d.1927), playwright and author of *Three Men in a Boat*, is buried in the churchyard.

IFFLEY. A southern suburb of Oxford. *St Mary.*

This is a magnificent Norman church comprising nave, chancel and central tower. The three-stage *west front*, restored in 1858, is particularly rich in Norman decoration. The dark narrow interior is no anticlimax; the tower arches are as charm-

Iffley, St Mary. The west front, rich in Norman decoration.

ingly decorated with chevrons, and on the west side with a floral design, as one could wish. *Glass* in the nave is C15/C16 and the east window of 1932 is by Webb; Sir Ninian Comper designed the pulpit, and the reredos of 1864 is by J.Buckler.

LANGFORD. 5m S of Burford off A361. *St Matthew.*

This is one of the county's rare Norman churches with even rarer Saxon carvings. The central tower is Saxon and the aisles and south porch c.1200. The

Langford, St Matthew. The exterior of the Saxon central crossing tower and porch of c.1200.

chancel is C13 but it was poorly restored in 1824; it was re-restored in 1864. The stone tunnel-vault beneath the Saxon tower would be one of three examples of Saxon vaulting in Britain, but it is more likely to be C13. In the south porch is a re-set *Saxon Crucifixion* and a headless *Christ Triumphant*. On the south wall of the tower are two *carved figures* which may have been part of a sundial. The dates of all of these carvings are disputed, but are likely to be C10. Inside, notice the delicate c.1200 capitals of the arcades and the rare C13 *aumbry* in the chancel north wall. Finally, in the south aisle is a wall-monument to the Howse family, with a punning epitaph.

OXFORD. 50m NW of London off M40. *Chapel,* All Souls College, High Street.
Dating from the 1440s it is T shaped in plan with the top of the T at the west end accommodating a two-bay ante-chapel screened from the nave by a magnificent wood screen of black and gold. However, the treasure of the interior is an amazing *reredos* of 1447 taking up the full eight of the east end. This was restored by Sir George Gilbert Scott in 1872-6 and the figures are by E.C. Geflowski of 1872. Take particular note of the C15 *stalls* with 42 carved *misericords* of 1442. There is much C19 glass by Clayton & Bell and the west window is by Hardman & Co of 1861; however, there is some good *glass* of 1441 in the ante-chapel. The timber roof with its hammer-beams and carved angels is original and was restored by Scott in 1872.

Chapel, Merton College, Merton Street.
What we see is only the choir, begun in 1290, with a crossing of c.1330, a south transept of 1367, a north transept of 1416-20, and a tower of 1448-9; the nave was never built. Even so it is a large chapel, with a magnificent east window of mainly heraldic C15 *glass.* Inside, it is a grand conception with a painted roof of 1850 by William Butterfield who also designed the sedilia; the *font* of Siberian malachite was given by Tsar Alexander in 1816. Sir Ninian Comper was responsible for the *altar* surround of 1923 and the painting of a Crucifixion is school of Tintoretto (1518-94). Note the elegant *pulpit* of c.1700, and the good, brass eagle *lectern* of c.1500. Covering the west window is a trompe l'oeil of the never-built nave by A.W. Acworth and R. Potter of 1968.

Chapel, New College, New College Lane.
Like All Souls Chapel this is T shaped with an ante-chapel in the top of the T at the west end, and the famous 'Reynolds Window' – a Nativity designed by Sir Joshua in 1771, filling the west window. Epstein's *Lazarus* tends to dominate the ante-chapel space. Completed by 1386 this, like many Oxford chapels, was heavily restored by Sir George Gilbert Scott in 1877-81; the roof, sedilia, piscina, much of the stalls, screen, and organ gallery, are all his.

However, the arms of the stalls are original together with 62, late-C14, carved *misericords*. Enjoy the El Greco (1541-1614) St James, a *painting* given in 1961. Apart from the west window all the *glass* of the ante-chapel is late-C14 and there is more in the main chapel with, mercifully, little of the C19. The ante-chapel has many C15 and C16 brasses of average quality.

St Mary the Virgin, High Street. One should not expect city churches to be untouched, and this is no exception. It is a mainly C15 church with an older tower of c.1300, all drastically restored in 1848-52, and again in 1894-6, when an attempt was made to put right the earlier mis-handling. The extravagant south porch of 1637 with its twisted columns is by Nicholas Stone. In the chancel, the *reredos* is all that remains of a C15 original, the stalls are C15. Most of the glass is C19, but notice in the south aisle a rare *window* by A.W. N Pugin.

Oxford, St Mary. This extravagant south porch was built in 1637 by Nicholas Stone.

RYCOTE. 3m SW of Thame off A329. *St Michael & All Angels.*
In the care of English Heritage. Built in 1449 as a chantry chapel with three priests, it became a private chapel when Edward VI dissolved chantries. Outside, the west tower, with a combined nave and chancel, has remained unchanged. The *interior* is unforgettable and a good example of the 'prayer-book' layout. The furnishings date from 1610-82 and are dominated by two vast, roofed *family pews*, one domed. The pulpit, west gallery, and screen with massive strapwork cresting, are all early-C17; the *reredos* with Commandment boards, Lord's Prayer and Creed, is of 1682. Older than anything else in the church is the C12 *font* bowl. The stalls with carved poppyheads, benches and font cover are all of 1449. Notice the painted ceiling in the west end restored with stars and clouds, the fireplace, the good C17 and C18 *monuments* and one to Colonel Hammersley (d.1929) with *lettering* by Eric Gill.

STANTON HARCOURT. 6m W of Oxford on B4449. *St Michael.*
An aisleless Norman church of c.1150 with a crossing tower. Transepts were added and the chancel enlarged in c.1250. The south Harcourt Chapel was built c.1470. The north and south entrances

are Norman, the nave roof with traceried spandrels is c.1400. Notice the *shrine* of c.1300 to St Edburg taken from Bicester Priory and the medieval *glass* of c.1250 in the chancel south wall; the glass in the Harcourt chapel is c.1450. Not to be missed is the rare mid-C13 *rood screen*. On the south end of the nave side is a C15 painted female saint. The Harcourt family is represented by many good *monuments* ranging from a stone effigy of c.1400 to one of 1861. There are two small *brasses* of the early-C16 in the chancel.

UFFINGTON. 6m W of Wantage on B4507. *St Mary.*
The unusual magnificence of this church is due to Abbot Faritous of Abingdon Abbey, cellerar to Henry I, who built the church with crossing tower in c.1250. It is one of the finest examples of the C13 in the country. The chancel was re-roofed in restorations of 1850. Parts of the C15 screen have been made into bench-ends. Other items to note are the works of an old clock, and a C15 chest. On the north wall there is a brass *plaque* to Thomas Hughes (d.1896), author of *Tom Brown's Schooldays.*

WHEATFIELD. 13m SE of Oxford off A40. *St Andrew.*
A small C14 church restored in the mid-C18 in a Classical/Gothic revival mixture. Standing stuccoed and whitewashed in a deserted and overgrown churchyard, although still used, its main purpose ended when the the adjacent Wheatfields House was burnt down in 1814 and it now has a romantically deserted atmosphere. Inside, the *furnishings* are all of c.1740 and unchanged. It glows with a warm

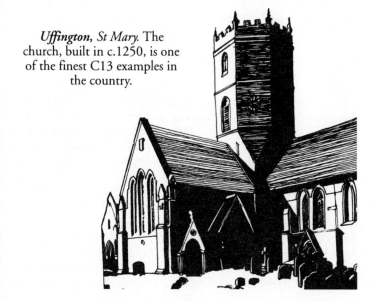

Uffington, St Mary. The church, built in c.1250, is one of the finest C13 examples in the country.

light from the coffee-cream paint of the walls. Note the *hat pegs* over the pews and stalls, the *Royal Arms* dated 1742, the fine *communion table* and the single *hatchment*.

WIDFORD. 1m E of Burford off A40. *St Oswald.*
Here is a small hidden medieval church of great interest built in the C13 on the site of a Roman villa. The nave and chancel are unmarked on its unassuming exterior except for a central bellcote. Inside, its charm is immediate for it has an unaltered 'prayer-book' *interior.* The windows still have their small Tudor diamond-shaped leaded lights, the *pulpit* is C15, the communion rail and the Commandment boards are C17 and the simple box pews are early-C19. The chancel floor has two sections of a Roman *mosaic* pavement *in situ.* On the nave north wall is a C14 *wall painting* of St Christopher partly obliterated by a C17 Royal Arms, while on the north wall of the chancel are *painted* the Three Living and the Three Dead (a warning that death is inevitable), with a Martyrdom above.

YARNTON. 4m NW of Oxford off A34. *St Bartholomew.*
This is a small Norman church rebuilt in the C13 and enlarged in the C17. It comprises nave, chancel, south aisle and south chapel, with a south-west tower dated 1611. Bench ends in the south aisle and nave are C15, as is the fine *reredos* of Nottingham alabaster. Above the chancel arch are fragments of a C15 *wall painting.* In the Spencer chapel of 1611, with its painted walls and roof, are some very good C17 *monuments,* and the biggest collection of C17 armorial *glass* in Britain. In the chancel, nave and south aisle, there are some panels of good Flemish and English C15 and C16 *glass* introduced in 1816. The only original panels are in one of the north wall windows.

Other Churches

BESSESLEIGH. 4m SW of Oxford off A420. *St Lawrence.*
A small part-Norman church, with C13 and C17 additions and restorations. The *interior* is unrestored C17 and C18, with box pews, font, gallery, pulpit and tympanum.

CHECKENDON. 5m SE of Wallingford off A4074. *SS. Peter & Paul.*
A small Norman church of flint and stone with an aisleless nave and apsed chancel. Some medieval *tiles* are in the chancel, which has the only original window. Particularly note the C13 *wall paintings* on the apse, the three C15 *brasses* and the 1960 memorial window by Laurence Whistler.

CHOLSEY. 9m SE of Abingdon off A329. *St Mary.*
Intrinsically a Norman church with a chancel lengthened in C13, built in flint and stone with central tower. The glass is by C.E. Kempe, 1891 and 1900, and note small brass of priest (d.1471).

Dame Agatha Christie (d.1976) is buried in the west of the churchyard.

CHURCH HANDBOROUGH. 7m NW of Oxford off A4095. *SS Peter & Paul.*

A spired church with a Norman nave, chancel and aisles, extensively remodelled in 1399. Over the north door is a C12 *tympanum.* Inside, the C15 *rood screen*, with painted loft, extends across both aisles. Note the C15 *brass* and the late-C15 *glass* in the chantry window and the south aisle, also the C15 patterned *wall painting* of white roses on red in the north chapel.

COTE. 10m W of Oxford on B4449. *Baptist Chapel.*

Maintained by the Historic Chapels Trust. A plain and simple chapel, the only concession to decoration on the outside being a scrolled gable head with plaque. In appearance it might be a small C18 factory. In fact it was founded in 1656 and built in 1739-40.

NUNEHAM COURTNEY. 5m SE of Oxford on A423. *All Saints.*

In the care of the Redundant Churches Fund. Built, very much as an eye-catcher, in the form of a Classical temple with a dome by Lord Harcourt assisted by James 'Athenian' Stuart in 1764. Inside are C17 and C18 Italian furnishings introduced in 1880. In the churchyard is a good C17 monument from an earlier church on the same site.

Nuneham Courtney, All Saints.
Built by the 1st Lord Harcourt
in 1764.

OXFORD. 50m NW of London off M40. *St Giles,* St Giles Street.

The tower, nave, and aisles are C13, the chancel late-C13, and the south chapel rebuilt 1850-2, all restored in 1920. The glass is C19.

St Mary Magdalen, Magdalen and St Giles Streets.

A church marooned on a traffic island close to the spot where Cranmer, Latimer and Ridley were burnt to death in 1556. Though C14, it was so over-restored in 1842 that it has the atmosphere of the C19. The tower was rebuilt in 1511. Inside, are two C17 Italian *reliquaries.*

SWYNCOMBE. 6m NW of Henley off B481. *St Botolph.*

A small early-Norman church of flint and stone consisting of an aisleless nave and apsed chancel. It was restored by Benjamin Ferrey in 1850 who took liberties by inserting lancet windows and two round-headed windows in the apse. Restored *wall paintings* in the chancel show an overall diaper pattern and scroll decoration. Screen and loft are of 1914.

WITNEY. 10m W of Oxford off A40. *St Mary.*

A large C13 church with a tall central tower and a Norman north porch, restored in 1865-9. Two chantry chapels were added on the north side in the C14 and the south transept enlarged in the C15. The tower has claims to be the finest of any parish church in the county. The interior was over-restored in the 1860s but there are a number of good C14 side chapels.

WOODEATON. 3m NE of Oxford off B4027. *Holy Rood.*

A church with a simple C13 nave and chancel, and a C14 west tower. C13 *piscina*, and built-out *sedilia*, C18 *reader's desk, pulpit* and *tester*, C15 carved *bench ends, rood screen* of c.1500. The C14 *wall paintings* are notable because the St Christopher has a scroll in Norman French: 'Who looks upon this image shall not that day die an ill-death.' Meaning that when they die it would not be without church rites.

SOUTH-EAST ENGLAND

Kent

A county composed of clay, sandstone and chalk, with some Kentish Rag, a limestone difficult to work. Caen, in France, proved a useful source of limestone for church building. Quarr stone from the Isle of Wight is also another source of limestone and both are used freely as dressings with flint.

As Kent is the gateway to France it is surprising that there should be so few surviving pre-Conquest churches; the mostly restored St Mary in Castro, at Dover, is the only example. Norman churches are far better represented, the three famous examples being St Nicholas, Barfreston, St Mary, Brook, and St Margaret, St Margaret's at Cliffe. The majority, however, are medieval of the C13 and C14, none of national importance. *All Saints* at Woodchurch has claims to being the most beautiful church in the county, but generally one is left with the impression that having erected the cathedral at Canterbury, inspiration was exhausted when it came to the humble parish church.

A surprising number of early shrine foundations survive and the body of one royal abbess, St Eanswythe, lies at Folkestone. For so large a county there is little medieval glass, but outstanding brasses are to be found at St Mary, Cobham,. while at St Mary, Chilham, the

Barfreston, St Nicholas. Built in Caen stone, this is the finest Norman church in the county.

SOUTH-EAST ENGLAND

Dartford

Gravesend

Sheerness

Margate

Herne Bay

Broadstairs

Chatham

Ramsgate

Canterbury

Sandwich

Deal

Staines

Camberley

Woking

Sevenoaks

Maidstone

SURREY

Leatherhead

KENT

Guildford

Dorking

Reigate

Dover

Godalming

Tonbridge

Royal

Ashford

Tunbridge Wells

Crawley

East Grinstead

Tenterden

Folkeston

Horsham

New

Hythe

Romney

Petersfield

Burgess Hill

EAST

SUSSEX

Rye

Lydd

WEST

SUSSEX

Lewes

Hastings

Havant

Chichester

Worthing

Brighton

Bexhill

Littlehampton

Newhaven

Eastbourne

Bognor

Regis

remarkable monuments are well worth a detour.

BADLESMERE. 5m S of Faversham on A251. *St Leonard.*
The church has a short west tower with a C13 chancel and an exterior rendered in the early-C19. The interior, of great beauty, includes C18 *box pews*, a three-decker *pulpit* and *altar rails*, the Ten Commandments, the Lord's Prayer and Creed painted on boards, an interesting *reredos*, the *Royal Arms* of George I, dated 1717, and one hatchment.

BARFRESTON. 6m NW of Dover off A256. *St Nicholas.*
Without doubt this is the finest Norman church in the county, part flint and part Caen stone with a wealth of fine carving. This is well worth a detour. It now consists of only nave and chancel, the latter rebuilt in 1839-42. Over the south door is a *tympanum* of Christ in Majesty (note the scratch dials on the door jambs). The magnificence of the east *wheel-window* is virtually without equal, although the glass is of c.1850. There are faded wall paintings in the north-east corner.

BROOK. 4m E of Ashford off A20. *St Mary.*
A small complete Norman church of c.1100, with massive square west tower, built of flint with Quarr and Caen stone dressing. In the tower is a first floor chapel with arches opening on-to the nave below and the remains of an altar with a C12 *wall painting* of Christ above. The sanctuary floor is patterned with old *tiles* and the chancel has two sets of mid-C13 medallion *wall paintings:* the Nativity and the Passion of Christ. In the nave is a C13 Life of the Virgin and over the north door is a large C13 St Christopher. Note the fine *screen* and pulpit.

BROOKLAND. 5m NE of Rye on A259. *St Augustine.*
Thankfully ignored by C19 restorers, this church is mainly of the mid-C13 with a surprising feature: a detached medieval timber *bell tower.* A second surprise is inside; the oldest (C12) and finest lead *font*

Brookland, St Augustine. The oldest and finest Roman font in Britain.

in Britain, covered with the signs of the zodiac and labours of the month. There are fragments of C15 *wall paintings* in the south aisle and C14 *glass* in the north aisle. Two curiosities are: a *tithe pen* in the north aisle and a sentry box *shelter* for the vicar at the graveside in wet weather.

CHILHAM. 6m SW of Canterbury off A28. *St Mary.*
Built of flint in the C16, except for the chancel of Bath stone, built in 1863. There is much original glass in the north aisle. The chief glory lies in the *monuments* which date from 1619 by such famous designers as Nicholas Stone, Sir Francis Chantrey, Sir Richard Westmacott, to Alexander Munro in 1858.

COBHAM. 3m W of Rochester on B2009. *St Mary.*
The west tower was built in the 1360s, the rest is C13 with some C12 detail. The notable C13 chancel accommodated a college founded in 1362 by Sir Roger de Cobham. Unique to Britain is a *loft* over the reredos (there are several in France). The amazing *brasses,* some eighteen in all, are unequalled in Kent; those to the Brook and Cobham families are outstanding. Following the restoration in 1862, only one *misericord* remains in the chancel.

ELHAM. 5m NW of Folkestone on B2065. *St Mary.*
This church is one of the county's gems, comprising a C12 nave, a C13 chancel, and C14 aisles, with a late-C14 tower, all tactfully restored in the early-C20 when the old *tiles* and C17 *text-boards* were preserved. Very good C20 furnishings include the organ loft, marble paving in the sanctuary, panelling and altar rails. The *lectern* is French C17 installed in the early-C20 along with the alabaster *triptych* and C15 and C16 *glass.* Note the *painting* of c.1500 by Rocco Marconi from the Palazzo Morosini, Venice.

GRAVENEY. 3m NE of Faversham off A299. *All Saints.*
This flint church is mainly C14 with an unrestored Norman chancel and good furnishings. Inside are C18 *box pews,* some incorporating original medieval benches. There are fragments of medieval *glass* in the chancel; a good C17 *pulpit* on a C19 base; an early-C16 rood screen and a superb *brass* to John Martyn (d.1436), a Justice of Common Pleas, and his wife.

HALLING. 3m SW of Rochester on A228. *St John Baptist.*
Basically a church of the C14 and C15 but excessively restored in 1889. However, the *wall paintings* of the Last Supper and scenes from The Passion over the chancel arch were mercifully saved. So too was the unusual, but coarsely cut, *brass* of Silvester Lambarde, a woman who died in 1587, sitting up in a four-poster bed.

HIGHAM. 1m N of Rochester off B2000. *St Mary.*

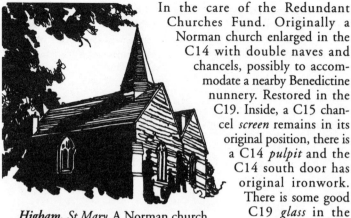

In the care of the Redundant Churches Fund. Originally a Norman church enlarged in the C14 with double naves and chancels, possibly to accommodate a nearby Benedictine nunnery. Restored in the C19. Inside, a C15 chancel *screen* remains in its original position, there is a C14 *pulpit* and the C14 south door has original ironwork. There is some good C19 *glass* in the chancel.

Higham, St Mary. A Norman church enlarged in the C14 with double aisles.

HIGH HALDEN. 4m NE of Tenterden on A28. *St Mary.*
To a C14 nave with aisles, the south aisle C15 with high quality arcading, the other rebuilt in the early-C16, and chancel built in rough stone is attached a remarkable *timber tower* and timber west porch. The entrance is through a timber passage lined with C14 oak panelling. The construction of the timber-work is well worth inspection. The church was restored by G.E. Street in 1868 when the east window with *glass* by Clayton & Bell, was inserted. Some C14 *glass*, including what is believed to be the earliest heraldic arms, is in another chancel window, and more in the south aisle. In the chancel are the remains of a C13 sedilia from an earlier building.

HILDENBOROUGH. 2m NW of Tonbridge on A245. *St John.*
Built in 1843-4 and Euan Christian's first church. The exterior is dull but the *interior* is remarkable. A vast arch-braced roof draws the eye to the crossing, with a wide space for preaching. The transept west *window* is by William Morris and that in the south transept by Sir E. Burne-Jones; the north window, by A.B. Joy, is dated 1876.

HYTHE. 4m W of Folkestone on A259. *St Leonard.*
The church has a Norman nave, remodelled in the C13, with a C13, though unfinished, chancel which is among the best of its kind in Kent. It was only completed in 1886 by J.L. Pearson. The church was restored earlier in 1874. The reredos of 1881, by G.E. Street, is vast and expelled to the south aisle. A *helmet* hangs high in the north aisle and there is a vast number of skulls in the ambulatory.

KEMSING. 3m NE of Sevenoaks off A225. *St Mary.*

A Norman church with later additions, a north aisle of 1890 and a surprising *interior.* The rood *screen* was reconstructed in 1894 but the figures are by Sir Ninian Comper in 1908, as are the *reredos* and *canopy.* He also did the chancel wall paintings in 1902. The *font* is Norman and the cover Jacobean. The Venetian lamp holder in the north aisle was copied in 1894. Among the noteworthy *glass* there is a C13 Virgin and Child in the north aisle and a jumble of C14 and C15 fragments. The east and west windows of 1902 are by Sir Ninian Comper. Other points include a good *brass* of 1347 and a C13 oak chest.

LOWER HALSTOW. 4m NW of Sittingbourne off A2. *St Margaret.* Built of flint with stone dressings and with a C13 south-west tower, the nave and chancel are completely Saxon. All were restored by W.D. Caroë in 1913 who added the south porch. The lead *font* is of c.1190, there are C14 painted leaves on the chancel arch and a C14 Coronation of the Virgin is *painted* next to the west window.

NEWINGTON. 3m W of Sittingbourne on A2. *St Mary.* The church built of flint with stone dressings has a C14 nave, a C13 chancel and a stone west tower of the C15. The interesting font *cover* is of c.1530, the same date as the linenfold panelling in the south aisle. The north aisle has faded C14 *wall paintings* of The Last Judgement and a Nativity, with saints in the window splays. Also note five *brasses,* the earliest of 1488.

RAINHAM. 4m E of Chatham on A2. *St Margaret.* This is a C13 church remodelled in the C14, with a C15 tower. Inside, above the screen the roof is panelled and *painted* with red roses, the emblem of Edward IV. The fine parclose *screen* of the C15 is carved with heads, animals and leaves. On the south wall of the nave are *paintings:* a Last Judgement; a damaged Annunciation; and a C15 St Christopher painted over a C14 St Christopher. Note the fine C14 *oak chest* with carved tracery, the four C16 brasses and two rather clumsy monuments to the 2nd and 3rd Earls of Thanet.

ROLVENDEN. 3m SW of Tenterden on A28. *St Mary.* With a tower of brown ironstone, the early-C14 nave and C13 chancel are built of dark-brown rubble sandstone. A first-floor *family pew* of the Gybbon-Moneypennys is well furnished with ten chairs, a table and a carpet, but notably with no view of the pulpit. There is good *glass* of 1848 in the east window. A *monument* to Henry Tennant (d.1917) is designed by Sir Edwin Lutyens who also designed the small medallion to H.J. Tennant (d.1936).

ST MARGARET'S AT CLIFFE. 4m NE of Dover on B2058. *St Margaret of Antioch.* This, the largest of the three Norman churches in the county, was built c.1140 in flint with Caen stone dressings. It is a building to be enjoyed for its early architecture, for there is little else. It consists of a wide nave; the aisle windows were inserted in restorations of 1864, but in the high clerestory the windows are original. The wide and simple chancel also has original windows. The font is dated 1663 and the glass is of c.1860.

STONE. 2m E of Dartford on A226. *St Mary.*
This memorable flint church is perched on chalk cliffs above the Thames and on the edge of a very active quarry. It is all of the late-C13, except for the chancel, rebuilt 1860, when the church was restored. Inside, the workmanship of the decoration is worthy of Westminster Abbey where much of the stone was carved. Comparable artistry is maintained in the excellent C13 *paintings* on the north wall, which include the murder of Becket.

UPPER HARDRES. 5m S of Canterbury off B2068. *SS Peter & Paul.*
Built of flint with stone dressings, this church has a Norman tower, with a C13 nave and chancel. The pulpit is C18 with fine marquetry tester. The *glass* is well worth coming to see: in the west window are three C13 roundels, damaged by fire in 1972, and two east lancet windows have C14 glass in brilliant colours and came from nearby Stelling church. Two *brasses*, one to John Street, rector (d.1405), is unique in that Street kneels at the foot of a bracket supporting two saints. There are good *monuments* to the Hardres family

WOODCHURCH. 4m E of Tenterden off B2067. *All Saints.*
One of the most beautiful churches of Kent. Built in the C13, enlarged in the C15 and restored by Ferrey in 1858. Bright light floods into the chancel from triple lancets where there is a double *piscina* and three *sedilia*. The piers of the nave seem to be marble but are polished and waxed freestone. Note the good Norman *font*, again waxed and polished, the C16 *pulpit*, two C14 *misericords* and the C13 *glass* in the south aisle, but particularly the fine cross *brass* of 1333.

Other Churches

DOVER. 15m SE of Canterbury on A2. Dover Castle, *St Mary-in-Castro.*
Dating from c.1000, this is the finest example of a late-Saxon church in Kent. Heavily restored by Sir George Gilbert Scott in 1860-2.

FORDWICH. 2m NE of Canterbury off A28. *St Mary.*
A simple unrestored church with plain C18 furnishings. Basically C13 with a C13 west tower and C14 aisle. Inside is good C14 glass, one C17 text painted on the wall, a *Royal Arms* of 1688, C18 box pews, a square Norman *font* and a Norman stone *sarcophagus* unique in Kent.

MINSTER-IN-THANET. 5m W of Ramsgate off A253. *St Mary.*
An abbey church rebuilt in the C12 and C13 on a huge scale. The
east window of 1861 is one of the finest by Thomas Willement. The
stalls have eighteen good *misericords* of c.1410.

TONGE. 1m E of Sittingbourne off A2. *St Giles.*
A flint built church and unusual in that a vast C16 nave roof sweeps
down over the two aisles. Otherwise the building is of all periods;
part Norman, part C13, with a
brick chancel of C16 and C18,
all restored in the C19. The
rood *screen* is early-C16 and the
north wall carries a faded C14
painting of St Christopher.

TUNBRIDGE WELLS. 30m
SE of London on A28. *St
Charles the Martyr.*
Begun in 1676 and twice
enlarged by 1690, with a chancel of 1882. A square, plain
brick exterior conceals a rich
interior. A five domed ceiling is
decorated with extravagant *plasterwork*. Galleries and seating are
original, with a C17 reredos
from St Antholin, London.

WESTERHAM. 5m W of
Sevenoaks on A25. *St Mary.*
A C13 church stiffly restored in
1854 and 1882. However, inside
is the second oldest *Royal Arms*
in the country; it is to Edward
VI and is the only one to survive
from his reign. Also much C19
glass and seven C16 brasses.

*Tunbridge Wells, St Charles the
Martyr.* This beautiful plaster
ceiling of 1690 is
by Wren's chief plasterer,
Henry Doogood.

Surrey

The north-west of the county is poorly supplied with building stone
and church builders were obliged to use materials that would not have
been considered in, for example, the Avon area. Pudding-stone,
composed of small pebbles set in sandstone which weathers badly,
and sarsens, a grey, unattractive sandstone, were all that was available
and so were used extensively. In the southern half of the county there
are wide varieties of sandstone, such as the good Reigate stone used for

the London Bridge built in 1176, Windsor Castle and Westminster Abbey. In the middle of Surrey are the chalklands of the North Downs and consequently the walls of many churches are of flint.

Surrey experienced prosperity in the nineteenth century and consequently many old churches were rebuilt, altered and spoiled. There is little in the way of Saxon work; the tower of St Mary's, Guildford, is the only substantial evidence remaining. There are several small Norman churches without aisles; these are not remarkable and nothing remarkable followed, either in the medieval era or later. However, Surrey boasts the earliest surviving brass (1277) in Britain – and certainly one of the best – at St Mary's, Stoke D'Abernon, where lies Sir John D'Abernon, seven feet long in chain-mail. Surrey also has an exceptional late-C12 wall painting at SS Peter & Paul, Chaldon, one of only eleven surviving from so early a date. Erroneously called a Doom, it shows hell and purgatory and should more properly be called The Purgatorial Ladder.

ALBURY. 4m E of Guildford on A248. *SS Peter & Paul.*
In the care of the Redundant Churches Fun, the church has a part Saxon and part Norman tower. Owing to a quarrel with the then owner of Albury Park, it was deserted by its parishioners in 1842. The now roofless chancel is C13, as is the south transept, restored by A.W.N. Pugin in 1839. Also by Pugin is the extravagant Drummond family mortuary chapel in the south transept. Note the *glass* by William Wailes and the ceiling by T. Earley.

CHALDON. 5m S of Croydon on B2030. *SS Peter & Paul.*
This small flint church has a Norman fabric but only one Norman window survives in the west wall; the rest is late-C12 and early-C13 with a C19 steeple. A C14 *Easter Sepulchre* in the chancel north wall and a rare *pulpit* dated 1657 sum up the secondary details of interest. However, the point of any visit should be to see the late-C12 century *paintings* on the west wall. The subject, which must be based on Byzantine sources, shows little souls scrambling up a ladder from hell, where two dog-faced devils stoke a cauldron, to purgatory and the Weighing of Souls. Chaldon was on the pilgrim route to Canterbury. The church has a rare C13 bell.

COMPTON. 3m SW of Guildford on B3000. *St Nicholas.*
A good Norman church with a pre-Conquest tower. The light and spacious interior has the extraordinary feature of a two-storey *sanctuary*, the only one in Britain. No satisfactory explanation for this has been found. The upper-sanctuary *guard-rail* is late-C12, a remarkable survival. Also remarkable is the trefoil of C12/C13 *glass* of the Virgin and Child in the lower sanctuary. The altar-rail, pulpit and former chancel screen, now the tower screen, are all of c.1620. The church was well-restored in the C19.

Watts Chapel.
Designed in 1896 by his widow for the painter, G.F. Watts. For admirers of Art Nouveau a visit to the 1901 interior is essential.

ESHER. 4m SW of Kingston on A3. *St George.*
This charming little church should not be missed. Only used occasionally, it is a rare example of a church built in the reign of Henry VIII, in c.1540. A brick south chapel was built by Sir John Vanbrugh in 1725-6 for the Dukes of Newcastle. At the same time the chancel was altered, a brick north aisle was built in 1812, and all is unrestored. The splendid *Newcastle pew,* with servants' box pews behind, is only entered from outside, this also is untouched. It became a Royal pew in 1816 when Princess Charlotte (d.1817) lived at Claremont. A *painting* of her apotheosis by Arthur Devis hangs in the church. Note the good *reredos* of 1722, the C18 three-decker *pulpit* (the only one remaining in Surrey), the west gallery of 1840-2 and the good monuments.

LINGFIELD. 3m N of East Grinstead off B2028. *SS Peter & Paul.*
The tower is C14, the rest was rebuilt in 1431 by Sir Reginald Cobham when he founded a college here. The plain exterior belies the interior. There are very good C15 furnishings: *font* and *cover, lectern* with chained Bible, *screen* and *stalls* with eight *misericords.* The best set of *brasses* in Surrey should not be missed, these are mainly to the Cobham family in the Lady Chapel. There are also many monuments to the Cobhams including one to the builder (d.1446), whose feet rest on a nasty looking sea-wolf, and one to Lord Cobham (d.1361), whose feet rest on a rather bored Saracen. Note the *Royal Arms* of Queen Anne and the C18 brass chandelier.

SHERE. 5m E of Guildford on A25. *St James.*
This cruciform church is basically late-C12 with a tower heightened in the mid-C13 and spire of the C14. In c.1300 the north transept was shortened and the south aisle extended, and in c.1350 the chancel was lengthened. All was sensitively restored in 1895 when the vestry was added. The *lychgate* is 1901 by Lutyens. The lack of building materials is underlined by the mixture of flint, rubble, Bargate stone, re-used Roman tiles, Tudor brick and Horsham slab, used in the building. Inside, the *font* of Purbeck marble is c.1200, the best in Surrey, and note the C13 'Crusader chest'. Unusual altar fittings are the stainless steel rail, the cross and candlesticks in wrought iron with bronze inlay and the bronze aumbry, all of 1956 by Louis Osman. Two good, but restored, C15 *brasses* should be noted; and in particular, the minute (2" high) C13 Madonna & Child, *painted* on a half pier north-west of the Bray Chapel, should not be missed; nor the carved St James on the east side of the crossing.

STOKE D'ABERNON. 4m W of Epsom on A245. *St Mary.*

At first one may think this is a C19 church. It is far earlier: the south wall is Saxon, the north aisle late C12, and the chancel C13. An unfortunate over-restoration in 1866, later rectified, is responsible for this mistaken impression. Don't miss the Norbury Chapel with its Tudor fireplace; coloured C17 Vincent *effigies*; the splendid D'Abernon *brasses* beginning with Sir John (d.1277) – the oldest in Britain – another Sir John (d.1327), and his son, all in full armour with traces of original blue; or the C13 *'Crusader chest'.* The outstanding *pulpit* is Elizabethan and, in the lancet windows, is good C15 *glass*; the *reredos* is C15 Flemish. Do not overlook the *wall paintings*, fragments of a C13 Adoration of the Lamb, in the chancel.

Stoke d'Abernon, St Mary. The 1277 brass to Sir John D'Abernon.

Other Churches

CHARLOOD. 2m E of Gatwick Airport. *St Nicholas.*
Tower, nave, and chancel all of C11, with a C15 screen and remarkable *wall paintings*.

GUILDFORD. 30m SW of London off A3. *St Mary.* Quarrey Street.
A church with a pre-Conquest crossing tower, with nave, aisles, chancel and chapels of c.1160. Note the curious east end comprising squints and passages, and the faded C12 *wall paintings* of St John in St John's Chapel.
Holy Trinity. High Street.
James Horne rebuilt the church in brick in 1749-63 after the tower fell. There is good joinery and ironwork, also many good *monuments* including one to Archbishop Abbott (d.1633), and two small Abbott *brasses*.

HAM HOUSE. 2m SW of Richmond off A307. *Chapel.*
In the care of the National Trust. In the NE corner of Ham House is the family chapel constructed in the 1670s and furnished in 1673 and 1674. Completely unaltered even to the rare altar cloth and the alms dish.

LALEHAM. 2m SE of Staines on B376. *All Saints.*
A C12 church with a brick tower dated 1732. Inside, is a large painting of c.1810 of Christ on the sea with St Peter, and a splendid *west window* by Wilhelmina Geddes. Matthew Arnold (d.1888) is

buried in the churchyard.

OCKHAM. 5m NE of Guildford on B2039. *All Saints.*

Mostly C13 with a C14 tower. The east end is famous for its seven lancet *window* of c.1250 (note the stiff-leaf capitals). The glass is of 1875. The King Chapel, added in 1735, has a white marble *monument* to Lord King (d.1734) by Michael Rysbrack. There are curious *bosses* in the 1530 roof and the brasses should not be overlooked.

WEST HORSLEY. 6m E of Guildford off A246. *St Mary.*

Basically a C13 church, with a pre-Conquest flint tower. Note the C14 alabaster *Nativity*, the fast fading C13 *wall paintings* on the nave west wall, the good C13 small medallions in *glass* and the many good *monuments*. The head of Sir Walter Raleigh (ex.1618) is interred here (see the west window). But St Margaret's, Westminster, makes an equal claim!

WOTTON. 7m E of Guildford on A25. *St John.*

The early-Norman tower, originally central, is attached to a C13 church with the chancel restored in the C19. The north chapel contains the C17 Evelyn family *mausoleum* and is the burial place of the diarist, John Evelyn (d.1706). Note the many Evelyn monuments from 1603 and the simple screen of c.1630.

Sussex

The church builders of Sussex were fortunate in that there was nearly always a local stone which, if not up to the quality of the Cotswold limestones, at least stood up to the weathering of centuries. There is sandstone in the Weald, and Downland churches are built of flint with stone dressings; at times chalk is used for interiors. There are many simple medieval timber roofs and one good ornate Elizabethan one at South Harting.

Sussex has many Saxon churches; Bosham and Sompting are two of the best. Of Norman churches, East Sussex possesses the best at Icklesham, Ifford and Lewes. But West Sussex has the earliest, at Steyning. The C13 is well represented: Ashurst, Boxgrove and Burpham are well-known examples. Thereafter there is little until the C19 when most were built in Brighton: St Peter in 1824-8, St Bartholomew (which runs the Royal Pavilion a close second in flamboyance) in 1872-4, and St Michael in 1893-5.

ARUNDEL. 10m E of Chichester on A27. *St Nicholas.*

A rare example of a total rebuilding some time after 1380 left the church belonging completely to one period. With Arundel Castle on the doorstep it is understandable that there is a Fitzalan Chapel for the Dukes of Norfolk, unused since the break with Rome and only entered from outside. It is separated from the church by an original iron grill. Inside the chapel are fourteen good C13 carved wood roof *bosses* remaining from an earlier roof, and some fine tombs of earlier Earls of Arundel, with monuments to C19 and C20 Dukes of Norfolk. In the church itself particularly notice the faded early-C15 *wall paintings* of the Seven Deadly Sins and the Seven Works of Mercy, also the numerous good C14 *brasses.* The Gothic stone *pulpit* with canopy is contemporary with the church.

BISHOPSTONE. 10m E of Brighton off A259. *St Andrew.*
Built of flint with stone dressings, architecturally one of the most interesting churches in Britain. Originally Saxon as can be seen by the west end of the nave and the *porticus* (not a porch but a side chamber). The west tower, the south doorway, the north aisle and the east end are Norman, the chancel arch and north arcade are c.1200. It was all restored in 1849 when the east window was renewed and the rib-vaulting above the altar inserted. However, there are many questions left unanswered to delight historians. In the south doorway gable is a sundial with the name *Eadric.* Is this Saxon? And why does the north aisle of c.1200 have small early-Norman windows? Architecture apart, notice the Saxon and Norman decoration and the beautifully carved *coffin-lid* of c.1200.

BOSHAM. 4m W of Chichester off A27. *Holy Trinity.*
Famed for being shown on the Bayeux Tapestry where Harold is seen entering the church before the Battle of Hastings. Of that church only the tower and *chancel arch* remain. The chancel was lengthened and the nave rebuilt in the C13, while in the C14 the aisles were widened; a restoration was carried out in 1845. It is built on a very old site; it is said to have been first a Roman basilica, then, more certainly, an Irish monastery before the Saxon church was built. The south door is C14 with original ironwork. Inside, the octagonal *font* is Norman and in the chancel south wall are the remains of a Norman *piscina.* The fragments of medieval *glass* came from Norwich Cathedral. Notice the mutilated, but high quality, C13 female *effigy* in the chancel.

Bosham, Holy Trinity. The part Saxon tower and Saxo-Norman chancel appear in the Bayeux Tapestry.

BOXGROVE. 3m NE of Chichester on A285. *SS Mary and Blaise.*
A flint-built church, with only one aisle in the south, and sturdy
flying buttresses supporting the clerestory. Only the C12 choir and
nave, the C13 transepts, central tower and part of the nave remain as
fragments of a ruined Benedictine priory. Nevertheless, the interior
with its slender columns of Purbeck marble has great dignity. The
surprise is the heraldry and foliage *painted* on the vaulted ceiling in
the mid-C16. A further surprise is the very ornate *De la Warr chantry*
of 1526; a successful example of Gothic trying to be Renaissance.
There are three other C18 monuments of mixed quality and one
from 1937 of Admiral Nelson-Ward in uniform. Note the *medieval
tiles* in the south chancel aisle and the C13 carved wooden *bosses* in
the aisle and choir.

BREDE. 5m N of Hastings on A28. *St George.*
A church with a Norman fabric buried in later additions and alterations. The south aisle is C13 and the north aisle c.1300. A Norman
chancel, rebuilt in c.1537, was changed in the C14 by the addition of
north and south chapels. Inside, one has to look hard for Norman
evidence but there is some dog-tooth decoration in the south aisle.
Notice the unusual east window with heraldic *glass* of c.1537, the
poor box dated 1687, the Stations of the Cross by W.T. Monnington
and the extravagant tomb to Sir Goddard Oxbridge (d.1537).

BRIGHTON. 50m S of London by M23. *St Bartholomew,* Ann
Street.
A very tall, aisleless, brick church built in the 1860s, the chancel was
never built. The *interior,* mostly designed by G. Wilson in 1895-
1910, is only for those who have a taste for Art Nouveau and
Byzantine marble.
St Peter, Victoria Gardens.
Built 1824-8 by Sir Charles Barry, whose design won a competition
when he was in his late twenties. It is in C15 Gothic style with an
adroit west tower combined with porch. The chancel, built in 1900-6,
was not part of Barry's plan. The nave and aisles are plaster-vaulted,
and thin piers give an impression of space and height. The *glass* is
1880s and 90s by C.E. Kempe.
St Paul. West Street.
Built 1846-8 by R.C.Carpenter in correct C13 Gothic. The narthex
or vestibule, and screen are by G.F. Bodley, so it is no surprise to
find Sir E. Burne-Jones responsible for the altar *retable,* a very early
design of 1861. One of the Magi is a portrait of William Morris. In
the south aisle is an early-C16 Flemish *retable.* Most of the other
glass is by A.W.N. Pugin.

ETCHINGHAM. 7m N of Battle on A256. *The Assumption &
St Nicholas.*

A church entirely of the C14 and built for Sir William de Echyngham (d.1389) who is buried in the chancel. The chancel is longer than the nave which marks it out as being a collegiate foundation. Once inside there is much to see. The C14 screen has lost its upper part leaving only one tier of pierced panels and in the chancel the floor *tiles* are contemporary with the building. There are eighteen C14 *misericords* in the stalls and note the fox in a friar's cloak preaching to geese. In the heads of many windows remains some good C14 *glass*, while the east window of 1857 is by J.R. Clayton. Notice the *funeral banner* and *helmet*, and the *brass* to Sir William de Echyngham and to others of his family.

MILLAND. 5m SW of Haslemere off A3. *Old Church.*
Under restoration by The Friends of the Friendless Churches. In 1878 the rather nasty *St Luke* was built, although the old church was used until c.1950; thereafter it fell into decay and it was in danger of collapse by 1973, when the Friends took a long lease. The church consists of a nave and chancel in one, with a north transept with porch and a south porch added in the early-C19. What has exercised many historians is the date of the structure and with its bones bared this has become less difficult; one authority claims it as Saxon. The interior was in an indescribable mess but the early-C19 *box pews* are being reassembled, the two-decker *pulpit*, on a single column, repaired and before long this small, church will be returned to its former charm.

PARHAM. 5m NW of Arundel off B2139. *St Peter.*
A small, originally medieval, church much rebuilt in 1545 and remodelled in the Gothic style in c.1820. The interior is unaltered since the 1820s, and the fretwork screen, the pulpit, the box pews and coved ceiling are all of that date. The whole of the north transept, with its *fireplace*, was the squire's pew; opposite, in the south transept, was the parson's pew. Note the rare lead *font* with Lombardic lettering and the small *Royal Arms.*

PENSHURST. 4m W of Battle off B2204. *St Michael.*
A lonely, late-C14, aisleless church built of Wealdon sandstone, with a stumpy west tower, and *untouched* since the C17, apart from some C19 fittings. Pulpit, reader's desk, box pews and nave panelling are all C17. The pulpit, however, may be from Long Melford, Suffolk. The C15 screen is the oldest fitting and there are some fragments of medieval glass in the east window.

SOMPTING. 2m NE of Worthing off A27. *St Mary.*
Well-known for having the only Saxon Rhenish Helm *spire*, of c.1000, a shape mainly seen in Germany. Apart from the tower, the church was rebuilt in the late-C12 by the Templars. The tower arch

has crude Classical acanthus capitals of c.1000 harking back to a dimly remembered Roman Britain. There are pieces of re-used Saxon sculpture set in the nave north wall and in the chancel. The south transept was originally a quite separate Templar chapel. Notice the C13 Christ in Majesty *sculpture* in the nave north wall and the early-C14 female head wearing a wimple.

SOUTH HARTING. 6m W of Midhurst on B2146. *SS Mary & Gabriel.*

Sompting, St Mary. This famous tower with its 'Rhenish Helm' spire is Saxon and Norman.

A large early-C14 church, repaired after a fire in 1576, with some evidence of being Norman. The tower and fantastic *roofs* are Elizabethan and therefore unusual for Sussex. The font is C13 with a Jacobean cover. In the south transept is a painted *monument* of c.1600 to two families. A good monument of 1846, by Richard Westmacott Jnr., stands in the chancel. Note the war memorial by Eric Gill. The village stocks stand outside the churchyard.

STEYNING. 10m NW of Brighton on A283. *St Andrew.*
This is one of the best Norman churches in Britain. The west tower is C16, but the west tower arch is c.1100. Entering by the south door, notice the original C12 ironwork. The nave is breathtaking; originally longer, four of the bays dating from c.1170. Each capital and round arch have different intricate decorations with tall, round-arched clerestory windows above them. The chancel is C19 and a sad foil to the exuberance of the Norman work The Sussex marble *font* is Norman. In the south aisle, note the *Royal Arms* of 1703 and the Mace and Staff of c. 1685.

TROTTON. 3m W of Midhurst on A272. *St George.*
This church with an early-C13 tower has an undivided early-C14 nave and chancel. The interior leaves an unusual impression because there is no chancel arch. The roof is original. A *wall painting,* c.1380, of The Last Judgement in red monochrome, covers the west wall,

the most complete survival of this subject, discovered in 1904. The oldest *brass* in England to a female, Lady Margarete de Camoys (d.1310), lies in the nave floor; notice the small dog crouching at her feet. In the chancel, on a large table tomb, is another splendid *brass* to Lord Camoys (d.1419), who fought at Agincourt, and Lady Camoys, great granddaughter of Edward III, showing them holding hands, with his Garter above him, an early representation of the order. Notice too the Norman *font*, box pews and a Royal Arms.

UP MARDEN. 8m NW of Chichester off B2141. *St Michael.*
A small and remote C13 church with a stumpy weatherboarded tower and a rendered exterior. This has been claimed to have the loveliest interior in Britain. It is well worth a long detour. The effect inside is of centuries of accumulation and nothing jars or clashes. The plain glass, white rendered walls, the plain brick floor and plastered waggon-roof give a feeling of infinite, unchanging rural peace. It is obviously a much loved church.

WARMINGHURST. 10m N of Worthing on B2139. *Holy Sepulchre.*
In the care of the Redundant Churches Fund. A small, remote and charming aisleless church. It is C13, refurbished in 1707 and left untouched until restored with great skill in 1959. The interior is

Warminghurst, Holy Sepulchre. A small C13 church
with C18 furnishings.

simplicity, from the *box pews* of c.1770, the three-decker *pulpit* of the same date, to the earlier 1707 *communion table* and barley-sugar baluster *rail*. The wood screen was inserted in 1707 to separate the chancel from the nave. At the same time the *Royal Arms* of Queen Anne were painted in the typanum. Note the three *hatchments*.

WEST CHILTINGTON. 9m N of Worthing off B2139. *St Mary.*
An unspoiled C12 church with shingled spire, a nave with south aisle and a roof of 1602. Apart from the charm of the building the point of any visit must be the *wall paintings* of two periods, the C12 and the C14; the life of Christ arranged in a series of arcades, and a warning to Sabbath Breakers, are two among the many faded subjects of high quality.

Other Churches

CLAYTON. 6m N of Brighton. *St John Baptist.*
A small C11 church with C19 chancel giving no hint of the treasures within. Like Hardham, this has a famous series of C12 *wall paintings* unique in England for their period and state of preservation. Note the C11 chancel arch.

GLYNDE. 3m E of Lewes off A27. *St Mary.*
A Palladian church in flint with Portland stone dressings, built for the Bishop of Durham in 1763-5. Inside, the box pews, communion rail, west gallery and pulpit are all of the 1760s. Unfortunate intrusions are the screen and glass of 1894 and 1900. It is a comfortable interior and the hessian wall hangings add to the impression.

HARDHAM. 1m S of Pulborough on A29. *St Botolph.*
A very small church built in the C11, with some C13 and C14 windows. Its simple exterior with C19 bell-turret and porch gives no clue to the riches inside: a famous series of late-C12 *wall paintings.* These were uncovered in 1866 and although faded still give a vivid impression of what an overall scheme looked like. The St George in the nave is C13 or C14.

LULLINGTON. 5m NW of Eastbourne off A27. *Church.*
The dedication is unknown, but this must be the smallest church in Britain; inside, the longest side measures only sixteen feet. However, a visit to this early-C14 church will not easily be forgotten.

NORTH MARDEN. 8m NW of Chichester on B2141. *St Mary.*
Do not be deterred by the farmyard access to this tiny *Norman* church with nave and apse, unaltered save for the C12 windows. Note the iron *Royal Arms* of George III, tiny in scale too.

SHERMANBURY. 8m S of Horsham on A281. *St Giles.*
A small, medieval aisleless church restored in 1710, when the nave was lengthened, and again in 1885. *Box pews* with names and farm addresses on them are unusual survivors. Notice the musical instruments in a glass case, formerly used by musicians in the gallery, and

the *Royal Arms* of Queen Anne.

WESTDEAN. 5m W of Eastbourne off A259. *All Saints.*

A church with an attractive exterior, part Norman (tower, lower stages and west window), part C14. Sir Oswald Birley (d.1952), the painter, is buried here. Note the *bronze head* by Sir Jacob Epstein.

WEST DEAN. 5m N of Chichester on A286. *St Andrew.*

Restored after a serious fire in 1934. It has a gabled west tower unique in Sussex, Saxon nave walls, and an interior that is admirable C20, with a fine, but fire damaged, monument to Sir Richard Lewknor (d.1616) and a recumbent bronze *effigy* of William James (d.1912) by Sir W. Gascombe John.

LONDON

N20
N14
N21
N9
Woodford
NW17
N12
N11
N13
N18
E4
N3
Muswell Hill
N22
N17
E18
NW4
NW9
N2
N10
N8
N15
Walthamstow
E17
NW11
N6
N4
E11
N19
N16
E10
NW2
Hampstead
NW5
N7
N5
E5
E12
NW3
E7
NW10
NW6
N1
E8
E9
Islington
E15
NW8
NW1
Acton
W10
W9
EC1
E2
E3
Stratford
E13
E6
W7
W13
W5
W3
Shepherd's Bush
W12
W11
W2
Mayfair
W1
WC1
WC2
City of London
EC2
EC4
EC3
Stepney
E1
E16
W8
W14
Victoria
Lambeth
SE1
E14
SE28
Chiswick
W6
SW7
SW5
SW3
SW1
Chelsea
SW10
SE16
SE11
SE17
SE8
Greenwich
SE2
W4
SW13
Fulham
SW6
Battersea
SW8
SE7
SE18
SE14
SE10
SW11
SW9
SE5
SE15
SE3
SW14
Putney
SW15
Clapham
SW4
Lewisham
SE4
SE13
SW18
SE24
SE22
SW12
SW2
SE21
SE23
SE12
SE9
Dulwich
Catford
SE6
Wimbledon
SW19
SW17
SE27
SE26
Streatham
Crystal Palace
SE19
SE20
SW16
SW20
SE25
Enfield
GREATER
LONDON
Romford
Uxbridge
Richmond
LONDON
Wimbledon
Bromley
Croydon

LONDON

London, including the City and greater London which took in parts of Essex, Kent, Surrey, and all of the old county of Middlesex, in the deplorable reshuffle of the boundaries in 1975, cannot be looked on as other areas of Britain. There is no natural stone and building materials were imported by sea from Caen in Normandy, Portland and Purbeck. During the rebuilding of the City after the Great Fire of 1666, brick was likewise brought from wherever it was conveniently available.

The Great Fire left only a few older City churches standing. Wren's rebuilding was responsible for fifty-one parish churches, mostly completed by 1686; then there are the seven built by Nicholas Hawksmoor and a few others constructed in the eighteenth century until, in the Victorian period, expanding London demanded more and ever more churches.

Many of the City churches were of course badly damaged by bombs in the Second World War. In many cases only the walls were left standing and the interiors were so damaged that only material which could be rescued from the ruins was added to the later-restored churches. In these cases I have not described what has been lost but only what is there now.

With so much wealth generated in the capital it is not surprising that there is scarcely a single church left in its original condition; to contribute to a restoration was, until the twentieth century, one way of buying space in heaven for the afterlife.

The City of London

All Hallows-in-the-Tower, Byward Street, EC3
The church, originally attached to Barking Abbey, was very badly damaged by Nazi bombs in 1940. Although most of the walls survived together with the crypt, the west tower of 1658-9, the porch of the 1880s and the undercroft of 1925, a reconstruction was not attempted. The style of the new is late-Gothic of the C16 by the Seely & Paget partnership and it was rededicated in 1957. In the undercroft are the remains of a Roman tessellated *pavement*, parts of three Saxon crosses and an altar stone from Palestine. In the north

aisle are exhibited fragments salvaged from the bombing. The superb *font cover* is by Grinling Gibbons (1648-1721), the Wren *pulpit* comes from St Swithun, London, destroyed by bombs in 1941. Note the three C18 sword rests. There are monuments to City worthies, three C15 *brasses* and six of the C16, by far the biggest collection in London, so one is not surprised to discover that this is a brass rubbing centre. It is also the chapel for HM Customs and Excise and the London World Trade Centre.

All Hallows, London Wall, EC2.

Built by George Dance the Younger in 1765-7, in the Classical style, in plain brick with stone dressings and with a low west tower. Considering that he was then only twenty-four, it is a remarkable building. The interior was refitted in 1891 and, after bomb damage in 1941, left derelict for twenty years. It was sympathetically restored in 1962 by Richard Nye. The elegant interior is in contrast to the plainness of the outside. Robert Adam only introduced neo-Classical decorative motifs in 1759, yet here, only six years later, Dance is using the style with enormous confidence. The wide nave, uncluttered by aisles,

London Wall, All Hallows. The west tower, built in 1765-7 by George Dance.

is lit by high semi-circular clerestory windows in the vaults of the plaster roof. Fluted Ionic columns lead the eye up to the decorated barrel-vault ceiling and to the coffered apse at the east end. The pulpit, placed in the centre of the north wall, is entered from the vestry behind. A very large painting over the altar is by Sir Nathaniel Dance-Holland: a copy of *Acts IX* by Pietro da Cortona, it was presented to the church by the painter. The two, many branched, brass *chandeliers* are contemporary with the church. It is now a Guild church, the headquarters of the Council for the Care of Churches, and contains the library for the Council for Places of Worship.

Bevis Marks Synagogue, Heneage Lane, EC3.
Built in 1700-1 by a Quaker, Joseph Avis, this is the oldest Jewish synagogue in Britain. The west front overlooks a courtyard with none of the piety of an Anglican church; the simple style of the building would do justice to a Nonconformist chapel. Inside, the rich *furnishings* are original: three galleries with a trellis balustrade, seven superb C18 Dutch *chandeliers*, the *Ark*, similar to a reredos, and the *rails* with spiral turnings are all of c.1700.

St Andrew, Holborn, EC1.
A large Wren church for what was a big parish when it was built in 1684-90. In 1704 Wren faced the building in Portland stone. It has a typical square Wren plan with a square west tower, though the decorative detail is more Baroque than is usual with his churches. The interior was dramatically altered in 1872 by S.S. Teulon; all was destroyed by firebombs in 1941, elegantly rebuilt by Seely & Paget and reopened in 1961. In the spacious and bright interior the sumptuous new fittings are in the Wren style, supplemented by pieces from St Luke, Old Street. The mid-C18 *organ case* is from the Chapel of the Foundling Hospital and a monument to its founder, Captain Thomas Coram (d.1751), is in the west end.

St Andrew-by-the-Wardrobe, Queen Victoria Street, EC4.
This was the last of the City churches designed by Wren after the Great Fire and built 1685-93. Unfortunately, it was badly damaged in 1940, leaving only the walls standing. It was restored 1959-61 by Marshall Sisson. Built in dark-red brick, originally rendered, with stone dressings, it is one of Wren's primary models with upper and lower windows. In plan it is square with a square south-west tower. The church now wears borrowed clothes: the weather-vane is from St Michael, Bassishaw; the splendid *pulpit*, marble *font* and cover from St Matthew, Friday Street; the *Royal Arms* of c.1685 from St Olave Jewry; the C18 organ was bought in 1961; and the C18 *glass* came from Bulstrode Park, Buckinghamshire. However, the c.1600 *sculpture* of St Andrew, the *sword rest* and C18 beadles' *staves* are original. Four south aisle windows are modern and by Carl Edwards. The aisles have been panelled off beneath the galleries to make chapels, vestry and offices. Additionally the church is the headquarters of the Ancient Monuments Society and the Redundant Churches Fund.

St Andrew Undershaft, Leadenhall Street, EC3.
One of only five City churches to have escaped the Great Fire and Nazi bombs but which, ironically, suffered IRA bomb damage in 1992. The C15 tower is the oldest part, the rest was rebuilt in 1520-32 in rough stone with ashlar dressings and restored in 1930. In 1949, the panelled roof was restored, and 125 carved and gilded early C16 bosses replaced. The iron *communion rail* is by J. Tijou in 1704,

the organ case is of 1696. Do not overlook the 1776 *scenes* from the life of Christ painted in the spandrels of the arcade, the C18 *sword rest* and the C17 *glass* in the west window.

SS Anne & Agnes, Gresham Street, EC2.

A small red brick church with stone dressings, rebuilt by Wren in 1677-80 and retaining the C14 tower from an earlier church destroyed in the Great Fire. The steeple was added in c.1714. All but the standing walls were destroyed in 1941 and restored in 1963-6 by Braddock & Martin Smith. The plan, based on the Greek Cross and only used by Wren in two other churches (see also St Mary-at-Hill & St Stephen Walbrook), gives a feeling of space in what is a small building. Charles II's *Royal Arms* is from St Mary, Whitechapel, the dark *reredos*, depicting Moses and Aaron, from St Michael, Wood Street, and the modern font is a copy from that at St Mildred, Bread Street. The church is now used by the Lutherans.

St Bartholomew-the-Great, West Smithfield, EC1.

One of the five City churches to escape the Great Fire of 1666 and Nazi bombs in World War Two. It is basically a Norman church which formed the choir and transepts of an Augustinian Priory founded in 1123. Unusually, it is built of flint with stone dressings. The clerestory windows are late-C14 and the Lady Chapel was added in c.1330. By the C18, the building had fallen into disrepair and was used as a workshop. It was restored in the 1880s. The magnificent interior with its short, stout pillars and round-arched clerestory is satisfyingly Norman. Note the *tomb-chest* of c.1500 to the founder, Rahere (d.1143), and the C15 octagonal *font* in which William Hogarth (1697-1764) was baptised.

St Benet, Paul's Wharf, Upper Thames Street, EC4.

This is also one of the few Wren churches to escape damage by Nazi bombs in World War Two. It has belonged to the Welsh population of London almost uninterruptedly since 1320 and is known as 'The Welsh Church'. It has also been the chapel of the Royal College of Arms since 1555. The first church was destroyed in the Great Fire, and the present building was designed in Wren's office and built in

Paul's Wharf, St Benet. The west end of a Wren church, built 1677-82.

1677-83; it was restored in 1836 but severely damaged by a fire in 1971. Built of dark red brick with white stone dressings and ornamental swags, and a north-west tower capped by a lead cupola, it stands on a constricted site. Inside it is, in Wren's phrase, a 'convenient auditory', whereby the pulpit is clearly seen from everywhere. Full of light, with heraldic banners and Charles II's finely carved *arms* in the lobby, it is a gracious and relaxing interior. There are many monuments to Heralds and a small *monument* to Inigo Jones (1573-1652) who was buried in the earlier church. Henry Fielding married his second wife here in 1747 and Shakespeare's Feste in *Twelfth Night* also refers to St Benet's: 'The Bells of St Benet's, sir, may put you in mind'.

St Giles Cripplegate, Barbican, London Wall, EC2.
The C16 Barbican church is large with north and south aisles and with a small wood cupola. It was much restored in the C19. It survived the Great Fire only to be severely damaged in World War Two. The furnishings are modern, supplemented by items from St Luke's, Old Street. Here Shakespeare witnessed his nephew's baptism in 1607, Oliver Cromwell married Elizabeth Bouchier in 1620 and John Milton (d.1674) is buried under the chancel.

St Helen, off Bishopsgate, EC3.
One of only five City churches to survive both the Great Fire and World War Two. Ironically it suffered severe blast damage in an IRA bomb explosion outside the Baltic Exchange in 1992. It was mainly built in the late-C13 of rough stone and stone dressings with a C17 bell-turret. The south *doorway* is dated 1633, a forerunner of the coming Baroque style. Its curious plan with an unusual double nave is due to the church having served both a Benedictine nunnery and as a parish church. The double nave had a screen down the middle separating nuns in the north nave from parishioners in the south nave. The screen proved inadequate, because in 1385 the sisters were rebuked for kissing parishioners! The *pulpit* with a large canopy is a fantastic example of Jacobean woodwork; and observe the Easter sepulchre with a squint beneath in the nuns' choir. Also noteworthy is the very early wood *sword rest* dated 1665 and the c.1600 *sculpture* of a small seated figure. The church is well known for the number of its monuments to civic notables, including one to Sir Thomas Gresham (d.1579) who founded the Royal Exchange, and another to Robert Hook (d.1703), an experimental philosopher. Note the three C15 and four C16 brasses.

St James Garlickhithe, Garlick Hill, EC4.
Designed by Wren and built 1676-83 of ashlar with the spire added later in 1713-17. It suffered damage in World War Two and was restored by Lockhart Smith and Alexander Gale when C19 additions

were removed to bring the church back to its original appearance. The workmanship of this restoration is possibly the best in the City and all but indistinguishable from the original. The plan is a repeat of St Stephen Walbrook without the dome. Nevertheless there is an impression of interior height. The finely carved *pulpit* and *tester* are original but the stairs are from St Michael Queenhythe. In the blocked east window above the altar is an Ascension by Andrew Geddes (1783-1844) given in 1815. Note the *hat stands* at the ends of the pews and the wrought iron *sword rests*. The magnificent glass *chandelier* of 1967 is by Andrew Montrose and based on an C18 model at Emmanuel College, Cambridge. Seven of the City's Livery Companies have their annual services here.

St Katherine Cree, Leadenhall Street, EC3.

Leadenhall St, *St Katherine Cree.* One of the ceiling bosses displaying the arms of the Fishmongers Company.

A very rare church for London, and one built in 1628-30 at a rare time for church building in England. The tower is earlier, of 1504, with a cupola added in 1776. It is also unusual in that it escaped the Great Fire and survived World War Two mainly unscathed. The short nave is lit by clerestory windows and divided from the aisles by slender Corinthian columns. Above, the rib-vaulted plaster ceilings carry large bosses painted with the badges of Livery Companies. A magnificent feature is the large east rose window with *glass* of 1630. The octagonal marble font was donated in 1646 by the Gayer family. An annual Lion sermon, endowed by Sir John Gayer, is given in thanks to his escape from being eaten by a lion in Syria in 1643, only due to a timely prayer. Note the two C18 iron *sword rests*, and the 1668 organ with its finely carved case. This is also the Guild Church for Finance, Commerce and Industry.

St Margaret Lothbury, Lothbury, EC2.
This is one of the few Wren churches to be undamaged in World War Two. Built of stone in a plain style on a constricted site in 1686-90, with a south-east tower on the street front, it appears to be a typical Wren City church. However, the interior is a feast of C17 furnishings collected from demolished churches now incorporated in the present parish. The wood chancel *screen* of twisted columns designed by Wren is a breathtaking display of woodcarving. Such virtuosity overshadows the equally fine pulpit and tester. The sumptuous *reredos* is flanked by paintings: one of Aaron and the other of Moses, c.1700. Notice the two magnificent wood *sword rests*, on the north and south pew ends. After so much splendour the simple C18 organ case and west gallery come as something of an anticlimax. In the chapel in the south aisle is a small *font* attributed to Grinling Gibbons, and nearby is a splendid monument and portrait bust to Ann Simpson (d.1784) by Joseph Nollekens.

St Mary Abchurch, Abchurch Lane, EC4.
The rather grimy brick exterior is relieved by the light fantasy of the spire which could only be by Wren who designed the church in 1681-6. Rectangular, with a central dome, it luckily escaped serious damage in World War Two and consequently the interior furnishings are mainly intact. The astonishing *reredos*, actually carved by Grinling Gibbons (1648-1721), was blasted into a thousand pieces in 1940 and painstakingly reassembled in 1948-53. Other original details are the heavily carved *pulpit, tester* and steps, the marble *font* with wood cover, the richly carved *pews*, the west gallery and doorcases and finally the carved *Royal Arms* of James II. The organ case of 1717 is from All Hallows, Bread Street. Note the *poor boxes, sword rests*, and the richly carved original *pews*. Those on the south side have alas, lost the dog kennels which used to be underneath them. The church is

closely associated with the Fruiters' Company, whose arms are in the south window.

St Mary-at-Hill, Lovat Lane, EC3.
Built of brick by Wren in 1670-6 and hemmed in by other buildings, the west end and tower of yellow brick in Lovat Lane is by George Gwilt in 1787-8, the side walls were rebuilt in 1826 by James Savage who restored the interior in 1848-9, and it was fortunately undamaged in World War Two. This uninspiring introduction gives no hint of the feast of surprises inside. The unusual plan is that of a square domed centre with cross-arms from the corners: a Greek Cross (see also SS Anne & Agnes and St Stephen Walbrook). The dome and ceiling plasterwork, renewed in 1826, are painted blue and gold on white. The furnishings are exceptional, particularly as they were restored in the mid-C19 by William Gibbs Rogers and his work is indistinguishable from the original. That said, the *pulpit* is original, but the backboard and canopy, the rector's pew and reader's desk are all dated 1849, and the *Royal Arms* are Queen Victoria's. However, the fine *altarpiece* is original to Wren, as are the *box pews*, a unique survival in the City. Note the six outstanding C18 *sword rests*, the best in the City. The trombone of the founder of the Church Army, Prebendary Wilson Carlile, rector from 1892-1926, is in the vestibule.

St Mary Woolnoth, King William Street, EC3.
Built 1716-27 by Nicholas Hawksmoor, and his only City church, on a restricted, triangular site, the church now faces a busy traffic junction. Its dramatic Baroque west front incorporates a rusticated entrance porch and a solid double tower capped by two Classical temples. The interior space is a cube with a blue star-speckled ceiling. Restorations in 1875 by William Butterfield removed the side galleries whose carved panels now hang strangely on the walls. For no particular reason he also raised the floor and lowered the pulpit. The *altarpiece* of twisted columns supporting a black canopy and communion *rails* are all Hawksmoor's. Notice the *helmet* and *gauntlets* of Sir Martin Bowes (d.1550) and the small organ case of 1665. This is the official City church for the government of British Columbia.

St Peter-upon-Cornhill, Cornhill, EC3.
The church was built to Wren's designs in 1666-70, with a rendered exterior, a big west tower with a small copper dome and spire, and restored in 1879-80. The three-storied south porch, refaced in 1873, is C15, the date of an earlier church on the site. In the large tunnel-vaulted interior there is more evidence of the earlier building: a tomb recess in the north chapel, and C15 niches on either side of the east window. It is unfortunate that the C17 pews and galleries, apart from the west gallery, were taken out in the C19 restorations. The

pilastered *reredos* is original, as is the marble *font* with cover, and the organ case is c.1670. The splendid *pulpit* with *tester* is likewise of the 1670s. Note the *Royal Arms* of Charles II and the vestry *screen* behind it. The Poulterers' Company hold their annual service in the church and it is associated with the British Sailors' Society.

St Stephen Walbrook, Walbrook, EC4. Designed by Wren and built 1677-81 of ashlar with central dome; its spire was added in 1717. The church was damaged during World War Two, restored by Godfrey Allen and reopened in 1954. The exterior is difficult to see but it is for the interior plan that the church is best known. This is one of three Wren churches built on a Greek Cross plan (see also SS Anne & Agnes and St Mary-at-Hill). The rectangular form with the dome floating on eight arches

Cornhill, St Peter-upon-Cornhill. The domed spire of the church rebuilt to Wrens's designs in 1677-81.

supported on eight Corinthian columns gives the interior an amazing impression of space. The reredos, *pulpit* and *tester*, the staircase with twisted balusters, and the stone *font* with a very elegant carved cover, are original fittings saved from the wartime devastation. The panelling of the west entrance lobby also escaped destruction. Note two *paintings:* one by Benjamin West (1738-1820), *The Burial of St Stephen*, and an *Adoration of the Magi* attributed to Ludovico Cigoli (1559-1613); also the wrought-iron *sword rest* dated 1710. The ten ton marble *altar* is by Henry Moore. It was installed in 1987 after much disagreement. The original for the 'Vicar of Bray' was Henry Pendleton, rector here in the C16.

Other Churches

St Botolph Aldersgate, Aldersgate Street, EC1.
A church rebuilt 1788-91 in red brick with a short slender west tower and cupola. One of the City churches originally built near the gates for travellers. The plan is similar to that of George Dance's All Hallows'. The elegant interior has east and west apses and a surprisingly blue, coved, plaster ceiling. Note C18 pulpit on a palm trunk, a contemporary *sword rest*, and four interesting *monuments*, one (1750) by L.F. Roubiliac.

St Mary Aldermary, Queen Victoria Street, EC4. *(32)
An earlier church, of which only the present tower remains, was finished in 1629 in time to be destroyed by the Great Fire. Wren followed the earlier building, and the rebuilding is one of his rare excursions into Gothic. Faced in stone, it was completed in 1682. The nave *ceiling* is a glory of fan-vaulted plasterwork. Most of the original furnishings vanished in a drastic C19 restoration leaving only the marble *font* of 1627 and the finely carved *pulpit* from the earlier church. The magnificent *doorcase* is from St Antholin, Budge Row, demolished in 1876. The annual service of the Skinners' Company is held here.

St Olave Hart Street, Hart Street, EC3.
This pre-Great Fire church of the C13 and C15 was badly damaged in 1941, although the medieval and C18 furnishings were saved. It was restored in 1954. Note the six C18 *sword rests*, two from All Hallows, Staining. The Clothworkers' Company holds its annual service here.

Greater London

All Saints, (Chelsea Old Church) Cheyne Row, Chelsea, SW3.
The church was so badly damaged by bombs in 1941 that it was almost totally rebuilt, leaving only remnants of the older church of 1667-74 preserved in the south-east More Chapel and the east end. Built of brick with stone dressings the heavy tower and nave are entirely of 1949-58. The simple *font* of 1673, the C17 *altar* and rails together with six *chained books* (the only chained books in a London church) are all from the older church. The pulpit is a copy of the original of c.1680. Always known for its monuments, many of which survived the bombing, the oldest is to Sir

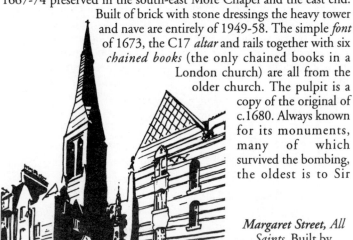

Margaret Street, All Saints. Built by William Butterfield in 1849-59.

Thomas More (d.1535) while the most interesting is to Sara Colville (d.1632) rising up in her shroud. Notice the bell in the porch given in thanksgiving in 1679 for the deliverance from drowning of 'William Ashburnham Esqvier Cofferer to his Majesties household'.

All Saints, Margaret Street, W1.

The church on the street front is hemmed in by its school building and the clergy house. It is a small and awkward site for so ambitious a project for this is the most important church in Marylebone. Built in 1849-59 by William Butterfield, then aged only thirty, it is the first great example of the High Gothic Revival and was built under the auspices of the Camden Society as a centre of Tractarian worship. One therefore expects something remarkable and there is no disappointment. Influenced by John Ruskin's *Seven Lamps*, published in 1849 ('beauty and effect of colour shall arise from construction and not from super additions'), it is built of dark-red brick with bands and patterns in darker colours, Inside all is religiously dark and highly decorated with painted wall patterns, stiff-leaf capitals and pointed architecture in the style of c.1200. The short nave with clerestory leads the eye through the steep chancel arch to a towering *reredos* of the 1860s by William Dyce, covering the entire east wall. The original reredos paintings quickly faded and these remaining are by Sir Ninian Comper in 1909. The Lady Chapel reredos is also his. The interior, although dazzlingly impressive, is not to everyone's taste, it was called ugly and even vulgar earlier in this century. However, you will not leave unmoved.

All Souls, Langham Place, W1.

The problem of visibility on a difficult site – on John Nash's processional route to Regent's Park, on the bend from Regent Street to Portland Place – was neatly solved by Nash by putting a circular portico supported by giant Ionic columns, so making it visible from each direction. Built in 1822-4 it now doubles as a recording studio for the BBC, after being cleverly adapted in the 1970s and repaired following damage in World War Two.

Langham Place, All Souls.
Built by John Nash in
1822-4 and now a
BBC studio.

Chapel Royal, St James's Palace, SW1.
Built in the 1530s by Henry VIII when he created St James's Palace,
the chapel consists of a T shaped space with an original ceiling
panelled in octagons on a blue background and dated 1540. The
lower decoration and furnishings are from c.1836. The display of
mainly C17 gold and silver plate is well worth seeing. Charles I took
Communion here before his execution in 1649, Princess Caroline of
Brunswick married the unwilling George IV in 1795 and Queen
Victoria married Prince Albert here in 1840. The chapel has also
witnessed countless royal baptisms.

Christ Church, Commercial Street, Spitalfields, E1.
Built by Nicholas Hawksmoor in 1714-15 in
magnificent stone, this is a church with a
chequered past. Built at a time when Huguenot
refugees brought prosperity to the area there
were financial problems and it was not consecrated until 1729. The Industrial Revolution
killed off the local prosperity and by 1958 the
building was considered dangerous and
demolition seemed inevitable. However,
Friends of Christ Church have raised
money and work is in hand to restore it to
its former glory. The building is
monumental in conception, with a
huge portico supported on four
Tuscan columns. Inside, a central
space with a flat roof lit by a clerestory
has barrel-vaulted aisles each side,
with east and west end screens on
Classical columns. The interior was
once Hawksmoor's most sumptuous
and the cost of restoration will be
huge. One wishes the Friends of
Christ Church success in this formi-
dable venture.

London, Christ Church.
The tall west spire focuses
the eye on the end of
Brushfield St, built in 1723-9
by Nicholas Hawksmoor.

Grosvenor Chapel, South Audley
Street, W1.
Built in c.1730 as an estate chapel in yellow brick and roundheaded
upper windows, with a slender spire and bell-turret above the west
entrance, this building is surprisingly in the New England Colonial
style. Inside, the nave has a coved ceiling, the aisles are groin-vaulted
and there are three galleries. Pulpit and communion rail are original
but the simplicity of the scheme was completely altered in 1912
when the high altar and open screen were inserted by Sir Ninian

Comper. Lady Mary Wortley Montagu (d.1762) and John Wilkes (d.1797) are both buried here.

Holy Trinity, Sloane Street, Chelsea, SW1.
Built in 1889-90 by John Sedding in a mid-C16 style, this was his last church, built at a time when high Gothic was going out of fashion. The front, of brick with stone dressings, with its vast west window and Tudor style turrets, looks as though it has strayed from Hampton Court Palace. The interior is another matter; here is a celebration of the Arts and Crafts of the 1890s: much Morris & Co *glass* of 1894-5 by Morris himself and Edward Burne-Jones, a Burne-Jones *frieze* above the arcades, an astounding metal *grill* of 1892 by Henry Wilson in the morning chapel, the chancel stalls by F.W. Pomeroy; and F. Boucher was responsible for the *font* of marble and onyx. Many more furnishings and paintings were contributed by other inspired members of the Arts and Crafts Movement. For those interested in the period this church should not be missed.

The Queen's Chapel, Marlborough Road, SW1.
One of only two places of worship in London by Inigo Jones and built 1623-7 in the then new Palladian style, using rendered brick-

Marlborough Street,
Queen's Chapel. A classical chapel built by Inigo Jones in 1623-7.

work with stone trim, its narrow west front is crowned by a massive Palladian architrave. The interior was wrecked during the Commonwealth but restored in 1662 for Catherine of Braganza, the Portuguese wife of Charles II. One enters beneath a deep gallery into a barrel-vaulted nave, its coffered vaults picked out in gold and white. The *reredos*, inserted in 1938, is an early painting by Annibale Carracci (1560-1609). Above the altar is a three-light Venetian window, said to be the first in Britain. The *east gallery, stalls, lectern* and south *organ gallery* are all of the 1660s. From Inigo Jones's time there remains only the *communion rail* and *overmantel* in the west gallery, once the Royal pew. George III married Princess Charlotte here in 1761, and until 1901 it was known as the German Chapel. It is open only for Sunday services, except in August and September.

St James, Piccadilly, W1.
Designed by Wren in 1676-84 as a new church for what was strangely enough 'a new suburb', and built in red brick with stone dressings. It was very badly damaged in World War Two and restored in 1947-54. The bright and spacious interior is covered by a plaster barrel-vault ceiling supported on slightly slender Corinthian columns on first floor galleries. The *reredos* with large segmental architrave is by Grinling Gibbons and the *font*, standing on a Tree of Knowledge, is also by him. The *organ* is remarkable in having been made by Renatus Harris for Whitehall Palace chapel in 1678 and given to this church in 1691. The *carved case* is by Grinling Gibbons. There are many good *monuments* including one to the caricaturist James Gillray (d.1815) and another to Van de Velde, the marine painter (d.1641). Outside in the north wall is a pulpit erected in 1902 but no longer used owing to traffic noise.

St James-the-Less, Thorndike Street, SW1.
This was the first and best London church built by G.E. Street, 1860-1. It is a heavy building in patterned red and black brick with stone dressings, and completely Gothic, with buttresses and a top-heavy spire. The interior is suitably and religiously dark where the brick patterns are repeated with red and yellow glazed tiles. Above the chancel arch is a good *fresco* by G.F. Watts. The *pulpit* is astonishing and heavily carved by T. Earp.

St John's Chapel, in the White Tower, Tower of London, EC3.
This small plain chapel is perhaps the most impressive Norman architecture in Britain. A rarity for this country is the tunnel-vaulted nave, with groin-vaulted aisles and galleries over, which curve behind the altar apse to make an ambulatory. It was used as a royal chapel until the Commonwealth, became a repository for state papers at the Restoration and continued so until the C19 when it was restored as a chapel. Here Mary Tudor married Philip of Spain by proxy in 1554.

Earlier, in Wat Tyler's Rebellion (1381), when rebels captured the Tower, Bishop Sudbury and three others were found at prayer before the altar and snatched away to be beheaded on Tower Hill.

St Luke, Sydney Street, Chelsea, SW3.

Authorised to be built by Act of Parliament in 1819 to accommodate the expanding capital, and recently restored. The church was built at great cost by James Savage in an impressive Gothic Revival style of solid stone and not, as was more common and cheaper, stone faced. It is also the first Revival church to have stone vaulting throughout. One enters, by way of a type of porte-cochère beneath a tall west tower, into a high, imposing nave with triforium and clerestory, and lined with wooden galleries. The east end has a seven-light window of 1959 *glass* by Hugh Easton and below it the altar with a large and dramatic 'Descent from the Cross' by James Northcote (1746-1831). The fine *organ* dates from 1824 and was played by John Ireland, organist from 1904-26. Charles Dickens married Catherine Hogarth here in 1836 and Charles Kingsley was curate in the 1830s. Note the military *monument* by Sir Francis Chantrey to Lt-Col. Henry Cadogan, killed at the battle of Vitoria in 1813.

St Pancras New Church, Woburn Place, WC1.

This is the earliest Greek Revival church in London; it was also the most costly to build after St Paul's Cathedral. Built of brick with stone facing by H.W. and W. Inwood in 1819-22, it uses numerous genuine Greek Classical details in its design; most striking, because it faces Euston Road, is the Erechtheum, an Acropolis temple, and the tower, which is adapted from the Temple of the Winds, Athens. Throughout, the historical detail is accurate; inside, six correct Ionic columns support the organ and there are six more in the east apse. The fittings are of the best, and whatever one might think of a pagan original for a Christian church, the visitor will applaud the result.

St Paul, Covent Garden, WC2.

One of only two places of worship in London by Inigo Jones, built 1631-3 and restored, after fire damage in 1796, by Thomas Hardwick the Younger. The east entrance front is all portico and Etruscan in style: a deep roof supported on four Tuscan columns. This front, originally brick, was stone-faced in the late-C19. The central entrance door is false. Inside, the west gallery, supported on Doric columns, is original but other galleries were removed in 1872 to make the altar colonnades. Fine carving on the pulpit is all early-C19. Grinling Gibbons (d.1721) is buried here and commemorated by a carved *wreath* of flowers by him on the west screen, which came from St Paul's Cathedral in 1965. Many famous actors and other personalities are buried here including Sir Peter Lely (d.1680), Thomas Rowlandson (d.1827) and Dame Ellen Terry (d.1928). The

Covent Garden, St Paul. Built in 1631-3 by Inigo Jones

church is the headquarters of the Actors' Church Union and known as the 'Actors' Church'.

St Peter ad Vincula, Tower of London, Tower Hill, EC3.
The present chapel replaces an earlier building and dates from the early-C16. It is a simple low building of rendered flint, with a small brick west tower; its five large windows overlook the Tower Green. The *organ* is one of the City's oldest and was made in 1679 for the Chapel Royal in Whitehall, while the C16 *font*, smashed in the Commonwealth, has been reassembled from four pieces. The chapel is chiefly famous for being the burial place of executed dignatories: Queen Anne Boleyn (ex.1536); Queen Catherine Howard (ex.1542); Edward Seymour, Duke of Somerset (ex. 1552); Sir Thomas More (ex.1535); John Dudley, Duke of Northumberland (ex.1553), his son Lord Guildford Dudley (ex.1554) and his daughter-in-law, Lady Jane Grey (ex.1554); Robert Dudley, Earl of Essex (ex.1601); James Duke of Monmouth (ex.1685) are only a few. Note the magnificent canopied *monument* to John Holland, Duke of Exeter (d.1447).

CROYDON, Canning Road, Addiscombe, *St Mary Magdalene.*
For those who love C19 eccentricities, then this church must be seen. Consecrated in 1879 and built by R. Buckton Lamb, who believed wholeheartedly in timber roofs, it was only finished in 1930 when the tower was completed. The interior gives the impression that the walls are of secondary importance; timbers everywhere reach upwards to the climax, a small lantern above the centre crossing. One leaves with the refreshing discovery that some C19 architects were not slaves to medieval detail.

DEPTFORD, High Street, SE8. *St Paul.*
Designed by Thomas Archer in 1713 this glorious church was not

consecrated until 1730, then restored in 1856, 1883, 1930s and 1970s. The dramatic entrance is beneath a huge semicircular portico with Tuscan columns supporting, by way of contrast, a slender steeple. The vast and theatrical interior is all one should expect of late-baroque style: a high square nave is divided from the aisles by colossal Corinthian columns, and both nave and aisles have flat ceilings of highly decorated plasterwork. Unfortunately the pulpit, altar and organ case have all been altered from Archer's original design. However, one can forget the furnishings and admire the magnificence of the neo-Baroque decoration. Notice the *monument* to Vice-Admiral James Sayer (d.1776) by Joseph Nollekens.

GREENWICH, Charlton Village, SE7. *St Luke.*
Built of brick in 1630, with a north aisle of 1639 and east end of 1870, this is still a more or less unspoilt village church, whose white-washed interior maintains an almost rustic atmosphere. The nave waggon-roof was restored in 1925, while that in the chancel is C17. The octagonal *pulpit* with scrolled panels is c.1630 and the stone font late-C17. One north window has interesting C17 heraldic *glass*. There are some good *monuments:* one to Lady Newton (d.1630) is by Nicholas Stone and another simple monument with a fine *bust* by Sir Francis Chantrey commemorates Sir Spencer Percival, the Prime Minister assassinated in 1812. Do not overlook the *hatchments.*

HAMPTON COURT PALACE. *Chapel Royal.*
Maintained by Historic Royal Palaces. The Chapel was built by Cardinal Wolsey before 1525 but completed by Henry VIII in 1535-6. Entering by the west door, with Henry VIII's arms and those of Jane Seymour on either side, into the ante-chapel beneath the Royal pew, one is unprepared for the splendour in the chapel itself. The ceiling is original and consists of gilded pendants and deep, close ribbed, lierne-vaulting (the stars were added by A.W.N.Pugin in the 1840s). Above the Royal pew the *ceiling* was painted by Sir James Thornhill in c.1711, a time when Queen Anne had the chapel refitted. The *reredos*, designed by Sir Christopher Wren, and carved by Grinling Gibbons, was brought from Whitehall in the 1690s. The windows date from the 1711 refitting when a *trompe l'oeil* was painted by Thornhill beyond the organ case by Gibbons. In 1894 a restoration returned the windows to their Tudor form. Thomas Highmore was responsible for the poorly painted decoration on the top part of the walls before 1712, Christopher Schrider made the *organ* and Sir Edwin Lutyens designed the brass *altar cross.*

HAREFIELD, Church Hill, Hillingdon. *St Mary.*
Still a rural church, set on the very edge of north-west Greater London. It is chiefly built of flint rubble, and of all periods, with a C13 chancel, a north-west tower of c.1500 refaced in brick and all

heavily restored in 1841. The two aisles are unusually the same height as the nave. Entrance is by the north door close to the tower. The interior gives the impression of a happy jumble of interesting items. In the nave and chancel the notable plaster ceilings were restored c.1700. In the north aisle is a restored screen of c.1500. The ingenious C18 *pulpit* amalgamates the reader's desk and parish clerk's pew. Note the *commandment boards* and *reredos* in the chancel. The glory of this little church is the *monuments* mainly of the C16 and C17. In particular, do not miss that by Grinling Gibbons to Mary Newdigate (d.1692). Lady Derby's (d.1637) is the largest and grandest, she lies beneath a four-posted canopy. In the Breakspear Chapel there are five *brasses* to the Ashby family, two of these are palimpsests.

HARROW-ON-THE-HILL, Church Hill, *St Mary.*
Built of flint-faced stone and placed high on a hill, its tall slender spire can be seen for miles. The lower courses of the tower are the oldest part, c.1130, and the spire was rebuilt in 1765. In chronological order came the early-C13 nave, aisles and chancel, then the transepts of c.1300, and finally the nave roof and clerestory of c.1450. All was relentlessly restored in 1846-9 by Sir George Gilbert Scott in the decorated style of c.1300 when the north chapel was added and the porch rebuilt. The interior lost most of its character in the restoration, but note the late-C12 Purbeck marble *font*, the good oak *pulpit* of c.1675, the *glass* by Kempe Studios in the chancel lancet windows and the east window by Sir Ninian Comper. There are many *monuments*, principally to past headmasters of Harrow School, one is by Richard Westmacott Jnr. Also note the ten *brasses* ranging from 1370 to 1603, but particularly that to the founder of Harrow School, John Lyon (d.1592); it is small and easily missed in the north arcade. In the churchyard, near a tombstone to Peachey, Lord Byron (1788-1824) as a schoolboy claimed 'this was my favourite spot'. His illegitimate daughter, Allegra, who died in Italy aged five in 1822, is buried near the south door.

ICKENHAM, High Road and Swakeleys Road, Hillingdon. *St Giles.*
A C14 village church enlarged in the C16, built of flint and rubble, and part rendered. One enters by a timber-framed porch of c.1500. The nave and chancel have good roofs of c.1500, and off the north aisle is a very unusual and small *mortuary chapel* of 1640-50 with niches for upright coffins, and Jacobean communion table and benches. There is good *glass* of 1956 and 1971 by Alan Younger in the west extension. Note the C14 *coffin lid*, the two C16 brasses and one of the C17. A marble baby in swaddling clothes, Robert Clayton (d.1665), lies incongruously on a windowsill. It was found buried in the churchyard in 1921.

KENSINGTON, Philbeach Gardens, SW5. *St Cuthbert.*

Built in 1884-8 by Roumieu Gough in the Gothic style of c.1300 in red and black brick, and remarkable for its Anglo-Catholic interior embellishments. In the east end is a vast reredos made in 1913-1; the Arts and Crafts *lectern* in wrought iron and copper is by Bainbridge Reynolds of 1897. A happy survival are the very early *light fittings* of 1887 and these, together with the silver-panelled altar frontal, communion rails, *Royal Arms*, candle sticks and much else, are also by Bainbridge. The carved pulpit, piscina and sedilia are original fittings of 1887, and the rood screen is of 1893. In total it is a noteworthy display of Arts and Crafts fittings.

LEWISHAM, Deptford High Street, SE8. (off A200). *St Paul.*
A magnificent Baroque church designed by Thomas Archer and built 1712-30 in the finest Portland stone. The west end is finished with a tall slender spire above a semicircular portico. Inside, the plan is that of a square 'preaching box', with vestries behind canted angles. Corinthian columns support a classically correct entablature beneath a richly decorated ceiling. The altar stands in an apse with painted curtains decorating the space above the entablature. The fittings are entirely original with a square late-Norman *font*. Thankfully ignored by the C19, the church was carefully restored in the 1960s.

LITTLE STANMORE, Whitchurch Lane (B461), Edgware, NW9. *St Lawrence.*
Once the church of the Dukes of Chandos at Cannons Park, this is one of the most extraordinary churches in Britain. There is a very ordinary C14 to C15 flint tower, but the rest of the church was rebuilt for Chandos in brick with stone dressings in 1715; attached to the north side is the Chandos Mausoleum of 1735-6. The unaisled interior is about as theatrically Baroque as was possible in England; deception is the key, for nothing is what it seems. The walls are completely *painted* by Francis Sleter, with illusions of niches containing the Virtues, and the vault is painted by Louis Laguerre (1663-1721) with scenes of the *miracles*. Box pews with prayerbook chains lead the eye to the east end and to the carved decoration of the *reredos* attributed to Grinling Gibbons. Behind is the *organ case*, also attributed to Gibbons. The door in the north wall leads one first into the Mausoleum ante-room by James Gibbs containing some unimportant wall-tablets and then into the Mausoleum itself, completely *painted* in architectural illusion by Sleter and G. Brunetti, except for the *monument* to the 1st Duke and his two wives by Gibbons. Again all is not what it seems, for marble is used only as a facing and the ducal monument is but a piece of scenery. Two later, and over-large sarcophagi, tend to spoil the duke's dramatic effect.

ORATORY OF ST PHILIP NERI, Brompton Road, SW3.
A Roman Catholic church built from 1878 by Herbert Gribble in a

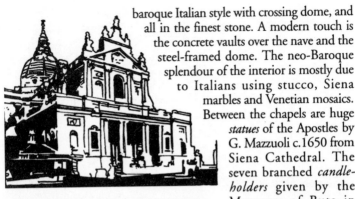

baroque Italian style with crossing dome, and all in the finest stone. A modern touch is the concrete vaults over the nave and the steel-framed dome. The neo-Baroque splendour of the interior is mostly due to Italians using stucco, Siena marbles and Venetian mosaics. Between the chapels are huge *statues* of the Apostles by G. Mazzuoli c.1650 from Siena Cathedral. The seven branched *candleholders* given by the Marquess of Bute in 1878 are by William Burges, – the two were rebuilding Cardiff Castle – and a reminder of Bute's conversion to Rome in 1868. There is much else to see in this opulent interior, but noteworthy are the *altar* and *baldacchino* of c.1710 from St Servatious, Maestricht, in the St Wilfred Chapel, two early-C18 *angels*, signed by A. Calegari, in the organ loft and, in the Lady Chapel, a costly *altar* and *reredos* of 1693 inlaid with semi-precious stones, from the Chapel of the Rosary in San Domenico, Brescia.

Brompton Road, Oratory of St Philip Neri. Magnificent Baroque Revival by Herbert Gribble begun in 1878.

PETERSHAM, Petersham Road, Richmond. *St Peter.*
Amazingly, for a church so near to London, this is untouched. The chancel is C13, attached to a nave rebuilt in brick in the C16, with transepts and tower added in the C17. Inside there are no Victorian 'improvements'; beneath a low flat C18 plaster ceiling the *box pews* and *galleries* are all of 1796, and the *pulpit* and reading desk are of the same date. The *font* of 1740 is the earliest fitting in the church.

WANSTEAD, Redbridge, off A114. *St Mary.*
The church, the park, now a golf course, and the club house, once the stables, are the only evidence of what was once the biggest house in Britain, Wanstead house, built in 1714-20 by Colen Campbell for Sir Richard Child the banker. It was demolished in 1824, but the church, built 1787-90, in a strict Classical style by Thomas Hardwick, still stands. A Tuscan porch leads one into an interior dominated by tall Corinthian columns with original wooden galleries, high *box pews*, and wrought-iron communion rails. The surprise is an astonishing *pulpit* with *tester* supported on two palm-tree columns (the Childs made their first fortune in the East India Company). Note the 1834 monument by Sir Richard Westmacott, another of 1745 by Peter Scheemakers and the magnificent memorial to Sir Josiah Child (d.1699) attributed to John Van Nost.

EAST ANGLIA

Cambridgeshire

A county now incorporating the former Huntingdonshire and Isle of Ely and not previously blessed with any suitable building stone. The redrawing of the county boundaries in 1974 brought the fine Barnack limestone quarries into Cambridgeshire, and the Ketton quarries are only just across the border with Lincolnshire. Making the best of the original lack of building stone, the local material, clunch, was utilised. Clunch is a chalk easily carved but quite unsuitable for exteriors as it weathers badly. Otherwise flint was the only native building material.

Understandably Ely Cathedral influenced the design of many of the county churches and Ely's octagonal towers are frequently repeated.

In the Introduction, mention was made of the influence of the Camden Society, founded in 1839 in Cambridge, which was responsible for removing so many historical fittings and altering the interiors of so many churches. The Camdenians unfortunately made an example of their own county and it is no surprise that Cambridgeshire has almost nothing left of older church interiors.

BOTTISHAM. 6m E of Cambridge on A14. *Holy Trinity.*
Tower and chancel C13 built of Barnack stone, nave c.1300-20. All restored in 1839. Note the cut-down Elizabethan communion table on the north wall of the sanctuary and the very unusual stone *rood screen* contemporary with the nave. In the south aisle is a small painted relief of a schoolboy, commemorating the gift of a school in 1730.

BURWELL. 10m NE of Cambridge on B1102. *St Mary.*
Built in the C15, of flint with Barnack limestone trim, in the grandest of styles competing with those of Suffolk. The west tower has a Norman lower storey. Enter by the fan-vaulted north porch and inside all is bathed in brilliant light from huge C15 windows emphasising the whiteness of the chalk clunch used for the interior. Both nave and chancel were re-roofed in the 1460s. The date 1464 appears on the east wall over the chancel arch and the carved wooden *bosses* include a pope, an emperor, a pelican and several birds including a

EAST ANGLIA

NORFOLK

Cromer

Wells next
the Sea

Hunstanton

North
Walsham

King's Lynn

Swaffham

NORWICH

Great
Yarmouth

Wisbech

Downham
Market

Wymondham

Lowestoft

Peterborough

Bungay

Beccles

Ramsey

Ely

Thetford

Diss

Southwold

CAMBRIDGESHIRE

Halesworth

Huntingdon

St Ives

Bury
St Edmunds

Eye

St Neots

Newmarket

SUFFOLK

Aldeburgh

Cambridge

Haverhill

Hadleigh

Ipswich

Saffron
Walden

Sudbury

Felixstowe

Harwich

Colchester

Braintree

ESSEX

Clacton
on Sea

Harlow

Chelmsford

Epping

Basildon

Southend on Sea

swan. Notice the brass dated 1542, this is a palimpsest; on the reverse are the figures of a canon and a deacon of c.1325.

ELY. 15m NE of Cambridge on A10. *Prior Crauden's Chapel.*
A tiny gem of a first floor private chapel built for Prior Crauden, off his new hall, in c.1321-5, exactly the time when the amazing Octagon, and Lady Chapel, in the Cathedral were being built, with which it has many similarities. Deserted after the Dissolution it later became part of the living quarters and was only restored in 1846. Richly decorated with carved ogee arches, niches, and canopies, it is famous for the tiled mosaic *floor* of which the portion before the altar shows The Temptation of Adam and Eve. The east window has what may be French *glass* installed in c.1850.

ICKLETON. 8m S of Cambridge on B1375. *St Mary.*
A church with a stumpy central tower and a perfectly preserved Norman nave and clerestory, re-roofed in the C14. The chancel was rebuilt in 1882-3. Inside on the nave north wall is a rare C12 series of true *frescos* depicting the story of the Passion. Below these are the martyrdoms of St Peter, St Andrew and St Lawrence. Above the chancel arch is a C14 *Doom* with, unusually, the Virgin topless.

ISLEHAM. 7m N of Newmarket on B1104. *St Andrew.*
An admirable church built of flint and pebble rubble in the early-C14, except for the insensitive C19 west tower by G.E. Street. The hammer-beam *roof* and clerestory were paid for by the local Peyton family in 1495 and recorded on the roof. In the chancel are eight *misericords* of c.1450. The unusual brass *lectern* was found in the Fen in the mid-C19 and is of the same type as those in St Mark's, Venice. A C17 funeral *helmet* is supplemented by two Italian *helmets* of c.1500 in the priest's chamber. There are a great number of good monuments and three brasses including a fine Peyton *brass* of 1484.

KIRTLING. 5m SE of Newmarket off B1063. *All Saints.*
The rich Norman south door, with Christ in Majesty in the tympanum, also has Norman *ironwork* on the door itself which leads into a C15 nave and a chancel of C13. The south-east chapel of c.1500 in brick, built by the North family, is particularly rewarding. There are many monuments to the Norths, the earliest is to the 1st Lord North (d.1564), the builder of the chapel. Good *hatchments* are worth noting, also a brass in the chancel to Edward Myrfin (d.1553).

LEIGHTON BROMSWOLD. 8m W of Huntingdon off A604. *St Mary.*
The chancel is late-C13, the rest was rebuilt in c.1630 and hardly altered since. This must surely be the oldest unaltered church *interior* in the country. It is complete with Carolean pews, stalls, lectern, litany desk, pulpit and reader's desk, all of the 1630s and decorated

Leighton Bromswold, St Mary. Hardly altered since
c.1630, the interior, east end.

with balusters and knobs from the turner's lathe. Even the roof has
matching knobs. Notice the *children's pews* in the west end from the
time when this was used as a school. In the south transept is a
damaged alabaster tomb to Sir Robert Tyrwhitt (d.1572) and his
wife who was Governess to Elizabeth I and a maid of honour to
(Queen) Catherine Parr.

ORTON LONGUEVILLE. SW suburb of Peterborough. *Holy
Trinity.*
Most of the church is early-C14 with a north chapel of c.1275 and
south aisle of 1675. Inside are box pews and a *wall painting* showing
the upper half of a good C16 St Christopher. Note the early-C17
funeral helm.

SWAFFHAM PRIOR. 8m NE of Cambridge on B1102. *SS Mary*
and *Cyriac.*

Two churches stand within yards of each other in one churchyard, built at a time when the village was two parishes. St Mary's was built in the C12 of flint with limestone dressings and a surprising Norman octagonal tower. The Norman nave has two C14 aisles and a chancel almost completely rebuilt in restorations of 1878. Four small brasses are of little interest but the *glass* of 1910-20 from St Cyriac is interesting and includes a scene from World War One. St Cyriac, also of the C12 with a fine C14 tower, and restored in the C19, is no longer used. The nave with *box pews* and a small west *gallery* is left to quietly decay.

Other Churches 5/96

CAMBRIDGE. 50m N of London off M11. *Holy Selpulchre,* Bridge Street
One of five round churches in Britain and dating from c.1130. Over-restored by A. Salvin under the Camden Society in 1841-4.
St Benet, Benet Street. Oldest church in the county: Saxon tower,

Cambridge, Holy Sepulchre. One of only five round churches in Britain; the Norman interior.

aisles and nave c.1300. Exterior over-restored in C19.

FLETTON. S suburb of Peterborough. *St Margaret.*
Mostly Norman but famous for C9 *Saxon carvings* on exterior chancel buttresses. These are unparalleled in Britain or Western Europe.

GODMANCHESTER. S suburb of Huntingdon on A604. *St Mary.*
Mainly C13, C14 & C15 with west tower of 1623 and good chancel of C13. Note twenty C15 *misericords* from Ramsey Abbey and the mass dial, a form of sundial to tell the time of the masses.

Essex

There are more than 350 medieval churches in the county and all of them are worth a visit. Because there is no source of good building stone in the county, the materials used vary, ranging from Saxon split timbers at Greensted, flint and puddingstone, ragstone from Kent, to deep red brick. Owing to the proximity of London, long timber became scarce by the late-Middle Ages and consequently there are no spectacular C15 roofs such as are found in Norfolk and Suffolk. However, Essex made a speciality of late-medieval timber towers, those at Blackmore, Margaretting and Navestock being three among many. Additionally, this skill in timberwork was applied to porches. Also noteworthy are the number of surviving wall paintings; those at Copford date from c.1140-50 and are remarkable, and two of the Virgin and Child — one of c.1250 at Great Cranfield and the other C14 at Belchamp Walter — are well worth a visit.

BELCHAMP WALTER. 4m SW of Sudbury off B1058. *St Mary.*
The west tower is C15 and the nave of c.1220 is exceeded in length by the chancel built a hundred years later. The interior was over-painted in 1860. However, only discovered in 1926 and therefore untouched, is a large *wall painting* of a C14 Virgin and Child and traces of a Wheel of Fortune on the south wall. Notice an interesting tomb of 1324 to Lord Boutetort and the C12 circular font.

BLACKMORE. 8m SW of Chelmsford off A414. *St Lawrence.*
An aisled Norman, Augustinian, priory church of c.1170, with the finest timber *tower* in Britain, built c.1480. The weatherboarded tower is supported on ten upright posts. Little remains of the Norman work, but the west wall is visible behind the timber tower and the north wall has Norman work in it. The church was restored in 1896-8 when the roof was renewed and the c.1400 *shields* restored. The octagonal Purbeck marble *font* is C13. Notice the good quality *monuments* (some, alas, damaged): Thomas Smyth (d.1594) and his wife, and the slab memorials in the floor, particularly that to Simon Lynch. In a glass case beneath the tower is a *cresset stone* (for holding holy oil).

CASTLE HEDINGHAM. 4m NW of Halstead on B1058. *St Nicholas.*

The west brick tower is dated 1616 but the rest is completely Norman and rich in decoration. Inside, the early-C16 double-hammer-beam nave *roof* is one of only four in the county. An ornate C14 chancel *screen* is also a rarity for Essex. On the south side are five C15 *misericords* including one of a fox carrying off a monk.

COPFORD GREEN. 5m SW of Colchester on A12. *St Michael & All Angels.*

An almost unchanged Norman church with squat tower, apsed east end, and late-C13 south aisle. Difficult to find, but persevere and you will not be disappointed. Unfortunately the Norman vaults in nave and chancel were removed. It is justly famous for its *wall paintings* contemporary with the church, which once covered every wall. These include Christ in Majesty in the apse and the Signs of the Zodiac round the arch leading to the apse. In the north aisle: The Healing of Jairus's Daughter, and the Battle of the Virtues and the Vices, with Virtue wearing armour.

FINCHINGFIELD. 8m NW of Braintree on B1053. *St John Baptist.*

A mostly C14 church with a huge Norman tower and unusual chancel clerestory. The early-C15 chancel *screen* is the county's best and

Great Warley, St Mary. Built in 1904, the interior is a celebration of Art Nouveau; the east end.

that in the south aisle runs a close second. In the south chapel there is a Purbeck marble *monument* with brass figures to John Berners (d.1523). Notice the Stuart Royal Arms and, on the window ledge in the south aisle, the peculiar scratched *device*: a diagram of 'Nine Men's Morris'. The Kempe Chapel has a good king-post roof and a carving of 'Scandal' with ass's ears at the base of the east arch.

GREAT CANFIELD. 3m SW of Great Dunmow off B184. *St Mary.*
A virtually Norman church with C15 belfry and porch. Inside are some surprises. The Norman *chancel arch* is one, and note on the left capital a face being pecked by two birds; another is one of the best *wall paintings* in Britain of a seated Virgin and Child c.1250. There are three C16 brasses.

GREAT WARLEY. 2m S of Brentwood on B186. *St Mary.*
This roughcast church, built in 1904 by C.H. Townsend, the architect of the Horniman Museum and Whitechapel Gallery, London, is modest enough, but the interior is a celebration of *Art Nouveau*. The chancel screen, decorated with luxuriously flowering trees, and the font on bronze angels, are brilliant. The apse is decorated with silver. All in all it is an experience not to be missed.

GREENSTED. 10m W of Chelmsford off A414. *St Andrew.*
This is one of the famous churches of Britain and the oldest wooden church in the world. It is also the only existing example of a timber Saxon church, although it was heavily restored in the C19. The nave, consisting of upright split logs, is Saxon and the plinth on which it stands belongs to restorations of 1848. Dendrological tests give a date of AD 845 to some nave timbers. One dormer on the north side is Tudor, the others date from re-roofing in 1892. The Tudor, brick chancel is C16. Note a small *painted panel* c.1500 of St Edmund, whose body rested here in c.1013, and a fragment of glass

Greensted, St Andrew. The exterior of the oldest wooden church.

of the same date, again possibly of St Edmund. There is also some notable carving on the C19 roof spandrels including one of a wolf guarding the head of St Edmund.

LITTLE BRAXTED. 7m SE of Braintree off A12. *St Nicholas.*
It is unusual when a C19 restoration results in something better than what was there before, but this small stone-built church with clay-tiled roof and wooden bellcote was actually turned into something jewel-like by the incumbent, the Rev. Ernest Geldart, in the 1880s. It has recently been restored to its C19 glory. Geldart only added a new north aisle and an organ chamber to a c.1120 church; his creativity went on decorating the *interior.* Every surface is covered with colour, and often complex designs. He designed the altar rails, pulpit, choir stalls, low chancel screen and font, all splendidly carved. This church interior is not to be missed.

LITTLE DUNMOW. 2m E of Great Dunmow off A120. *St Mary.*
The church was once the Lady Chapel of an Augustinian priory. Lavish remodelling in 1360 has left us with richness unusual among parish churches. Inside, and below the east and south windows, is blind arcading decorated with animals and natural growth. This is the home of the Dunmow Flitch and the *Chair*, made up from part of a C13 stall, is to be found in the chancel. A flitch of bacon is awarded annually to any married couple of Dunmow who can prove that they have not quarrelled or repented of their marriage within a year and a day after its celebration. It was first awarded in 1445. There are two very good mid-C15 alabaster *effigies* on a tomb chest.

LITTLE MAPLESTEAD. 2m N of Halstead off A131. *St John Baptist.*

Little Maplestead, St John.
Exterior, built in c.1340 by the Knights of St John of Jerusalem

One of only five rare round churches and originally built by the Knights of St John of Jerusalem on the plan of the Holy Sepulchre at Jerusalem, and rebuilt in 1334. However, most of what is there today is the result of restorations of 1851-7. Built of rough stone with lime-stone dressings its walls are buttressed to hold the conical roof crowned by a five-sided belfrey. Entering by the C14 porch one gets an impression of the original interior, although the roof is C19. Beyond the round nave is a C14 chancel with apse.

THAXTED. 6m SE of Saffron Walden on B184. *St John Baptist.*
Built in the C14, C15 and C16 and one of the most imposing churches in the county. The church is constructed of pebble rubble and the proud spire is 181 ft high, two feet less than its length. Both north and south porches have parvises above. Inside there is an impression of uncluttered space. The medieval roofs of the nave and aisles have good *bosses* and there is early-C16 *glass* of assorted saints in the north aisle and a late-C14 figure in the south transept. The east window of 1900 is by C.E. Kempe. Conrad Noel, vicar from 1910-42, to whom the present interior appearance is due, promoted a campaign for Christian Communism and pioneered the revival of Morris dancing. Gustav Holst played one of the organs here for some years.

WALTHAM ABBEY. 5m S of Hoddesdon on A121. *Holy Cross & St Laurence* .
The still superb church is all that remains of what must have been an impressive abbey. The crossing tower fell in 1552 and was replaced by the west tower in 1555-6. The splendid *nave* is the earliest Norman example in Britain, but the east and west ends are sadly interfered with. Noteworthy details are the reredos and pulpit of 1876 by W. Burges, the traces of a Doom on the east wall of the C14 Lady Chapel, and the brilliant *east window* of 1861, an early one by Burne-Jones. A *whipping post and pillory* are kept in the south chapel. King Harold, vanquished at Hastings in 1066, is buried here.

Other Churches

BOWERS GIFFORD. 3m E of Basildon on A130. *St Margaret.*
A small church with a weatherboarded spire and tower supported by a large buttress. The chancel screen of 1926 is by Sir Charles Nicholson. See here the best *brass* in Essex of a large knight with no head, dating from 1348.

CHICKNEY. 7m NE of Bishop's Stortford on B1051. *St Mary.*
A pre-Conquest church with *Saxon nave*, chancel of c.1200 and a lovely C15 *font* and cover.

STRETHALL. 4m W of Saffron Waldon off B1039. *St Mary.*
A small late-Saxon church with C11 chancel arch.

Norfolk

For church enthusiasts Norfolk is a goldmine; there are over 650 medieval churches! Flint is the main building material often used with stone flushwork. Saxon buildings, of which there are few, are distinguished by round towers, but over seventy churches have Norman work in them. The greater part, and the glory of the county, are the C15 churches where the expanse of window is extended to the full and interiors are flooded with light and covered by hammer-beam roofs, all financed from the wealth of the wool trade.

Norfolk is a county of round towers: some 119, of which seventy-eight are pre-Conquest.

ATTLEBOROUGH. 14m SW of Norwich on A11. *St Mary.*
The east end and crossing tower base are Norman. A college of chantry priests was founded here in 1368 and the nave was built for the parish. The surprise is the survival of the original 19 ft high *rood screen*, together with its loft, stretching across nave and aisles, still with a lot of original colour, all made c.1475. Over the chancel arch are the clear remains of a *wall painting*, an Annunciation of C15. In the south aisle is a St Christopher. Surviving from the college are two C15 *misericords* in the stalls. What glass survived the Civil War is set in the west window.

BALE. 7m NE of Fakenham off A148. *All Saints.*
This unprepossessing village church with C14 tower, C15 nave and C13 chancel gives no hint of the surprises inside. The original arch-braced *roof* of the nave survives; at the east end there is a *pulley* for lifting a rowel light to the rood. The font, decorated with emblems of the Passion and Trinity, is of c.1470. Notice the iron-bound chest of c.1500, the Royal Arms of c.1660, later re-used and the king's initials and date changed, and the seven *consecration crosses*, most with leafy frames. The greatest gem of the church is the C14 and C15 *glass* in the south-east nave window, re-set in 1938.

BYLAUGH. 4m NE of East Dereham off B1147. *St Mary.*
A secret church hidden by trees, with a round, C14 tower, C15 nave and a chancel of 1809-10. The *interior* is untouched since 1810: box pews, family pews, chancel panelling, communion rail, table and a three-decker pulpit, are all of this date. Also notice the Royal Arms, a *hatchment*, the *reredos* with the Commandments, Lord's Prayer and Creed and (a nice touch) two *fireplaces* in the transepts.

CAWSTON. 3m SW of Aylsham on A1145. *St Agnes.*
A vast church, enlarged at the expense of the Earl of Suffolk (d.1414),

with tall west tower of grey freestone. Only the chancel of c.1300 was unchanged. The hammer-beam and angel *roof* with *bosses* is C15. The C15 bell-ringers' gallery has an amusing *inscription*. There are traces of a *wall painting* of St Agnes with the donor (the Earl of Suffolk) in the north transept. Notice the three C15 *misericords*, the C15 benches, a C15 *poor box*, a medieval *chest* and some medieval glass. The glory of the church is the C15 *rood screen*. Lofty and still with its doors, it has twenty painted panels, including one of St Matthew wearing glasses!

CROSTWIGHT. 2m E of North Walsham off B1150. *All Saints.*
An early-C14 church with renewed windows and a tower reduced in 1910. Inside is a C13 Purbeck marble font and the remains of a C15 rood screen. Notable are the C14 *wall paintings* showing a tree with the Deadly Sins, the Passion, St Christopher and others undecipherable. Some of the detail is similar to the paintings in St Nicholas, Hoxne, Suffolk.

EAST HARLING. 8m NE of Thetford on B1111. *SS Peter & Paul.*
This majestic church is mainly C14, altered in the C15 at the cost of Anne Harling (d. 1498). The nave is covered by a good, steep, *hammer-beam roof*, and the east tie-beam still carries a pulley for the rowel light for the rood. In the south aisle is a magnificent *parclose screen* with most of the original colour. The remains of a once beautiful C15 *rood screen* are in the west end. Notice the stalls with animals and figures as arm-rests and six C15 armorial *misericords*. There are indistinguishable remains of a wall painting in the north aisle, perhaps St George, and the *Royal Arms* of Charles II in the west end of the same aisle. The C15 Norwich *glass* of the east window is the jewel of the church. There are twenty panels depicting scenes from the life of Christ, with figures of the two donors, Sir Robert Wingfield (d.1462) and Sir William Chamberlain (d.1482), two of Anne Harling's three husbands.

GREAT WALSINGHAM. 6m N of Fakenham on B1388. *St Peter.*
A particularly beautiful church built c.1320-40 and the centre of the great pilgrimages to Our Lady of Walsingham. The chancel unfortunately went in the C16. Surprisingly, the interior remains untouched. The original C15 *benches*, forty in all, stand on their original curbs. There are: a C15 *poor box*, a Royal Arms of George I, a C17 Communion rail, a C15 *pulpit* painted in 1613 and fragments of C14 Norwich *glass* in both aisles.

KING'S LYNN. 40m W of Norwich on A47. *St Margaret.*
A Norman church rebuilt in the C13, with the nave, crossings and transepts rebuilt in the Gothic style in 1744 after the spire fell. The stalls have good C14 *misericords*; there is also an assortment of fine

C14 screens, a excellent early-C18 inlaid *pulpit*, and a modern aluminium altar of 1936 in the sanctuary. Notable is the rococo Snetzler *organ* of 1745. In the south chapel are two magnificent Flemish *brasses*, of 1364 and 1365, the biggest in Britain.

NORWICH. 100m NE of London on A11.

Octagon Chapel. The striking octagonal building of 1754-6 by Thomas Ivory (1709-79) began as a Presbyterian chapel but became Unitarian in 1820. A good interior. Notice the five *sword* and *mace rests*.

St Giles. Built late-C14 with the tallest tower (1737) in the city, and a chancel of 1866-7. A beautiful and unusual hammer-beam *roof* covers the nave. Notice the good C15 *monuments*, five sets of *sword rests* and two good C15 *brasses*.

King's Lynn, St Margaret. A Flemish brass of 1364 and one of the biggest in Britain.

St Helen. Part of the Great Hospital founded in 1249, but built c.1480. Unusually it was split into three in the mid-C16: two men's wards in the west end, two women's wards in the chancel, and the south transept became the parish church. The chancel *ceiling* was painted in 1392 with 252 spread eagles in honour of Anne of Bohemia. Because the parish church was in the south transept, that is where the altar is placed beneath a good Georgian *reredos* by Thomas Ivory (1709-79). There are good *bosses* in the south transept chapel. Notice C18 *sword* and *mace rests*, the banner staff locker, the gothic Ivory pew dated 1780, and the C16 bench-ends.

St Peter Mancroft. A magnificent church dominating the colourful market place, built all-of a-piece in 1430-55 and restored in the mid-C19. There are many carved wood *bosses* including an Agnus Dei, and a *reredos* of 1885 enlarged by Sir Ninian Comper in 1930. The font has a rare C15 *canopy* (it is not a cover) cleverly restored in 1887. In the stalls are two C15 *misericords*. Notice the pulleys to hoist the

Lenten Veil to cover the rood in Lent, the C15 Flemish tapestry in the south aisle, three sets of *sword* and *mace rests* and the *brass* to Sir Peter Rede (d.1568) in late-C15 armour - a palimpsest of a good late-C15 Flemish brass.

SALLE. 4m SW of Aylsham off B1145. *SS Peter & Paul.*
This church built from c.1400 to 1450 lays claim to being the finest in Norfolk. Under the west window is a row of royal shields dating from 1400-13, while above the window are angels in feathered tights! Both porches have vaulted ceilings with bosses. Inside, the roofs look disappointing but they are contemporary with the building and have a great number of good carved *bosses*. The 'wineglass' *pulpit* catches the eye immediately and, although converted to a three-decker in 1611, it is actually C15. The dado of a fine *rood screen* remains with eight painted panels; the stalls have twenty-four notable *misericords*. The east window and the south window in the south transept have impressive Norwich *glass*. There are five C15 *brasses*, including one to the grandparents of Anne Boleyn.

STOW BARDOLPH. 2m NE of Downham Market on A10. *Holy Trinity.*
A Norman west tower and the church rebuilt 1848-9. Inside, there are: a carved *Royal Arms* of Charles II, two *misericords* in the stalls and, in the Hare Chapel, an alabaster *monument*, in an exuberant design, to Sir Ralph Hare (d.1623), together with other monuments. Most remarkable, and surely unique in Britain, is a life-sized figure in wax of Sarah Hare (d.1744) in a cupboard. Her will stipulated the *effigy* as well as the clothes it is dressed in!

WALPOLE ST PETER. 5m NE of Wisbech off A47. *St Peter.*

Walpole St Peter, St Peter. Interior looking east of the 'the cathedral of the fens', built c.1350-1400.

This also claims to be the finest church in Norfolk and is called 'the cathedral of the fens'. Built c.1350-c.1400 with large windows the interior is flooded with light. Notice the animal *bosses* in the south porch, particularly those of dogs gnawing bones. The pulpit dates from c.1605 and the nave benches and the west screen are all of c.1630. Only the dado of the rood screen survives with its painted figures. The eagle *lectern* is early-C16 and the *poor box* is dated 1639. A faded *wall painting* of a Doom is over the chancel arch, and the stalls have four C15 *misericords*.

WARHAM ST MARY. 2m SE of Wells-next-the-Sea off A149. *St Mary.*

The church, built of flint, appears lost in trees. It has a C14 tower, Norman north door and C13 nave and chancel. The C18 brick Turner chapel is the newest part of the building. The airy, white painted, *interior* is unaltered since 1800. From the box pews, stained red, and the three-decker pulpit with tester, to the commandment boards and communion rail, all date from the same period except for the Royal Arms of George IV, c.1820-30. Four *hatchments* decorate the white walls.

WESTON LONGUEVILLE. 9m NW of Norwich off A1067. *All Saints.*

The tower is C13, the chancel C14, the nave C13 and the two aisles C14. This church has two claims to fame: Parson Woodforde, who wrote *The Diary of a Country Parson*, was rector from 1776-1803 and his portrait and memorial are still there; the C14 *wall painting* of the Tree of Jesse in the north aisle is outstanding. Notice the Apostles painted in the south aisle windows and the small *brass* to Elizabeth Rokewoode (d.1533).

WILBY. 12m NE of Thetford off A11. *All Saints.*

Mostly C14 but the *interior* was re-fitted in 1633 after a fire and it remains unaltered. The three-decker pulpit, family pews, box pews, west gallery, benches, almsbox, communion rail and table all date from 1637. On the north wall is the top half of a C15 St Christopher.

WORSTEAD. 3m SE of North Walsham off A149. *St Mary.*

One of the grand Norfolk churches. Its nave and tower were begun in 1379; the chancel is earlier. The tall, badly restored, *rood screen* with original coving, is dated 1512. The tower screen, dated 1501, was painted in the C18. There are good *box pews*, and *painted canopies* on the east wall of the nave and in the south arcade. There are also three fair brasses.

WYMONDHAM. 8m SW of Norwich on A11. *SS Mary and Thomas of Canterbury.*

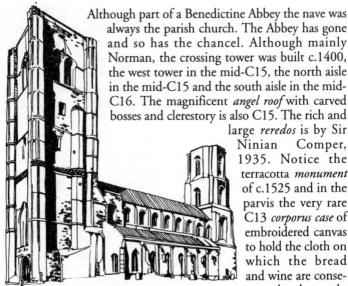

Although part of a Benedictine Abbey the nave was always the parish church. The Abbey has gone and so has the chancel. Although mainly Norman, the crossing tower was built c.1400, the west tower in the mid-C15, the north aisle in the mid-C15 and the south aisle in the mid-C16. The magnificent *angel roof* with carved bosses and clerestory is also C15. The rich and large *reredos* is by Sir Ninian Comper, 1935. Notice the terracotta *monument* of c.1525 and in the parvis the very rare C13 *corporus case* of embroidered canvas to hold the cloth on which the bread and wine are consecrated; the only other one known in Britain is at Hessett, Suffolk.

Wymondham, SS.Mary & Thomas. Exterior of the magnificent abbey church built in the C14 and C15.

Other Churches

BOOTON. 6m SW of Aylsham off B1145. *St Michael.*
A unique church eccentrically built in 1876-1900 by the then Rector Whitwell Elwin. He had no architectural training!

CLEY-NEXT-THE-SEA. 11m W of Cromer on A149. *St Margaret.*
A squat C13 tower, a rare C14 clerestory, ruined transepts, and a magnificent C14 west doorway contribute to a remarkable building. Inside, the wide aisled nave gives spaciousness and above the arcades are niches with carved figures. Note the good *brass* to John Symondes (d.1505) and the medieval *glass.*

KENNINGHALL. 10m E of Thetford on B1113. *St Mary.*
Norman south door, C15 nave and c.1300 chancel. Royal Arms of Elizabeth I removed from the tympanum to the north aisle. Arms of Charles I in west end.

LITCHAM. 6M NE of Swaffham on B1145. *All Saints.*
Basically a church of c.1300 but drastically renovated in c.1400, with a brick tower of 1668. There are: good *box pews,* two *misericords,* Flemish *glass* in the east window, the remains of a C15 painted rood screen, Royal Arms, and a C15 almsbox in the porch.

NORTH RUNCTON. 3m SE of King's Lynn off A47. *All Saints.*
A rare classical church for the county. Built 1703-13 in stone with

brick dressings. Much of the original *interior* survives.

SCULTHORPE. 2m W of Fakenham off A148. *St Mary & All Saints.*

This C19 church was rebuilt 1860-1 and its chancel in 1847. The *organ case* of 1752 is by Snetzler. There is very good early Morris and Burne-Jones *glass* in the south aisle.

TIVETSHALL. 15m SW of Norwich off A140. *St Margaret.*

Nave of C14 and chancel of c.1300. The interior is remarkable for the huge, and rare, *Royal Arms* of Elizabeth I filling the tympanum in the space left by the demolished rood.

Cley-next-the-Sea, St Margaret. The C14 south porch.

Suffolk

Not a county blessed with good building stone but with an abundance of flint. The churches are mainly flint with stone or brick trim, consequently round towers, needing no costly cut stone for the corners, are normal on early churches. However, by the fifteenth century Suffolk cloth merchants had made fortunes and many churches were completely rebuilt, such as those at Long Melford and Lavenham, with huge windows flooding the interiors with light. Suffolk specialised in porches and many of them have upper floors. The porch was important in that marriages and baptisms were conducted in them, some having piscinas in the wall. The glory of Suffolk churches is in the timber roofs and no county has finer or richer examples. Unfortunately, during the Civil War, William Dowsing, a Puritan iconoclast, and his thugs mutilated many of the roofs, pews and decorations. The county also possesses some of the earliest and finest brasses, such as those at Acton (c.1302) and Burgate (c.1410).

ACTON. 2m NE of Sudbury off B1115. *All Saints.*
One might well wonder what has brought us to this undistinguished

church, mainly of c.1300 with west tower base of which upper parts are of 1913-23. The principal reason must be to see one of the oldest and finest *brasses* in Britain. Sir Robert de Bures (d.1302) lies in chain mail with surcoat and shield, with crossed legs his feet rest on an amiable lion; the brass is all of 6ft 6ins and was made c.1320. Another brass of Alyce de Bures (d.1435) is slightly less fine but completely outshone by her earlier namesake. In the north chapel there is a very large and splendid *monument* to Robert Jennens (d.1745), adjutant of the Duke of Marlborough. Look for the bench-end carved as a pair of moorhens.

BLYTHBURGH. 12m SW of Lowestoft on A12. *Holy Trinity.*
The finest C15 church in Suffolk. The north and south doors, both original, still have *shot holes* from Dowsing's men when they forced their way in, in 1644. The interior is light and bright and covered by a cambered roof supported by angels in the centre, also shot at, alas, by Dowsing's men. The C15 *bench-ends* are carved to represent the Deadly Sins, the pulpit is Jacobean, the wood *lectern* c.1450. There is an interesting Jack o'Clock of c.1652 (where a figure can be seen hitting a bell with an axe). The old brasses, alas, were ripped out by Dowsing.

Blythburgh, Holy Trinity. The C15 nave roof supported by angels.

BRENT ELEIGH. 6m NE of Sudbury off A1141. *St Mary.*
Built of flint with stone trim in the C14 and C15. Jacobean and C18 box pews, Jacobean pulpit, but the gem is the *Crucifixion* of c.1300 painted on the wall as a reredos above the altar. To the right are fragments of a C16 Harrowing of Hell.

BURGATE. 4m SW of Diss off A143. *St Mary.*
This mainly C14 church restored in the C19 offers little in the way of interesting architecture and that is not the point of a visit. Inside, on a good tomb-chest, is one of the best Suffolk *brasses* to Sir William

Burgate (d.1409) and his wife, both standing beneath a crocketted canopy, he with his feet upon a satisfied-looking lion. The pulpit is Jacobean and the communion rail C17, but they are an anticlimax after the brass.

DENSTON. 10m SW of Bury St Edmunds off A143. *St Nicholas.*
A village church rebuilt in 1475 to accommodate a 'college' of three chantry priests, consequently the east end is grander than the nave which belonged to the village. Notice the four *misericords*, one of the Christian crane, and the two family pews in the choir indicating the important difference in religious and social status. The *rood beam*, a rare survivor, remains, but the screen was reduced to dado height in the mid-C16. The *Royal Arms* of Queen Anne hang over the tower arch and high in the south aisle hang a *helmet*, *sword* and *tabard* of the Robinson family. There are two C16 brasses

GISLINGHAM. 6m SW of Diss off B113. *St Mary.*
The red brick tower of 1639 was the last addition to the C15 nave and the C14 chancel. A splendid double hammer-beam *roof* covers the nave and by good luck the three-decker pulpit and box pews, all C18, were spared in the C19. Parts of the screen survive under the tower and elsewhere, sufficient to show its faded magnificence. A *peel-board* dated 1822 shows the names of the ringers with the tools of their trades.

HADLEIGH. 8m W of Ipswich on A1071. *St Mary.*
The west tower is early-C14 and the rest C15. In the chancel west wall is a simple Easter sepulchre of c.1500 and some finely carved bench-ends. Some brasses, of which one of 1555, to a Protestant martyr, is a continental *palimpsest.*

HESSET. 5m E of Bury St Edmunds off A14. *St Ethelbert.*
An entirely C15 church except for the C14 chancel, to which is attached a two-storey vestry with a *fireplace* in the upper room. There is much medieval *glass* in the aisles including a scene showing St Nicholas blessing small boys, one of whom holds a golf-club. On the south wall are *paintings*: a St Christopher over the south door and St Barbara. And on the north wall are the Seven Deadly Sins c.1400 and the awful C15 Warning to Sabbath-Breakers. However, the treasure of the church is the *corporus case*, on loan to the British Museum. It is one of only two in Britain; the other may be seen at SS Mary & Thomas, Wymondham, Norfolk.

IPSWICH. 70m NE of London on A12. *St Margaret.*
One of the finest of Ipswich's churches, richly decorated, with much flint flushwork. Inside there is a spectacular double hammer-beam *roof*, painted in the C17 and all recently restored. In the vestry is a large Prince of Wales Feathers dated 1660.

Unitarian Meeting House, Friars Street.

Daniel Defoe (1661-1731) referred to this chapel: 'As large and as fine a building of that kind as most on this side of England ... London not excepted'. He was right; this rendered timber-framed building is one of the most unspoilt and finest meeting houses in Britain. It began as a Presbyterian chapel and was built at a cost of £257 in 1699-1700. The change came at the end of the C18 when the congregation became Unitarian. Notice the spy hole in one of the handsome double doors, a left-over from times when Nonconformists were persecuted. The furnishings are all original from the circular communion table in the centre to the hexagonal one-handed clock and the hat pegs in the galleries. The fine carving on the pulpit is said to be by a pupil of Grinling Gibbons. All in all this is an unforgettable interior.

ICKLINGHAM. 7m NW of Bury St Edmunds on A1101. *All Saints.*

In the care of the Redundant Churches Fund. Unused for over 100 years this large thatched village church escaped the C19 restorers. Unusually the tower is at the west end of the C14 south aisle. The walls of the nave are early-C12. There is some good medieval *glass,* recovered from the churchyard in the C19. Most of the pews and benches date from the C14 and C15 and by the south door is a C17 family *box pew.* The floor of the chancel and sanctuary consist of C14 *tiles.* Until recently there were original hassocks cut from reed; these are now kept at St James's, a half-mile to the north-west. Notice the C14 iron-bound chest.

KEDINGTON. 15m SW of Bury St Edmunds off A143. *SS Peter & Paul.*

The typical Suffolk exterior of C14, with a strangely cut-off roof, gives no hint of the magically rustic *interior* untouched by the C19 Camdenians. Nothing seems vertical or horizontal, the oak pews lean this way and that, all strangely lit by overhead roof windows. The three-decker pulpit and musicians' gallery are of c.1750 and in the west end are children's benches, with hat pegs for the boys; from when this end of the church was used as a school. The Barnardiston family pew is made up from the old rood screen and retains some original colour. The present folding *screen* is dated 1619. Good Barnardiston monuments.

LAVENHAM. 6m NE of Sudbury on A1141. *SS. Peter & Paul.*

Built mainly in the C16 of flint and stone, at the expense of the 13th Earl of Oxford and cloth merchant Thomas Spring, with a mid-C14 chancel. This church is acknowledged to be the most beautiful of all the Suffolk 'wool' churches and has the tallest tower in the county. It is one of the best examples of 'more glass than wall' and the interior is flooded with light. Its bells are also famed in the ringing world. The tenor bell, weighing 21 cwt and made in 1625, is described as the 'finest toned bell in England, probably the world'. The *rood screen* is a rare survivor for c.1340 and is contemporary with the chancel. There are five good C15 *misericords* in the stalls, including one of the Pelican and its young. The *Spring Chapel* is splendid and was intended to be the Lady Chapel. Note the fantastic <u>screen</u> and C17 communion table. Over the south door are three Royal Arms: George II, George III and Elizabeth II. Don't overlook the *brass* to Thomas Spryng (d.1486) in the vestry and that of a swaddled infant in the chancel.

1523

LONG MELFORD. 3m N of Sudbury on A134. *Holy Trinity.*
Like Lavenham this is a vastly impressive 'wool' church. It was rebuilt in the late-C15 of flint and stone with a C16 brick porch. The tower, rebuilt in 1903, encases a brick tower damaged by lightning in c.1710. Where Lavenham has the highest tower this is the longest church in the county. The north aisle has some of the best C15 *glass* in Britain. Set in the north wall note the alabaster *relief,* of the Adoration of the Magi, older than the church, and dug up from beneath the chancel floor. Here, too, is the Clopton Chapel with the tomb of John Clopton the founder of the church. The arch of the recess is painted with figures of the Clopton family. In the chancel the Clopton tomb doubles as an Easter Sepulchre.

The Lady Chapel is only accessible from outside. Unusually this is the only parish church, never to have been an abbey, to have a Lady Chapel. Notice the C18 multiplication *tables* from when the chapel was used as a school. Notable are the Clopton *brasses,* the exceptional *monument* to Sir William Cordell (d.1580) and the *'Lily Crucifix'* in the Clopton Chapel window.

MENDLESHAM. 6m NE of Stowmarket off A140. *St Mary.*

Long Melford, Holy Trinity. Exterior of the longest church in the county, built in the late-C15.

A church mostly of the C13 with C15 windows. The surprises are inside: a magnificent *font cover* of 1630, with pulpit of the same date, a good *brass* of 1417 and another of 1720. Medieval *glass* from the redundant Rishangles church has recently been installed. Best of all is the *armoury* above the south porch, containing the finest collection of English armour in any parish church, ranging in date from c.1470 to c.1610.

MILDENHALL. 8m NE of Newmarket off A11. *St Mary.*
A glorious church standing in the middle of the town and rightly famed for the beauty of its hammer-beam roof. The earliest part is the east end, c.1240-1300, with unusual east window. The rest is C15 including the 120ft tower with fine fan-vaulting in the entrance. The early-C15 nave *roof* is an example of a late-medieval heaven with carved angels all about: some sing, others play instruments, while some perch on the tie beams. They must once have been coloured. The aisles' roofs are no less ambitious with swans and antelopes in the south aisle, both symbols of Henry V.

In the south of the churchyard are the ruins of a charnel house and chapel founded in 1387.

NEEDHAM MARKET. 3m SE of Stowmarket on B1113. *St John Baptist.*
Externally all of the C15, uninteresting and restored in 1885. Inside it is another matter. The *roof* has been called 'the culminating achievement of the English carpenter'. The construction of the hammer-beams, posts and tie-beams leaves one astonished. Unfortunately, it was damaged when covered by a Georgian plaster waggon-vault ceiling. This was removed in the 1880s and the roof skilfully restored to its original splendour.

POLSTEAD. 7m E of Sudbury off A1071. *St Mary.*
Basically a C12 church rebuilt in the C14 and the only Suffolk church to have a medieval stone spire. However, its fame has another aspect and mystery; the arches of the Norman aisles are in brick and support a clerestory, also built with some brick. The bricks are not Roman and may be the earliest C12 English bricks. There are many fragments of C15 *glass* in the chancel, and note the remains of a *wall painting* of a bishop on the nave north wall and the two small C15 *brasses*, one in the chancel wall and the other before the pulpit.

RUSHBROOKE. 3m SE of Bury St Edmunds off A134. *St Nicholas.*
A small brick church built in the C16, with tower of the C14. Inside, the nave pews face each other as in a choir, an arrangement from the 1840s. There is good C16 *glass* in the east window and a highly decorative *rood beam* survives. The tympanum above the beam contains the oldest *Royal Arms* in the country and uniquely that of Henry VIII.

Needham Market, St John Baptist. Interior,
the early C15 nave roof.

SHELLAND. 3m W of Stowmarket off A14. *King Charles the Martyr.*
The charm of this delightfully eccentric small church, built of rendered flint in 1767, is within. Little has changed *inside* since 1767. Box pews, panelling, chancel rail, communion rail, table, pulpit and musicians' pew are all original, even to the small *carved arms* of George III. The green walls and blue coloured roof with orange tie-beams and a fabric covered chancel, are astonishing. It should not be missed.

SOUTHWOLD. 11m S of Lowestoft on A1095. *St Edmund.*
With its massive 100ft tower, and rebuilt of flint flushwork in 1430-60 after a serious fire, this runs close to Blythburgh as the finest Suffolk church. Like Blythburgh, it has a Jack o'Clock, and Jack is dressed as a man-at-arms of c.1480, when he was made. The *screen* of 1460 has thirty-six original, coloured, gesso figures in the dado. The bench-ends are something different: in place of poppy-heads there are figures. In the south aisle is a very rare Elizabethan, round *communion*

table. The chancel has two amazingly carved *parclose screens* and an east window of 1954 is by Sir Ninian Comper. The reredos is by F.C. Howard in 1930. Notice the arms of George III over the south door and the fourteen late-C15 *misericords*.

THORNHAM PARVA. 4m SW of Diss on A140. *St Mary.*
Here is one of those rarities: an all-thatched church. The south and north doorways and the south window are all Norman and the circular high placed west window is Saxon, as is the masonry of the nave walls, and the chancel is early-C14. Inside, the gem of this gem of a church is the famous Thornham Parva triptych *retable* of c.1300, given by Lord Henniker in 1927 and which may have come from the Dominican monastery at Thetford, because it shows St Dominic and St Peter Martyr who was a Dominican friar. On the north and south walls of the nave are the two-tier remains of a C13 *wall painting,* perhaps telling the story of St Edmund on a background of painted masonry pattern. Note the three consecration crosses. The southwest nave window has some medieval glass and two 1980 panels by Laurence Whistler. Sir Basil Spence (1907-76), architect of Coventry Cathedral, is buried in the churchyard.

UFFORD. 3m NE of Woodbridge on B1438. *St Mary.*
Part Norman, part C15 with what must be the tallest and most remarkable *font cover* in the world. The Gothic cover of c.1450 reaches to the high roof and has a pelican on top. The whole is cunningly contrived to telescope into itself. How this escaped Dowsing's vandalism is a mystery. The once fine, unusual *bench-ends* didn't and some were mutilated. Note the three C14 *misericords*. The village stocks are beyond the churchyard west wall.

WINGFIELD. 7m E of Diss off B1118. *St Andrew.*
This is a memorable grouping of C14 church, moated castle and college. The interior owes much to the Wingfield family. In the chancel is the *tomb* to Sir John Wingfield, who died of the Black Death in 1361; his effigy wears full armour. By marriage the estates went to the de la Pole family, and the glory of the church is another *monument* in the chancel to Michael de la Pole, Earl of Suffolk (d.1415). Notice the fifteen identical early-C15 *misericords* and the remaining dado of the once magnificent *screen*. The parclose screens are original. There is the unusual feature of a *'sentry box'* to shelter the vicar at a rainy burial. (See also a similar one at Walpole St Peter, Norfolk.)

Other Churches

CROWFIELD. 3m NE of Needham Market off B1078. *All Saints.*
This is the only Suffolk church to have a timber-framed chancel. The nave has a good hammer-beam *roof* and note the carved wall plates.

Ufford, St Mary. The Gothic font cover of c.1450.

DENNINGTON. 3m N of Framlingham on A1120. *St Mary.*

All of C15 with C14 chancel, Elizabethan pulpit, four C15 *misericords*, C18 box pews, a rare *rood beam* and complete parclose *screens* to chapels, with lofts and parapets, C15 animal bench-ends.

EARL SOHAM. 5m W of Framlingham on A1120. *St Mary.*

The builder's name, Thomas Edward, is on the buttresses and the date is c.1475. Good hammer-beam *roof* supported on figures beheaded in the Civil War, *Royal Arms* of Charles II, carved animal *bench-ends.*

GIPPING. 2m N of Stowmarket off B1113. *St Nicholas.*

A private chapel built c.1483 for Sir James Tyrell (who may have murdered the Princes in the Tower in 1483) in fine flint flushwork. Bright, light interior, some original *glass* in east window. One original *kneeling bench.*

HOXNE. 4m N of Stowmarket off B1113. *St Nicholas.*

Impressive C15 west tower, chancel rebuilt 1879, the rest is C15. On the north wall are painted: a defaced St Christopher, the Seven Deadly Sins, six scenes from Works of Mercy, and the remains of a Last Judgement, all c.1400, and similar in detail to those at All Saints, Crostwight, Norfolk.

LITTLE SAXHAM. 4m W of Bury St Edmunds off A14. *St Nicholas.*

A notable Norman round tower with two-light bell openings marks this church, the rest is C14. Jacobean pulpit, animals on bench-ends and a C17 *bier* in the north aisle.

WALPOLE CHAPEL. 3m SW of Halesworth on B1117. *Congregational Chapel.*

In the care of The Historic Chapel Trust. One of the first Congregational chapels in Britain. Two cottages of 1607 were converted in 1647. Unspoilt, simple interior, with pulpit and reader's desk in centre of one side, pews and galleries on three sides. No longer used.

EAST
MIDLANDS

Derbyshire

Derbyshire and the 'Peak District' are almost unremittingly stone country offering a variety of limestones and sandstone. Clay for bricks is found to the south of Derby. Saxon architecture is best represented by the crypt at Repton, while Norman work survives in the noble magnificence of Melbourne, with a smaller superlative, but heavily restored, example at Steetley. For early Gothic the chancel at Ashbourne takes some equalling and of later Gothic date Tideswell is completely of the C14. St Saviour, Foremark, although 'Gothick', was built completely in 1662 and the furnishings remain. All Saints, Dale is a tiny church of enormous charm and should not be missed; its jumbled interior has furnishings of the C15 and C17. The chapel at Haddon also has original fittings of the C17, and wall paintings of the C15. Nearby is the magnificence of the ducal chapel at Chatsworth, unaltered since completed in the 1690s. Finally there is the early Pugin church of St Mary at Derby consecrated in 1839 and now hemmed in by a city ring road.

ASHBOURNE. 13m NW of Derby on A52. *St Oswald.*
This is one of the noble churches of Derbyshire, perfectly sited at the end of Church Street, with an astounding C14 crossing tower and spire 212ft high. The dignified wrought iron gates of c.1730 to the churchyard are attributed to Robert Bakewell. The nave and aisles are c.1300, and the oldest part, the chancel, is c.1241. Notice, in the south aisle, good leaf *capitals* of c.1300. The glass is mainly C19 by various makers and of little note except for the brilliant Arts and Crafts *glass* of 1905 by Christopher Whall, on the left as you enter, and the big west window of the *Tree of Jesse* by John Kempe of 1902. In the Boothby Chapel crowded C18 Boothby monuments displace those of the earlier extinct Cockayne family. Here is Thomas Banks' *monument* to little Penelope Boothby, exhibited in 1794 at Somerset House where Queen Charlotte was moved to tears.

EAST MIDLANDS

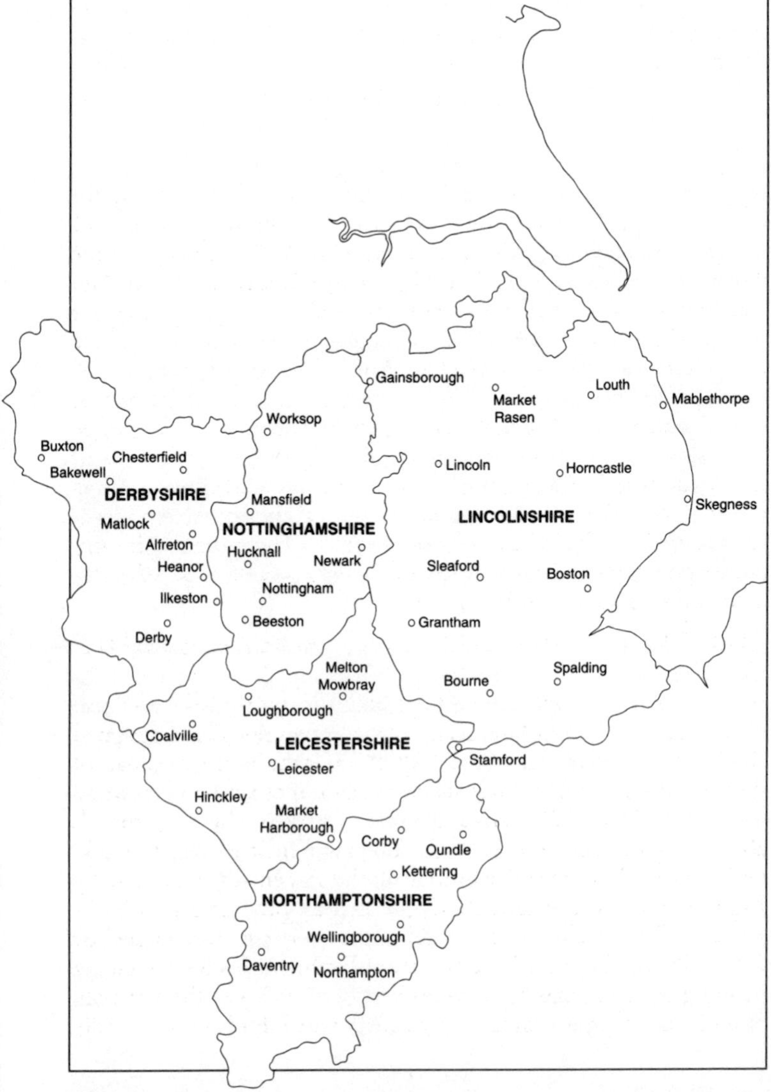

Buxton
Bakewell
Chesterfield

DERBYSHIRE

Matlock
Alfreton
Heanor
Ilkeston
Derby

Worksop
Mansfield

NOTTINGHAMSHIRE

Hucknall
Newark
Nottingham
Beeston

Gainsborough

Market
Rasen

Louth

Mablethorpe

Lincoln
Horncastle

Skegness

LINCOLNSHIRE

Sleaford
Boston

Grantham

Spalding

Melton
Mowbray
Bourne

Loughborough

Coalville

LEICESTERSHIRE

Leicester

Stamford

Hinckley

Market
Harborough
Corby
Oundle
Kettering

NORTHAMPTONSHIRE

Wellingborough
Daventry
Northampton

AULT HUCKNALL. 5m NW of Mansfield off A617. *St John Baptist.*
One could easily overlook this small Derbyshire church but it is well worth seeing. Unusually, it has a crossing tower supported on a Norman west arch and an C11 east arch. On the west front is an C11 *tympanum* depicting a fight with a dragon, and a devil. The nave and north aisle are early-Norman, with a C14 roof, and a beakhead decorated chancel arch. William Butterfield restored the church in 1885-7 when he installed the pulpit, *font* and simple pews. The south chapel contains a remarkable Italian style *tomb* to the wife (d.1627) of the first Earl of Devonshire. A black floor slab commemorates the death of Thomas Hobbes (d.1679), philosopher, author of *Leviathan* (1651) and tutor to generations of Cavendishes, who lived to the then remarkable age of 91!

BAKEWELL. 11m SE of Buxton on A6. *All Saints.*
Originally Norman and collegiate, dating from c.1200, with a C13 chancel, a C14 crossing tower reconstructed in 1841-52, a C14 octagonal spire, and a C14 nave rebuilt in 1852. The interior of the chancel was restored in 1879-82 by George Gilbert Scott Jnr who was responsible for the floor, choir stalls, altar and reredos. Better work is the *reredos* in the north aisle by Sir Ninian Comper. Notice the three C14 *misericords* in the chancel stalls, the sundial on the south porch, and the *glass* by John Hardman in the north transept (1881) and in the Vernon Chapel (1859). The alabaster Foljambe *monument* dated 1377 is the only surviving example of a type of medieval wall monument in which demi-figures look down as if in a theatre box. Other monuments to the Vernon and Manners families are worth examining. Finally, the headstones in the south porch carry occupation symbols and are part of the largest collection of early-medieval monuments in Britain.

CHATSWORTH HOUSE. 7m W of Chesterfield off B6012. *Chapel.*
Built in the south-west corner of the house, this is the private chapel of the dukes of Devonshire, rising through two floors and designed and built by William Talman in 1688-99. It is the least altered part of the great house. Panelled to first-floor height in cedar with limewood carvings by Samuel Watson and London carvers, there are murals above by Louis Laguerre (c.1693) showing Christ healing the sick, and overhead, a central roundel of the Ascension (c.1693) by Laguerre and his assistant Ricard, which all provide a rich background. The vast altarpiece of Derbyshire alabaster was designed by C.G. Cibber who carved the figures of Faith and Justice flanking a painting of St Thomas by Antonio Verrio, c.1693. On the east wall, opposite the altar, is a large family gallery which leads off the family

drawing room and apartments. The twenty-one chairs are contemporary with the chapel and covered with needlework by the 6th Duke's female relatives. Two large brass candlesticks on either side of the altar were bought in London for £60 in 1691. After 300 years there is still a lingering scent of cedar from the panelling.

DALE. 7m NE of Derby off A6096. *All Saints.*
This is one of the smallest and strangest churches in Britain because it shares a roof with a part stone and part half-timbered farmhouse. The building had little or nothing to do with the nearby ruins of the C12 Premonstratensian Dale Abbey; it was a mid-C12 chantry chapel and only after 1480 became the infirmary for the abbey. The nave masonry is Norman and the details are C15. Inside is a quaint jumble of joinery: C17 *box pews* and C15 *benches* seem assembled without logical thought. As if this were not enough there are beams, braces and posts to confuse the eye. The three-decker *pulpit* behind the altar, the west *gallery*, the *communion table*, and the *family pew* are all of c.1634. Note the late-C13 *paintings* on the north wall.

FOREMARK. 7m S of Derby off B5008. *St Saviour.*
Unusual in that it was built complete in 1662 as the estate church for Foremark Hall. The exterior is totally Gothic with crenelated west tower and an aisleless nave. Inside, however, most of the original C17 furnishings survive: a three-decker *pulpit*, twenty-seven *box pews*, and

a glorious *rood screen* in a backward looking Jacobean style, with a C17 panel of coloured *glass* in its pediment. The east window was inserted in 1891. Note the Creed boards, the *Royal Arms* and the Burdett *hatchments*. The brass candelabrum in the west end is from Westminster Abbey.

HADDON HALL. 5m NW of Matlock on the A6. *Chapel.*
The small chapel is built into the south-west corner of the lower court. Two C12 lancet windows in the south wall give a clue to its

Haddon Hall, Chapel. Chapel interior showing the C14 St Christopher wall painting on the south wall.

age. On entering, one sees ahead a C14 *wall painting* of St Christopher, for it was believed that the sight of the saint would ward off the plague. St Nicholas, to whom the chapel is dedicated, calms a rough sea on the north wall, and the Three Quick and Dead cavort on the west wall. The roof is dated 1624, the same date as the *box pews* and three decker *pulpit*. Notice that all the furnishings show remnants of original colours. An oak Jacobean cover crowns the simple Norman stone font. The splendid Nottingham alabaster *reredos* depicting the Easter story was acquired when the house was restored earlier in the C20 Some good C15 *glass* survives in the east and south windows. A white marble tomb to a boy, Lord Haddon (d.1894), was designed by his mother Violet, Duchess of Rutland.

KEDLESTON. 5m NW of Derby off A52. *All Saints.*
In the care of the Redundant Churches Fund. This is really the chapel to Kedleston Hall which stands close by. It is a late-C13 stone-built building with crossing tower, and a splendid Norman south door. A Curzon chapel by G.F. Bodley was added in 1907-13 making a north aisle. Inside, the *family pew, box pews* and *communion table*, are all late-C17. Wooden lids set in the chancel floor conceal an early-C14 mailed knight and his wife. A mid-C15 Chellaston alabaster tomb to John and Joan Curzon stands in the south transept. Other Curzon monuments were designed by Robert Adam (1728-92), and sculpted by John Rysbrack (1694-1770) and Peter Scheemakers (1691-1781). In the banner-hung north chapel is a superb gleaming white Italian marble monument by Sir Edgar Mackennall to Lord Curzon, Viceroy of India and Foreign Secretary (d.1925), and his first wife, Mary Leiter (d.1906). The curious public is barred by elegant wrought iron grills by P. Krall. Note the 'Baptism of Christ' by Antonio Correggio (d.1534), and the Madonna by Francesco Mola (d.1666). And don't overlook the brilliant *glass* of c.1910.

MELBOURNE. 7m S of Derby on B587. *SS Michael and Mary.*
One of the finest Norman churches in Britain and certainly the best in the county. It was restored by Sir George Gilbert Scott in 1862. With twin, unfinished, west towers and a tall crossing tower, this particularly grand church may have been built from 1133 for the Bishop of Carlisle, who moved here to escape Scottish attacks on Carlisle. Yet, tantalisingly, some of it may also predate the C12. The interior is magnificent, with a five bay nave supported on drum pillars that have arches decorated with zigzag motif. Above the clerestory is a C17 timber roof. Unusually, the chancel was two-storied, as the upper windows over the arch show. Note the C14 *painting* on the north-west pier of the tower: two women accompanied by horned devils – the traditional warning to gossips. On the opposite pier are the remains of a Passion series. The simple font is

Norman and the two C19 *hatchments* are to the first and third Viscounts Melbourne. Notice also the good C19 *glass.*

NORBURY. 5m SW of Ashbourne on B5033. *St Mary.*
This is the most satisfying of Derbyshire churches, both for the building itself and the beauty of the surroundings which adjoin a C17 manor house. A small stone-built church consisting of a C14 nave, a lone C15 north aisle, and a delicious C15 chancel. Eccentrically, the short C14 tower is on the south side and its lower stage is the porch. It was restored in 1842. Inside, both chancel and nave have C15 timber roofs. Note the two Saxon crosses set in the nave floor and go straight to the chancel. Here there is an unusual collection of medieval *glass:* the east window is a collection of C15 pieces, the rest is C14 with many heraldic details. The Fitzherbert *tombs* crowding the space are magnificent, two are exceptional late-C15 alabaster tomb-chests. Note the C16 palimpsest *brass.* George Eliot's parents (Evans) are buried in the churchyard.

STEETLEY. 10m NE of Chesterfield off A619. *All Saints.*
This lonely Norman chapel is one of the best examples of its kind in Britain. Built in c.1150, roofless throughout most of the C19, it was sympathetically restored in 1880, and consists of a nave, with a narrower chancel and vaulted apse. Some detail is C19: the south portal for example, which has a very rich display of Norman decoration. It is worthwhile studying the carved decoration of the *capitals* which have animals, leaves, human figures and the inevitable beakheads. Note the Anglo-Norman grave slab, and the C19 panel painted with saints on the north wall.

TIDESWELL. 6m E of Buxton on B6049. *St John Baptist.*
Rightly known as 'The Cathedral of the Peaks', this impressive church was built 1340-1400, and restored in the 1870s. The pinnacled west tower adjoins an aisled nave and transepts, with the chancel beyond, the last part of the church to be completed.

Steetley, All Saints. The richly decorated C12 south door.

Inside, the nave *roof* is original, the north aisle roof is 1632-5, while the chancel roof has C14 carvings of angels holding shields. The light-flooded chancel is one of the finest in Derbyshire. Behind the altar is a stone *reredos*, its niches were refilled with coloured statues in 1950. On either side of the chancel arch are stalls with two C15 *misericords*, and in the Lady Chapel in the north transept are ten plain C14 *stalls* with uncarved misericords. In the south transept the Lytton Chapel has a C14 bell, painted *hatchments*, and a large modern alabaster tomb-chest with a good mid-C15 *effigy*. Note the big *brass* in the chancel to John Foljambe (d.1383), a copy made in 1875, the nearby *brass* to Bishop Pursglove (d.1579), and the painted Creed, the Lord's Prayer and the Commandments in the north and south aisles. The glass is C19.

Other Churches

CASTLETON. 8m NE of Buxton on A625. *St Edmund.*
A Norman church with a C15 tower that suffered a severe restoration in 1837 when the aisles were removed! Good Norman chancel arch with large zigzag decoration. *Box pews* dated C17 and, unusually, a large C18 library with several rare books.

DERBY. 120m NW of London off M1 at junctions 24 & 25. *St Mary*, Bridge Gate.
An early work of A.W.N. Pugin, a Roman Catholic church consecrated in 1839. A large building in C15 Gothic style with a narrow west tower. Inside there is a vaulted choir with apse and the Lady Chapel of 1854 is by Pugin's son E.W. Pugin, with original stencilled wall decoration. The glass is mainly by Hardman, 1919-31.

REPTON. 5m NE of Burton on B5008. *St Wystan.*
An abbey was founded here in 660 and the church is of all dates from the C9 with a fine tall C14 west spire, and chiefly famous for its Saxon crypt beneath the east end. The crypt is a square of three bays supported by pillars carved with a spiral decoration.

Leicestershire

The county, incorporating Rutland since 1974, can be classified in two parts as far as building materials are concerned. In the west are churches built of grey sandstone, dating from the early C14, while in the east lies iron limestone extending from Northamptonshire, with churches of the C13. This is a simplification because there are, of course, the largely Norman church at Morcott, the Norman tower at Breedon and Norman work at St Mary de Castro, Leicester. There is very little pre-Norman work, apart from the well-known collection at St Mary, Breedon-on-the-Hill, and at St Nicholas, Leicester. Like

Northamptonshire, this is a county of stone spires.

Two ecclesiastical buildings of importance stand out: the small C16 chapel at Withcote with almost all its glass of c.1530 intact, and the backward-looking Commonwealth church at Staunton Harold, with most of its C17 interior fittings, for which its builder, Sir Robert Shirley, was imprisoned.

BOTTESFORD. 8m W of Grantham on A52. *St Mary.*
The imposing spire and nave are C15, and the chancel was rebuilt in the C17 to house flamboyant monuments to the Earls and Dukes of Rutland. The church was restored in 1847 and the interior says everything about it. Entering by the south door the chancel gives the impression of a crowded cocktail party at which no one moves, for there are splendid Rutland *monuments* filling every available space. One is to two children who died through *witchcraft.* Two others, to the 7th and 8th Earls, are by *Grinling Gibbons.* Notice the pulpit and reading desk dated 1631, the good 1404 *brass*, the five, inevitably Rutland, *hatchments* in the nave, the two sets of funeral *armour,* Queen Victoria's *Royal Arms* in plaster over the chancel arch and the recently discovered, and fragmentary, remains of a Doom *painted* over the chancel arch – alas, too decayed for restoration.

BREEDON-ON-THE-HILL. 8m SE of Derby on A453. *SS Mary & Hardulph.*
The church cannot be missed on its high hill, now half-quarried away. It is an old site, once an Augustinian priory, and before that a Saxon monastery built on an Iron Age camp. The west tower, originally the crossing tower, is Norman; the nave, once the priory chan-

Bottesford, St Mary. The chancel packed with magnificent Manner's tombs.

cel, is C13, with a C15 clerestory. Throughout the church are some good C9 Saxon *sculptures*, that are unparalleled in Britain or Europe. The largest, the 'Breedon Angel', is in the ringing chamber and can only be seen by appointment. The vaulted north aisle has a remarkable *squire's pew* dated 1627 and Shirley family *monuments*. The box pews, reader's desk, pulpit and west gallery are all c.1793.

BROOKE. 2m S of Oakham off A6003. *St Peter.*
A remote church, rebuilt in 1579, incorporating some original C12 Norman detail, with a C13 west tower, and all restored in 1879. Outside, it presents a lop-sided appearance because the steeply pitched roof of the north aisle is not balanced by any south aisle. However, the purpose of a visit is to see the *interior*, unchanged since 1579. Of the furnishings, only the C12 font is older. The details are too many to list but even the roof is of the same period and it is very unusual to see a church interior in which all the parts form such a harmonious whole. Notice the Norman strap-hinges inside the north door.

EMPINGHAM. 6m E of Oakham on A606. *St Peter.*
This C14 church, with C13 nave and C15 roof, has a surprising grandeur. The *piscina* and *sedilia* are mid-C13, and some C14 *glass* survives in the north transept. Over the south door is ornamental *wall painting* with more in the south transept where there is the faded remains of a Virgin.

EXTON. 5m E of Oakham off A606. *SS Peter & Paul.*
This large limestone church occupies a very rural situation. The tower was struck by lightning in 1848, and the whole restored in 1852. It is in essence a C19 church. However, it has the finest collection of monuments (9) in the county after Bottesford. A vast baroque edifice in the north aisle by Grinling Gibbons (1686) shows the two wives and many children of the 3rd Viscount Campden. A beautiful alabaster *tomb-chest* to John Harrington (d.1524) in the south aisle has two splendid recumbent figures, still showing traces of original colours. In the south transept is an outstanding *monument* to Robert Kelway (d.1580). Banners and funeral armour of the C16 and C17 have been removed for repair and renovation.

GADDESBY. 5m SW of Melton Mowbray on B674. *St Luke.*
A church worth a long detour. What is visible dates from 1290-1340 but covers an earlier fabric. Outside, the south aisle is a riot of uniquely luxurious decoration which spreads to the south front, and the north aisle is tame by comparison. The interior is unrestored rustic with medieval benches and brick floors, with a Victorian rood screen. A remarkable celebration of battle is demonstrated in the *monument* by Joseph Gott to Col. Cheney (d.1848), who sits astride

a nearly life-sized, collapsing, white marble horse, one of four shot from under him at Waterloo!

KING'S NORTON. 6ms E of Leicester off A47. *St John Baptist.*
This is one of the outstanding Gothic Revival churches in Britain. Built by John Wing Jun. in 1757-61 for Squire William Fortrey (d.1783), who is buried in the churchyard, his monument abutting the east window. It is an aisleless church with a brick west tower faced with the Ketton stone which is used for the rest of the church. There was a tall spire until it was struck by lightning twice in the C19, the last time in 1850. Do not be deterred by the unusual C18 latch on the west door; lifting the plate releases the catch. The interior is miraculously unchanged. The furnishings are of good-quality Norwegian oak, with a *pulpit* placed centrally before the altar. Unlike the Gothic exterior, some of the fittings have Classical details. Notice the *Royal Arms* in the west gallery.

LEICESTER. 16m S of Nottingham on A6. *St Mary de Castro.* Castle Street.
This is a church for those who enjoy architectural problems for it is of all periods from Norman to C19 but not always clear cut as to dates. The nave is c.1107, the chancel c.1160 with a sumptuous, completely Norman, *sedilia*. In the C14, the north aisle was rebuilt, the same date as the extremely wide south aisle, creating a space which makes for an awkward interior. Sadly the furnishings are mid-C19, when Sir George Gilbert Scott restored the building.
St Nicholas. St Nicholas Circle.
An early-C7 Saxon church built on a Roman site with an C11 tower, restored in 1904-5. Notice the re-use of Roman bricks in much of the exterior. Most of the nave is Saxon apart from the huge brick arch inserted on the south side in 1829. The chancel is mainly Norman with evidence of a Saxon north wall. Most of the remainder is Norman, apart from the C13 south aisle and chapel, and the north transept of 1888. The north aisle was demolished in 1697 and rebuilt in 1875-6.

LUTTERWORTH. 11m S of Leicester on A426. *St Mary.*
A large church of the C13 and C14 with a spire of c.1710. The interior has two important C14 *wall paintings*: a big Doom over the chancel arch and Three Kings in the south aisle, both extensively re-touched. Note too the Elizabethan *altar table* in the north aisle, an early *brass* of 1403, the east window by Clayton & Bell (1884), and the marble relief dated 1837, by Richard Westmacott Jnr. John Wycliffe (c.1320-84), the religious reformer, was once buried here. He was later exhumed, cremated and his ashes scattered on the River Swift.

NOSELEY. 7m N of Market Harborough off B6047. *St Mary.*
This is a very private chapel and difficult to find, but perseverance
will bring reward. The owners, who live at the hall next to the chapel,
like to have a written appointment. It is a large chapel, completed by
c.1305 with a C15 roof. The interior reminds one of a decayed
college chapel. There are many monuments to the Hazleriges of the
Hall, some amazing *stalls* of the 1470s, and the east window has good
glass of c.1306. Just inside the west door a painted screen *door* of
c.1306 is haphazardly propped against the wall. The screen has long
since gone.

STAUNTON HAROLD. 11m W of Loughborough off B587. *Holy
Trinity.*
In the care of the National Trust. After so much Commonwealth
destruction, this church comes as a welcome relief. Over the west
door is an inscription: 'In the yeare: 1653 when all ₍hings sacred were
throughout the nation Either demollisht or profaned Sir Richard
Shirley Barronet founded this church' Shirley died in the Tower for
his impudence in maintaining the Protestant religion. It is no surprise
that the style is late-Gothic. What is surprising is the unchanged
interior in a then old-fashioned Jacobean style, from the box pews,
pulpit, *Communion table*, and tower *screen*, to the west gallery. Only
the organ case (1686), and the chancel iron-work screen by Bakewell
(1711) are later. The best of all features is the boarded ceiling painted
as heaven with balloon-like clouds.

*Staunton Harold, Holy
Trinity.* Built complete
in the 1650's.

STOKE DRY. 2m S of Uppingham off A6003. *St Andrew.*
A small remote stone-built church of immense charm. Mainly C13, with Norman features from an earlier building, and a C15 clerestory. The chancel is C12 and the slender west tower is of c.1300. Inside, the nave roof is dated 1574 and a c.1300 south chapel contains good *monuments* to the Digby family. The gem of this church are the *wall paintings*. The earliest are late-C13 in the chancel, with C14 in the south chapel, while those in the nave are C16. It is claimed that the Gunpowder Plot was planned in the room over the porch. The story springs from Sir Everard Digby, one of the conspirators who was hanged in 1609. Alas for romance, it is untrue.

STOKE GOLDING. 14m SW of Leicester off A5. *St Margaret.*
One of the finest and most beautiful churches in the county, it is the result of a major rebuilding between c.1290, when the south aisle was built, and the completion of the tower and spire in c.1350. Apart from the chancel, rebuilt in 1882, the church was passed over by Victorian restorers. On the north wall, in Latin, is a C16 copy of an earlier inscription hinting at when the rebuilding was undertaken: by Robert de Campania and his wife in the reign of Edward I (1272-1307). Note the *roof-bosses*, the good double *piscina*, the massive C17 chest in the south aisle, and the c.1350 *font* showing the patron saint and a kneeling donor, perhaps Robert de Campania.

TEIGH. 5m N of Oakham off A606. *Holy Trinity.*
The west tower (the lower stage C13 and the upper C14), was kept when the 4th Earl of Harborough rebuilt the church in 1782. Externally it is Gothick, internally it is unchanged late-Georgian. Pine *box pews* rise in three tiers facing each other across the unaisled nave. Over the west door is the pulpit framed by a *painted* window with trees seen through it! Two readers' desks, one on either side of the pulpit, are balanced by Commandment and Creed boards, again on either side. The *font* is a magnificent mahogany vase, once attached to the altar rails. Note the *altarpiece*: a C17 Flemish Last Supper.

TICKENCOTE. 9m E of Oakham off A1. *St Peter.*
A C12 church, rebuilt in 1792 in the Norman style by S.P.Cockerell when the original Norman *chancel* was restored and a south tower and vestry added. The church is famous for the lavish unrestored Norman *chancel arch* leading into an unexpectedly stone-vaulted chancel of c.1160. Note the Norman stone font of c.1200.

WITHCOTE. 12m E of Leicester off B6047. *Chapel.*
In the care of the Redundant Churches Fund. The chapel is a rare surviving example of a detached Tudor private chapel of c.1500. Restored in 1744 and again in 1864, the whole reminds one of a

Cambridge college chapel dropped into a rural scene. Miraculously much of the original outstanding *glass* survives, comprising eight Apostles and ten Prophets, all dating from c.1530. The interior was re-fitted in the C18. Note the *painting* of Mary washing Christ's feet by Francesco Bassano (1548-91).

WYMESWOLD. 12m N of Leicester on A6006. *St Mary.*
This is a C14 church with a C15 west tower, but more remarkable is the sensitive restoration by A.W.N. Pugin in 1844-6. Here is a feast of Pugin design. The roofs are Pugin's with the gold-starred ceiling in the chancel. Note the original *bosses* in the nave. The screen, font, stone pulpit, sedilia, candle sconces and chandeliers are all Pugin's. The east window and the ornate bier are also his.

Other Churches

NORMANTON. 6m E of Stamford off A606. *St Matthew.*
A unique position in a reservoir! Originally built in 1764, with a Baroque west portico, and tower modelled on St John, Smith Square, London, added in 1826. The nave and chancel were rebuilt in 1911 in a style matching the tower.

TIXOVER. 8m SE of Oakham off A47. *St Mary.*
A massive Norman west tower with arch, all of c.1140, is attached to a late C12 nave and south aisle, with a C13 north aisle. The roofs are early C17. Original stone seating lines the chancel walls, the benches with poppy-heads are early C17, and do not overlook the *monument* dated 1623. No electricity, and still lit by oil lamps and candles.

Lincolnshire

For one of the biggest counties in Britain, nearly 50 miles long, south to north, Lincolnshire is surprisingly little known. There is a wide variety of unspoilt countryside, from the low fenlands in the east to the limestone lands and undulating views of the west side. The county is fortunate in having the most famous of building stone at Ancaster: freestone, a fine limestone deposit that stretches from the south-west of the county to Lincoln and which for centuries has been easily transported by water. Consequently, many of Lincolnshire's churches are built of Ancaster stone. In the far south of the county, around Stamford, is another freestone called Stamford Grit, used extensively for the town's rebuilt churches. To the east of Lincoln and halfway to the sea is green sandstone, and in the north around Caistor, ironstone.

There are over 600 churches in Lincolnshire and those of the C14 (the Decorated period) are the best of any county. To begin with the earliest, six are Saxon: St Mary at Stow is the most impressive of any county. There are only remnants surviving from the C12 and C13. In the C14 we are on surer ground: the Decorated south porch and chancel fittings of St Andrew, Heckington, is unsurpassed in any parish church; St Botolph, Boston, apart from its C15 tower, is as complete and fine an example as one could wish to find. The C14 monument, or Easter Sepulchre, at St Andrew, Irnham is well worth a detour, neither should the very grand Cecil monuments at St Martin, Stamford, be overlooked. At Hannah-cum-Hagnaby, St Andrew has an unaltered C18 interior, and SS Peter & Paul at Lanton-cum-Partney, and St Andrew at Well, both have similar C18 unaltered interiors of good quality.

In the county reshuffle of 1974 Lincolnshire lost part of its northern boundary to Humberside. As the division is completely artificial I have ignored Humberside and the two churches involved are here back in Lincolnshire but marked with (H) after the place name.

BARTON-ON-HUMBER. (H) 15m NW of Scunthorpe on A15. *St Peter.*
In the care of English Heritage. The church has a place in history as being the first to be recognised, in early-C19 debate, as pre-Conquest. To us, the tower is obviously Saxon, with an C11 top stage. This is all that remains of a small apsed, late-C10 church. Of the rest, the nave, north aisle and chancel are mid-C15, and the south aisle C13. The interior is stripped of its furnishings, replaced by an exhibition. However, the east window has two splendid panels of C14 *glass*, the C15 *screen*, with a late-C19 Rood loft, has been restored, and the C15 north door survives with its original iron-work. Note the mid-C14 heads in the nave arcades.

BOSTON. 30m SE of Lincoln on A16. *St Botolph.*
This is one of the largest and grandest of British parish churches and built almost completely in the C14 of Barnack stone. Justly famous for its 'stump', the amazingly

Boston, St Botolph. Built complete in the C15, the Boston 'stump' dominates the flat landscape

gracious and excessively high 272ft C15 west steeple visible for many miles, it was restored by Sir George Gilbert Scott in 1845-7, by G.G. Place in 1851 and again by Scott in 1857. For the best effect enter by the west door, and 137 ft above is lierne stone-vaulting and many bosses inserted in 1851. The nave and aisles were re-roofed in 1928-33 and the chancel roof is of 1781. In the chancel, the *stalls* have sixty-two carved *misericords*, and carved elbow-rests, dating from c.1390, with canopies of 1860. Two important *brasses*, one to Walter Peacod (d.1398) and his wife, and the other to a priest of c.1400, are also in the chancel. The *pulpit*, dated 1612 with restored tester, is exceptionally fine work, and the *font* of 1853 is by A.W.N. Pugin. Note the Corporation *mace holder* of 1727 in the front pew. Although altered in 1853 the wrought iron *communion rails* of 1754 are particularly fine. The south, west and north doors are all C14. On the tower south door there is a C13 door knocker of a lion's head with two lizards. The glass is all C19 and C20. Notice the ten *hatchments* under the tower, the two *Royal Arms*, and the C15 chest.

BRANT BROUGHTON. 7m E of Newark off A17. *St Helen.*

Built of Ancaster stone and dating from the late-C13 to late-C14, with a 198ft crocketted west tower, this church was restored in the 1870s by G.F. Bodley, who also rebuilt the chancel. There is much lavish carving on the exterior which reaches a climax in the south and north stone-vaulted porches. Inside, the effective C19 restoration is apparent; Bodley's work is always sympathetic: almost all the fittings, and the roof which was returned to its original colouring, are by him, as is the splendid *reredos*, with a late-C15, German Ascension. Beneath the tower is a sculptured C14 Trinity and the glass in every window is all late-C19.

COATES. 10m NW of Lincoln off B1241. *St Edith.*

Is this the smallest church in the county? It comprises a Norman chancel, and a C13 nave, both sympathetically restored in 1884. The *screen*, restored at the same time, is now complete with loft, parapet, and tympanum with painted figures, the only one remaining in a Lincolnshire parish church. There are good furnishings: the *family pew* is early-C17, with a C15 *pulpit* and bench-ends. Note the *Royal Arms* dated 1635, some pieces of medieval *glass*, a late brass of 1590, and two monuments.

CORBY GLEN. 12m N of Stamford on A151. *St John Evangelist.*

This is a church of all dates from Norman, through the C13, C14 and C15, to the C19 chancel. Built of Ancaster stone, it has a nave, two aisles, and a C15 west tower. Inside, there are *box pews* in the aisles. Note the C18 *Royal Arms*, and the C15 door in the parvis chamber over the south porch. Of particular note are the extensive early-C15 *wall paintings* discovered in 1939; some are fragmentary, but all are clearly recognisable.

CROFT. 4m SW of Skegness off A52. *All Saints.*
One of the important Lincolnshire churches, built of greenstone mainly in c.1350, with late-C14 windows. The west tower has an upper stage of greystone rebuilt in 1665. The church was restored in 1838, 1881, and 1894 and it contains a wealth of C15 woodwork. The *pulpit* is dated 1615, and note the C15 bench ends and *screens.* There is also a good C15 *brass*, and an eagle *lectern.*
The main point of any visit is to see the fine quality *brass* of c.1300; a knight wearing chain-mail, one of the five earliest in Britain.

GRANTHAM. 25m S of Lincoln on A607. *St Wulfram.*
With its C14 tower this is rated as one of the twelve best and grandest parish churches in Britain and a glory of Gothic architecture. The nave is part C12 and part C13, with a late-C12 north aisle, C13 south aisle, and a C14 chancel. The building was restored by Sir George Gilbert Scott in the 1860s. Entering by the south door, note the stiff-leaf *capitals* of c.1230. Inside, the nave and aisle roofs, and the rood screen, are all by Scott. Most of the furnishings are C19 except for the wrought-iron *mace screen* of c.1766 in the south chapel, five *hatchments*, an early *Royal Arms* dated 1586, and another with the arms of Charles II. All the glass is C19, some of it good. Do not overlook the crypt with a rare medieval altar (most altars were replaced after 1550).

HANNAH-CUM-HAGNABY. 11m SE of Louth on A111. *St Andrew.*
Small, humble, and completely rebuilt of greenstone in 1753, with nave and chancel under one pantile roof, a west porch, and tiny bellcote on the west end, the crowded Georgian atmosphere of this church is undisturbed; plain *box pews*, two-decker *pulpit* and tester, *commandment boards*, and *communion rail*, are all contemporary. The Venetian east window, brick floor and simple font are

Grantham, St Wulfram.
A perfect C14 Gothic spire is attached to one of the best and grandest churches in Britain.

perfect foils to a charming interior. Only the C15 west doorway remains from the earlier church.

HECKINGTON. 4m E of Sleaford off A17. *St Andrew.*

Even in a county so rich in good C14 church architecture, this one is remarkable. Built of Ancaster stone in the C14, at the time of the best Decorated style, this is an outstanding gem. It was restored in 1888. The south porch is but a delicious overture to what is to come. Go straight to the chancel and there wonder at the *Easter sepulchre, double piscina, triple sedilia* and *founder's tomb.* Although all have lost their original paint, and the wall paintings and original glass are all gone, the effect is magical. The seven-light east window is one of the glories of C14 Decorated architecture. Such richness is due to the founder, Richard de Potesgrave, rector here in 1308-45 and later chaplain to Edward III. The rest of the church comes as an anticlimax, but there is much more to admire.

IRNHAM. 10m SE of Grantham off A151. *St Andrew.*

A large church of Ancaster stone in the grounds of the Hall, with a nave and C15 clerestory, a late-C13 chancel and north aisle, (the south aisle is demolished), and a late-Norman base to a west tower, with early-C14 upper stages. The prize of the interior is the C14, richly decorated *monument*, or Easter Sepulchre, moved to the east end of the north chapel during restorations in 1833. Notice the *Royal Arms* of 1759, the *hatchment* of 1859, and the magnificent *brass* to Sir Andrew Luttrell (d.1390).

LANGTON-BY-PARTNEY. 3m N of Spilsby off A16. *SS Peter & Paul.*

A small but simple, classical church built in the 1720s of brick with stone dressings, a widely overhanging roof and an extraordinary stump of a bell turret added in 1825 over the west end. The entrance is a surprise: a small vestibule has twin stairs leading to the west gallery and the ringing chamber with a hand-cranked *carillon*. The interior is especially grand, with *box pews* arranged college-chapel fashion, facing across the nave, and a fine plaster ceiling with a heavy dentilled cornice. It is similar to St Margaret at Well. A high, panelled *reredos*, with a recess for the altar, covers the east end; a tall three-decker *pulpit* with tester dominates the space; small brass candlesticks are fixed to the pews. Note the three *hatchments*. Dr Johnson worshipped here when he visited the now demolished Hall.

LINCOLN. 130m N of London on A46. *Chapel*, The Gaol, Lincoln Castle.

Pevsner called this 'a unique and terrifying space'. Indeed it is. Built, along with the gaol, by John Carr of York in 1787, it has a very ingenious plan. In the suitably gloomy interior deal cubicles, like narrow loose boxes, raised in steep crescents, focus on the pulpit. They are constructed so that prisoners could only stand and see only the preacher. Their self-locking doors are hinged so that only one prisoner at a time could exit from the rows of cubicles. Debtors were kept in slightly more comfort in cages on either side of the pulpit. This is the only surviving example of an C18 gaol chapel.

St Benedict, High Street.

This C13 church just survived the Civil War, when the tower was destroyed and the nave badly damaged. It was threatened with demolition in 1928. Only the chancel and north chapel survive of the C13 church, the tower nave and north aisle are C17. The surviving C13 work is distinguished by stiff-leaf *capitals*, and an incomplete lancet window in the east end of the south wall. Fittings include a fine C14 *sedilia*, a good double *piscina*, and a small c.1530 statue of Mary Magdalene holding a jar of ointment. The *Royal Arms* of 1734 was repainted in 1819.

St Mary-le-Wigford, High Street.

The oldest church in the city, with a tall, thin, late-Saxon *tower*, and an early-C13 nave and chancel. The south aisle is of 1877, and it is unusual in having its original C11 dedication stone set in the exterior wall of the tower. The original west door, now blocked, is over-restored, and entrance is by way of a north porch of 1972. The interior is a beautiful example of early-C13 work, with a feast of stiff-leaf *capitals*, shafts with moulded rings, and delicate pointed arches. The ceilings are modern, however, and restoration work here won the European Architectural Heritage Year award in 1975. This included the unfortunate south aisle offices. Fragments from other Lincoln churches are set in the west wall of the vestry. On the south wall of the tower is a Saxon cross shaft. Note the brass *chandelier* of 1720, the alabaster *tomb-chest* to Sir Thomas Grantham (d.1618) and his wife, from St Martin's church, and a small *brass* in the south nave arcade to John Jobson (d.1525), a fishmonger, showing his tools, an axe and knife. Other items displayed are from St Mark, demolished in 1972.

LITTLE BYTHAM. 7m N of Stamford on B1176. *St Medard.*

This stone-built church has Saxon work in the south-west and south-east corners of the nave, with a Norman chancel. Above the chancel south door is a uniquely curious *tympanum* consisting of two eagles on either side of an empty roundel which, it is said, once contained the skull and arm bone of St Médard (c.470-c.560), bishop of Vermandois. The chancel is also unusual in having a stone bench running round the walls. In the north wall of the nave is a C12 Norman door. The tower arch supporting a C13 tower is also Norman. The reredos is C19, and the pulpit base is dated 1590.

SLEAFORD. 20m SE of Lincoln on A17. *St Denys.*
This is another of the Lincolnshire churches famed for the lavishness of its C14 decoration. Built of Ancaster stone with a squat, rather plain, C13 tower, it is of the late-C12 and C13, and was rebuilt in the C14, with a C15 clerestory. With north and south aisles it has a curious extra north aisle addition of 1853. The great north aisle *west window* with its flowing C14 tracery overlooks the market place. The interior appears to be entirely of the C14, with the original *rood screen*, but with *loft* and *rood* of 1918 by Sir Ninian Comper. At the west end of the north aisle there is a desk with fifteen chained books, a C17 dole cupboard in the north transept and, in the north aisle, a rare C17 Sheldon *tapestry.* The glass is all C19 except for one piece of 1900 in the south aisle by Morris & Co. There are many monuments, but particularly note that to Sir Edward Carre (d.1618) by Maximilian Colt, and another by Sir Richard Westmacott.

STAMFORD. 20m S of Grantham off A1.
All Saints, All Saints Place.
A prominent church on a dominating site, which at first appears to be C15 but on closer inspection is basically of c.1230. Enter by the C15 porch, noting the warning to bell-ringers, and the C13 date is apparent from the sumptuous stiff-leaf *capitals* in the three-bay south arcade. The rest is a rebuilding of the late-C15. The reredos, and screen of Mexican onyx, are of 1878, the vestry of 1886, but the *hourglass stand* is C17. Of particular note are the many *brasses* to the Brownes who rebuilt the church. On the north wall of the tower is a *painted* memorial to a ringer, in verse dated 1694.
St Martin, High Street St Martin's.
Whatever was here before the late-C15 was completely demolished when the present church was rebuilt on the site. The nave roof with angels and bosses is from this date, but the chancel's plaster ceiling is C18. It is impossible to miss the important *Burghley tombs.* Elizabeth I's Lord High Treasurer (d.1898) lies commemorated in alabaster in full armour beneath a glorious tabernacle supported on six Corinthian columns. Behind, is a huge monument executed in Rome in white marble to the 5th Earl of Exeter (d.1700). After these, the remaining good Cecil monuments appear tame stuff. Do not miss the four Cecil *hatchments,* and the C15 *glass,* mainly from churches at Tattershall and North Yorkshire. In the churchyard is a slate gravestone to 52 stone Daniel Lambert who died in 1809.
St Mary, St Mary's Street.
It is difficult to see this stone-built church with a heavy tower without being run over, for it juts out into what once was the Great North Road. Its structure is late-C13 with some C14 work, and a nave and aisles extensively rebuilt in the C15. All was restored in the 1850s.

The restoration of the chancel under John Dando Sedding in 1890 is good Arts and Crafts. To him we owe the painted ceiling, the screen and choir-stalls. In the Corpus Christi Chapel is the glory of the church: a gilded and painted waggon-roof of the 1480s with 380 gilded *bosses*. Note the outstanding female figure *sculpture* of c.1330 in the north chapel, and do not overlook the Arts and Crafts *glass* (1891) by Christopher Whall in the north chapel. The parish library is particularly interesting in that it was started in the early C17 and has early-C16 books.

STOW. 10m NW of Lincoln on B1241. *St Mary.*
This deserves to be better known for it is surely the most impressive, and largest, of late-Saxon churches. Stone-built and consisting of an unaisled C12 nave and chancel, with C11 transepts and a C14 central tower, it is almost cathedral-like. The building was well restored in 1850-2. One's first impression of the interior is that it is Norman but inspection of the transepts, crossing and arches shows them to be Saxon work of c.975. The nave is high, plain and narrow with decoration reserved for the chancel where the convincing groin-vaulting is C19. Particularly note the *graffito* of a Scandinavian long-ship on the north side of the south-east crossing pier, which must date from c.1000, the early-C13 wall *painting* of St Thomas à Becket on the east wall of the north transept, and the C15 *brackets* with carved figures of musicians on the east walls of both transepts. There are also late-medieval benches in the nave and the stalls include parts of a medieval screen.

Stow, St Mary. One of the largest of the late-Saxon towers.

SWATON. 7m SE of Sleaford on B1394. *St Michael.*
One of the finest churches in a county rich in fine churches. It is a cruciform plan consisting of a C13 crossing tower, with early-C14 nave and aisles built in good ashlar and an early-C13 rubble-stone chancel, all restored in the mid-C19. The south wall of the south transept has a blocked Norman window and in the north transept is a C14 piscina. Part of the C15 *screen* survives in the south transept and note the C15 bench-ends. In the south aisle is the remains of a C15 Wheel of Fortune *wall painting.* The north aisle has a C14 effigy of a female figure with a sleeping dog at her feet.

TATTERSHALL. 7m S of Horncastle on A153. *Holy Trinity.*
One of a unique grouping of buildings that include the massive tall keep of the brick Castle, built by Lord Cromwell, Treasurer to Henry VI, begun in 1435 and visible for miles across a flat plain.The church, built of Ancaster stone from 1469, stands next to almshouses founded by Lord Cromwell in 1440. It consists of nave, aisles, chancel and transepts, with a west tower of the 1480s, and was large enough to accommodate a castle garrison. The interior is plain and light, with most of the coloured glass taken to St Martin's, Stamford in 1757. The nave *pulpit* is of c.1450, the stone *screen* of 1528. A glass case in the south aisle preserves pieces from the original wood screen and two c.1470 *misericords.* A little original glass is arranged in the east window. Note the *brasses* in the north transept.

WELL. 7m NE of Spilsby off B1196. *St Margaret.*
Rebuilt in 1733, to improve the view from Well Hall, with a temple-like west front in the style of Inigo Jones. The satisfying interior belongs entirely to its period with no later intrusions; as at SS Peter & Paul, Langton-by-Partney, *box pews* are arranged facing across the nave and dominated by a three-decker *pulpit.* Two family pews flank the altar and a rich architectural *reredos* covers the east wall beneath the window. Overhead is a fine stucco ceiling. Note the *Royal Arms* of George II. The font, alas, has been stolen.

Other Churches

ADDLETHORPE. 5m N of Skegness off A52. *St Nicholas.*
Stone-built in the C14, its chancel was demolished in 1706. Opulent south porch. Good, simple, *angel roof* excellent *screen* and note *Royal Arms* and C18 *glass.*

BELTON. 4m N of Grantham on A607. *SS Peter & Paul.*
A small church on the Belton estate with a Norman north arcade, over-restored in 1816. However, the Brownlow and Cust *monuments* are worth a visit. Note the *Royal Arms* in the south porch, the Commandment boards and the Flemish *glass* in the vestry.

BIGBY. 3m E of Brigg off A1084. *All Saints.*

A stone-built church with an early-C13 chancel and nave, a C13 south aisle, a late-C13 west tower, and a brick, north wall of 1780, in the north aisle. All was heavily restored in 1878, the date of the east window. However, note the tall *tomb-chest* to Sir Robert Tyrwhit (d.1581) and his wife; around the tomb are shown 22 children! and a Wild Man at his feet. There is also a *brass* of 1632 to a priest and his wife, with an amusing epitaph.

LINCOLN, Park Street. *Friends' Meeting House.*

Interesting in that it is a cottage dated 1689, the year of the Toleration Act permitting such chapels. The dais has its original gallery, and the three-arched gallery is C18.

STAMFORD, Browne's Hospital, Broad St. *Chapel.*

Attached to the almshouses founded by William Browne in 1475 it still has original fittings. The 1475 *glass* is of remarkable quality. The screen and *stalls*, with angel armrests and six *misericords*, are all of c.1480.

THORNTON-CURTIS. (H). 4m SE of Barton-on-Humber on A1077. *St Lawrence.*

Mainly C14 and a fine church. It possesses one of the ten Norman, black Tournai marble *fonts* in Britain. Jacobean *pulpit* and altar *table*, C18 *Royal Arms*, c.1200 *ironwork* on south door, north door *ironwork* c.1350, *collection shoe* dated 1661.

Northamptonshire

A notable feature of the churches of Northamptonshire is the many fine stone spires. This is due to the excellent limestone of many colours found in abundance, which has been quarried from distant times at Weldon and King's Cliff and, just across the border with Lincolnshire, at Barnack and Ketton.

Brixworth, the Anglo-Saxon church, is the largest and best of its kind north of the Alps and consequently is outstanding. As for Norman churches, there is nothing of importance outside Northampton which has St Peter and The Holy Sepulchre. The C13 was important here because many churches were rebuilt with nave, aisles, and the distinctive, mostly east-Northamptonshire, stone spires, a rebuilding that carried over to the early-C14. Thereafter church-building peters out. Of the C15 there is little, Fotheringhay and the piece-meal rebuilding of Lowick are the exceptions, both having lantern-towers. The C16 is even more barren with the single exception of Whiston, although a number of family chapels were built in these years. The C18 saw the emergence of many Nonconformist chapels.

ALDWINCLE. 5m SW of Oundle off A605. *All Saints.*

Aldwincle, All Saints.
The impressive C15 tower.

In the care of the Redundant Churches Fund. Built in the C13 and C14 with an impressive C15 tower, this church is noted for the fact that the poet, John Dryden, born in the vicarage, was baptised here in 1631. Note the remains of c.1490 *glass* in the Chambre Chapel, the small *brass* of 1463 to William Aldwynkle in the corner of the chancel, and the iron-bound chest on the south side of the chancel.

ASHBY ST LEDGERS. 4m N of Daventry off A361. *St Leodegarius.* This church is possibly C13, with C14 alterations and north tower. The point of any visit must be to see the unaltered interior, and the very faded late-C15 *wall paintings* representing the Passion of Christ; one of the most complete cycles of the subject. By the chancel arch is an earlier, c.1325, Flagellation of St Margaret. Note the C18 *box pews* facing into the nave and the Jacobean *pulpit*. Otherwise the fame of the church is due to the Catesby family; there is a fine *brass* to William Catesby, captured and executed at Bosworth Field in 1485. There are other good Catesby monuments but nothing to Robert of the Gunpowder Plot. However, there is a splendid Gothic one by *Lutyens* to Lord Wimborne (d.1939).

BRIXWORTH. 7m N of Northampton on A508. *All Saints.* It is not going too far to claim that this is the most outstanding Saxon church in Britain. Built c.675 or 750, of stone rubble and some Roman and even Saxon brick and tile, in a recently Christianised area, it was originally a monastery but ceased to be monastic after the

Danish invasion of 870. Miraculously, the church is relatively untouched by medieval alterations, except for the Verdun Chapel attached in c.1300 and a new belfry with spire in the early-C14. A major restoration was undertaken in 1864-6, when a medieval chancel was replaced by the present polygonal apse, and the roof given a steeper pitch. On the west jamb of the Norman south porch is a c.800 *Saxon Eagle of St John* in relief. The interior is surprisingly light, and impressively simple. The presbytery arch replaced a Saxon triple arch in the early C15. Near the pulpit, in an iron cage, is a rare c.1300 stone *reliquary* which was found containing a throat bone in the south wall of the Verdun Chapel in 1821.

COTTESBROOKE. 8m N of Northampton off A50. *All Saints.*
A cruciform church built all-of-a-piece in c.1300, restored in the C18 and again in 1959-60. The nave roof is ceiled but those in the chancel and transepts were exposed in 1960 revealing a C15 roof. The reredos and communion table are also from 1960. The good three-decker *pulpit* and *box pews* are C18. Notice the staircase leading to a family pew fitted out with a *fireplace*. Some good *monuments*.

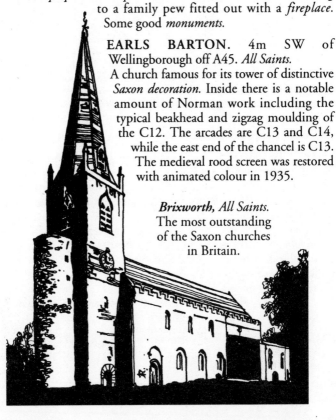

EARLS BARTON. 4m SW of Wellingborough off A45. *All Saints.*
A church famous for its tower of distinctive *Saxon decoration.* Inside there is a notable amount of Norman work including the typical beakhead and zigzag moulding of the C12. The arcades are C13 and C14, while the east end of the chancel is C13. The medieval rood screen was restored with animated colour in 1935.

Brixworth, All Saints.
The most outstanding of the Saxon churches in Britain.

FOTHERINGHAY. 4m NE of Oundle off A605. *St Mary & All Saints.*
Founded in 1411 by Edward Duke of York, killed at Agincourt in 1415, the church was completed after his death. The duke's *monument* stands south of the altar. Even though it lost its chancel in 1573, this is a noble church with a *lantern tower*, and visible for many miles. Inside, note the C18 box pews and the splendid C15 *pulpit* with a fine vaulted C17 *tester*. The font is C15 with a cover made up of two seats from the stalls. The late-medieval glass was removed in the C19 and has recently been found smashed in an undercroft beneath the porch. The York window was dedicated in 1975. Nearby are the remains of Fotheringhay Castle where Mary, Queen of Scots was beheaded in 1587.

GREAT BRINGTON. 6m NW of Northampton off A428. *St Mary.*
The mainly C13 exterior of this church, with C16 chancel and north and south chapels, gives little hint of the grandeur of the *monuments* in the Spencer Chapel, built in 1514. In the chancel south window there is some *glass* of 1532, some late William Morris *glass* in the Spencer Chapel and one *window* by T.Ward. A *tombstone* with a brass inlay dated 1616 in the chancel is to Laurence Washington, an ancestor of George Washington, the first President of the USA.

LOWICK. 8m E of Kettering on A6116. *St Peter.*
A C13 church rebuilt in 1370-99, with chancel and north chapel rebuilt c.1415, south chapel of c.1467 and lantern-tower of c.1500. With Fotheringhay, this is the only C15 church in the county. The

Lowick, St Peter. One of only two C15 churches in the county and famed for its medieval glass.

point of seeing this church is for the miraculous survival of so much medieval *glass* in the north aisle, and the splendid *monuments* running from 1417 and culminating in Sir Richard Westmacott's to the 5th Duke of Dorset (d.1843). Note the *Royal Arms* painted over the chancel arch and the two *hatchments* in the south chapel.

MIDDLETON CHENEY. 2m E of Banbury on A422. *All Saints.*
This mainly C13 church with C15 tower, all restored by Sir George Gilbert Scott in 1856, is famous for the *glass* by William Morris, Rossetti, Ford Madox Brown and Burne-Jones, which is all early-Pre-Raphaelite and unforgettable. The Rector of the time, W.C. Buckley, was a friend of Burne-Jones. Additionally, there is earlier *glass* by Clayton & Bell of 1859, a Norman font, a *Saxon wheel-cross head,* and a faded *Doom* over the chancel arch.

NORTHAMPTON. 65m NW of London off A1. *Holy Sepulchre.*
This is the best preserved of the four surviving C12 round churches modelled on that at Jerusalem. It has a C14 west tower and a C13 chancel, heavily restored by Scott in 1860, and was re-roofed in 1868 and 1879.
St Peter.
Built in c.1150, this is the best Norman church in the county. The tower was rebuilt in the early-C17 and the east end by Sir George Gilbert Scott in 1850. The interior is spectacular: richly decorated *capitals* lead the eye directly up to the altar, a view uninterrupted by any rood-screen. The reredos dates from 1875. In the south aisle are fragments of *Saxon* carving and an early-C14 tomb recess.

OUNDLE. 10m NE of Kettering on A605. *St Peter.*
A fine church, mainly of the C13, with tall C14 spire. A vast sum of money has recently been spent on restoration, and apart from the removal and sale of some late medieval pews the result must be applauded. The interior is light, bright and shining with cream paint and polished floors, revealing medieval detail formerly lost in murky gloom. The C15 oak *pulpit* glints in colours that enhance the carved details. A rarity is the C15 eagle *lectern,* similar to those at Urbino and at Newcastle Cathedral, Southwell Minster, Long Sutton, Lincolnshire, and Oxburgh, Norfolk. A large brass chandelier with candles in the nave, and dated 1685, is matched by smaller versions in the aisles.

STANFORD-ON-AVON. 11m N of Daventry off B5414. *St Nicholas.*
An impressive church rebuilt c.1300-50 and restored in 1908. The point of a visit must be to see the wealth of medieval *glass* dating from c.1307 to the C16, and the fifteen restored *monuments* dating from 1558 to 1896, including one in the north aisle by Richard

Titchmarsh, St Mary. Mainly C15 with 'the finest tower outside Somerset'.

Westmacott Jnr. (1799-1872). Notice the single *misericord*, the pulpit made up from the rood-screen, the *embroidered* altar frontal, claimed to be of 1613, the C17 organ case and the panelled stalls. Do not overlook the *hatchments*, nor the late-C16 or early-C17 organ case said to be from the Royal Chapel, Whitehall.

TITCHMARSH. 6m S of Oundle off A605. *St Mary.*
The mainly C15 church has what has been called 'the finest tower in England outside Somerset'. Unusually, it is surrounded on three sides by a ha-ha. It also has the peculiarity of a C17 *family pew* placed over the porch. Note the re-set Norman arch in the chancel, the good, painted, C18 *monuments*, and a *bust* to the poet, John Dryden, who lived here as a boy. An interesting C18 plaque in the south aisle, west end, records that Hugh Richards, a servant, saved his master's life from an attempted assassination, but no date is given. The chancel *wall paintings* of the Annunciation were done in 1861 by Miss Anson. There are two small *glass* panels by C.E. Kempe in the south aisle.

WADENHOE. 4m SW of Oundle off A605. *St Michael & All Angels.*
A church in a wonderful position above the village and close to a supposed Saxon village. With a Norman saddle-back tower, this is a church of c.1250, except for the south aisle which is c.1290. For those who enjoy an architectural puzzle look at the three-bay C13 arcading on the outside of the tower north wall and speculate on its purpose. The nave roof is dated 1844, which is possibly the date of the restored east window. There is a good C13 *font*, and note the

C16 pews in the aisles. Notice too, a wall plaque in the north aisle to Thomas and Caroline Hunt who were 'both cruelli shot by banditti' in 1824. They were on their honeymoon in Italy and had just visited Paestum. Three banditti were later executed for the murder.

Other Churches

AYNHO. 5m SW of Brackley on A41. *St Michael.*
Rebuilt in 1725, it looks like a Baroque house and not at all like a church, were it not for the C15 tower. The original *pulpit, box pews* and west *gallery* survive. The east window, dated 1857, is by Thomas Willement.

EASTON NESTON. 1m NE of Towcester off A43. *St Mary.*
A late-C13 church, with C15 tower, noted for the C18 two-decker *pulpit, box pews* and *organ case.* There are some fine *monuments* to the Fermor family including brass *palimpsests.* Inevitably there are Fermor *hatchments*

LAMPORT. 10m N of Northampton on B576. *All Saints.*
A church rebuilt in the C13 and the interior classicised in 1740, with a chapel of 1673. The west tower is late-Norman. In reality it is a private Isham family chapel and noted for the Isham *monuments.*

NORTHAMPTON. 65m NW of London off A1. *St Matthew.*
A large church of 1894 of no note except for the fact that it contains a beautiful Madonna and Child of 1944 by *Henry Moore* in the north transept, and a Crucifixion by *Graham Sutherland* installed in the south transept in 1945. There are also other works by modern artists.

STOKE DOYLE. 1m SW of Oundle. *St Rumbold.*

Stoke Doyle, *St Rumbold.* A C18
plaster angel above the
east window.

The decayed state of a C13 church was responsible for the rebuilding of this in 1722-5, unusually in the Classical style. The interior still retains C18 box pews, pulpit and font. There are some good *monuments*, in particular one of 1725 by the then young John Rysbrack in the north chapel.

WELLINGBOROUGH. 10m NE of Northampton on A45. *All Hallows.*
A church rebuilt in the late-C13 to early-C14 with a tower of c.1300-50, all restored 1861. There is good C20 glass including a north aisle window designed by *John Piper* in 1961, six very interesting C14 carved *misericords*, a *wall painting* of 1952 by Hans Fiebusch in the south transept and a carved C17 *Royal Arms.*
St Mary, Knox Road.
Built in the grandest C16 style by Sir Ninian Comper from 1908 to 1930 and only consecrated in 1968. It was Comper's favourite church; his wife is buried in the north chapel.

Nottinghamshire

Early building works are in Nottinghamshire sandstone and the distinctive red Mansfield sandstone. Limestone is found in the north-west of the county on the border with Derbyshire. The best building stone, however, comes from Ancaster in Lincolnshire and this is sometimes used. What timber buildings survived were replaced by brick in the eighteenth and nineteenth centuries using the abundant clay left in the last ice-age. Tythby church for example has a brick tower but stone nave and chancel. Spires are found in the south of the county but otherwise the towers are square and short.

The Norman nave of SS Mary & Martin, the remaining fragment of Blyth Priory, is the largest and almost only Norman work in any parish church in the county. St Catherine, Teversal, has re-used Norman detail and is almost the only C13 church to survive; and, apart from St Leonard, Wollaton, the C14 is equally unrepresented. The C15 is better interpreted by the magnificence of St Mary, Newark, one of the largest churches in England, and St Mary in Nottingham.

There is almost nothing in the way of wall painting and most interiors were cleared out in the C19. This is in part made up for by the chapel at Clumber built in the 1880s, and the 1890s interior by Sir Ninian Comper in the little church of St Mary at Egmanton.

BLYTH. 6m NW of Retford on A634. *SS. Mary & Martin.*
All that remains of the once important Priory of Blyth is a fragment of Norman severity. The chancel and transepts were demolished after the Dissolution. However, the interior is very well worth a visit just to

Blyth, SS Mary & Martin. The Norman nave,
with a south aisle added in c.1300 and a late-C14 tower.

see the recently discovered and restored *wall painting* of the Last
Judgement covering the whole of the east end. It was painted by
Italian, or near-eastern, artists, from the evidence of the detail it was
done shortly after the first English Bible of 1525. There are also: a
painting attributed to *Fra Bartolommeo* (1475-1517), seven *hatchments*, mainly to the Mellish family, and some eighteen C15 painted
panels set in the screens, rescued from the rood screen.

CLUMBER. 4m SE of Worksop off A614, in Clumber Park.
St Mary the Virgin.
In the care of the National Trust. A chapel built for the 7th Duke of
Newcastle in 1886-9 by Bodley & Garner at a cost of £30,000. The
exterior is a perfectly proportioned example of the late-Decorated
style. Often called a 'miniature cathedral', it must have given the
Anglo-Catholic Duke enormous pleasure. Bodley unfortunately fell
out with his patron and the interior was finished by Ernest Geldart.
The screen and rood, for example, are by Geldart. In the south aisle is
a statue of the Virgin by Sir Ninian Comper, and a poignant *monument* by Sir Richard Westmacott to Georgiana, a duchess who died in
childbirth in 1822. The church has recently been restored at the
expense of the Coal Board who caused serious damage to the stone
vaulting, paid for in the first place out of coal revenues.

EGMANTON. 11m NW of Newark between A1 & A6075.
St Mary.
One could easily miss this gem; the modest and undistinguished exterior with C15 tower gives no hint of the glory within. The brightly

painted *rood screen* and canopy with rood above, the *organ case*, and open work *pulpit* of 1896-8 are by Sir Ninian Comper and were financed by the ardently Anglo-Catholic 7th Duke of Newcastle.

HAWTON. 2m S of Newark off A46. *All Saints.*
The tower was built in 1482 at the same time as the clerestory and south aisle. The C13 north aisle is the oldest part of the church. Here is the finest *chancel* in the county, built c.1330, and, another prize, a magnificent *Easter Sepulchre*. In the panel below are four Roman soldiers in C14 armour asleep, while the upper panel shows the Ascension with the Apostles looking upwards. It is all deeply carved in luxurious flowing lines.

NEWARK. 19m NE of Nottingham on A46. *St Mary Magdalene.*
One of the grandest churches in England. The tall spire of the C13 and C14 towers over the busy market place; it was hit by a cannon ball in the Civil War and the hole can only be seen from one spot in Appleton Gate. The nave is entirely C15, the chancel was remodelled in late-C15 and the transepts begun after 1500. Inside, there is much to see. The bowl of the C15 font was destroyed by Parliamentarians when Newark surrendered in 1646. Replaced in 1660, it leaves C15 saints with C17 heads, moustaches and beards. The black *rood screen* of 1508 is the only surviving work of Thomas Drawsword of York.

Egmanton, St Mary. The brightly painted rood screen of 1896 by Sir Ninian Comper.

Newark, St Mary Magdalene
The tall spire of one of the grandest
churches in England.

Beyond is a glittering gold *reredos* of 1937 in C14 style by Sir Ninian Comper. Notice too in the Markham chapel two naively painted C16 stone panels of the Dance of Death, and re-set medieval glass of c.1300 and the C15 in the chancel chapel east window. In the choir are twenty-four *misericords* of c.1524 and a large outstanding Flemish *brass* dated 1363 in the north choir aisle.

NOTTINGHAM. *St Mary.*
A large cruciform C15 church marooned in the old Lace Market, for the modern centre of the city has moved away. West end by W.B. Moffat (1845-53), chapter house by G.F. Bodley (1890) and south chapel by Temple Moore (1912-13). Inside, the chancel roof of 1872 by Sir George Gilbert Scott was decorated by Lawrence Bond in 1965. The choir stalls are also Scott's of 1872. The reredos and screen is by Bodley & Garner, 1885. There is much C19 stained glass

including Clayton & Bell and Kempe, many tattered regimental banners and a carved wooden Lion & Unicorn of c.1710 in the west end. On the SE crossing pier hangs a late-C15 *Madonna and Child* in the style of Fra Bartolommeo, given in 1839. The octagonal C15 font has in Turkish the longest known *palindrome* of twenty-five letters in a church: it translates as 'wash my sins not only my face'.

TEVERSAL. 4m W of Mansfield off B6014. *St Catherine.*
Late-C12 and C13 with re-used Norman detail, such as the remarkable south door. Adapted for C17 worship, the interior remains almost unchanged. The reader's desk is of 1908 and the Georgian *Royal Arms* are before 1801, but the rest, the communion rail and table, the box pews, squire's pew, commandment board, stalls and west gallery, are genuine C17. Notice too the large Molyneux *hatchments* hanging beneath the south clerestory.

Other Churches

BLIDWORTH. 5m SE of Mansfield on B6020. *St Mary of the Purification.*
C15 square tower, Classical nave 1739-40, chancel 1839. Famed for the *Rocking Cradle* used at a 'Rocking' service in February. On the reverse of the hymn board King David painted and signed 'Shepperd 1779'.

HOLME PIERREPONT. 4m E of Nottingham off A52. *St Edmund.*
Considering its closeness to the city this is a surprisingly remote church standing next to the Hall. Basically C13 but rebuilt in 1666 with a chancel of 1878-91. Inside there is a C13 arcade and many good Pierrepont family monuments including one to 'Princess' Gertrude (d.1649), a flattering Baroque reference to the Duchess of Kingston.

THURGARTON. 3m S of Southwell on A612. *St Peter.*
A magnificent fragment of an Augustinian Priory built c.1230. Some few, very good, salvaged fittings: bracket and canopy of c.1330 and four C15 *misericords.*

TYTHBY. 2m S of Bingham off A52. *Holy Trinity.*
Brick C19 tower with nave of two dates, the north side is C14 and the south C18. The interior is very unusual in that it was shared by Tythby north of the nave and Cropwell Bishop south of the nave. The interior was refurbished in 1825. Cropwell's box pews date from then but Tythby's side is Victorian of c.1837. *Squire's pew*, *Royal Arms* of George III, and west *gallery* are worth noting.

WINKBURN. 2.5m N of Southwell off A617. *St John of Jerusalem.*
Once a manor of the Knights of St John. A small church with an *unaltered* C17 century interior. Tower rebuilt 1632, Norman decoration, squire's pew, and *box pews.*

WOLLATON. 2m W of Nottingham. *St Leonard.*
Early-C14 chancel, late-C14 nave, tower and spire. Wall plate to
Robert Smythson (1614), the first to be called 'architector', builder of
Wollaton Hall. Good Willoughby *monuments* and brasses.
WYSALL. 10m S of Nottingham off A60. *Holy Trinity.*
Norman north wall, C14 chancel, C13 tower. The tower *ladder* may
well be C13. There are four *misericords* and a small brass cande-
labrum of 1773.

WEST MIDLANDS

Cheshire

Cheshire is not a county blessed with good building materials. There is a red, or buff, sandstone that weathers badly and blackens from soot, otherwise it is brick, and timber. Two timber-framed churches survive, the earliest longitudinal timber church buildings in Europe: one, St Oswald at Lower Peover, perhaps from the C12, and the other, SS James & Paul at Marton.

Little survives of Norman architecture apart from the nave and crossing of St John, Chester, a cathedral until 1541, and a chapel at Prestbury largely rebuilt in 1747 and therefore not included here. St Mary at Nantwich represents the C14 with a feast of gargoyles and pinnacles in red sandstone; it has the only stone lierne-vaulting in the county. At Malpas, the C15 St Oswald has an astonishing angel roof with the details of the bosses picked out in gold and is certainly worth a detour. St Chad, Tushingham, was built, unusually, in the late C17 with a unique timber roof. From the C19 is Alfred Waterhouse's chapel at Eaton Hall, which must be the richest private chapel in Britain. Although this county does not boast a great range of worthwhile churches it does possess some outstanding items.

ASTBURY. 2m SW of Congleton on A 34. *St Mary.*
Pevsner was excited by this church and indeed we should be also. It is a C15 rebuilding, in millstone grit, of a C14 church, with a spire rebuilt in 1838, and a tower of 1366 attached to the west end of the north aisle. Nave and chancel are undivided and the long crenelated parapet gives the impression of a castle. The interior is rightly famed for its woodwork. The nave and south aisle *roofs*, completed in c.1500, are incredible examples of the woodcarver's skill: bosses and pendants (one above the altar for the pyx shows the five wounds of Christ) and, in the south aisle, angels bearing shields, all have their detail carefully picked out in gold paint. In the nave are C17 *box pews* each with different strapwork decoration. The *rood screen*, with C15 fan-vaulting, is the finest in the county, and notice the C17

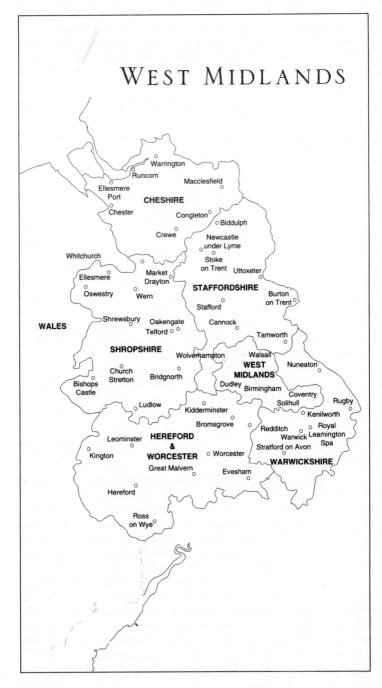

WEST MIDLANDS

Warrington

Runcorn

Macclesfield

Ellesmere
Port

CHESHIRE

Chester

Congleton

Biddulph

Crewe

Newcastle
under Lyme

Whitchurch

Stoke
on Trent

Uttoxeter

Ellesmere

Market
Drayton

STAFFORDSHIRE

Burton
on Trent

Oswestry

Wern

Stafford

WALES

Shrewsbury

Oakengate
Telford

Cannock

Tamworth

SHROPSHIRE

Wolverhampton

Walsall

**WEST
MIDLANDS**

Nuneaton

Church
Stretton

Bridgnorth

Dudley

Birmingham

Coventry

Bishops
Castle

Solihull

Rugby

Ludlow

Kidderminster

Kenilworth

Bromsgrove

Redditch

Royal
Leamington
Spa

Leominster

**HEREFORD
&
WORCESTER**

Warwick

Kington

Worcester

Stratford on Avon

WARWICKSHIRE

Great Malvern

Evesham

Hereford

Ross
on Wye

wooden eagle *lectern* with fearsome talons. In the north wall of the clerestory is a c.1500 wall *painting* of the Virgin knighting St George, and a coat of arms. Above the west gallery, with its pierced balustrade, is the painted *Royal Arms* of Charles II. The glass is late-C19 and early-C20.

CHESTER. 35m SW of Manchester end of M53. *St John Baptist*, Vicar's Lane.

This seemingly Victorian church with a sandstone exterior is not all it appears to be. Although the exterior is C19, it is the major Norman architectural work of the county, and was a cathedral until 1541. The C13 north porch was rebuilt when the tower fell in 1882, the north-east bell tower was built in 1886 and the south aisle is 1859-66. Inside, the early-C12 Norman nave piers support a c.1200 triforium and a C13 clerestory. Beyond, is a splendid Norman *crossing* supported on simple arches. In the north aisle there are stone *effigies*, one of c.1300, in chain-mail with crossed legs. The reredos of 1876, with a 'Last Supper', was designed by John Douglas, and the pair of brass chandeliers in the sanctuary were given in 1722. Note the faded wall *painting* of St John Baptist in the north aisle. The Lady Chapel has C17 oak gates and fine wrought-iron railings. Here the reredos is made-up from the old high altar reredos of 1692, and on the south wall is a *monument* of 1693 showing the upright skeleton of Diana Warburton holding before her the winding sheet with her obituary on it! The glass is all C19, and the organ was first used for the coronation of Queen Victoria in 1838 at Westminster Abbey, London.

CHOLMONDELEY CASTLE. 11m SE of Chester off A49. *Chapel*.

Dedicated to *St Nicholas*, this chapel has a complicated building history. Originally a timber-framed, late-C15 chapel, it was restored in the 1650s, and the chancel was encased in brick in 1717 when the rest was rebuilt, with the transepts added in 1829. However, it retains its C15 hammer-beam chancel *roof* and many furnishings from the mid-C17, the most complete of its date in the county. The box pews are of 1829 but the carved oak *pulpit, clerk's desk, lectern, altar rails* and *Commandment boards* are all of the 1650s. A novelty is that the chancel screen of 1655 supports the carved arms of Cholmondely and of Leinster. The painting of 'The Adoration of the Shepherds' is attributed to Pietro da Cortona (1596-1669). However, two others, one of the 'Holy Family with Saints', and the other, 'The Rest on the Flight to Egypt', are simply School of Pietro da Cortona. A finely turned stair leads to the State Gallery (family pew) at the west end, and note the six *hatchments* ranging from 1827 to as recently as 1968. The east window contains small Flemish *glass* roundels.

EATON HALL. 4m S of Chester off B5130. *Chapel*.

Although the vast house remodelled for the dukes of Westminster by Alfred Waterhouse in 1870-83 has gone, his chapel, built 1873-84, remains and it must be the finest C19 private chapel in Britain. In style, it is French Gothic of the C12 and C13 and built of sandstone, with a 175ft high tower with four clock faces and a memorable carillon of 28 bells with a repertoire of 31 tunes! Inside, the pink sandstone walls rise to rib-vaults with gilded bosses, and blank arches in the south wall are filled with mosaics. Understandably, the furnishings are opulent and most were designed by Waterhouse. The *pulpit* and *screen* are of pink-veined alabaster decorated with pierced panels filled with foliage. In the chancel the *crucifix* of silver, copper and enamel, was designed in the mid-1880s by A.H. Mackmurdo and made by the Century Guild; behind is an open-work alabaster reredos. On the south side is a white alabaster effigy of the first Duke's first wife (d.1880) by Sir Joseph Boehm. The *glass*, made in 1876, is by Frederic James Shields.

ECCLESTON. 3m S of Chester off A483. *St Mary.*
This is one of G.F. Bodley's finest churches, rebuilt in 1899 in C14 style at the first Duke of Westminster's expense. The exterior in red sandstone does not distinguish the chancel from the aisled nave with clerestory supported by delicate flying buttresses. The buttressed west tower has a crenellated parapet. Inside, the furnishings are Bodley's; the screen, extending the full width of the church, the pulpit and tester, are all of carved oak. A remarkable stone *reredos* behind the high altar is richly carved, painted and gilded with two tiers of figures. The glass is by Burlison and Gryllis. In the churchyard is a bronze *tomb*, by Detmar Blow and Fernand Billerey, to the Earl of Grosvenor (d.1909).

LOWER PEOVER. 11m W of Macclesfield on B5081. *St Oswald.*
Dating perhaps from the C12, this church, with Marton, claims to be the oldest longitudinal timber church in Europe. The stone-built west tower dates from c.1500 and all was much restored, altered and re-roofed by Anthony Salvin in 1852-4. It is a grander conception than Marton, with more sophisticated patterns of timber-work, and consists of a nave and two aisles. It was originally all under one roof, Salvin gave it three! The chancel has a south chapel of c.1610 and a north chapel of c.1624. Inside the dark interior, the *font cover, patron's pew* and *screens* are all Jacobean. The north chapel screen is dated 1624. The pulpit and lectern were made-up by Salvin from a three-decker pulpit. Near the font are breadshelves for endowed bread charities, dated 1720 and 1739. Simple C17 oak box pews fill the nave, some bearing the Shakerley crest, while pews next to the tower have canopies. The glass is all C19, and note the C13 dug-out chest.

MALPAS. 5m NW of Whitchurch on B5069. *St Oswald.*

Malpas, St Oswald. Brereton chapel and tomb of
Randal Brereton (d.1522).

This is one of the best examples of C15 work in the county.
Although some details in the chancel are C13, the whole church was
rebuilt on C14 foundations. The church, comprising nave, two aisles
and chancel, with a west tower, is built of red sandstone, with a brick
vestry of 1717. Inside, all is space and light; overhead is a breathtaking angel *roof* with painted and gilded bosses, restored in 1957-66. In
the chancel three C15 oak stalls remain, each with a *misericord*, while
in the south aisle are six of the original *box pews* of 1680, and a splendid C13 oak *chest* covered with gorgeous iron scroll-work. Above the
chancel arch hangs a large painting of 'St Peter's Denial of Christ' by
Francis Hayman (1708-76) given in 1778. Two pretty C15 screens to
the Brereton (south) and Cholmondeley (north) chapels conceal a
magnificent alabaster *tomb-chest* with effigies to Randal Brereton
(d.1522) in full armour, and his wife, in the south chapel. In the
north chapel is another alabaster tomb-chest to Sir Hugh
Cholmondeley (d.1605) and his wife, with their six children represented on the sides of the chest. Note their baby in swaddling clothes.
Sir Richard Westmacott is responsible for the tablet to Lady

Cholmondeley (d.1815). There is some good *glass* in the north chapel; a c.1500 panel, and some C16 Flemish panels and C17 Flemish medallions. All other glass is C19.

MARTON. 6m SW of Macclesfield on B5085. *SS James and Paul.*
With Lower Peover, this claims to be oldest longitudinal timber-church in Europe, dating from c.1370. Even the shingled bell-turret is timber-framed; its interior, like an aisled barn, is a fascinating jumble of posts and braces. Pews and font date from a restoration of 1871 but the *pulpit* is dated 1621. On the west wall are outlines of a lost wall *painting.* The painting of Moses and Aaron holding the tablets is the only surviving part of the former reredos.

NANTWICH. 4m SW of Crewe on A534. *St Mary.*
A cruciform church, collegiate from c.1330, with octagonal crossing tower and built of the local red sandstone in the C14, with good decorative detail of gargoyles and pinnacles, extensively restored in 1854-61 by Sir George Gilbert Scott. Inside, a C19 roof is carried on angel corbels, and the chancel has very fine C14 stone lierne *vaulting,* with many good carved stone bosses, the only medieval examples in the county. The sedilia, piscina and *aumbry* are all early-C14. A treasure of the church is the late-C14 *stalls* with canopies, and twenty carved *misericords.* Hanging in the south aisle is a small painting by Jules Bouvier, 'The Widow's Mite'. There are original fragments of C14 *glass* in one chancel window, and in the north transept is good glass of 1876 by C.E. Kempe, of 1862 by Hardman & Co, and of 1877 by Clayton & Bell.

SHOTWICK. 5m NW of Chester off A550. *St Michael.*
Basically a Norman church with a decayed Norman south door, a C13 chancel and a west tower of c.1500. It is unusual for England in having two naves, and so much C17 and C18 furnishing. The three-decker *pulpit* is c.1740, the very unusual *churchwardens' pew* with canopy is dated 1709, the *communion rail* is C17 and the box pews C18. Note the late-C18 brass chandelier. *Glass* in the north aisle east window shows a C14 Annunciation and the splendid C15 door may have come from a church in Chester.

TUSHINGHAM. 4m NW of Whitchurch on A41. *Old St Chad.*
A small church built of brick in 1689-91 and paid for by donations, principally from John Dod, a London mercer. The plan consists of a nave and chancel in one, with a built-in, stumpy west tower with pyramid roof. Ball finials on gable ends and apexes make up nice exterior detail. Notice the lion-headed knocker on the south door. (One enters with the impression of stepping back in time.) Inside, the roof *trusses* are remarkable for Cheshire, and set with star-shaped openwork panels. Traditionally the floor is covered in straw, a nice

Tushingham, Old St Chad. The small brick church built for John Dod in 1689-91.

touch. The simple benches are original, as are the Benefaction board, the three-decker *pulpit,* two *family pews, screen* and west *gallery.*

Other Churches

RAINOW. 3m NE of Macclesfield on A5002. *Jenkin Chapel,* Saltersford.
Remote and difficult to reach, built in 1733, with a short west tower of 1754 with a saddle-back roof. Inside, the *box pews,* west *gallery,* and two-decker *pulpit,* are contemporary with the building.

WILMSLOW. 6m NW of Macclesfield on A538. *Unitarian Chapel,* Dean Row.
A pleasing low building with leaded two-light windows, built of brick in 1693; in appearance it might be a large farmhouse. Access to the galleries is by exterior stairs on either side of the façade. Simple interior with box pews. Similar chapels at Adam's Hill, Knutsford (1689) and King Edward Street, Macclesfield (1689).

Hereford and Worcester

These two counties, bludgeoned into a forced marriage in the 1970s, do not make an ideal couple when it comes to churches, although both are united in the use of red sandstone for building. Herefordshire was very much affected by its Welsh neighbours and its Norman architecture is decorated by Hereford carvers with a strong Celtic flavour, as may be seen at SS.Mary & David, Kilpeck, and St George, Brinsop. It also has two of our remotest churches: St Bartholomew, Richards Castle, and St Clydog, Clodock, with relatively unchanged interiors. The incomparable Abbey Dore, really only a shred of its original Cistercian self, has its original C17 fittings untouched. A surprise is the Gothic Revival interior at Shobden which is the best of anything of its time and should not be missed. Mercifully, there was no spare nineteenth-century wealth for rebuilding and many churches were left slumbering for us to rediscover. The exception is St Catherine, Hoarwithy, where J.P. Seddon created an Italian fantasy in 1875. St George, Brinsop, was left to Sir Ninian Comper to restore in the 1920s, and for the Arts and Crafts few parish churches can offer more than All Saints, Brockhampton.

Worcestershire was affected by the Industrial Revolution and its proximity to Birmingham meant that wealthy industrialists wrecked more by well-meaning restoration than is the case in Herefordshire. There are fragments of Norman work in many churches, and not a few Norman fonts, but pride of place must go to St Cassian at Chaddesley Corbett with its deeply carved dragons snarling around the bowl. Great Malvern has a gem in its former Benedictine priory church which has the finest collection of medieval glass in Britain as well as the only medieval wall tiles. What is undoubtedly the finest Baroque interior is at Great Whitley where Lord Foley is remembered for this Italian extravaganza in gold and white. Croome d'Abitot is unique in having a church built by two masters, Lancelot Brown and Robert Adam, and its Gothic revival interior is only excelled by that at Shobden.

ABBEY DORE. 10m SW of Hereford on B4347. *St Mary.*
After the Dissolution, this Cistercian Abbey of the C12 and C13 was left in increasing ruin for nearly a hundred years until the church, built of red sandstone with grey limestone dressings, was restored in 1632-4 by Viscount Scudamore. Restoration is hardly the word, for what he did was drastic; the nave and aisles were demolished and the transepts, presbytery and ambulatory became the parish church, with a west tower set in the angle of the south transept. Inside, the roof and most of the fittings are from 1634: the unusual nave *screen* made by the 'King's Carpenter', the *pulpit*, almsbox, communion rail, *reader's desk*, *Royal Arms*, stalls and west gallery are all of that date.

The splendour of the church is the late-C13 double *ambulatory*, a forest of sandstone columns with the best foliate *carving* in Britain, lit by fragments of C16 and C17 coloured *glass*. Note the two *hatchments*, and the C13 hinges on the north ambulatory door.

BESFORD. 8m SE of Worcester off A4104. *St Peter.*
This is a mid-C14 timber-framed church, the only one in the county, with a C15 porch, and a stone chancel built in 1881 when it was restored. A *rood loft*, contemporary with the church, remains intact with its original colouring, while the communion rail and panelling are C17. Note the funeral *helmet* with an animal crest. Among the monuments is a *triptych* of c.1588 to a member of the Harwell family who died young. Closed, its doors shows shields and when opened it shows the deceased painted with figures and scenes above them.

BRINSOP. 6m NW of Hereford off A480. *St George.*
This unimpressive church comprises a nave, a north aisle and chancel, all built c.1300-50, and a small C19 bellcote. However, it contains some good Norman sculpture datable to 1150-60. The *tympanum* has a large St George with two birds and a lurking lion and there are fragments of a *frieze* of birds and other pieces. Additionally, there are defaced C14 *wall paintings*, an Annunciation and Visitation in the chancel and a Crucifixion above the south door. The *reredos* is alabaster with much gold-leaf; the rood figures and several windows of the 1920s are by Sir Ninian Comper. Notice the Dorothy Wordsworth window by Comper; her parents lived nearby.

BROCKHAMPTON-BY-ROSS. 5m N of Ross-on-Wye off B4224. *All Saints.*

Brockhampton-by-Ross, All Saints. A splendid celebration of the Arts and Crafts by W.R.Lethaby in 1901-2.

The only church built by W.R. Lethaby, an Arts and Crafts architect, in 1901-2. This building is so remarkable that we can only regret its uniqueness. Consisting of nave, low crossing tower, short transepts, chancel-all thatched-and heavy porch with a weatherboarded pyramid roof, it is not a building to be overlooked. The interior is even more remarkable and completely original in concept. A succession of steeply pointed concrete arches lead the eye beyond the crossing to the brightly lit chancel and the *east window* of SS Margaret and Cecilia by Christopher Whall, who is responsible for all the other brilliantly coloured *glass*. One altarpiece is early-C16 Flemish, the other C15 Sienese, and the two *tapestries* in the chancel are designed by Sir Edward Burne-Jones and made by Morris & Co. Note the 48 panels of the *choir stalls* each carved with a different wild flower, repeated on the altar cloth. Note the *pulpit* with the carved figure of Christ preaching. See this church at the same time as nearby Hoarwithy.

CLODOCK. 4m W of Pontrilas off A465. *St Clydog.*

A Norman church with a late-C12 chancel and a stumpy C15 tower, all built in red sandstone, in a remote setting in one of the most beautiful parts of Britain. A late-C13 east window and two C15 south windows do not distract and, in fact, allow more light into what must have been a gloomy Norman nave. The inside is almost untouched late-C17, from the panelled *box pews* to the three-decker *pulpit* with tester. The west gallery, however, is c.1715 and the benefaction table 1805. A quaintly unconvincing Gothic *frame* with finial is painted round the north chancel window. Note the Lord's Prayer, the *Royal Arms* and the newly-painted texts of the Ten Commandments.

CROOME D'ABITOT. 7m S of Worcester off A38. *St Mary.*

In the care of the Redundant Churches Fund. This stone-built church runs a close second to St John, Shobdon, in Gothic fantasy, but is unique in that it is the only church to be built by Lancelot Brown with an interior by Robert Adam. Built from 1763 for the 6th Earl of Coventry as an ornament to his park, it is architecturally more correct in its medieval window tracery than Shobdon. Entering beneath the west tower, the interior is completely satisfying, and even if the white-painted nave is less of a fantasy than Shobdon, it is Gothic all the same, with an ogee chancel arch complete with crockets. A high *pulpit*, with intricately carved tester, has panelling matching the pew ends, and a jewel of a *font* by Adam in carved wood, stolen in 1988 but recovered, is unlikely to be left unprotected again. A narrow chancel is overcrowded with Coventry *monuments* which include one by Grinling Gibbons to the 4th Lord Coventry (d.1687). Note the two *hatchments* and the

Commandment boards in Gothic frames in the chancel arch.

GARWAY. 9m NW of Monmouth off B4521. *St Michael.*
Built of sandstone rubble and originally a circular Templar church of c.1180. Of this only the chancel arch remains; the present C13 rectangular nave was built over it. Off the chancel is a late-C13 south chapel. Most eccentric of all is the detached C13 west tower, actually south-west, set at an angle to the nave and connected by a C17 passage. Inside, the nave walls are painted pink, giving a warm light, with a C14 *roof*; the hefty benches are C16. Note the masons' marks, the C12 dug-out *chest* in the tower, the *graffiti* on the C12 *piscina* in the south chapel, the carving on the chancel arch that may be copied from the Bab el Foutouh (c.1090) in Cairo, and the carved hand of God set on the nave north wall.

GREAT MALVERN. 8m SW of Worcester on A449. *SS Mary & Michael.*
The church of a former Benedictine priory built in pinkish stone in 1420-60 and restored in 1860. It has a short Norman nave, a part-Norman crossing tower with transepts, and a C15 chancel. Inside, the nave, with short massive columns, shows its Norman origins while, above, are huge clerestory windows of c.1450 and a flat timber roof. One gets a clear view through to the great east window and its *glass* of c.1440. Dispersed throughout the church is one of the finest collections of late-medieval *glass* in Britain. In the chancel is another fascination: the only surviving medieval C15 wall tiles in Britain, numbering about 1200. Notice also the twenty-two *misericords* of c.1480 in the stalls.

GREAT WITLEY. 9m NW of Worcester on A443. *St Michael.*
In the care of English Heritage. Standing next to the ruin of Whitley Court burnt out in 1937, the church, built in cream-coloured ashlar for Lord Foley in 1735, is attributed to James Gibbs. The exterior is unremarkable but the interior is a breathtaking Italianate extravaganza in white and gold. Pietro Bagutti was the *stuccadore* and the ceiling detail is in papier mâché. Antonio Bellucci painted the twenty-three *ceiling panels* which, with ten *windows* (dated 1719) by Joshua Price, and the organ case, were bought from the Duke of Chandos's Canons Park when it was demolished in 1747. The pews, font, pulpit, etc., were inserted in the 1850s and are a C19 Gothic conception of Italian high Baroque! One cannot overlook the vast *monument* by Michael Rysbrack to the 1st Lord Foley (d.1735) which is surely one of the biggest in Britain.

HOARWITHY. 7m N of Ross-on-Wye off A49. *St Catherine.*
In 1875, J.P. Seddon was commissioned by the rector to encase in stone a humdrum brick box of a church only built in 1843. The

Hoarwithy, St Catherine. Built 1875.
Looking up at the tower between ilex trees
one might be in Italy.

result is a dramatically astonishing conception borrowed from Southern Italy. The approach is also dramatic, up steps flanked by ilexes, along a columned cloister and in through the west door shadowed by a tall bell-tower. Inside, all is mosaic floors, gold inlay, marbles and lapis lazuli seen through Byzantine arches, with Byzantine lanterns, originally heated by a hypercaust. The climax of the theatrical interior is in the Byzantine east end with a mosaic of the Pantokrator in the apse. It all took thirty years to complete, an act of reverence we can greatly admire today. See this church at the same time as nearby Brockhampton.

KILPECK. 6m SW of Hereford off A465. *SS Mary & David.*
This small Norman church is one of the great treasures of Britain and should be seen at least once in a lifetime. Apart from Saxon masonry in the north-east corner of the nave, a Jacobean gallery, some late-medieval windows and the restored C19 bellcote everything dates from 1140-80. The decoration is sumptuously extravagant because this was near a Benedictine priory founded in 1134, and the nearby motte-and-bailey castle was important in its day. The south door is heavily decorated with one crisply carved column filled with vine leaves hiding two Viking warriors, framed by sinuous serpents. In the *tympanum* is the Tree of Life and, above it, some marvellously varied beakheads. The corbels in the eaves are carved with myriad beasts and figures almost beyond imagination. On the

west front are dragon-heads and a window with interlaced bands. Inside, there is something of a simple contrast; the chancel arch carries three devout figures on each side. Beyond is an apse of three bays with rib-vaults joining overhead with four frightening heads.

This brief introduction to a famous church cannot do justice to every wonder to be found there. The joy of discovery will be the prize gained by every visitor.

LEOMINSTER. 12m N of Hereford on A49. *SS Peter & Paul.*
Built of local sandstone this is one of the great parish churches of Britain. Once a Benedictine priory church, only the nave and west door of c.1130 remain. The south nave was rebuilt in 1239, and the central tower, transepts and east end apse all went after the Dissolution. A serious fire in 1699 resulted in the rebuilding of the south nave aisle. All was restored in 1886. The west portal has some fine capitals of c.1150 and the south-west porch has good *stiff-leaf* carving. The great drum-like pillars of the nave (the original parish church) indicate the Norman work, contrasting with the blank east wall built after the Dissolution. Note on the north wall the *painting* of the Wheel of Life of c.1275. Little furniture survived the fire, but the organ case is of 1739 and there are some C14 tiles in

Kilpeck, SS Mary & David. The south door guarded by two Viking warriors and framed by sinuous serpents.

the south nave. The C19 glass is unremarkable, but there is a nice window of 1948 in the Lady Chapel.

MONNINGTON-ON-WYE. 9m W of Hereford on A438. *St Mary.*
Built of local sandstone in a simple nave and chancel plan in 1679, apart from the C15 west tower. Inside, little has changed: the *screen*, *communion rail* and cut-down *pulpit* are all of the 1680s, and fitted with twisted columns; the font is dated 1680 and the carved *Royal Arms* are those of Charles II. Note the upright Nonconformist settles. By legend, Owen Glendower (d.1416) is buried in the churchyard

RICHARDS CASTLE. 6m N of Leominster on B4361. *St Bartholomew.*
In the care of the Redundant Churches Fund. A large and lonely hilltop church built of rubble stone originally rendered, with a Norman nave, an early-C14 south aisle, a C14 chancel and north transept and, unusually for Britain, a freestanding bell-tower of c.1300. Within are *box pews*, one dated 1688, a *family pew* in the north chapel, and a banked *west pew*, with some medieval *glass* fragments in the transept, south aisle and chancel windows. On the south wall are traces of C18 wall paintings. Note the two *hatchments*.

ST MARGARETS. 13m SW of Hereford off B4347. *St Margaret.*
A small lonely church on a hilltop, consisting of nave, chancel and weatherboarded bell-turret. What is noteworthy about this building is that it has one (c.1520) of only three remaining screens with an *independent rood loft* still intact. Moreover, it is very finely carved but unpainted, apart from recently restored black lettering texts. Note the churchwardens' duties in English and Welsh.

SHOBDON. 6m W of Leominster on B4362. *St John Evangelist.*
In the 1750s the Hon. Richard Bateman of Shobdon Court, a friend of Horace Walpole, then converting Strawberry Hill to Rococo Gothic, added to a C13 west tower a Rococo Gothic nave and chancel. The exterior looks interesting but nothing like so interesting as the Gothic fantasy inside. Furthermore it is unchanged. A stunning *pulpit*, with a gorgeous white tester and original red velvet hangings, is worth coming to see in its own right. The *pews*, *reader's desk* and *lectern* are painted white with blue details. Indeed, everything is white, giving the impression of an iced wedding cake. Bateman, however, retained the original Norman *font*. Note the elaborate *fireplace* in the south transept and do not overlook the east window *glass* of 1907. Although Bateman destroyed an outstanding Norman church, he left the two doorways standing north of the church as an eye-catcher. One leaves this amazing interior forgiving Bateman for destroying a Norman church, for what he gave us in return is an incomparable gem.

WORCESTER. 25m SW of Birmingham on A38. *St Swithun.*
In the care of the Redundant Churches Fund. A perfect example of an C18 town church, built in the classical style in 1736 and retaining a C15 west tower. The east front, overlooking the street, has an imposing Venetian window in a fine classical façade. The interior is fantastic: plaster Gothic Revival *vaulting* covers the aisleless nave, *box pews,* mayor's throne with *sword rest* and *west gallery* are all of the 1730s. Most amazing of all is the three-decker *pulpit* of the same date, with a *tester* crowned by a pelican feeding her young, and an anchor swinging below her. Note the *font* and the splendid wrought-iron *altar table* also of the 1730s.

Other Churches

CHADDESLEY CORBETT. 5m SE of Kidderminster on A448. *St Cassian.*
Except for the west tower of 1779, the church is C14 with a brilliant chancel, the best in the county, all restored in 1863. Do not miss the Norman *font* of c.1160, vigorously carved with five sinuous drag-

Shobdon, St John. The interior looking west is a fantasy of Gothic Revival created in the 1750s.

ons, the *brass* of 1511, the limestone knight's effigy c.1290 and the vividly restored C17 *monuments.*

SHELSEY WALSH. 9m NW of Worcester off B4204. *St Andrew.*
Built of tufa, a porous rock, with a Norman nave and C13 chancel, but heavily restored in 1859. Notable *roof* to chancel, original, decorated *rood beam*, and fine late-C15 *screen.* Note the C15 floor tiles and the wood *tomb-chest* of 1596.

STRENSHAM. 5m N of Tewkesbury on A38. *SS Philip & James.*
Unimpressive exterior, but its *screen* of c.1500 with 23 painted panels is preserved as part of the west gallery. C15 tiles in the nave, two excellent *brasses* of 1390 and 1405, C18 two-decker *pulpit*, early-C16 *panelling* and benches with hat-pegs. Good *monuments.*

TYBERTON. 7m W of Hereford on B4352. *St Mary.*
Rebuilt in 1719-21, the exterior has been spoilt by windows inserted in 1879. Enter by the Norman doorway and it is another story. The *reredos* is magnificent and contemporary with the church, as are the furnishings and monuments. Note the *Royal Arms* dated 1720.

WARNDON. 3m NE of Worcester off A449 and Jct 6 of M5. *St Nicholas.*
A small C12 church with C15 timber-framed west tower and porch. Untouched interior with C17 *box pews* and *communion rail*, some C15 *glass* fragments with an early-C14 Virgin in the east window.

Shropshire

Sandstone is the principal building material in Shropshire and it comes in colours ranging from red through pink to white. The red, when blackened with the smoke of ages, can look depressingly drab, but there are many gems of churches in the county and, notwithstanding outside appearances, one should persevere.

There are more than a few Norman churches, starting with the early-Norman Holy Trinity at Much Wenlock, St Mary at Shrewsbury, and the two small treasures of the lonely Heath Chapel and St Leonard at Linley. Of the early-Gothic, there is again St Mary at Shrewsbury. St Bartholomew at Tong is as good an example of the late-Gothic as one could wish for and its large collection of tombs is famous.

A timber-framed church is a rarity in Britain, yet Shropshire has two, a chapel at Halston, and St Peter at Melverley. Both are well worth a visit. There must have been many more, but Victorian industrialists from Birmingham and Manchester discovered the rural peace of Shropshire, bought estates and rebuilt churches in fits of piety. At Peplow, in deeply rural Shropshire, Norman Shaw built a sympathetic vernacular-revival chapel in 1879. St Michael at Llanyblodwell, rebuilt in 1845-60 by the vicar, is best treated as a serious joke.

In all, Shropshire is a rewarding county for its untouched 'prayer-book' interiors and its wide variety of architectural styles.

BURFORD. 8m SE of Ludlow on A456. *St Mary.*
Built of red sandstone with west tower, a C14 nave and chancel with Norman masonry, the church was heavily restored in 1889 by Sir Aston Webb. The interior is suitably dark and religious with the chancel roof, sedilia, the Art Nouveau lighting and lectern all by Webb. The screen, of dark-red wood and gilded iron-work, is from Louvain, and the *reredos* is dated 1871. The point of any visit is to see the unusual *monuments* and in particular that to Richard Cornwall (d.1568). It opens out as a painted triptych signed by Melchior Salaboss and dated 1588, with three full-length figures above a panel painted with a figure in a shroud. Lady Caroline Rushout (d.1818) by Sir Richard Westmacott lies on a couch supported by two angels. Don't overlook the 6ft *brass* to Princess Elizabeth (d.1370), daughter of John of Gaunt.

CLAVERLEY. 5m E of Bridgenorth off A454. *All Saints.*
A large church built of red sandstone with a Norman base to the west tower, a Norman north aisle and a mid-C14 chancel. The rest is of all dates and styles. The point of a visit is to see the important wall *painting* on the upper north wall of the nave. This was done in c.1200 and only discovered in 1902 when the church was restored. At first sight it looks like the Battle of Hastings, originally with fifteen fully armoured knights, three of whom are falling from their horses, all very much in the style of the Bayeux Tapestry. In fact it is a common subject, the battle between the Virtues and Vices. Note the simple tub-shaped Norman *font*, the late Arts and Crafts communion rail of 1912 and the alabaster tomb to the Speaker of the House of Commons, Sir Robert Broke (d.1558), with his two wives and their seventeen children!

HALSTON. 4m NE of Oswestry off A495, behind Halston Hall. *Dedication unknown.*
If you enjoyed the other timber-framed church at Melverley then don't miss this chapel, it's a jewel. It is smaller than Melverley, with a Georgian brick west tower, and a half-timbered nave and chancel that may be c.1600. Enter by the tower west door and beneath the west gallery to discover an almost untouched interior with panelled walls, two-decker *pulpit* dated 1725, a small C17 *credence table*, facing *box pews, squire's pew*, a Royal Arms, and seven *hatchments*. A *helmet* and armorial *shirt* hang over the *Christening pew*. It is a chapel with everything, even *paintings* of Aaron and Moses, with a Creed board and Lord's Prayer behind the altar. Notice the animals carved on the spandrels of the roof and the magnificent brass nineteen

branched *chandelier* of 1725.

HEATH. 10m SW of Bridgnorth off B4368. *Dedication unknown.*
This is a small, lonely Norman chapel with nave and smaller chancel all built of pink sandstone, and rare because it is unaltered except for a C17 nave window. Enter by the south door, noting the C12 hinges and zigzag decoration, and discover the rugged interior; of the furnishings none is later than the C17. The roof could be C13 and the plaster walls have traces of paintings flaking badly. The *pulpit, readers' desk, squire's pew* and *box pews* are all no later than C17, and the plain tub-shaped *font* is Norman.

LANGLEY. 1¾m SSE of Acton Burnell off A49, 6m S of Shrewsbury. *Dedication unknown.*
Maintained by English Heritage. A small chapel in a lonely setting, built of stone with a bell-turret, and consisting only of a nave with chancel. Outside is the date 1564, and the roof is dated 1601. It could have been built at either time. The simple Puritan interior has furnishings contemporary with the building, except for the communion table which is a replacement of 1969; the original was stolen. A curiosity is the movable *pulpit.* The chancel, with its kneeling benches set Puritan fashion round three sides of the table, is floored with medieval tiles.

LLANYBLODWELL. 7m SW of Oswestry off B4396. *St Michael.*
An eccentric church rebuilt by an eccentric vicar, the Rev. John Parker, from 1845-60. Original features are the C15 south wall and

Llanyblodwell, St Michael. Rebuilt in 1845-60 by an eccentric vicar, the interior is a riot of colour and lettering.

north arcade, and a Norman south door. In form it has a nave and north aisle only. The rest of the building is Parker's from the wild south porch to the extraordinary spire with a convex curve. It stands free of the building like a campanile. The overwhelming impression is one of colour, blue, red and gold. Almost every surface has been covered with black lettering and painted stencil designs. Whatever one may think of Parker's achievement one has to agree that it is lively. He left the C15 screen alone, only repainting it. The coloured font is of c.1660. One leaves with some admiration for his self-confidence.

LONGNOR. 8m S of Shrewsbury off A49. *St Mary.*
A small stone church of c.1270 and really a private chapel for the nearby Hall. The nave and chancel are one unit with a charming wood belfry and an outside stair to a west gallery. Inside is unaltered C18: pulpit, box pews dated 1723 each having a single wooden *candle-holder, reader's desk, squire's* and *vicar's pews* with much original clear glass. Note the five Corbet *hatchments*, and the sundial on the south wall dated 1718.

LUDLOW. 25m S of Shrewsbury on A49. *St Laurence.*
The largest parish church in the county, originally collegiate, with a tall crossing tower, built in pink sandstone and mainly of the C15. Inside, note the good remnants of *screens* and the chancel stalls of 1447 with twenty-eight amusing carved *misericords*. There is also much *glass* of varying quality with good C19 glass by Thomas Williment and John Hardman, and some good Renaissance *tombs.*

LYDBURY NORTH. 15m NW of Ludlow on B4385. *St Michael.*
A large cruciform church, built at two Norman periods, with a C13 west tower, a C14 north transept and a C17 south transept. All was remarkably restored in 1901 by R.J. Micklethwaite, an Arts and Crafts architect. The south porch was rebuilt in 1901, when the room above the south transept was restored. The interior is bright with pink plastered nave walls, and above is a fine C15 roof discovered in 1901. Filling the north transept is a Roman Catholic chapel; it is unusual for an Anglican church to be used by both denominations. Note the delicate Arts and Crafts *light fittings.* In the *tympanum* above the restored screen are the Creed and Commandments in black lettering dated 1615. On the altar is a rare pair of wooden *candlesticks* of c.1640. The *box pews*, carved with dragons, and the *pulpit*, are of 1624. The Walcote chapel has *hatchments* of the Clive family. Clive of India (1725-74) bought nearby Walcote Hall in the 1760s and took over the chapel. In all, this is a very pleasing visit in beautiful border countryside.

MELVERLEY. 9m W of Shrewsbury off B4393. *St Peter.*

One of only two timber-framed churches in the county – the other is Halston – it stands suspended above the river Vyrnwy. Probably built in the C15 and restored in 1878 when the windows were inserted, it nevertheless retains its late-medieval charm. Small and low, looking like a Shropshire barn were it not for the bell-tower and church porch, it deserves a visit. Inside, nothing is straight. A huge roof truss comes low and is utilised for the simple screen with dado across the square nave; it looks like an untidy barn. In the entry skewed stairs lead from a medieval tiled floor to what may be the oldest west gallery in Britain, of 1588.

MINSTERLEY. 8m SW of Shrewsbury on A488. *Holy Trinity.*
Built of brick and stone in a rustic baroque style at an unusual date for Shropshire, 1689. Its grand west front with clock, topped by an elliptical pediment and crowned by a wooden belfry, is so exuberant as to carry a skull and crossbones. The rustic style is carried inside to the good quality wood fittings; the pews, unfortunately, are C19. On the west gallery hang six *maidens' garlands* dating from 1726 to 1794. A seventh garland is exhibited, and explained, in a glass case.

SHREWSBURY. 40m NW of Birmingham on A5. *St Chad*, Murivance.
An impressive town church built in yellow ashlar in the Greek Revival style by George Stuart in 1790-2. It is an unusual building; the west tower rises over the entance porch from a square base, becomes an octagon and finishes in a tall round cupola. Behind this is a circular nave. Entering is rather like the processional way in a large house: a circular vestibule leads into a circular space with a fine

Shrewbury, St Chad. A round church built in 1790-2 in the Greek Revival style.

staircase, before one enters the nave which is the third, and largest, circular space. Here, all is white with gilded ironwork and dark circular pews, alas cut down from their C18 height. Cast-iron Ionic columns carry a near circular gallery interrupted by a sanctuary arch supported on Corinthian columns. The reredos of 1923, the pulpit of c.1890, and east window of 1844, are out of step with the regularity of the Classical interior, nevertheless it is a church worth visiting. It is unfortunately closed on weekday afternoons.

St Mary, St Mary's Place.

In the care of the Redundant Churches Fund. Why the best medieval church in the city should be redundant is a mystery. It is a fine cruciform church, built in red sandstone, with a west tower and one of the tallest spires in England. Much Norman masonry is evident from an earlier church, particularly at the base of the tower, in the transepts and the south porch. Inside, the space is remarkable; the two aisles added in the early-C13 have magnificent arcading with stiff-leaf *capitals* supporting Norman masonry, and C15 clerestories. The roofs are of the same date but heavily repaired in 1894 after the spire fell. The carved *bosses* in the chancel roof are original but in the nave many are replacements although the musical angels are original. The fine *font* is C14 and the best feature in the church is the remarkably fine *glass*. Over the altar is a mid-C14 Jesse window from Old St Chad's, the best in the county; the remainder is good continental glass from many sources. Several *monuments* are worth noting: one to Admiral Benbow (d.1702) made in the 1840s, another to Col. Cureton (d.1848) by Sir Richard Westmacott, but particularly that to Cadman (d.1739) who, as his verse tells us, tried to fly from the tower across the Severn and failed!

TONG. 6m E of Telford on A41. *St Bartholomew.*

A collegiate church built in 1410 by Lady Isabella Pembruge in memory of her three husbands. The collegiate buildings were to the south of the church. It is impressive, built in red sandstone with a squat central tower and a south chapel of 1515. The interior is atmospheric with antiquity mainly due to the many excellent *tombs* which crowd the chancel and spill out into the nave. Note especially the good alabaster effigies. The Golden (south) chapel to the Vernons still retains traces of gold leaf in the vaults. The *pulpit* is dated 1629. Don't overlook the sixteen carved *misericords* in the chancel, all of c.1410. The *Royal Arms* of Coade Stone in the north aisle commemorates the Peace of Paris, 1814. There is good *glass* of 1900 by Charles Kempe in the east window, and an embroidered velvet *vestment* of c.1600. Note the figure of St James on the tomb of Sir Richard Vernon (d.1451) telling us that he made the pilgrimage to Compostela.

UPTON CRESSET. 4m W of Bridgnorth off A458. *St Michael.*
In the care of the Redundant Churches Fund. This small basically
Norman church, lying at the end of a track, is built of stone with a
charming wooden bell-turret and an unfortunate south chapel added
in the C19. The simple interior has a Norman chancel arch richly
decorated with zigzag motif and three orders of shafts. Notice the
brass dated 1640, unusual in that it is signed. The east window has
roundels of C16 Flemish *glass.*

Other Churches

BERWICK. 3m NW of Shrewsbury on B5067. *Dedication unknown.*
Built in 1672 as a chapel to Berwick House and remodelled in 1892,
with a west tower of c.1731. The west gallery, *pulpit*, and box pews
are all original. Note the two good monuments of 1814 and 1818 by
Sir Francis Chantrey.
CLUN. 5m N of Knighton on A488. *St George.*
Mainly Norman, over-restored and partly rebuilt by G.E. Street in
1877, with an oddity of a massive Norman west tower with pyramid
roof. There is a fine wooden *canopy* above the altar and a Jacobean
pulpit and *reredos* in the north aisle, and a good C15 roof.
LEEBOTWOOD. 9m S of Shrewsbury on A49. *St Mary.*
A medieval church of rendered stone, standing on a wooded hill,
with nave and chancel as one and a niggardly Georgian west tower.
Inside are box pews with *hat pegs*; some C17 panelling, with rustic
attempts at classical pilasters. The east window is of c.1845 and note
the fragments of wall painting on the north wall.
LINLEY. 3m NW of Bridgnorth on B4373. *St Leonard.*
An almost complete Norman church consisting of nave and chancel
with a hefty west tower. Both the south door and the chancel arch are
Norman and decorated with a simple zigzag design. The east window
is C19 and the tub-shaped *font* is Norman. Note the 'Green Man' in
the tympanum of the blocked north door.
MUCH WENLOCK. 6m NW of Bridgnorth on A458. *Holy
Trinity.*
A large church, mainly Norman with a C13 chancel and C12 addi-
tions. The west front, with an impressive portal of two orders and
zigzag ornament, is the best exterior feature. The door carries late-
C12 ironwork and the pulpit is Jacobean.
PEPLOW. 12m SE of Whitchurch on A442. *Chapel of the Epiphany.*
A simple vernacular-revival chapel built by Norman Shaw in 1879 in
one of his lively designs of half-timbering with brick nogging and a
sweeping roof. Inside, the chancel walls have imposing *murals* painted
in 1903, and the *screen* is a masterpiece.

Staffordshire

To the average traveller the county means the Potteries and the Black Country, but away from industry there are some treasures to be discovered in this mainly sandstone county.

There are no Saxon churches, but the Norman period is represented by St Mary, Tutbury, and St Chad at Stafford. Although both were extensively restored in the C19, the interiors are still satisfyingly Norman. The Gothic style is found throughout the county but the best is the C14 St Editha at Tamworth. Alabaster carving at Burton-on-Trent flourished until the end of the C17 and consequently there are many finely detailed tombs, and the C14 and C15 screens at St Andrew, Clifton Campville, are well worth seeing. There is little in the way of brasses and few misericords.

Prosperity came to the county with the Industrial Revolution and consequently the C19 saw the rebuilding of old churches and building of new. The most ambitious of almost any church is A.W.N. Pugin's St Giles at Cheadle, built regardless of cost by the 16th Earl of Shrewsbury, where every inch of its amazing interior is covered with a rainbow palette of colour.

CHEADLE. 5m E of Longton on A521. *St Giles.*
This Roman Catholic church with a 200ft spire built in 1841-6 was A.W.N. Pugin's masterpiece, and is well worth a long detour. The almost

Cheadle, St Giles. The interior is Pugin's masterpiece of 1841-6.

unlimited wealth of the 16th Earl of Shrewsbury ensured a richness of decoration unequalled by any other Gothic Revival church. Built in red sandstone in the Gothic style of c.1300 the interior is far more lavish than any parish church of that time could ever have been. The interior is suitably and religiously dim, so muting the riot of colour covering every foot and designed throughout by Pugin. The south aisle is basically red and the north aisle blue, signifying Our Lord and the Virgin Mary respectively. Throughout, Minton and Wedgewood tiles cover the floors, and yellow and blue glazed tiles form a 4ft dado on every wall. Above the chancel arch is a Last Judgement, leading the eye to the brilliantly colourful chancel beyond Pugin's rood and screen. His too are the reredos, pulpit and font. The *glass* is entirely by William Wailes.

CHECKLEY. 5m NW of Uttoxeter on A522. *St Mary & All Saints.* A church of all dates: the tower begins as Norman, rises to c.1320 in the middle, and finishes as C15. The clerestory windows and the north and south aisle windows are all C17, and the chancel late-C13 with a magnificent east *window.* Enter by the south doorway of c.1300 and note the Norman *font* with basic decoration including a donkey and a lamb in a vat. Above, the roofs are all C17. Sir Ninian Comper was responsible for the south chapel parclose screen of 1922. The stalls are of c.1535 and there is some good late-C14 *glass* in need of attention in the north-east and south-east windows, which includes the Martyrdom of St Thomas à Becket showing Henry II being scourged at the tomb. In the churchyard near the south door are the remains of three Saxon crosses.

CHEDDLETON. 7m NE of Stoke-on-Trent on A520. *St Edward.* The C13-C15 church would pass with little comment were it not for a restoration by Giles Gilbert Scott in 1863-4 which used much very early work by William Morris. Morris's friend Thomas Wardle, a dyer, was churchwarden here at the time. There is a great deal of *glass* of 1864-9 by Morris, eight beautiful little figures of 1864 by Ford Madox Brown in the chancel, and Edward Burne-Jones designed the *glass* in the west end of the south aisle as well as three large angels, also in the south aisle. The amazing brass eagle *lectern* is C15 Flemish. The painted chancel roof is probably Scott's.

CLIFTON CAMPVILLE. 8m E of Lichfield off B5493. *St Andrew.* This is possibly the best medieval church in the county and certainly it has one of the finest steeples. Mostly built c.1300-50, it is one of the few churches in Britain to have a garderobe, the medieval toilet, in its north-east annex, not for an incontinent congregation, but part of the living accommodation for a priest. The stalls have seven early-C14 *misericords* and, on a C14 bench-end, a carved angel in feathered tights. In the south aisle in a large semi-circular recess is a mid-C14 *painting* of Christ seated in Glory. In the south chapel are very fine and early *screens* of c.1300. Michael Rysbrack was responsible for two *monuments*, of 1721 and 1724, to the Pye family, and Sir Richard Westmacott for that of Charles Watkins (d.1813).

ELFORD. 5m E of Lichfield off A513. *St Peter.*
The tower is dated 1598, but the rest is of 1848-9 by Anthony Salvin, except for the south chapel and aisle, rebuilt by G.E. Street in 1869-70. The church turns its best side towards Elford Hall. The only reason for a visit is for the surprising monuments: a child effigy to John Stanley, c.1460, killed by a tennis ball; a knight of c.1370 in full armour; Sir Thomas Arderne (d.1391) and his wife; the best of them is that to Sir William Smythe (d.1525) and his two wives. Do not overlook the roof by Salvin, with heraldic corbels, gilded capitals, and the blue and red lettering round the arches.

INGESTRE. 5m E of Stafford off A51. *St Mary.*
The church may or may not be by Christopher Wren; if not him then by someone in his office. The attribution comes from a drawing

Ingestre, St Mary. Possibly designed by Wren in 1676.

for a never-built tower lantern. Built in 1676 as a chapel for the Hall, the drab, square, stone exterior, with an over-large west tower, does not prepare one for the interior. Quality is the keynote throughout. Enter through the west door beneath the tower and one might be in a London church. The nave has a flat ceiling with splendid stucco decoration and is divided from the aisles by four-bay arcades supported on clusters of four Tuscan columns. A magnificent carved rood *screen* is crowned by a huge *Royal Arms* of Charles II, and beyond is a barrel-vaulted chancel with a highly decorated plaster ceiling. The *reredos*, composed of figures of the Annunciation inserted in 1871, has a garland that is probably original. Two large angels by Thomas Willement are in a window in the north wall of the chancel. A north *window* is by Morris and Co of 1897, immediately after Morris's death, who, when his firm became established, never put his glass in old churches. The chancel is packed with *monuments* to Chetwyns and to the Talbots, Earls of Shrewsbury. Later interments over-spilled into the aisles. Notice a touching monument to Lady V.S. Talbot who died at Naples in 1857. This is a church not to be missed and very well worth a detour.

MAVESYN RIDWARE. 12m SE of Stafford off B5014. *St Nicholas.*
A large brick Gothic nave of 1782 is attached to a C15 west tower and an earlier north aisle. This sounds uninteresting, but the surprise is in the interior because here is an extreme of early Romanticism: the Mayvesyn Chapel. Portrait family tombs in alabaster line the walls, with three reliefs showing battles fought by the family. In the centre stands the tomb-chest of Sir Robert Mayvesyn (d.1403), killed at the battle of Shrewsbury; there are also a *helmet, gauntlets* and *shield* hanging in the chapel. It looks authentically ancient. In fact all this is bogus, and dates from 1785-1812 when it was fashionable to add antique glory to family ancestry. Genuine enough are the Norman *font,* the C15 and C16 tombs of the Cardon family, and two C13 knights lying in separate recesses. Unfortunately, the plaster has been scraped from the walls exposing re-used stonework never intended to be seen.

MAYFIELD. 1m SW of Ashbourne off A52. *St John Baptist.*
A part Norman church with a west tower dated 1515 and C14 chancel. Enter by the c.1500 south door porch: the door is c.1500 in a late-Norman doorway, the south arcade is also Norman. The north arcade and aisle were rebuilt in 1854. Unusually the *benches,* dated 1630 and 1633, are of the same date as the *pulpit* and chancel panelling. The communion rail is of c.1650. Note the font dated 1614 and the two good C18 memorials.

RUSHTON SPENCER. 5m NW of Leek on A523. *St Lawrence.*
This small church, marooned in fields, is a rarity that must once have

been common; beneath the stonework it is a timber-framed building. The exterior is C17 and early-C18, with a quaint weatherboarded, saddleback bell-turret. The east window is dated 1690 and the south door 1713, but otherwise the building appears to be early C17. Inside, the church is still lit by oil lamps. The north aisle is divided from the nave by timber posts of c.1200; this was previously an outer wall. The Gothic *roof* is the little church's glory; two original trusses with king-posts survive, and Georgian texts are painted across the tie-beams. The west gallery is supported on the westernmost truss. Note the Jacobean *pulpit*, the squire's pew, and the *hatchments*.

STAFFORD. 12m S of Stoke-on-Trent on A34. *St Chad*, Greengate Street.
In 1650 the church was said to be ruinous. Nevertheless, restoration began in 1854 and was completed by Sir G. G. Scott in 1875. The west front is entirely by Scott, as are the aisle walls, the north transept is of 1886 and the crossing is C15. However, the nave with its drum piers and clerestory is impressively and genuinely Norman, and the chancel arch is splendidly rich in Norman decoration. On the top of the north-east pier of the tower is a very rare Latin *dedication* to the builder: 'He who founded me is called Orme'. The heavily restored chancel retains some excellent blind *arcading* on the north and south walls. Inevitably, for so huge a restoration, the fittings are almost all of the 1880s. Do not be taken in by the seemingly Norman font, it is of 1856! A magnificent *reredos* of 1910 is by Sir Walter Tapper and the Rood was presented in 1922.

St Mary,
This was the first restoration undertaken by Sir George Gilbert Scott in 1840-4. Today, with better ideas of preservation rather than restoration, we should say that Scott rebuilt the church, although, when he started work, two important parts of the building had collapsed. The sizable nave, covered by a Tudor roof, is c.1200 with C15 clerestory windows and arcades of the early-C13; the capitals are by Scott. The crossing arches were rebuilt by Scott, as were the south transept and the chancel south aisle, but the north transept of c.1340 remained untouched and the finest part of the building. A jewel of the fittings is the Norman *font* of Mediterranean inspiration, c.1148. Two inscriptions read 'You carry divine water from Jerusalem, giving me beauty and grace'; and the sensible warning 'It is discreet to run from lions'. In the north aisle a C19 memorial bust reminds us that Isaac Walton was baptised here in 1593. In the north transept are two good alabaster tomb *figures* of Sir Edward Aston (d.1568) and his wife. There is a noteworthy organ by John Grieb of 1789-90. Some fragments of medieval glass are in the north aisle, and the west window there was designed by A.W.N. Pugin in 1846.

TAMWORTH. 14m NE of Birmingham on A453. *St Editha.*
The church suffered a serious fire in 1345 and most of what we see is
of the mid-C14 rebuilding, although parts of the old structure
survive. The tower originally stood over the crossing, supported on
two surviving Norman arches. The building suffered no less than
three restorations in the C19, beginning with Sir G.G. Scott in the
1850s. Enter through the tower doorway and pass the impressive
Baroque, Ferrers *monument* of 1680 designed, but not carved, by
Grinling Gibbons. A benefit from the C19 restorations is the early
Morris & Co *glass* of the 1870s designed by Edward Burne-Jones
and Ford Madox Brown in the chancel clerestory and the north
chapel. Both the font and reredos of the 1850s are by Scott, but the
elegant, and altered, wrought-iron screen is C18. The tower has a
very unusual double spiral stair rising in opposite directions and
never meeting. If this is locked ask for the key!

TUTBURY. 5m NW of Burton on A50. *St Mary.*
Once part of a Benedictine priory founded in 1080. This accounts
for the splendour of the west front with a very rich doorway,
comprising five arches of beakheads, of which the outer arch has the
first use of alabaster in England, and a west window of c.1160. The
nave and arcades are early C12 while the north aisle is 1820 and the
south aisle C15. Note the *boar hunt* on the south door lintel. G. E.
Street, never one to resist putting back what had vanished, put in
the present apse and crossing tower in 1866. This may look accept-
able from outside but the
apse and chancel inside
are an unhappy pastiche
when compared with the
magnificence of the
Norman nave. The rere-
dos, pulpit, stalls and
font are all Street's.

Tutbury, St Mary.
The glorious west front
of a Benedictine priory
founded in 1080.

Other Churches

ALREWAS. 4m NE of Lichfield on A38. *All Saints.*
A church of all dates with two re-set Norman doorways, and a C13 chancel. Very good C19 *glass* by Charles Kempe and Henry Haliday of 1877 – his best. Decayed C15 wall painting in chancel; *reredos* by Basil Champneys (1893), pulpit dated 1639.

ALSTONEFIELD. 4M E of Leek off A523. *St Peter.*
Another church of all dates, built in sandstone and limestone. Norman south door and chancel arch; Jacobean woodwork and remarkable *pulpit* dated 1637; *box pews,* Cotton *family pew* painted green; and small Anglo-Saxon sculptures.

BURTON-UPON-TRENT. 12m SW of Derby on A38. *St Chad,* Hunter Street.
The best building in the town and G.F. Bodley's last church. Begun 1910 at the expense of Lord Burton in style of c.1300. A serene interior.

Warwickshire

with West Midlands

Sandstone is the principal building material here, ranging from an unattractive dark red to a buff colour. Unfortunately, it weathers badly. In the south-east, where Warwickshire joins Oxfordshire and the Cotswolds, is found the only good limestone. For a county long famed for its trees there is, disappointingly, nothing special in the way of roofs.

Pre-Conquest architecture is represented by the late-Saxon central tower at St Peter, Wootton Wawen, and at St Gregory, Treddington, by the nave and the remains of a wooden west gallery. St John Baptist, Berkeswell, and St Mary, Stoneleigh, are the most complete of Warwickshire's Norman churches, with smaller examples at Ryton-on-Dunsmore, Corley and Wyken. At Merevale the Cistercian abbey has left us remnants of a thirteenth-century church. St Alphege at Solihull is almost completely early-fourteenth century, and SS John, Lawrence & Anne at Knowle is early-fifteenth century. St Mary, Warwick, was rebuilt in c.1700 in early Gothic-Revival style, with intricate vaulting patterns.

For an industrial county the nineteenth century inevitably saw a great deal of building, most of it instantly forgettable. Among the best are St Peter at Hampton Lucy, built 1822-6, and Holy Trinity, Rugby, built by Sir George Gilbert Scott in 1852-4. Certainly not in the same class, but a curiosity, is All Saints, Leamington Spa, begun in 1843 by Dr John Craig, a vicar obsessed with building his own church, and mainly designed by him. For a remarkable interior of c.1900 with overtones of the Arts and Crafts there is St Agatha at Sparkbrook.

For the sake of simplicity the pre-1973 boundary of Warwickshire has been used to include Birmingham, a city which is now in what is called West Midlands.

ARBURY HALL. 3m SW of Nuneaton off B4102. *Chapel.*
This sumptuous Baroque chapel, completed in c.1678, was mercifully not Gothicised by Sir Roger Newdigate in the late C18 when the house was completely transformed into a Gothic fantasy. An amazing plaster *ceiling* displaying fruit, foliage and flowers in swags and sways was completed in 1678 by Edward Martin, who had worked for Sir Christopher Wren. The *reredos* is C15 Flemish and was brought back by Sir Roger while on a Grand Tour. On either side are Commandment boards dated 1631. Note the door lock of c.1680.

ASTLEY. 4m SW of Nuneaton off B4102. *St Mary the Virgin.*
This large aisleless church is only the chancel of a vast collegiate church built in 1342. The nave and central tower had already gone when Sir Richard Chamberlain reinstated the building as a parish church in 1607; the west tower and chancel, in a convincing C15 style, are his. Remaining from the original church are the remarkable stalls with eighteen *misericords* of the 1340s. The backs of the stalls are painted with the Apostles and the Prophets and each carries a scroll, re-worded in 1624. Of the same date are the Commandments in the chancel and the Lord's Prayer and Creed, with other biblical texts painted on the walls. The finely carved pulpit and lectern are late C17, and don't overlook the fine alabaster figures under the tower.

BERKSWELL. 4m E of Solihull off A452. *St John Baptist.*
Unlike many villages bearing the word 'well', where the water supply has long since dried up, there is an active well to the south-east of the

Berkswell, St John.
A Stumpy late-C13 tower is attached to a part-Norman nave and a Norman chancel.

church; a 16ft square cistern restored in 1851. The church is the most interesting in the county for its Norman chancel and two Norman crypts. The square, stumpy west tower is late C13 and the nave part Norman and part c.1300. One enters beneath a charming C16 half-timbered, two-storied porch and by a Norman south door. Inside, the floor rises to the east to accommodate the crypts beneath. A surprise is the rare octagonal west crypt of the late C12 beneath the east end of the nave. The east crypt beneath the chancel was used as a chapel in the C14 and has *paintings* at the east end where the altar would have been. Both crypts have strong rib-vaults carried on short wall-shafts. Back on ground level, note the remaining C18 *box pews* and the two excellent C18 *monuments;* one is by Sir Richard Westmacott (1775-1856) to twenty-nine-year-old Mrs Wilmot (d.1818).

BIRMINGHAM. 120m NW of London on M1. *St Paul,* St Paul's Square.

Built of stone in 1777-9 to accommodate worshippers in the Newhall Estate, it is rectangular with a squared apse and west tower. Inside, most of the furnishings are contemporary. The east window, by Francis Eginton from designs by Benjamin West, is a very good example of C18 *glass.*

St Agatha, Stratford Road, Sparkbrook.

Built of brick with stone dressings in 1901, in Gothic style, and transformed by the Arts and Crafts into one of the most satisfying and original churches of its period in Britain. Tympana depict the life of St Agatha, including the final scene of her burning. Inside, cream facing brick gives brightness to the vast nave; lozenge shaped piers support a clerestory and steeply pitched, painted, timber roof. The east end was rebuilt in 1959 after a serious arson attack. Note the particularly fine slate *altar* made in 1964. The east window is by Leonard Evetts, 1961.

BURTON DASSETT. 7m NW of Banbury off A41. *All Saints.*

Basically a Norman church built of Hornton limestone. Two Norman doorways lead into the Norman nave, with a C13 north aisle, north transept, and chancel of c.1300, all sensitively restored in 1890. The interior is a memorable spatial experience. The C13 capitals of the arcade are carved with foliage, and animals following each other: some are upside down! Note the abundance of C14 tiles, and the recently discovered C14 *wall paintings* in the nave and chancel.

CASTLE BROMWICH. 5m NE of Birmingham centre, exit 5 on M6. *SS Mary & Margaret.*

Built entirely of brick in 1726-31 in a Classical provincial style, and extraordinarily, encasing an older timber church which was only discovered during restorations in 1891-2. The old roof is hidden above the plaster ceiling. Thankfully, the restoration left the early-C18 *box pews*, *squire's pew*, *vicar's pew*, three-decker *pulpit* and west *gallery* untouched.

COMPTON WYNYATES. 8m W of Banbury off B4035. *Chapel.*
A chapel standing to the north of the house and unusually built c.1665 using fragments from an earlier church wrecked in the Civil War, with an earlier tower. It is also unusual in having twin naves with two east windows. Fragments of the painted ceilings show that they once depicted night in one aisle and day in the other. *Box pews* and *font* are of c.1665. Monuments from the earlier church are sadly mutilated. Note the funeral *gauntlets*, *dagger* and *spurs* of the 1st Earl of Northampton (d.1630) and the *banner* and *helmet* on the south wall brought from St George's Garter Chapel, Windsor. A sword belonging to Lord Spencer Compton, killed at Ypres in 1915, lies on a shelf.

GREAT PACKINGTON. 8m W of Coventry off A45. *St James.*
This is remarkable in that it does not look like either a church or anything else, and it must be the most extraordinary place of worship in Britain. Built of brick, with stone dressings, by Joseph Bonimi (1739-1808), in 1789-90 for the 4th Earl of Aylesford. If the architect had built nothing else he deserves to be remembered for this. It is square with four domed corner turrets joined by large broken pediments over high lunette windows and entirely Classical with Greek detail. Inside, the church is vaulted throughout and the fittings are justifiably extravagant. The *altarpiece* has a central *painting* of an Ascension, with 'IHS' written by angels in the sky, by J.F. Rigaud (1742-1810), an Italian painter who is buried in the churchyard. It is surrounded by marble columns and pediment. For an Anglican church the iconography is surprisingly Jesuit. All this stands behind a marble communion rail. The pulpit is of marble and far in advance of its time; it could be of the 1850s. The organ of c.1750 was reputedly used by Handel and came from Gopsall Hall, Leicestershire.

HONILEY. 5m NW of Warwick off A4177. *St John Baptist.*
A very Baroque church, built in 1723 of white limestone, consisting of an audacious west tower, crowned by a short spire, with nave and apse. Two marble pilasters in the apse support nothing! The original furnishings of *box pews*, west *gallery*, supported on marble columns, *pulpit* and *reredos*, remain almost untouched.

KNOWLE. 1m SE of Solihull on A4141. *St John Baptist.*
Although built in a piecemeal fashion over twenty years from 1396 it is all satisfyingly in the early-Perpendicular style. A chapel was founded here in 1396; added to in 1412, it became collegiate in 1416, when further additions were made. Inside, the church seems

unusually long due to the lack of any chancel arch. A curiosity is the canted east bay of the chancel with a processional subway blocked in the 1740s. This leaves the sedilia and piscina placed high and dry in the wall. The stalls have eleven early-C15 *misericords*, and by the pulpit is a small late-C17 *hourglass*. The fine and elaborate *screen* is contemporary with the church and in the north chapel are some fine ceiling *bosses*. Before leaving, notice the two dug-out chests, impossible to date, but obviously very early.

RUGBY. 11m E of Coventry on A428. *School Chapel.*
Built 1867-72 by William Butterfield this is an amazing high-Victorian, Gothic confection in polychrome brick and stone, well buttressed, apsed and gargoyled, with a monumental crossing tower. The large, high interior effectively continues the decorative polychrome patterns, and high in the hammer-beam roof over the nave the tie-beams are painted in black and white. The central space made by the transepts allows the pews to be inward facing. Above the apse is a mosaic of 1883 by Antonio Salviati of Venice. There are many memorials to old boys and to three past headmasters: the famous Dr Thomas Arnold (d.1842), and his predecessors, Dr James (d.1824), and Dr Wool (d.1829) by Richard Westmacott Jnr. Some of the glass is C16 Flemish, from Aerschott near Louvain, cleverly copied by Thomas Willement in the north transept. There is Morris & Co glass of 1902 in the south aisle and in the west window, designed by H. Dearle.

STRATFORD-UPON-AVON. 8m SW of Warwick on A46. *Holy Trinity.*
Although the overwhelming reason for the majority to visit this church is to see Shakespeare's tomb (d.1616) in the chancel, the building has other attractions. Dating from the early-C13 to the late-C18 it has some worthy architecture. Everything west from the crossing is after the C14, and the wide nave has the peculiarity of not having the same axis as the C15 chancel. The stalls have twenty-six late-C15 *misericords* that are well worth one's time, and the C15 Clopton Chapel has a magnificent *monument* to the Countess of Totnes (d.1635) by Edward Marshall who became master mason to Charles II. The monument carries some realistic guns and powder kegs referring to the Earl who was Master in Ordnance to James I. Note the two *sword rests*: one is C18, the other was made in 1920 in the C18 style. The church was restored in 1888-92 and again in 1898.

WOOTTON WAWEN. 5m NW of Stratford on A3400. *St Peter.*
The church boasts a tower with the only Saxon work in the county. It has the appearance of having grown around the central tower, which is exactly what happened. The upper stage of the tower is C15, the

nave is C12 and south aisle C13, while the large Lady Chapel is of c.1330, and the chancel may be C12 with C13 features. There are traces of Norman work and a Norman window in the north wall. Beneath the four arches of the tower is an unaltered Saxon *sanctuary.* The Lady Chapel has traces of C13 wall *painting* of small red roses, probably once part of an over-all pattern. It contains some impressive *monuments*, among them the fully armoured Sir Francis Smith (d.1605), and the poet William Somerville (d.1742) who composed his own epitaph. Note the C14 wooden *chest,* the two complete C15 parclose *screens,* the four *hatchments,* the Georgian *Royal Arms* over the south door, and the 1958 Yorke memorial window by Margaret Traherne.

Other Churches

HAMPTON LUCY. 3m E of Stratford off B4086. *St Peter ad Vincula.*
An ambitious church built 1822-6 and one of the grandest C14 Gothic revival churches of the C19. The ornate apse is of 1856 by Sir G.G. Scott. A plaster vaulted interior has an 1837 east *window* by T. Willement.

RUGBY. 11m E of Coventry on A428. *Holy Trinity.*
Built of grey stone in 1852-4 by Sir George Gilbert Scott at a cost of only £7,250 – good value for such a vast church. The style is C13 Gothic, with a crossing tower. The glass of 1892 is by C.E. Kempe.

SPARKBROOK. 1m SE of Birmingham centre off A34. *St Agatha.*
Built in 1899-1901 by W.H. Bidlake, at the best time of the Arts & Crafts, in a C15 Gothic-Revival style of the very foremost quality, in brick with stone dressings and rated as one of the best examples of its time. Unfortunately, almost all of the original furnishings have been destroyed.

STONELEIGH. 5m NE of Warwick on B4113. *St Mary.*
A Norman church in red sandstone with C14 south arcade and C18 south chapel. The *font* is Norman, the box pews, pulpit, organ and west gallery all early-C19. Note the early-C19 cast-iron *Royal Arms.*

TREDDINGTON. 6m SE of Stratford on A34. *St Gregory.*
Fundamentally a Saxon church, with late-C12 Norman alterations and C14 chancel. There are: a good C15 *screen* on a stone base, a low and rustic communion *table,* and a superb Jacobean *pulpit.*

NORTHERN ENGLAND

Cumbria

This is another county owing its existence to the bureaucratic reorganisation of 1975. It is probably more of a complete county than any of the others created at the same time because the two former counties it comprises, Westmorland and Cumberland, shared many common features. Even Pevsner's *Buildings of England* published both old counties together in one volume.

Limestone and pink and red sandstones are the principal building materials. The Shap quarries are famous for good quality building stone useful for ornamental detail. The red and pink sandstones are the characteristic Lakeland building materials. Granite and slate are used in areas where limestone and sandstone are lacking. Westmorland stone is famous for roofing and is used in large and small slabs of split stone.

The area was first civilised by monastic houses. However, they suffered cruelly from Danish raids and consequently there are only a few Saxon artifacts rescued from the first monastic foundations. Normans re-established the ruined monasteries and built more of their own, but these too were overrun by invading Scots. St Mary, Kirkby Lonsdale, with its Norman west end and tower base, represents the Norman interest here, together with the tiny Norman chapel at Ireby. The C12 and C13 centuries are firmer ground and St Mary, Lanercost, and SS Mary & Bega, St Bees, represent monastic examples of the apotheosis of Cumberland's ecclesiastical architecture. Wool wealth provided the impetus for late-medieval church expansion and the five aisles of Holy Trinity, Kendal, along with Kirkby Lonsdale's extra north aisle, are examples of this trend. All Saints, Boltongate, rebuilt in the late-C16 by the Earl of Westmorland, is the most exciting church in the county, possessing a unique stone tunnel-vaulted nave.

Lady Anne Clifford (1590-1676) was responsible for rescuing and rebuilding many churches; All Saints, Appleby, and St Ninian and St

NORTHERN ENGLAND

Berwick
upon Tweed

Alnwick
Amble

NORTHUMBERLAND

Ashington
Morpeth
Bedlington — Blyth

Whitley Bay
Newcastle upon Tyne — South Shields
Hexham — Gateshead — **TYNE & WEAR**
Sunderland

Carlisle
Consett — Stanley — Seaham

Peterlee
Maryport — Durham
Cockermouth — **DURHAM** — Tow Law — Hartlepool
Workington — Penrith — Bishop Auckland — Aycliffe — Stockton — Redcar
Keswick — Barnard — on Tees — Middlesborough
Whitehaven — **CUMBRIA** — Appleby — Castle — Darlington — **CLEVELAND** — Whitby

Ambleside

Windermere — Richmond

Kendal — Northallerton — Scalby — Scarborough
Ulverston — Filey

NORTH YORKSHIRE

Barrow in — Malton — Bridlington
Furness — Morecambe

Lancaster — Harrogate — Knaresborough — Great Driffield
Fleetwood — Skipton — Ilkley — York — **HUMBERSIDE** — Hornsea

Blackpool — **LANCASHIRE** — Keighley — Beverley
Lytham — Preston — Burnley — Bradford — Leeds — Selby — Kingston upon Hull — Withernsea
St Anne's — Blackburn — Halifax — **WEST** — Hedon
Southport — Rawtenstall — **YORKSHIRE**
Chorley — Wakefield — Pontefract
Formby — Ormskirk — Rochdale — Huddersfield — **SOUTH** — Scunthorpe — Grimsby
MERSEYSIDE — St Helens — Bolton — **GREATER** — Barnsley — **YORKSHIRE** — Cleethorpes
Wallasey — Wigan — **MANCHESTER** — Doncaster
Liverpool — Manchester — Rotherham
Birkenhead — Stockport
Sheffield

Wilfred at Brougham are due to her benefactions. Her furnishings of the latter two survive. The earliest pulpit (1616) is at St Mary, Kirkby Lonsdale. The C18 is here represented by St James, Whitehaven, which has the finest Georgian interior in the county.

Sarah Losh, daughter of John Losh, an industrialist, though unusually of a landed county family, built the touchingly unique small church of St Mary at Wreay, consecrated in 1842, in memory of her sister. It is like no other in Britain and should be seen without fail by anyone visiting the county. St Martin, Brampton, Philip Webb's only church, built in the 1870s, glowing with Morris & Co glass designed by Burne-Jones in a style forecasting the coming of Art Nouveau is a certain visit for those dedicated to the Arts and Crafts; and there is more, slightly later, Morris & Co, glass by Burne-Jones at St Mary, Lanercost. Finally, for those who enjoy a puzzle, St Wilfred's Chapel at Brougham is filled with continental furnishings collected by Lord Brougham in the 1840s, though exactly what there are and which piece came from where, can never be satisfactorily answered.

APPLEBY. 12m SE of Penrith off A66. *St Lawrence.*

A large church in pink sandstone with a stumpy west tower. All that remains of a Norman church is the lower stage of the tower. Burnt by the Scots in 1174 and in 1388, it was successively repaired and rebuilt. In 1645 Lady Anne Clifford rebuilt the chancel and the whole was restored in 1861-2 when the aisle windows were inserted. Inside, the aisle arcades are C14, the plaster ceiling is early-C19, and a C15 chantry chapel was incorporated into the south aisle in the C17. In the nave west end is what is claimed to be the second oldest

Appleby, St Lawrence. One of the churches restored in 1645 by Lady Anne Clifford.

working *organ* in Britain. Originally in Carlisle Cathedral where it was installed in the mid-C17 it was brought here in 1683. The case is c.1542 and the base is 1836, but the rest is of 1684. Notice the C18 *sword rest*, the *Royal Arms* of 1660, and the C15 carved screens behind the choir stalls. Two important *monuments* are in the north chapel: one to the Countess of Cumberland (d.1617), the mother of Lady Anne Clifford, and the other to Lady Anne herself (d.1676).

BOLTONGATE. 10m NE of Cockermouth on B5299. *All Saints.*
This must be the most exciting small church in Cumbria. Replacing a Norman church, it was built in sandstone rubble by the Earl of Westmorland in the late-C15, and is distinguished by its stone vaulted *roof.* The interior is dominated by a steeply pointed stone tunnel-vault over the aisleless nave and repeated in the small transepts which were once chapels. Corbels in the west wall carry capitals from the Norman church. The glass is all C19 with the lower west window attributed to Thomas Willement.

BRAMPTON. 9m NE of Carlisle on A69. *St Martin.*
Built in red sandstone in 1874-5, in the C12-C14 Gothic style, at the expense of the 9th Earl of Carlisle by the Arts and Crafts architect, Philip Webb, and his only church. Due to shortage of money the tower was not finished until 1906. Webb was a close friend of William Morris, and it is no surprise to find that all fourteen *windows*, glowing with colour, are by Morris & Co, designed by Burne-Jones. The east window, showing the Good Shepherd, includes a Pelican in her Piety, a forerunner of the Art Nouveau style.

BROUGHAM. 1m SE of Penrith off A66. *St Ninian.* Follow Right of Way signpost on the left.
In the care of the Redundant Churches Fund. The long, low, stone-built church overlooks a bend in the river Eamont and was completely rebuilt in 1660 in the Gothic style by Lady Anne Clifford. Nave and chancel are in one and, apart from the 1841 porch, all is C17. The interior is unaltered: *pulpit, font, screen, benches* and *family pews* are all of the 1660s. Note the fine *roof,* the *poor box* dated 1663 and the three *hatchments..* A grave slab in the chancel is said to mark the grave of Odard and Gilbert de Burgham (d.c.1200) *St Wilfred Chapel.* SW of the castle.
Another restoration by Lady Anne Clifford, of 1658, but in direct contrast to St Ninian. It was unsympathetically restored in the 1840s by Lord Brougham who altered the windows and fitted the west rose window. He also filled the church with high-quality carved *wood-work* from the Continent. However, the *font* bowl is 1660s and the pulpit is embellished with pieces of 1600s woodwork. The *stalls* are undeniably French, but made-up, and the splendid medieval-style *lectern* is mid-C19. The *reredos* of gilded oak includes Flemish and

German pieces of the C15. The discerning can enjoy themselves here picking out what is what.

CARTMEL. 10m SW of Kendal on B5277. *St Mary, Priory Church.* A priory of Augustinian Canons was founded here in c.1190 and from the beginning there was provision for a local parish church in the south transept. Remaining from the C12 is the north wall of the nave, the transepts, and chancel. The nave is mainly C14. Left ruined after the Reformation it was restored in c.1620, and again in 1859-70 by the 7th Duke of Devonshire. Inside, the roofs and seating of the nave are all of 1870, the chancel roof and screen are c.1620, and the choir stalls (the backs are c.1620) with twenty-six carved *misericords* are of c.1440. Some C15 *glass* is preserved in the east window and there is a mid-C14 glass *Tree of Jesse* in the south choir aisle. The Harrington tomb of c.1350, with some original *painting* on its ceiling, is claimed to be the best of its date in Britain.

GRASMERE. 9m NW of Windermere on A591. *St Oswald.* A difficult church to date because the evidence is covered with pebbledash rendering. The battlemented west tower, however, is medieval, and the nave is possibly c.1300. The astonishing and unique single span *roof,* covering aisle and nave, gives an amazing impression of space to the white painted interior. When the north

Grasmere, St Oswald. Although difficult to date, the tower is medieval. Wordsworth is buried in the churchyard.

aisle was built in 1652 the old north wall had large openings punched through, and in the C17 the wide-span roof was built, supported by an upper arcade built on top of the old north wall. Overhead is a fascinating and complex lattice of beams and posts. Note the *poor box* dated 1648, the *hatchments*, and the monument to the poet William Wordsworth (d.1850) by Thomas Woolner. To the east of the church Wordsworth is buried with Dorothy his sister and his wife Mary

GREYSTOKE. 4m W of Penrith on B5288. *St Andrew.*
A C13 church consisting of nave, aisles, and chancel was made collegiate in 1382. From an inscription it is clear the chancel was repaired in 1645 by the Earl of Arundel. The broad west tower is C14, but said to have been wholly rebuilt in 1848 when the church was restored. There are twenty late-C14 and early-C15 carved *misericords* dating from its collegiate time. Note the Flemish inspired carving of the stalls. The east window is of C16 *glass* reassembled in 1848. In the north aisle is C19 glass by C.E. Kempe.

KENDAL. 30m S of Penrith on A6. *Holy Trinity.*
This is a stone-built church that grew with the expanding town. The nave and west tower are mid-C15 to early-C16; to this were added no less than five aisles, three on the north and two on the south. All was drastically restored in 1850. Inside is a forest of pillars, supporting four arcades, giving constantly changing vistas. A black marble font is late-C15, and there are some good *monuments* in the Bellingham Chapel, a late-C13 coffin-lid, two C16 brasses, and a tablet of 1787 by John Flaxman. Against the west wall is a memorial to George Romney (1734-1802) the painter, who was born and died at Kendal, but buried at Dalton-in-Furness.

KIRKBY LONSDALE. 12m NE of Lancaster on A65. *St Mary.*
By its exterior this Norman church gives the impression of being later than it is. The lower stages of the west tower are Norman with a magnificent *west door.* The west end is also Norman, as can be seen by the sturdy Norman pillars of the arcading, and the chancel is C13. The interior is marked by having aisles and a C16 north outer aisle. The six-sided *pulpit* dated 1619 is part of an original three-decker cut down in extensive restoration of 1866. Note the sanctuary chair of 1629 and cupboard made from the vicar's pew.

LANERCOST. 3m NE of Brampton off A69. *St Mary Priory Church.*
Of the Augustinian priory founded in 1169 by Robert de Vallibus (de Vaux) little survives. The present church was the nave, and the east wall marks the old transepts and crossing. The base of the south wall is c.1200 and the rest c.1250. After the Dissolution the church

had a mixed history. First it was a residence, when the north aisle was the parish church, and it was only reunited with its nave in 1740. The west front is impressive with a fine mid-C13 *statue* of St Mary in the gable niche. Inside, the aisle arcade is C13, and note the three Morris & Co *windows* in the north aisle, designed by Burne-Jones in 1875, 1890 and 1893.

ST BEES. 4m S of Whitehaven on B5345. *SS Mary & Bega.*
This is the church of a Benedictine Priory founded in c.1120 on the site of a C7 nunnery destroyed by the Danes in the C9, and built of red sandstone on a cruciform plan, with a central tower of c.1200 and clerestoried nave of c.1250. After the Dissolution, the buildings fell into decay until the early-C17 when the church was restored. There was further restoration by William Butterfield in 1855-8. Although badly weathered after 800 years the west door is still imposing. The interior is very impressive. A magnificent and outstanding wrought-iron *screen* by William Butterfield dominates the interior. Note the dragon on the Norman *lintel* opposite the west door and two C14 tomb-effigies.

Wreay, *St Mary.* The Romanesque chancel in Sarah's Losh's church built in the 1830s.

WREAY. 5m SE of Carlisle off A6. *St Mary.*

An idiosyncratic church rebuilt in the 1840s by Sarah Losh (1785-1853) as a memorial to her sister Katherine who died young in 1835. The two had travelled in Italy and had shared an interest in architecture which clearly shows in this intimate stone-built church in the Romanesque style. The symbolic detail, most evident in the decoration in the west end, is drawn from a large range of sources and Sarah's own invention. Inside, a small rectangular nave leads the eye to an apse lined with Romanesque columns. The windows are glazed with fragments of old French *glass*. There is too much in this exceptional church to list here. There is only one way to discover its fascination: go and see it! Katherine's cyclopean mausoleum stands nearby.

Other Churches

IREBY. 8m N of Keswick off B5299. *Ireby Old Chancel.*

In the care of the Redundant Churches Fund. A small stone-built chapel with a bellcote on the west gable. Built in the C12 and extended to the east when the lancet windows were inserted.

MILLOM. 5m SW of Broughton-in-Furness on B5093. *Holy Trinity.*

A late-Norman church built of red sandstone, with a C13 south aisle rebuilt in the early-C14. All was restored in the C19 to which is owed most of the too-crisp detailing. The chancel was rebuilt in 1930 when the west gallery was added. The *box pews* are C18.

ULPHA. 5m N of Broughton-in-Furness off A595. *St John.*

A small chapel with nave and chancel in one, and a C17 east window. *Wall paintings* of the C17 and C18 were discovered in 1936 and include *Royal Arms* of Queen Anne.

UPPER DENTON. 5m NE of Brampton off A69. *Dedication unknown.*

A small Saxon church built with stone from the Roman wall and incorporating a Norman chancel arch brought from Birdoswald.

WHITEHAVEN. 8m S of Workington on A595. *St James*, Queen Street.

Built 1752-3 in sandstone, with a wide four-stage west tower, and the finest Georgian interior in the county. The entrance is under the tower into a lobby with an elegant double staircase to the galleries. The spacious nave and aisles, with an apsed east end, are painted in cream and pale pastel shades.

WITHERSLACK. 5m E of Newby Bridge off A590. *St Paul.*

Built c.1670 with a west tower and nave and chancel in one, originally with a roughcast exterior. Inside, the white coved ceiling reflects light from clear-glazed windows. Ionic columns, inserted 1768, mark the sanctuary. The pulpit was a three-decker, cut-down in 1880. Note the many *hatchments*, the Stanley *monument* of a white marble baby clutching a poppy, and the good C17 heraldic *roundels* set in the windows.

County Durham

This is a county with no shortage of good building stone. By far the most common is sandstone which extends from the north of the county to as far south as Bishop Auckland. In the south and west there is millstone grit which is often mistaken for sandstone. While the south-east has a soft, porous red sandstone, used at St Cuthbert, Billingham, for example, it weathers badly and is frequently replaced. From Darlington to the coast magnesian limestone is found; it was used at St Andrew, Roker, in 1906-7. In the unpopulated west carboniferous limestone is abundant.

Due to the early Christian foundations, some of the earliest Saxon work in Britain is found here, and St John, Escomb, is one of the three finest Saxon churches in Britain. It is unfortunately sited in a modern housing estate but is well looked-after as result. Norman evidence is also frequent, and St Lawrence, Pittington, has four late-Norman arcade columns carved with great vigour, and some good C12 wall paintings. Other Norman churches are St Andrew, Haughton-le-Skerne, and All Saints, Lanchester. St Cuthbert in Darlington is one of the grandest late-C12 Gothic churches in the county. But the noblest Gothic building is the Castle chapel at Bishop Auckland in a church made out of the early-C13 Bishops' Hall. St Andrew, South Church, is late-C13, and SS Mary & Cuthbert, Chester-le-Street, possesses a rarity: an intact C14 anchorite's cell, the best preserved in England. In the same church, a historical curiosity is the collection of Lord Lumley's spurious ancestors lined up in the north aisle, some with their feet amputated to fit into the space. Medieval glass is rare in the county, but there are early-C13 French panels at All Saints, Lanchester.

The C15 is represented by the chancel of St Brandon at Brancepeth. There was little building in the C16 and C17, but the Castle chapel, Bishop Auckland, has one of the finest untouched interiors of the 1660s. Other notable interiors are those at St Brandon, Brancepeth (1638), and St Andrew, Haughton-le-Skerne (1620s). All are due to Bishop Cosin's energetic influence.

The best of Georgian interiors is at Gibside Chapel where the fittings date from 1812. Slightly earlier is the apologetic Roman Catholic church at Esh Laud, built c.1800, which, to escape notice, pretends to be a farm complex. The finest parish church in the county is the 'Cathedral of the Arts and Crafts' of St Andrew at Roker built by E.E. Prior in 1906-7.

Finally, Cleveland, a bureaucratic creation, has been ignored; churches north of the Tees are listed in County Durham, while

Kirkleatham with its incomparable chapel and church has been returned to Yorkshire where it belonged for centuries before 1974.

BILLINGHAM. 2m N of Stockton on A19. *St Cuthbert.*
A remarkable Saxon tower of c.1000 is attached to a C12 nave incorporating earlier Saxon masonry, with a chancel rebuilt in 1847, and again in 1939. The north aisle is C12 and the south aisle C13. Inside, the tall and narrow nave suggests an early Saxon date of the C7 as the probable date of the tower doorway. The *screen* is dated 1625, a likely date for the *font cover*. Note the fragment of a C7 cross set in the north tower wall, a C7 grave-cover on a south windowsill, and the headless *brass* to a priest (d.1480). Chancel window by Marion Grant, 1939.

BISHOP AUCKLAND. 9m SW of Durham on A688. *Castle Chapel.*
The former bishop's aisled Great Hall was converted to a chapel by Bishop Cosin in 1661-5. Its fabric is early-C13, altered in the C14. In the alterations of the 1660s, the south front was faced with ashlar and given new windows, the clerestory windows enlarged, and Gothic tracery inserted. The interior shows what must have been a magnificent medieval hall: the aisles are marked off, each with four fine pointed arches supported on slender quatrefoil shafts. The mid-C17 roof is now held up by over-large C19 angels. At the west end was the dais with fragments of blank arcading distinguishing its importance. Reading desk and pulpit face each other halfway down the nave, while in the chancel are two canopied stalls and six c.1660 carved *misericords*. The reredos is of 1884. Three splendid baroque *screens* divide off the chancel and aisles. Original C17 *glass* is now only at the west end. An unrestored *organ* of 1688 is still used. Note the Classical *monument* by Joseph Nollekens to Bishop Trevor (d.1775).

BRANCEPETH. 4m SW of Durham on A690. *St Brandon.*
A large sandstone church standing in the park of the Castle and consisting of nave with late-C12 aisles, transepts, west tower, and a long chancel with a south chancel chapel, both rebuilt in the C15. Bishop Cosin was rector here in 1626-40 and refitted the interior in c.1638. The effect is overwhelming. A number of carved *bosses* can be seen on the C15 nave roof, and the c.1368 chancel roof has unique Laudian *bosses* with angels holding inscribed plaques. The splendid chancel *screen*, the *pews*, fourteen carved *misericords*, *pulpit*, and *font cover* are all Cosin's. Note two fragments of medieval *screens* above the chancel arch, the *Royal Arms* of James I, a wooden *effigy* in the north transept to the 2nd Earl of Westmorland (d.1484), two *brasses*, and the chain-mailed knight, Robert Neville (d.1319) in the centre of the chancel.

CHESTER-LE-STREET. 4m S of Gateshead on A167. *SS Mary and Cuthbert.*

Although this church is now entirely C13, with a good c.1409 west spire, unusual for the county, the site had a sandstone church in 1056 and before that it was a monastic cathedral from 883 to 995. In 1286 it became collegiate. It is also remarkable in having the best preserved anchorite's cell in England, now a museum, and inhabited from 1383 to the Dissolution. An unusual window with *squint* is in the original upper cell. The long nave, without a clerestory, is consequently gloomy, the east window is C19 and the chancel arch 1862. To mark the millenary in 1883 the chancel was refitted along with the screen and choir stalls. An unusual feature is the fourteen Lumley *effigies* laid closely together in two rows in the north aisle. Lord Lumley (d.1609) was obsessed with his illustrious ancestry, and although most of the early ones are bogus, and two were taken from Durham Cathedral graveyard, one knight of c.1260 in chain-mail may be Sir William Lumley. On the north side is the *Lambton pew* built over the Lambton crypt in 1829. A blocked arch at the east end marks the entrance to the 'charnel house.' Note the *brass* to Alice Lambton (d.1434) in the chancel south wall.

DARLINGTON. 20m S of Durham off A1. *St Cuthbert.*

This is one of the grandest late-C12 churches in the county. Originally a collegiate church with a dean and four canons, it was built in dark grey stone by Bishop le Puiset and is cruciform in plan with a sturdy central tower, a tall spire, chancel and transepts. All was restored in 1862-5 by Sir G.G. Scott. A stone rood *screen* of c.1400 marks off the chancel, in which is an early C14 *sedilia* and C15 stalls with eighteen carved *misericords*: numbers 3-7 on the north side are modern, the rest are c.1430. The marble pulpit is 1852, the mosaic reredos of the 1870s, and the Bishop's chair, vicar's chair, altar rails and the crossing altar are modern, by G.G. Pace. The glass is entirely C19, mainly by Clayton & Bell. Note the C13 female *effigy* in the south transept, and fragments of *wall painting* in the transepts.

ESCOMB. 2m W of Bishop Auckland off B6282. *St John Evangelist.*

This small church is one of only three complete Saxon churches to survive in Britain. Built in the C7, of now deeply blackened stone, some of which came from Roman Binchester, it is unfortunately surrounded by a colliery estate which creates an unlikely contrast. Fully restored in 1875-80, it was refurnished in 1965, and consists of a small nave and tiny chancel, with a tall narrow chancel arch. Five original windows survive with grooves for shutters, not glass. Two thin lancets in the nave and chancel are C13 and the three large windows are C19. The interior, now painted white, was probably plastered from the start, as would have been the exterior. Note the

Escomb, St John. The white-painted interior
and chancel arch.

Saxon sundial on the nave south wall, the red rustic C15 painted
scrolls above the chancel arch and further fragments on the nave north
wall. Notwithstanding the surroundings, this tiny and impressive
building is well worth a detour.

GIBSIDE. 6m SW of Gateshead off A694. *Chapel.*
Maintained by the National Trust. Built by James Paine as a chapel
with mausoleum beneath for the Bowes family in 1760-9, it was not
completed until 1812, when it was consecrated. This is the finest
Palladian church in the north-east of England. In plan it is a Greek
cross with a dome above the crossing, and is entered by a double
portico. The spatial effect of the interior is breathtaking, and it is

decorated in pastel pink with the early-C19 detail picked out in white. A magnificent c.1800 three-decker mahogany *pulpit*, in the crossing, with double stairs and an unusual umbrella-like tester, quite eclipses the centrally placed, railed-in, altar below it. Visitors' and servants' *box pews* are in the side apses, with family, agent and chaplain accommodated in the corner *boxes*, all made in the finest cherrywood.

HAUGHTON-LE-SKERNE. 1m NE of Darlington on B6279. *St Andrew.*

A stone-built, Norman church, except for the transepts, vestry and south porch, added in 1895, with a sturdy west tower, and

Gibside, Chapel. Built by Paine in the 1760s, this is the finest Palladian church in the north-east.

remodelled in the early-C15. Inside, what is obviously a Norman chancel arch has a C15 arch above it, and other Norman work can be picked out, such as the chancel windows. However, its glory is the woodwork, dating from 1662 and like that at St Brandon, Brancepeth, wainscotted throughout, together with *choir stalls, clergy stalls, reading desks, pulpit, altar rails, box pews* and an altered *reredos*, all of the same period. Notice the C10 and C11 fragments of cross-shafts in several parts of the church.

JARROW. 5m E of Newcastle on A185. *St Paul.*
This should be one of the most hallowed places of prayer in Britain for it was the church of the Venerable Bede (d.737). It is also unique in having the oldest dedication stone in Britain, dated 23 April 685. Originally two churches, east and west, linked by a late-C7 chamber heightened as a tower in the late-C11, the west church was rebuilt in 1783 and the nave and north aisle again rebuilt in 1866. The east church, now the chancel, is the original late-C7 church, confirmed by the three small Saxon windows in the south wall.

LANCHESTER. 6m NW of Durham on A691. *All Saints.*
This sandstone church is mainly Norman, with a chancel widened and rebuilt when the church was made collegiate in 1283, and a C15 west tower. Note the fine sculpture of the headless Christ in the tympanum over the vestry door. In the south porch is a good Roman altar with other Roman fragments. Once inside it is the chancel which takes our attention. There are six C15 stalls with carved *misericords*, one with a grotesque head, the remainder foliage. Corbels with carved heads are at odd intervals in the chancel walls; these were used to hold candles. The Communion rail is Jacobean. There is fine early-C13 *glass*: one piece, the Adoration of the Magi, is probably French. Do not overlook the early-C14 priest *effigy* in a recess.

PITTINGTON. 4m NE of Durham off A690. *St Laurence.*
Pevsner calls this one of the most exciting pieces of architecture in the county. He refers to the six-bay north arcade with four exuberant late-Norman columns supporting a Saxon wall and windows. The west tower is also late-Norman, the south aisle C13 with what is possibly a Saxon sundial on the outer wall, and the chancel rebuilt in 1846-7. Well worth seeing are the C12 *wall paintings* of St Cuthbert, which are unusually clear, surrounding the westernmost Saxon window. Note the small stone C13 *monument* of two boys carrying toy swords.

ROKER. 2m N of Sunderland on A183. *St Andrew.*
Unexpectedly for the area, this is a magnificent church, built in 1906-7 by E.E. Prior in neo-Gothic style, and faced in rough stone. A

Roker, St Andrew. Built in 1906 by E.E.Prior, the interior has good contemporary fittings.

short heavy tower hangs over the east end which projects outwards to make the chancel. The interior of the nave is exactly like an upturned boat: pointed arches in reinforced concrete faced with stone, supported on small paired columns, reach across the space. In the chancel the ceiling was *painted* by Macdonald Gill in 1927 on the theme of the Creation and restored in 1967. The *reredos* boasts a tapestry by Morris & Co, designed by Burne-Jones, the Adoration of the Magi, and the *carpet* has a Morris design. Ernest Gimson was responsible for the chancel furnishings; notice particularly his delicate *lectern* of inlaid ebony and silver. Eric Gill undertook much of the *lettering* throughout the building. There is also Burne-Jones designed *glass* made by Thomson & Snee of Gateshead in the east wall of the south transept, and the east window is by H.A. Payne of Birmingham. One can see why this is known as 'the Cathedral of the Arts and Crafts'.

STAINDROP. 9m W of Darlington on A688. *St Mary.*
A large church and the most impressive in the county. A Saxon nave was lengthened westwards at the same time that the aisles and tower were built in the C12. The chancel was rebuilt in the C13 when the transepts and north vestry were added. Both aisles were widened in the C14 when Ralph, Lord Neville (d.1367),founded a chantry. The church became collegiate under its founder the first Earl of Westmorland (d.1425), from 1408 to the Dissolution. It was exten-

sively restored in 1849-51. An upside-down Saxon *sundial* has been incongruously set in the north-east corner of the nave above the chancel arch; C15 stalls have twelve original carved *misericords* of c.1408; and the glass, apart from some medieval fragments in the south aisle, is all of 1865 by Clayton & Bell. *Monuments* to the Nevilles are in the west end of the south aisle. The founder's fine alabaster tomb-chest shows him with his two wives, and the fifth Earl of Westmorland's (d.1540) *effigy* is of blackened oak. Note the monument to Mary Lee (d.1813) by Joseph Nollekens and another to the first Duke of Cleveland (d.1842) by Sir Richard Westmacott. In the churchyard is a Cleveland mausoleum designed in 1850 by William Burn.

Other Churches

ESH LAUDE. 5m NW of Durham off B6302. *St Michael.*
Deliberately disguised as a farm courtyard this is a Roman Catholic church with a nave built 1798-1800, with presbytery of 1802 and outbuildings. An apsed chancel was added in 1850, a porch in 1910, and the altar of 1865 is in memory of Cardinal Wiseman.

MONKWEARMOUTH. 5m E of Gateshead on A1231. *SS Peter with Cuthbert.*
The remains of a Saxon monastic church of 674 are in the west end of the nave, the lower stage of the slender west tower, and in the plan of the nave and chancel. The tower was successively heightened up to the C10. The rest of the church is C13 and C14, the nave was rebuilt and enlarged in 1875. Note the showcases in the north aisles containing an inscribed *grave-marker* of c.700, two lion bench-ends of c.674, and various other items of interest.

SEAHAM. 10m NE of Durham on B1404. *St Mary.*
On a lonely site on the cliffs this long, low church has a late-C7 nave and early-C13 chancel and west tower. Note the double *piscina* with a carved hand raised in blessing, a late-Norman circular font, and 1580s *pulpit*. The church register lists the entry of the ill-fated marriage of Lord Byron the poet, which took place in Seaford Hall in 1815.

SOUTH CHURCH. 1m SE of Bishop Auckland off B6282. *St Andrew.*
This is the largest parish church in the county. Impressive and almost entirely c.1300, it consists of a west tower, aisled nave, transepts and chancel. Note the twenty-eight stalls with carved *misericords* 1416-17, fragments of C8 cross, and an oak *effigy* of a cross-legged knight, c.1340.

Lancashire

The red sandstone of the county is not, unfortunately, of the best quality, moreover when blackened by industrial soot it can present quite a depressing picture. In the south-west of the county the stone weathers badly and in many churches there is extensive repatching. Along the border with Yorkshire and in the north, however, is limestone, the best of building stones. Slate for roofing is also found in the north of the county. Some building brick was made from c.1700, and by 1800 brick of a harsh dark-red colour, Accrington Reds, was ousting stone.

There is nothing of Norman work in the county. St Mary, Whalley, an abbey church, is almost all C14 with some of the best C15 choir stalls of any parish church. St Mary, Lancaster, is almost all of the mid-C15 with some good C14 choir stalls, and St Andrew, Slaidburn, another C15 church, has C16 and C17 fittings. The C16 is represented only by the Sherburne Chapel of 1594 at Great Mitton. Some rebuilding occurred in the C18, but it was the following century that saw the greatest changes.

Inevitably, in such a prosperous industrial area churches were demolished and rebuilt in the C19, and others were built for an expanding population. Many late-C19 churches are by Paley and Austin. H.J. Austin joined E.G. Paley in 1886, and their distinctive buildings are dotted throughout Lancashire, and Cheshire too. There are only two of them listed here: St George, Stockport, a large, town church, and totally different from St Peter, a small rural church in Finsthwaite. There are a few of their other churches that are worth visiting: St Chad, Kirkby (1869-71); SS Matthew and James, Mossley Hill, Liverpool (1870-5); St Mary, Prestwich (1888-9); Christ Church, Waterloo (1891-4). In Bolton alone there are four: All Souls, Astley St (1880-1); St Margaret, St Margaret's Rd (1887); St Saviour, Dean Rd (1882-5) and St Thomas, Eskrick St (1875).

For simplicity Greater Manchester and Merseyside, two new counties, are included in Lancashire.

ASHTON-UNDER-LYNE. 6m E of Manchester on A670. *St Michael & All Angels.*
A large church of limestone begun in the early-C15 and completed in the early-C16. After the north side was reconstructed in 1821, it was almost completely rebuilt in 1840-1, and the tower rebuilt in 1886. The result is that it looks like a C19 church, and the interior is undisturbed since the 1840s: the three-decker *pulpit* is central on the north side of the nave with *box pews* placed to face it. There is good C18

plasterwork, and the best collection of medieval *glass* (1460-1517) in the county.

EUXTON. 6m S of Preston on A49. *Dedication unknown.*
It seems strange that this charming small, sandstone church, with bellcote, a C16 aisleless nave and 1837 chancel, should have no dedication. However, until the early-C19 it was a private chapel founded in the C14, the date of the north door. The rest of the building is C16 and although the date 1513 can be read above the west door, the date-stone is later, and evidence points to 1573 for the rebuilding. The nave roof is C16. Inside, the nave is unfortunately stripped of plaster, the pulpit is c.1724 and in the south wall of the nave are a C16 piscina and sedilia.

GREAT MITTON. 8m NE of Blackburn on B6246. *All Hallows.*
Built of brownstone rubble with C13 nave and chancel, a C15 west tower, and a remarkable chapel of 1594. Inside, the superb C13 *roof* is rich with carving, and the chancel is glimpsed through a fine C15 *screen.* The exceptional *Sherburne Chapel* has a fine series of family monuments, including an alabaster *tomb-chest* with effigies, of 1594. Note the Elizabethan *font cover*, the late-C17 *pulpit* and the late-medieval *tiles.*

LANCASTER. 22m N of Preston on A6. *St Mary.*
A Benedictine priory, a cell of Séez, Normandy, was founded here in 1094 but suppressed in 1428 and the monks transferred to Syon, Middlesex. It was then given to Brigittine nuns who, with the parishioners, built this large gritstone church from 1431, consisting of an aisled nave (the north aisle rebuilt in 1903), chancel, and west tower rebuilt in 1775. An apse just to the east of the chancel arch may be Roman and there is a Saxon door at the east end of the south aisle. The furnishings are particularly noteworthy: fourteen C14 *stalls* with beautifully carved canopies, each with a carved and mainly mutilated *misericord* which may be from Cockersand Abbey, a carved *pulpit* dated 1619, a matching *font cover* of 1631, and a *reredos* of four painted panels of 1919. Note the *monument* of 1753 by L.F. Roubiliac, a *Crusader's casket* and a set of four *Coptic crosses* of the C5.

LIVERPOOL. *All Saints*, Childwall.
With a C14 nave and chancel, a west tower of 1810-11 and Salisbury Chapel of 1739-40, this is the only remaining medieval church (it even keeps its lych-gate) in Liverpool. Restored in 1851-3, the box pews with doors are from that date; the Gasgoyne family pew is now in the vestry. An C18 octagonal font has been made round and its cover carries the Stanley crest. Note the *Royal Arms* of 1664, the *brass* of 1524, the brass *chandelier* dated 1737, the fragment of a Saxon

cross in the porch, and the numerous good monuments. In the churchyard is a castellated *hearse house* of c.1810.

St Agnes, Ullet Road, Sefton Park.

Built in red brick in a C13 Gothic style by J.L. Pearson in 1883-5, high with aisles and no tower, this claims to be the noblest church in Liverpool. The interior is, by contrast, faced with white ashlar and the stone-vaulting gives the impression of a scaled down cathedral. The Lady Chapel *reredos* and *screen* are by G.F. Bodley. Note the amusing corbel-heads, which include a horse falling down Horsfall Hill.

Unitarian Church, Ullet Road, Sefton Park.

Built of pink brick in 1896-9 by Percy Worthington with C13 Gothick detailing, this is a simple church with a bellcote and no tower. It is also one of the most delightful and praiseworthy Unitarian churches in Britain. The interior is ashlar faced, with Art Nouveau *light fittings* and Morris & Co *glass:* the earliest, of 1897-8, is in the apse. Do not overlook the *frescos* by Gerald Moira of 1902; in the library, is his 'The Pursuit of Truth', and 'The Cardinal Virtues' in the vestry. Note the beaten copper west doors.

St Clare, Arundel Avenue, Sefton Park.

Built of purple brick with stone dressings in 1888-9 by Leonard Stokes, this is a striking church in the Gothic style, with a high nave and no tower. The interior is bright with cream paint which unfortunately has obliterated the subtle stone detail. Like Bodley's *St Augustine*, Pendlebury, the deep wall-buttresses are side chapels as at Albi Cathedral, while above are high pointed clerestory windows.

MANCHESTER. SE of city centre to the east of A34. *First Church of Christ Scientist*, Victoria Park.

Built in 1903 on a Y plan by Edgar Wood, Manchester's Art Nouveau architect, this is one of the most remarkable buildings in Britain. Built of brick with white rendering, it is homely and comfortable with a sharply gabled west end with canted sides, a deep set west entrance having a cross shaped window above. It hardly looks like a church and in fact it is now Manchester Polytechnic theatre. The main hall has an open roof with trusses exposed, lit by huge dormer windows. At the far end is a marble mosaic 'reredos', and thin green tiles decorate part of the walls. Over the entrance is the organ loft behind a strange wood screen and off the main hall are small, perfectly proportioned, intimate rooms.

St Ann, St Ann's Square.

Built in 1709-12, of red sandstone, with a stunted west tower that originally had a three-stage cupola. It was restored in 1886-91 by Alfred Waterhouse who made the choir in the nave. The three galleries, the cut-down pulpit (the remains of a three-decker), and the box pews are original. Note the marble octagonal *font*, and the *paint-*

ing of the 'Descent from the Cross' by the Bolognese painter, Annibale Carracci (1560-1609).

PENDLEBURY. 5m NW of Manchester on A666. *St Augustine.*
A tall mass of a brick-built church and G.F. Bodley's greatest achievement. Built in 1871-4 at a cost of £33,000, it has claims to be the finest of the C19. The interior was inspired by the cathedrals of Toulouse and Albi and it is breathtaking in its majesty. The Dürer-like *reredos*, the *organ case, sedilia* and *rood screen* are all by Bodley. Down the side walls are what would be chapels at Albi but here they are recesses with finely painted saints overhead. The *glass* is some of the best of the C19, by Burlison and Grylls, designed by Bodley, and each with a different leading colour. Notice the paintings high up on the east sides of the wall-piers.

PILLING. 6m NE of Blackpool off A588. *St John Baptist.*
In the care of the Redundant Churches Fund. This small stone church, with bellcote and slate roof, is difficult to find up a track to the west of the main road. The date, 1717, with sundial is above the south door. Deserted for the new church in 1887, it is a rarity for the county, an unaltered interior. One *box pew* is dated 1719, but those in the north-west corner are of c.1812, the same date as the north and west galleries. Commandment boards, *Communion rails,*

Pilling, St John. The south door of a small, unaltered church of 1717.

two-decker *pulpit* and *Royal Arms* of George I are all of c.1719. The original Communion table was stolen. The rustic benches are probably also of 1719. It is a perfectly preserved 'prayer-book' interior.

SAMLESBURY. 3m E of Preston on A59. *St Leonard.*
Originally a small C14 sandstone church much enlarged in 1558, with further alterations in the C19 and a tower on the north-east built in 1899. It now consists of north and south aisles with nave and chancel in one. The interior walls have been mercilessly stripped of plaster but thankfully the C17 and C18 *box pews*, the earliest of which is dated 1678, were left in place. Note the two pew *candlesticks*. The two-decker pulpit has been moved from the centre of the south arcade. Notable features are the C12 *sanctus bell*, the *Royal Arms* of George II, the *boards* of 1728 with the texts of the Lord's Prayer, Commandments and the Creed, and the funeral *helmet*, *sword* and arms of Sir Thomas Southworth (d.1573).

Samlesbury, St Leonard. Helmet, sword and arms of Sir Thomas Southworth who died 1573.

SLAIDBURN. 7m N of Clitheroe on B6478. *St Andrew.*
This village used to be in Yorkshire until 1974, but is now part of Lancashire in the beautiful Trough-of-Bowland. The C15 church is a complement to the area, built of rendered sandstone with a square west tower contrasting with the low nave and aisles. The interior is unaffected by the C19 Tractarians; many of the fittings are late-C16 to C18, among them *Benefaction boards*, C17 *box pews*, family pews, some of them initialled, C17 oak *pews*, two *Royal Arms*, an Elizabethan *font cover*, an C18 three-decker *pulpit*, a fine early-C17 *screen*, and thirteen brass chandeliers. There is a good east window of 1848. Note the two *dog whips* for breaking up dog fights during a service!

STOCKPORT. 5m SE of Manchester on A6. *St George.*
A major work of the late-Gothic revival by Paley & Austin, built 1893-7, and their best work. The church is a magnificent cruciform building of red Runcorn sandstone in C15 Gothic style, with a crossing tower crowned by a 236ft spire. The lofty interior has a magnificent oak hammer-beam *roof* with Art Nouveau detail, and the white ceiling beneath the tower is decorated with red and green stencils

and gilded bosses. A Derbyshire alabaster *reredos* is carved with the crucified Christ flanked by the Virgin and six saints. The east window above it has Christ in Majesty. There is much else to note, from the richly carved *choir stalls*, the Derbyshire alabaster *font*, the chancel *screen*, to the elaborate *organ case*.

TARLTON. 8m E of Southport on A565. *St Mary.*
In the care of the Redundant Churches Fund. Deserted since a new church was built in 1866, this simple church of 1719 is built of hand-made brick, with porch, vestibule and vestry of 1824, the date when the bellcote was heightened with stone. The simple interior with angled apse, stone-flagged floors, *box pews*, and an L-shaped gallery, lit by oil lamps, retains many of its original fittings, with an interesting black stove. The pulpit, however, is not original.

UPHOLLAND. 5m W of Wigan on A577. *St Thomas.*
Part of a vast, never completed, church of a Benedictine Priory founded in 1317. The present magnificent nave was intended to be the original chancel, and the late-C15 tower marks where the crossing should have been. Now it consists of a nave with aisles, transepts, and a chancel built in 1882-6. The benches, dated 1635, are unusual for the time because box pews were more generally popular. Note the uncommon *churchwardens' pew* dated 1679, the pieces of medieval *glass* in a south window. and the pleasing plaster ceiling of 1752.

WHALLEY. 6m N of Blackburn on A59. *St Mary.*
On the site of this large parish church, rebuilt in 1330-80, there once stood a Cistercian abbey founded in the late-C13. It consists of an aisled nave, chancel, and west tower. A Norman south door is all that remains of an earlier building. At the Dissolution the church was enriched by twenty-four *choir stalls* of 1418-34 with intricately carved canopies from the abbey, together with twenty-two carved *misericords*, though some of these date from 1866. The chancel, north and south chapel *screens* are all mainly C15, but more interesting is the surprising *box pew* called 'St Anton's Cage' dated 1534, 1610, and 1830, the date when it was altered. There are other dated *box pews*: a carved example of 1702, a *churchwarden's pew* of 1690, and a *constable's pew* dated 1714. In particular, notice the fine oak benches in the nave. The organ case was made in 1729 for Lancaster Priory. In the south aisle is *glass* designed by A.W.N. Pugin in 1847, and lifeless, late Morris & Co *glass* of the 1890s.

Other Churches

FINSTHWAITE. 10m S of Windermere off A590. *St Peter.*
Built of slate in 1873-4 in Romanesque style with a central tower, and one of the best of the Paley & Austin churches. There is an outstanding *reredos* by the Venetian, Antonio Salviati.

LIVERPOOL.

St John Baptist, West Derby Road, Tue Brook.

Built 1868-71 by G.F. Bodley in red sandstone with a long nave and aisles, a lower chancel and west tower. The interior is furnished throughout by C.E. Kempe who also did the stencilling on the clerestory, the nave *wall paintings*, and the painted panels of the roof. *Reredos* and *screen* are by Bodley. Note the early Morris & Co *glass* of 1868 in the east window.

RIVINGTON. 7m NW of Bolton on B6227. *Holy Trinity.*

Built of stone in c.1540, and rebuilt in 1666, this small aisleless church with bell-turret has a c.1540 *pulpit*, an C18 brass *chandelier*, and the Pilkington genealogical picture (copy). A detached C16 *bell house* is now a tool store.

SALFORD. 3m W of Manchester centre on A57. *Sacred Trinity.*

Liverpool, St John. Built by G.F.Bodley in 1868-71 in a faultless C14 Gothic style.

Dirty and grey, this small ashlar faced church, lost in a maze of bridges, was built in 1752 replacing an earlier church of 1635 of which the tower remains, and restored in 1871-4. Inside, three galleries are decorated with armorial shields and the *Royal Arms*. A flat plaster ceiling was removed in 1886 exposing a fair C18 timber roof, from which dusty banners hang. Note the silver-topped *staves*, the black and gold donation *boards*, and the carved shields on the pew ends.

STONYHURST COLLEGE. 6m N of Blackburn off B6243. *Church.*

Built by J.J. Scoles in late-Gothic style in 1832-5 for the Jesuit College, with most of the fittings by J.B. Capronnier. The attraction lies in the amazingly rich, historic *vestments*: Henry VII's Cope, worn by Henry VIII at the Field of the Cloth of Gold; the Dalmatics and Chasuble of Queen Catherine of Aragon; the Lucca Chasuble of c.1460; Louis XV's Cope; and the St Dunstan Chasuble of the mid-C15.

Northumberland

Early Northumberland was the cradle of English Christianity. St Aidan founded a small monastery at Holy Island in 635 and established churches on the mainland, and St Wilfred founded a monastery at Hexham in c.671-3. A hundred and fifty years later, the land was continuously fought over; first by the Norse invaders; followed by the ruthless suppression of the North by William I, and then overrun by Scottish invaders, the turmoil lasted until the C16. It is no surprise, therefore, that sturdy, defensive west towers, such as that at St Anne, Ancroft, and stone vaulting, (perhaps a fireproofing measure) such as the C13 chancel at St Gregory, Kirknewton, are found in Northumberland's churches.

The first churches of the Northumbrian school were generally built of wood and consisted of a narrow aisleless nave and a narrower square-ended chancel. These were later rebuilt in stone. Typical of this type of building is St Andrew, Corbridge. There are several churches with Saxon towers attached to later Norman naves, which began as narrow Saxon naves. There is also an abundance of surviving Norman evidence – the unusually complete church at St Lawrence, Warkworth, for example – and of C13 rebuilding, such as the early C13 SS Peter & Paul at Brinkburn. Due to the unsettled political conditions there was little building of late-medieval churches, the exception being St Michael, Alnwick. A tradition of tunnel-vaulting survived, as is witnessed at St Cuthbert, Bellingham, where the vaults of nave and transept date from after 1609.

Few churches were built until the C19, the exception being the

'Oval Church', Newcastle, 1786-9. Later came the churches financed by the Industrial Revolution in expanding Newcastle, and the urgent restoration of many rural churches. Tyne & Wear, that wretched bureaucratic creation, has been ignored and its churches given back to Northumberland, where they rightly belong.

ALNWICK. 18m N of Morpeth on A1. *St Michael & All Angels.*
Political instability meant that there was almost no C14 and C15 church building in the county. This is the exception; it is in lavish late-Gothic, and is the most important C15 church in Northumberland. It was much restored in the C19; first in 1825, again in the 1860s and finally in the 1890s. Built of what is now blackened stone, with a typical stumpy Northumberland west tower, it had a five-bay nave with wide aisles and a slightly higher chancel of four bays with chapels. The interior is marked by its unusual width and richly foliated capitals of the north arcade, one having vines, fetterlock and crescents of the 4th Earl of Northumberland. Note the late-C15 *sculpture* of Henry VI and St Edmund, the early-C14 Flemish vestry *chest*, and C15 *glass* in the north aisle. The remaining glass is all C19 with three windows by Clayton & Bell.

AMBURGH. 5m E of Belford on B1342. *St Aidan.*
Founded in c.1230 but now of the C12, C13 and C14, it was assigned to the Augustinian canons of Nostell in Yorkshire, which would account for the very wide C14 south aisle with separate entrance; this may have been the parochial church. The arm of St Oswald was once preserved here. The nave predates c.1200 when the north aisle was added, and the crossing arches were rebuilt at the same time. In c.1230 the chancel was rebuilt and later in that century the south arcade. Two chantries were founded in 1316 and 1333. In the south transept a large *squint*, with early-C14 tracery, gives a view of the high altar. Beneath the chancel is a two-chambered *crypt* with unusual stone vaulting. Note the grouping of sedilia and piscina in the chancel south wall, and the cross-legged knight c.1320. Above hang the *breast plate, gauntlets*, and *helmet* of Fernandino Forster (d.1701). Noteworthy is the *monument* by Sir Francis Chantrey made in 1839. The churchyard has a Gothic monument to Grace Darling (d.1842).

ANCROFT. 5m S of Berwick on B6525. *St Anne.*
A small Norman church built of Ancroft stone with a neo-Norman chancel arch and chancel of 1870. All the windows are neo-Norman of 1870, as are the interior fittings. However, the west tower is an early-C14 'vicar's Pele', or fortified tower consisting of a stone tunnel-vaulted undercroft with rooms above, one having a fireplace.

BERWICK-ON-TWEED. 60m N of Newcastle on A1. *Holy Trinity.*

Berwick, Holy Trinity. A rarity because it was built in 1648-52, during the Commonwealth.

This rectangular stone-built church in a mixture of Gothic and Classical styles, with no tower, is a rarity because it was one of the very few built during the Commonwealth, being built in 1648-52, by the Governor of Berwick, Col. George Fenwick, after Cromwell's Scottish campaign. A chancel was added in 1855. Venetian windows and Gothic battlements mark the nave and the clerestory has a mixture of both Classical and Gothic windows. Inside, only the west gallery survives.

BRINKBURN. 10m NW of Morpeth off B6344. *SS Peter & Paul.*
A priory for Augustinian Canons was founded here in c.1135 and the church dates from 1190. After the Dissolution it was used until 1683; it then fell into ruin and was only restored in 1858. The east end, transepts, tower, and nave with a north aisle only, all date from c.1190, the west front is C13, and the roof, with the south-west corner of the nave, is 1858. The plan is cruciform with a central tower. Note the Norman nave *north door* which is richly decorated; the two south doors led into the cloisters. The nave arcade carries a triforium with paired Norman round-headed arches, and the clerestory windows are round-headed. The transept aisles are stone-vaulted, and the chancel, unusually, had an upper chamber, removed in 1858. The fittings are all of 1858.

CORBRIDGE. 4m E of Hexham off A69. *St Andrew.*
After Hexham this is the most important Saxon building in the county. The lower stages of the west tower are c.780, forming the west porch made of a sturdy re-erected Roman arch, with the original west window above it. The upper stages of the tower are C11, and

the south door is Norman. Aisles, transepts, and chancel were added to the narrow, high, Saxon nave in the C13, making a cruciform plan. In a recess in the north transept is a slab tombstone to Hugh, son of Asil (d.1296). A collection of fragments of coffin lids and grave stones are assembled in the porch. On the south of the church-yard is a medieval vicarage with a vicar's Pele tower of c.1300 built of Roman masonry.

EDLINGHAM. 5m SW of Alnwick on B6341. *St John.*
A small Norman stone-built church of two periods, with a sturdy west tower of which the lower stage is late-C12. The chancel arch and tunnel-vaulted porch (unusual for England) are early C12, the north aisle is late-C12, and the wooden window tracery was inserted in 1902. The base of a stone screen remains across the chancel arch.

Edlingham, St John. A small Norman church.

HALTWHISTLE. 14m W of Hexham on A69. *Holy Cross.*
Although the exterior looks forbidding with its slender lancet windows pierced through rough masonry walls, west bellcote, nave with aisles and chancel, this is an exceptionally complete C13 church, carefully restored in 1870. The interior is particularly satisfying and spacious. In the chancel the painted roof dates from 1881, and the stepped, three-stalled *sedilia* is unusually beautiful. Note the *font* dated 1676 and the C7 circular *stoup*. The *glass* of 1797-8 in the south aisle is by Morris & Co who may also have supplied the east window. There is a mutilated knight effigy of c.1389 and C14 coffin lids carved with foliate crosses.

HEXHAM. 20m W of Newcastle-on-Tyne on A69. *St Andrew.*
One of the biggest churches in the county, founded by St Wilfred in c.671-3, sacked by the Danes in the C9, and rebuilt as an Augustinian priory in 1113. Of the original church of 680 only the *crypt* remains. The transepts and east end of the nave are C13; the east end was rebuilt in 1858, the nave and north aisle in 1907-9. The interior is marked by a wood veranda *rood screen* of c.1500, the most complete of any English monastic church. St Wilfred's C7 throne, a cut-out square stone seat, stands in the centre of the chancel, and above a C15 painted pulpit are *paintings* of the Dance of Death and the Passion. Higher still is an early-C16 former *reredos*

Hexham, St Andrew. The night stairs.

with seven painted Bishops. There are thirty-eight carved *misericords* in the stalls: six are modern, the rest c.1425. Above the altar is a painting after Andrea del Sarto (1486-1530). The south transept still has the broad and gentle-stepped night stairs. Note the fragments of Saxon and Norman sculptured masonry set in the south and west walls of the nave and the Roman *glass* in the north-east aisle window.

HOLY ISLAND. 5m N of Belford off A1. *St Mary.*
A small stone-built late-C13 church with an C18 bellcote. Only accessible by causeway at low-tide, this magnificent site, on a small island, is important in early Christian history. St Aidan founded his monastery here in 635 at the invitation of King Oswald, but it was laid waste by the Danes 250 years later. Inside, the three-bay north arcade is C12, the south arcade and simple west front c.1300. In the long narrow chancel the altar carpet shows a page from the Lindisfarne Gospels, made by lady parishioners in 1970. Note the *hatchments.*

KIRKNEWTON. 5m W of Wooler on B6351. *St Gregory.*
From outside this stone-built church looks entirely of the C19. It was restored in 1860 and the tower is later, but inside it tells another story. The chancel and south transept have C13 stone tunnel-vault-

ing, arching to a shallow point overhead. Perhaps this was a fireproof measure. Note the *font* of 1663, and a rustic C12 sculptured relief of The Adoration of the Magi.

NEWCASTLE-UPON-TYNE. Manor Chare, *All Saints*.

Known as the 'Oval Church' because of its shape, this is a fine Classical structure built 1786-96, with a south tower and spire. Now deconsecrated it is used as an urban studies centre. The entrance is under the tower into a domed, circular space; beyond is an oval nave, with galleries on Doric columns round three sides, which is entered from the south. The walls, once painted, are now white, and the ceiling has been recently re-painted. To the east a domed apse marks where the altar stood. Columns and panelling are all of mahogany.

Trinity House, Broad Chare. *Chapel.*

The has an interior is almost untouched since 1635. To go in by way of an entrance hall, through a grand Jacobean *screen*, is a promising introduction to this intimate and scrupulously maintained chapel. A panelled two-decker *pulpit* two thirds of the way down one side faces a *reader's desk* across the nave, both flanked by splendid *box pews*; all are of 1635. The roof was replaced in 1651 and the wall panelling is early-C20. Decorated with flags and plaques, and woodwork carved with lively detail, it is a pleasure to find such a gem of an interior.

NORHAM. 9m SW of Berwick on B6740. *St Cuthbert.*

Once an important Norman church of which only the chancel and south arcade remain, the rest being a rebuilding of 1846-52, including the oblong west tower. The exterior of the chancel south wall, with its rhythmical spacing of five round-arched Norman windows decorated with beak-heads, is a delight. The east end was rebuilt in c.1340 after damage during a siege of the castle. Inside, the late-C17 carved *pulpit* and *stalls* are from Durham Cathedral, and the clergy stalls are made from a C17 family pew. In the south side of the chancel is a time-worn *effigy* of a cross-legged knight. Note the deeply carved *Royal Arms* of Charles II (it was never coloured) and the column made up of recently discovered Saxon sculptures.

SEATON DELAVAL. 6m NE of Newcastle on A92. *Our Lady.*

A small Norman church ,with a west porch of 1895 and a damaged tympanum over a Norman west door, which, in essence, was a private chapel for the Delaval family. Inside, a wide Norman chancel arch frames an identical Norman arch leading to a chancel extension of c.1300, replacing a Norman apse. A timber roof is hidden above an C18 plaster ceiling. Note the C14 piscina, the *hatchments*, two C14 *effigies*, and eight medieval, carved stone heraldic *shields* of high quality.

WARKWORTH. 6m SE of Alnwick on A1068. *St Lawrence.*

A large Norman church left unusually complete. A strong west tower

Seaton Delaval, Our Lady. Interior looking east.

was built c.1200, with a broach spire of c.1400, and the C14 south aisle has C15 windows. All was restored in 1860 when the clerestory was unaccountably destroyed. Inside, the rarity is the stone rib-vaulted C12 chancel. The fittings are mostly from the 1860 restoration but the wrought-iron Communion rail is c.1710 and the reading desk and pulpit are of 1920. Note the splendidly worked, and undamaged *effigy* of a cross-legged knight (c.1330), and on the outer south wall a wall tablet to a mason who died in 1794, carved by himself.

Other Churches

BELLINGHAM. 13m NW of Hexham on B6320. *St Cuthbert.*
An interesting stone-built church with west tower and an unusual stone barrel-vaulted nave and early-C13 chancel. After 1609 both nave aisles were demolished and stone vaults inserted: fifteen in the nave and seven in the transept. Note the C17 font.

BYWELL. 5m SE of Corbridge on A4692. *St Andrew.*
The best Saxon tower in the county with a c.1000 upper stage, attached to a C13 nave and chancel, with north aisle rebuilt in the C19. Note the remains of a Saxon cross in the chancel and the coffin lids built into the exterior wall of the north transept.

PONTELAND. 7m NW of Newcastle on A696. *St Mary.*
A church mainly rebuilt in the C13, the date of the chancel and transepts, with a sturdy Norman tower and evidence of Norman

masonry in the nave. The north aisle was rebuilt in 1810. There is medieval *glass* in the south chancel windows. Note the fine C14 *font* and the *Royal Arms* of George III.

STAMFORDHAM. 10m NW of Newcastle on B6309. *St Mary.*
Basically a C13 stone-built church, over-restored in 1848, consisting of nave with aisles, chancel and west tower. Note the rustic C14 *reredos* in the south aisle with a roughly carved crucifix, two mutilated knights' effigies of c.1300 and c.1400 and the collection of coffin lids in the porch.

Yorkshire

Taken as a whole, this is a county with a very varied supply of building stone, mainly limestone. Along the west and north borders is millstone grit. From Leeds southward is sandstone, the famous York stone, which is not from York at all but should instead be called Yorkshire stone. Running in a straight line north and south through the middle of the area is magnesian limestone. York itself lies in the middle of north-south line of clay, but it is narrow, and nearby to the east is a fine line of limestone separated from the sea by chalk. Further north, at Whitby, is oolite limestone.

Yorkshire is well provided with early architecture. St John, Kirk Hammerton (NR), is a complete Saxon church of nave and chancel; unfortunately it is now the south aisle of a larger church built in 1890-1. All Saints, Ledsham (WR), is also Saxon, disguised as a C15 battlemented church. These two venerable Saxon survivors apart, there are many Saxon crosses. The oldest (c.800) is at St Agatha, Easby (NR), and St Gregory, Kirkdale (NR) has a Saxon sundial. St John, Adel (WR) is an almost complete Norman church with a remarkable Norman bronze door-ring, and at St Cuthbert, Fishlake (WR) is the finest Norman doorway in Yorkshire. The C12 was a period of monastic expansion and the century is poorly represented in parish church building.

The C13 saw the building of St Giles, Skelton (NR), a church built entirely c.1240. Other churches were added to and chancels rebuilt, as at All Saints, Arksey (WR), where the transepts and chancel are C13, and the rebuilding of the Minster at Beverley (H) which began with the chancel in 1220. St Peter, Howden (H), has a perfect example of the C14 in its nave completed in c.1350. Beverley Minster (H) also has an example of the C14 in its nave, completed in 1390. A charming, small chapel was built on Wakefield Bridge (WR) in c.1350. The C15 was a century of rebuilding. At St Wilfred, Cantley (WR) the nave and tower are C15, St John, Leeds (WR) was almost entirely rebuilt; and St Oswald, Methley (WR) was remodelled in the C15. At SS Peter & Paul, Pickering (NR) are amazing C15 wall paintings. The C16 century is here represented by fittings and monuments which are scattered throughout many churches, such as the C16 screen with Catherine of Aragon's badge on it at St Mary, Swine (H).

A remarkable C17 survival is the interior of the unprepossessing St Thomas Becket at Beauchief (WR), whose interior is little changed since 1664 when it was fitted out. St Giles, Bramhope (WR) is another remarkable example with a completely undisturbed interior of 1649. At Leeds (WR), St John was built in the 1630s but suffered drastic restoration in the 1860s when box pews were cut down and other irrepairable damage was done. The C18 has other examples of unaltered interiors as in the extraordinarily memorable interior of Whitby's (NR) St Mary.

The C19 has some exceptional work, as in William Burges's two brilliant churches, St Mary at Studley Royal (WR) and St Helen at Skelton (NR), both built in the 1870s, and the interior of St Martin, Scarborough (NR), by G.F. Bodley, begun in 1861 and containing much early work by the William Morris firm. Sir George Gilbert Scott always considered All Souls, Halifax (WR), built 1856-9, to be his best church. St Stephen at Aldwark (NR) is a unique church built in 1846-53 by E.B. Lamb, and is better seen than described.

Kirkleatham has been taken from Cleveland and returned to North Yorkshire where it properly belongs. Humberside is about to be abandoned and returned to Yorkshire and Lincolnshire. I have anticipated this and used the three old East, North and West Ridings. Humberside goes to the East Riding. However, entries which are ex-Humberside are marked with (H) after the place name.

East Riding

BEVERLEY. (H) 6m NW of Hull on A164. *Minster, St John of Beverley.*
One of the best Gothic churches in Europe and collegiate until the Dissolution of the colleges under Edward VI. It is the third church on the site, begun in 1220, the date of the chancel; the nave was completed in 1390, and the west front by 1450. It was restored by Sir George Gilbert Scott in 1866-78. In plan it has a long aisled nave, aisled north and south transepts, and an aisled chancel with north-east and south-east transepts. In the nave, note the sculpted *musicians* over the piers: they are everywhere, over 70 of them. To the left of the altar is the luxuriant *tomb-canopy* of, it is thought, Lady Eleanor Percy (d.1328). The C14 *reredos* was heavily restored in 1826, the choir stalls of c.1520 have sixty-eight carved *misericords*, and overhead is a

panelled *ceiling* of 1445 painted with forty English kings. In the roof, above the vaulting of the central stub-tower, is an C18 tread-wheel used for lifting. In the nave south aisle is a Norman *font* from the first church, and near the altar is the stone *Sanctuary Chair* of c.937. The privilege of sanctuary for fugitives from the law extended to two miles' radius around the Minster

BOYNTON. (H) 3m W of Bridlington on B1253. *St Andrew.*
A church with an unprepossessing exterior and a brick nave and chancel built in neo-Classical style with Gothic detail in 1768-70, and attributed to John Carr of York. A C15 stone west tower remains from an earlier church. The interior is another matter. Decorated in a pale green, the nave glows with light from four Gothic-revival windows. Over the west end is a gallery: the Stricklands' *family pew.* Double screens of Corinthian columns mark off the chancel and sanctuary. There are many Strickland *monuments.* Note the 1770s *glass* signed by William Peckitt.

GARTON-IN-THE-WOLDS. 3m W of Great Driffield on A166. *St Michael.*
A noteworthy Norman church of the 1130s consisting of an aisleless nave, C15 chancel, and a west tower with a top of the C15. Restored in the 1850s by J.L. Pearson, to whom is owed much of the interior, and by G.E. Street in 1865. To the latter are due the C13 style *frescos* by Clayton & Bell (recently restored in memory of Sir Nikolaus Pevsner, and the *reredos.* Note the painted *roofs.*

HEMINGBOROUGH. 12m S of York on A63. *St Mary.*
Built mainly in the C13 of Tadcaster stone with a stumpy central crossing

Beverley, St John. A rare sanctuary chair of c.937.

tower crowned by a slender early-C15 spire 190ft high, it became collegiate in 1429. A peculiarity is that the north aisle is wider than the nave itself. The *pulpit*, although appearing to be Jacobean, is dated 1717, and in the south-west corner is a tub-shaped *font* of c.1190. There were originally four stalls in the choir from which only one *misericord* survives, dated as c.1200, and it may be the earliest in Britain. The church contains the largest number of C16 bench-ends in the county. Two further points of note are the late-C15 cadaver *monument* in the north chapel and the C15 carved stone *table* in the north transept.

HOLME-UPON-SPALDING-MOOR. (H) 11m NE of Goole on A614. *All Saints.*

A church, standing high and alone on the only hill for miles, of which three bays of a C13 nave remain, rebuilt in the C15 and C16, and all sympathetically restored by Temple Moore in 1906-11. Consisting of a nave, north aisle and chancel, with a late-C15 west tower, and built in a variety of stone and C17 brick. The interior has considerable charm and is unspoilt: a *gallery* of 1767 built for a choir and orchestra now has a C17 *barrel organ;* C16 black-letter texts decorate the east wall, and more *wall paintings* are in a tower niche where a crowned figure holds souls in a sheet; and there is a fine Jacobean *pulpit* with *tester*. In the churchyard notice particularly the gravestone to Jane Alcock: 'She was a virtuous but unloving wife'.

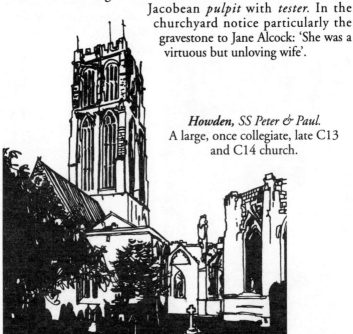

Howden, SS Peter & Paul.
A large, once collegiate, late C13 and C14 church.

HOWDEN. (H) N of Goole on A63. *St Peter.*
A large, once collegiate, cruciform church, late-C13 and C14, restored in 1843 and 1854. The original choir collapsed in 1609. The nave, completed c.1320, is a perfect example of its period. A splendid C15 *reredos* was formerly the pulpitum. Note the *parish coffin* of 1664, the eagle *lectern* and the very large *Royal Arms* of 1718 in the north aisle.

KINGSTON-UPON-HULL. (H) 6m SE of Beverley on A1079. *Holy Trinity*, Market Place.
The largest church in Britain. The C14 chancel, transepts and lower stage of the tower are built of the earliest medieval brick in Britain, and the nave, built of limestone, is 1389-1418. All was restored in 1841-5, and again in 1859-72 by Sir George Gilbert Scott. The interior is vast enough for a cathedral. The college-style arrangement of the pews in the nave dates from 1841. There are some good C14, C15 and C19 bench ends in the choir, and in the north chancel aisle is a *Last Supper* by James Parmentier, 1711. In the retro-choir is a fine Rococo *table* with a back panel showing cherubs' heads and religious vessels. There are a good number of monuments but nothing of note; the earliest is to Eleanor Box, Mayoress of Hull (d.1380). There is no earlier glass than the C19 except for a C15 *fragment* in the vestry. Note the C14 *font* of coloured marbles and the *brass* of 1451.

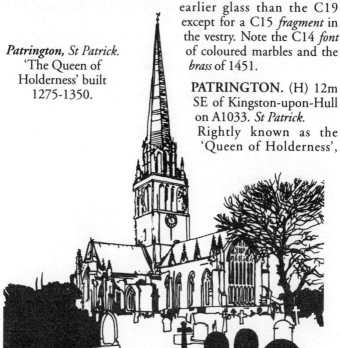

Patrington, St Patrick.
'The Queen of Holderness' built 1275-1350.

PATRINGTON. (H) 12m SE of Kingston-upon-Hull on A1033. *St Patrick.*
Rightly known as the 'Queen of Holderness',

this magnificent church was built between c.1275 and c.1350; first the transepts, then the nave with north and south aisles, and finally the chancel. It was finished off with a tall 189ft central spire. Entering by the north porch note the many masons' marks incorporating the letter 'A'. The interior is flooded with light for there is little coloured glass, and unusually the transepts have aisles. There is much here to compare with Hawton in Nottinghamshire, where the chancel is contemporary with the notable Easter Sepulchre, though Patrington is far grander. The C14 *screen* is much restored. In the north wall of the chancel is a rare C14 *Easter Sepulchre*, and in the south wall delicately decorated and crocketted *sedilia* and *piscina*. By far the most impressive fitting is the spectacular *reredos* of gilded oak made to designs of J.H. Gibbons in 1936. Above is the gloomy coloured glass of a 1884 east window. Note particularly the faint fragments of C14 *wall paintings* in the south aisle, the *pulpit* dated 1612, some pews of 1684, a badly weathered, but fine, C13 Virgin, and in the south chapel a *reredos* with a lamp pendant carved with the Annunciation.

SWINE. (H) 4m NE of Hull off A165. *St Mary.*
A rich c.1200 fragment of a vanished Cistercian nunnery, with fine traceried windows and an C18 tower. Note the eight carved *misericords* of c.1500, the fine C16 *screen* with the badge of Catherine of Aragon, and the alabaster tomb *effigies*.

Other Churches

BAINTON. 5m SW of Great Driffield on A163. *St Andrew.*
Almost all of this delightful church—the nave with aisles, large chancel and west tower—was built in the 1340s. The exception is the c.1300 SW corner of the chancel. Note the monument to Sir Edmund de Mauley (d.1314) whose soul is shown held in a napkin, also the *brass* to Roger Godeale (d.1429) and a painted wall memorial to an ejected rector, Robert Faucon, dated 1661, 21 years before his death!

NUNBURNHOLME. (H) 5m NW of Market Weighton off A1079. *St James.*
A Norman nave and chancel, with a tower of 1901 by Temple Moore who re-used the chancel arch to support his tower. Note the late-C14 fragments of *glass*, and the two rejoined parts of the best *Saxon cross* in Yorkshire.

North Riding

CASTLE HOWARD. 12m NE of York off A64. *Chapel.*
This is the private chapel built in the newer wing of Castle Howard (1700-26) and added in 1735-59 to John Vanbrugh's great house.

The chapel was remodelled with High Victorian fervour in 1875-8. The tall Corinthian columns, the sanctuary screen, and the flat *trompe-l'oeil* coffered *ceiling*, a copy of the St James's Palace chapel ceiling of the 1530s, are original. In the remodelling the floor was lowered, the coved ceiling inserted, pupils of C.E. Kempe painted the *frescos* of saints, and Kempe did the altar painting. Morris & Co *glass* by Burne-Jones is on hinged panels in the windows. Behind the altar is a plaster polychrome *bas-relief* by Andrea Sansovino (c.1467/70-1529).

COXWOLD. 6m SE of Thirsk off A19. *St Michael.*
An attractive C15 church in limestone with an octagonal tower; the chancel was rebuilt in 1774. Inside, the C18 box pews were cut down in 1906 and the former three-decker pulpit with tester was likewise tampered with. However, the C18 west gallery and flat ceiling survive. Note the good C15 *glass* in the heads of the nave windows. Around the chancel arch are coats of arms and above it, the *Royal Arms* of George II flanked by Fauconberg arms. This is the introduction to the astonishing Fauconberg, and the earlier Belassys, *monuments* that have taken over the chancel. The oldest is to Sir William Belassys (d.1603) and signed by Thomas Browne, and the most recent is to Rear-Admiral Lord Adolphus Fitzclarence (d.1856), illegitimate son of William IV, whose body lies in the Fauconberg vault. A memorial stone to Laurence Sterne (d.1768), who wrote the first modern novel, *Tristram Shandy*, stands outside the south wall of the nave.

EASBY. 1m SE of Richmond off B6271. *St Agatha.*
The church stands close to the gatehouse of the considerable abbey ruins. It is built of limestone with a late-C12 chancel, altered in the

Easby, St Agatha. A mid-C13 wall painting of the Expulsion from the Garden.

C13, when the nave was either built or remodelled. It is a long, low building with a small bellcote and a C14 tunnel-vaulted south porch. The church possesses the finest *Saxon cross* in North Yorkshire. Dated c.800, it is in the Victoria & Albert Museum, but a cast of it is in the church. On the nave north wall are C13 *paintings* of subjects taken from the Old Testament. There is more decorative painting on the south arcade arches. Do not be taken in by the chancel arch; it is not C13, but of 1869 by Sir George Gilbert Scott! Note the small C14 figures in the *glass* of the east window, the *hatchments*, and the Norman *font*. The nave roof is C19 supported on unusual *corbels*.

KIRKDALE. 4m W of Pickering off A170. *St Gregory.*
A small late-Saxon church notable for the best Saxon sundial in the country. It is above the south doorway with an inscription which dates it as c.1060. The nave, tower door, and chancel arch are c.1060, the north aisle c.1200; the chancel was rebuilt in 1881, and the church restored in 1907-9 by Temple Moore. Note the two Saxon coffin lids, one C7 and the other C11, the large Saxon *cross*, with other Saxon stone fragments, the *glass* by Kempe & Co in the east lancets, and the late-C14 *Virgin* in the north aisle.

KIRK HAMMERTON. 9m W of York off A59. *St John Baptist.*
Ignore the greater part of this church, built 1890-1, and concentrate on its south aisle, for this was a Saxon church comprising a tower, nave and chancel. Originally it had a C12 north aisle but this was demolished in 1890. It is built of very large masonry blocks, with a slender unbuttressed south-west tower, and west and south doors of two orders. Inside, the west end has a tall tower door. The chancel arch is a simple construction, and in the chancel is a Saxon window blocked by two later Norman windows.

KIRKLEATHAM. 6m E of Middlesbrough on A174. *St Cuthbert.*
A church rebuilt in finely tooled ashlar in a strict neo-Classical style by John Carr of York in 1763, with an earlier west tower of 1731. A Baroque *mausoleum*, built by James Gibbs in 1740, is attached to the north side of the chancel. The interior is modest, with a plain ceiling supported on Tuscan columns and a large, Venetian east window. Earlier box pews and the triple decker pulpit were cut down in alterations of 1855; the chancel fittings and altar are all C20. Do not overlook the *chest* of 1348, decorated with monsters, in the north aisle, or the *monument* to John Turner (c.1740) by Peter Scheemakers. In the octagonal mausoleum is an elegant *monument* by Scheemakers to Marwood Turner who died in 1739 on the Grand Tour, and for whom the mausoleum was built. Later Turner statues stand around in wall niches.
Turner's Hospital. Chapel.
This delightful small Baroque chapel was built in 1742 by James

Gibbs. The stone-faced entrance is beneath an octagonal clock-tower. In plan the interior is a Greek cross, and the groin-vaulted ceiling is supported by four fluted Tuscan columns. North and south galleries are linked by a stepped balcony in the west end with splendid wrought-iron *railing* above the entrance. To the left and right of the entrance two pews have noteworthy Rococo carved *doors*. The east window has Flemish *glass* of the Adoration of the Magi, flanked by mid-C18 glass showing John Turner, and Sir William Turner, the donor. Notwithstanding the unprepossessing surroundings, this elegant chapel is worth a detour.

LASTINGHAM. 6m NW of Pickering off A170. *St Mary.*
Of the monastery founded by St Cedd in 645 and destroyed by the Danes in the C9 nothing remains. But of the refounding in 1078, there remains an unforgettable and unique crypt; the church was partly built when the monks abandoned the site in 1086 and moved to York. It became parochial in 1228 when it achieved its present form, obviously far smaller than the planned abbey church. The crypt,

Kirkleatham,
Turners Hospital.
The west end.

apse, presbytery, and crossing are of 1078-86, north aisle C13, south aisle C14, with a C15 west tower. The chancel vault and south porch are restorations of 1879 by J.L. Peason.

PICKERING. 15m W of Scarborough on A170. *SS Peter & Paul.* A church sadly over-restored in 1878-80, but basically mid-C12 to C13, with an early-C13 west tower. It possesses one of the most complete sequences of C15 *wall paintings* in Britain. They are still remarkably vivid, although much restored in the 1880s. Near the lectern is a c.1340-50 cross-legged *effigy* holding a heart, and in the south chapel are two good alabaster *effigies*. Note the C18 brass *chandeliers*, and a banner in the Bruce Chapel. The chancel screen is C20.

ROBIN HOOD'S BAY. 5m SE of Whitby on B1447. *St Stephen Old Church.*
In the care of the Redundant Churches Fund. Built in 1821 this small, oblong, stone-built, aisleless church with cupola was deserted in 1870. Consequently its interior remains an undisturbed 'preaching box', with north and west *galleries, box pews*, a superb three-decker *pulpit* placed in the centre of the south side, and an organ in the west gallery. The *maidens' garlands*, formerly here, are now with the Yorkshire Museum and Art Gallery Service .

SCARBOROUGH. 30m NE of York on A64. *St Martin*, Albion Road.
A large, solid church built in now sombre limestone by G.F. Bodley in 1861-2. Bodley was the first customer of William Morris and the building went up at the right time – Morris and his friends began their work in 1861. The vast, high interior has fittings designed by Bodley and the decoration is by the Morris firm. The chancel and north chapel *ceilings* are distinctively Morris. The *glass* is entirely theirs and was designed by Rossetti, Burne-Jones, Morris and Ford Madox Brown. Behind the altar is Bodley tracery with an Adoration of the Magi by Burne-Jones with natural decoration by Morris. The gem of the interior is the *pulpit* with ten panels designed by Morris, Rossetti and Brown, but painted by George Campfield – notice the lilies becoming birds. In the vestry are more panels of St Martin by the trio of friends.

SHERIFF HUTTON. 10m N of York 3m E of B1363. *St Helen & Holy Cross.*
The limestone and sandstone tower and nave are Norman, with aisles added in the C14, C13 chancel, and a C15 five-light east window with glass of 1861. Inside, *box pews* from the C17 to C19 fill the nave and aisles; the Communion rail is Jacobean; and note the C14 *glass* in the heads of the north windows, and the *hatchments* in the south chapel. The tomb in the north aisle is said to be that of Edward

Prince of Wales (d.1484), son of Richard III; it is dated, however ,as early-C15. The *brass* in the north chapel is to John and Dorothy Fiennes (d.1491) who died in infancy. They are in swaddling clothes.

SKELTON. 4m NW of York on A19. *St Giles.*
A remarkably small church of limestone, only 44 by 32 feet, and an exceptional building completely of c.1240, with amazing detail that may be the result of a restoration by nineteen-year-old Henry Graham in 1814-18. The nave and chancel are in one, but the division is marked on the exterior by a double bellcote. The *south porch* is richly decorated by many shafts with stiff-leaf capitals, good enough for a cathedral. Indeed it was under the patronage of the York Cathedral Treasurers for centuries. However, the porch is of 1814-18! The roof is a replacement of c.1880, but the interior is no less rich than the porch; a short two-bay nave has substantial piers to the east which may originally have been intended to support a crossing tower. In the chancel a fine *piscina* has stiff-leaf decoration, and a neat arrangement of shafted, triple lancets lights the east end; the C19 *glass* is by Lavers, Barraud & Westlake. By the north door is a monument to Henry Graham (d.1819), aged only 24.

WHITBY. 15m NW of Scarborough on A171. *St Mary.*
Standing on a high cliff above the very attractive fishing town, one needs stamina to reach this church; there are 199 steps up Church Stairs. It is very well worth the effort. The church is Norman (c.1120), with a simple nave, chancel, and tower of c.1190, to which long transepts were added in the C13. In 1818 the nave was extended

Whitby, St Mary. A Norman tower, nave and chancel with C13 additions.

northwards making a large square space, and the south porch was added in 1821-3. The exterior is unimpressive but the interior is one of the most astonishing in Britain. In 1744 the north transept was remodelled, the south transept followed in 1759, more refitting continued until 1764, and it is to these years that the surprising charm of the unexpected interior is due. It is also untouched by C19 restorers, but sympathetically restored by W.D. Caroë in 1905. Galleries are on every side; in the transepts, in the nave and in the north aisle; all are C18 and painted white. The late-C17 *Cholmley pew* on barley-sugar columns presumptuously replaced the Rood Screen. A tall narrow three-decker *pulpit* of 1778 with a tester, raised perilously to gallery height, makes certain that the vicar is seen by all his congregation. *Box pews* are of many dates: those with finials are C17, others are C18 and early-C19, and to the left of the chancel arch is a C17 *family pew*. C18 *Commandment boards* decorate the walls, a *Royal Arms* of 1840 hangs above the chancel arch, and five steps lead into a murky chancel with east window *glass* of 1907 by C.E. Kempe. The interior is said to be like below decks in a large sailing ship, which is very likely since so much of the woodwork was made by shipwrights. This is a memorable church and is still lit by candlelight.

Other Churches

ALDWARK. 10m NW of York off B6265. *St Stephen.*
Built in 1846-53 by an unconventional architect, E.B. Lamb, using handmade herring-bone brickwork, flint, and cobbles, with freestone dressings. It comprises a short nave, with crossing and polygonal ended transepts, and a short chancel, all covered by a vast roof, with an extraordinary vaned south tower. Inside, the open timber roof, made mainly on medieval principles, but with quirky effects, defies description; it is better to see it. The interior has an intimate atmosphere filled with speckled light,
HORNBY. 9m W of Northallerton off A684. *St Mary.*
A large church of various coloured limestone with a late-C12 chancel, of which the east wall is 1877 by J.L. Pearson, an early-C14 nave, and a tower of which the lower stages are C11 and the belfry C15. Inside are an early-C16 painted parclose *screen*, good medieval *monuments*, C15 *glass* and a 1489 *brass* in the south chapel.
INGLEBY ARNCLIFFE. 6m NE of Northallerton on A172. *All Saints.*
A small church rebuilt in 1821 in a rustic Classical style with nave and chancel, and a west tower with C18 sash windows. The interior is painted white, setting off the deep red of the *box pews* with their original numbers. A *sailing ship* hangs from the roof. Note the two *Royal Arms* of William III and George VI, the medieval *monuments* and *glass* fragments from Mount Grace Priory.

West Riding

ADEL. 4m NW of Leeds on A660. *St John Baptist.*
The best and most complete Norman church in Yorkshire, consisting
of an aisleless nave and a lower, square-ended chancel, with a 1838
'renewed' bellcote on the west gable, and a sumptuous *south portal*
with 37 different beak-heads. The roof is modern, the two windows
in the nave south wall are C16, and the exceptional bronze *door-ring*
is Norman. The unplastered interior is dominated by a fine Norman
chancel arch of three orders, with capitals carved *in situ* showing the
Baptism of Christ and the Crucifixion. In the nave hang three *paintings,* Crucifixion, Ascension, and a smaller Gethsemane, by John
Vanderbank (1694-1739), given in 1745. Eric Gill made the *font
cover* in 1921, and Henry Gyles of York designed the arms of Charles
II (1681) in the east window, and the memorial window in the chancel to his friend Thomas Kirke (d.1706).

ALLERTON MAULEVERER. 6m S of Boroughbridge off A1.
St Martin.
In the care of the Redundant Churches Fund. Once a Benedictine
priory founded in the C12, the church was rebuilt in 1745 in a
Classical style, but retaining the four-bay C14 south arcade of the old
church. The rebuilding is attributed to James Paine. With central
tower, aisled nave, transepts and chancel, and some neo-Norman
decorative detail, the church has great charm. The impressive
hammer-beam *roof, pulpit, box pews, benches,* the Lord's Prayer and
Creed *panels,* and the framed *painting* of Moses and Aaron above the
chancel arch, are all of 1745. In the east window is C18 *glass* by
William Peckitt showing two small views of the original church. The
north transept has two early-C14 oak *effigies* of cross-legged knights
and an unusual *brass* of Sir John Mauleverer (d.1400) and his wife.

ARKSEY. 2m N of Doncaster off A19. *All Saints.*
A large cruciform Norman church with aisled nave and a C13 south
aisle, transepts and chancel. A north chapel was built c.1300, the
south chapel is C15, and the south doorway C13, the same date as
the upper stages of the tower. Good detailing throughout. Restored
by Sir George Gilbert Scott in 1869-70 who 'improved' the east wall.
The furnishings are worth noting: the *pulpit* and *pews* are 1634, and
the *font cover* in the Jacobean style is dated 1662. Note the many
interesting pieces of heraldic *glass.*

BEAUCHIEF. 4m S of Sheffield off A621. *St Thomas Beckett.*
Of the Premonstratensian Abbey founded c.1175 there is nothing
left but the tower. Against the tower east wall a chapel was built in
c.1662 with a four-light east window with Gothic revival tracery.

The tower is impressive, unlike the rest of the exterior. Enter under the tower west door and there is an immediate contrast; little has changed since 1664. The carved *box pews* with decorated finials, panelled *family pews* for rector and squire, a three-decker *pulpit*, and Communion *table* are all of 1664 and in the original arrangement. Note the Gothic monument to Mrs Pegge Burnell (d.1844), the squire's wife.

CAMPSALL. 6m N of Doncaster off A1. *St Mary Magdalene.*
A large limestone, early-Norman cruciform church, with a fine C12 west tower, aisled nave, transepts and chancel. In the west bay of the south aisle is C13 rib-vaulting with a rare priest's room above. There is good zigzag Norman decoration throughout, and the chancel has C13 lancet windows, although the east window is C19 with glass of 1964. Pride of the church is the superb C15 oak *rood screen* with its original coving and a long rhyming inscription. Note the stone altar by A.W.N. Pugin in the south transept and the Yarborough family *monument* (1803) by John Flaxman.

CANTLEY. 4m E of Doncaster off B1396. *St Wilfred.*
The church consists of a C15 west tower and nave, C14 south aisle, 1894 north aisle, and C12 chancel with a Norman priest's door with *tympanum.* The interior is almost entirely by Sir Ninian Comper in a correct Gothic style: a brilliantly coloured creation of 1894. Most noteworthy are the gilded *screens* painted green and red. Comper also designed the 'English altar' with hanging pyx and canopy, and the *glass* of the sanctuary south window. To see this interior is to gain an idea of the effect of medieval colour. Recently the north side of the church has been sympathetically extended to accommodate a larger congregation.

FISHLAKE. 7m NE of Doncaster off A614. *St Cuthbert.*
Built of millstone grit this is a church of many periods, a late-C13 south aisle, a C14 chancel, and a C15 west tower with a C13 base. It also has the finest Norman *doorway* in Yorkshire in the south door. Richly carved with figures, the Virtues fighting the Vices, it is surprisingly well preserved. Note the sculpture of St Cuthbert in a niche above the tower west window. The C14 font has a Jacobean cover.

HALIFAX. 5m SW of Bradford on A58. *All Souls*, Haley Hill, Boothtown.
In the care of the Redundant Churches Fund. Considered by Sir George Gilbert Scott to be his best church, it was built in millstone grit with limestone dressings in 1856-9, using C13 and C14 Gothic detail. Its north-west spire is 236 feet, and it has an aisled nave, transepts, and chancel with south chapel. It was built to outshine the Square Congregational Church. The wrought-iron *screens* are by

Francis Skidmore and the glass of 1859 is by Clayton & Bell, and John Hardman. Clayton & Bell also painted the Choir of Angels on the chancel ceiling. The alabaster *reredos* and the inlaid Caen stone *pulpit* are by J.B. Philip.

St John Baptist, Church Street.
A vast, mainly C15 church, built of blackened stone, with a tall C15 west tower and some C12 and C13 work on the north aisle. It consists of nave and transepts, both aisled, with chancel. The furnishings are noteworthy: a splendid C15 *font cover* with a spire; nine C15 carved *misericords* in the chancel; an outstanding *communion rail* of 1698; *Royal Arms* of Queen Anne; *box pews* of c.1633; the fine wood *ceilings* in nave and chancel dating from 1636, and an unusual *poor box* of 1701 carried by a life-size carved figure, older than the box, known as 'Old Tristram'.

KIRKBY MALHAM. 8m NW of Skipton off A65. *St Michael.*
Replacing an earlier church, this was built in the late-C15, ashlar-faced and consisting of nave and chancel in one, with chapels, and a west tower. The south door is older than the church and has a sanctuary ring (sanctuary from the law was claimed by those holding the ring). Inside, the floor slopes gently east, and the arcade piers have niches for saints' statues, removed at the Reformation, when the C12 stone *font* was thrown into the churchyard and found a century ago. Family *pews* are C16 to C17; one is dated 1631, and the *box pews* are early-C19. Note the small German *glass* panel of 1589, and the C15 chest in the west end. The chancel panelling was inserted in 1923.

LEDSHAM. 10m E of Leeds off A1. *All Saints.*
Hidden behind C15 battlements, pinnacles, and spire, is an C8 Saxon church comprising the lower stage of the tower, nave with north and south upper chambers, and a small chancel. The upper stages of the tower are Norman, and the tower door is C11 Saxon but much restored in 1871. Finally, the north aisle and Lady chapel are late-C14. The best of the *monuments* are in the Lady chapel: Lady Betty Hastings (d.1739) by Peter Scheemakers, and Lady Mary Bolles (d.1662), who was made a baroness in her own right, and has a recumbent, and shrouded, marble *effigy.*

LEEDS. 40m N of Sheffield on M1. *St John Evangelist*, New Briggate.
In the care of the Redundant Churches Fund. Built in 1632-4 of millstone grit in the Gothic style, and the largest of its date in England, it comprises a double nave with a north-west tower rebuilt in 1838. The church suffered a drastic restoration by Norman Shaw in 1866-8, but the serious damage was reversed in the early C20. The interior shines with dark polished oak. Cut down C17 *box pews*, minus their doors, fill the double naves, and note the sumptuous

Leeds, St John. The C17 interior.

C17 two-decker *pulpit* and tester. Dominating the east end is an elaborate C17 double *screen* topped with a *Royal Arms* in the south nave, and a scroll-surrounded cross in the north, both supported by generous strapwork. Decorated plaster *panels* fill the roof spaces between the timbers and the tie-beams are supported by angels and musicians. The north chancel has an elaborate *reredos* by Antonio Salviati of Venice. There is a *monument* in the south nave to John Harrison (d.1656), the founder of the church, whose portrait hangs on the west wall. Note the carved *Royal Arms* taken from the north nave *screen.* The glass is all of the C19. There are many wall plates.
St Saviour, Ellerby Road.
Built in 1842-5 for Dr Pusey, a leading Tractarian (see Introduction), it consists of an aisled nave, crossing tower, transepts and chancel. (G.F. Bodley added the Pusey Chapel in 1890.) With such a founder it was always 'high church', and the interior confirms this. A.W.N.Pugin designed the *glass*, and two windows, one in the north porch and the other in the north aisle, are by Morris & Co, 1875-80. The *reredos* is of 1921 by Temple Moore.

METHLEY. 7m SE of Leeds on A639. *St Oswald.*
This is an interesting church, notwithstanding the overworked restorations of 1876. It is built of York sandstone in the C13, remodelled in the C14 and again in the C15, with a chancel rebuilt in 1926, and comprising nave, chancel and C14 south aisle with a C15 west tower. The south chapel is important because it can be exactly dated 1483-4. The interior has much to interest to us: a C16 *font*

cover, a good *pulpit* made in 1708, a remarkable Flemish *lectern* of c.1500 with a C19 eagle, and many good *monuments*. Near the chapel are good alabaster *effigies* of Sir Robert Waterton (d.1424), the founder of the chantry, and his wife. There is a moderately good monument by Peter Scheemakers to Charles Saville (d.1741) and his wife; a better one is to Sir John Savile (d.1606) and his son, attributed to Maximilian Colt. Note the C15 *glass* in the chapel east window. The head corbels of the chancel arch are said to have inspired Henry Moore in his early career.

MIDHOPESTONES. 10m NW of Sheffield off A616. *St James.*
A tiny church built c.1705 of millstone grit and consisting of nave and chancel in one, with a minute bellcote on the west gable end. The interior has furnishings all of c.1705, *box pews* (two named), *west gallery*, a neat gallery *stair*, with nicely turned balusters, *wall panelling* and *pulpit*. It is a completely charming interior, so unaffected by style changes that it might have been built in 1625 rather than 1705.

SELBY. 11m S of York on A19. *SS Mary & Germaine.*
This is a rare survivor, an abbey church unspoiled by the Dissolution.

Selby, SS Mary & Germaine. The nave,
built 1290-1335.

It was begun in c.1100 and completed c.1230; the chancel was rebuilt c. 1280, the nave clerestory and galleries in 1290-1335. The collapse of the central tower in 1690 damaged the south transept, and the whole was restored in 1871-3 by Sir George Gilbert Scott. The south transept was rebuilt in 1889-90, a serious fire damaged the building in 1906, and the crossing tower was rebuilt in 1908. The nave is reminiscent of Durham Cathedral with round-arched arcades, galleries and clerestory, with a great deal of zigzag decoration. Although the nave ceiling was badly burnt some sixty carved bosses were rescued and replaced. In the chancel north aisle are c.1280 carved stone bosses, while in the south aisle are C20 replacements. Note the magnificent C15 *font cover*, the four-seat *sedilia* of c.1350, the C15 alabaster panel in the *sacristy*, and the many *monuments*, including a C14 cross-legged knight in the south aisle. The restored Jesse window in the east end has notable *glass* of c.1330.

SKELTON. 3m SE of Ripon off B6265. *Christ the Consoler.*
Built in 1871-2 in C13 Gothic style by William Burges for Lady Mary Vyner, mother of the Marchioness of Ripon (see Studley Royal), in memory of her son kidnapped and murdered by Greek brigands. It was paid for out of the unredeemed ransom money. With a north tower and spire, a steeply-roofed aisled nave and clerestory, and a lower rib-vaulted chancel, it is worthy of Burges, but less ornate than his nearby masterpiece at Studley Royal. The interior was richly carved by T. Nicholls, and the four-bay nave has arcading shafted with black Purbeck marble, similar to that at Salisbury Cathedral. Filling the space above the chancel arch is Nicholls' *sculpture* of the Ascension, leading the eye beyond into a colourful chancel. Throughout, the remarkable *glass* is by Frederick Weeks, obviously influenced by William Morris.

STUDLEY ROYAL. 2m W of Ripon off B6265. *St Mary.*
In the care of the National Trust, maintained by English Heritage. Built 1871-8 in C13 Gothic by William Burges for the Marchioness of Ripon, daughter of Lady Vyner (see Skelton). This church, larger than that at Skelton, is a masterpiece, consisting of an aisled nave, south porch, west tower with spire, an aisleless chancel and a vestry to the north-east. The interior is similar to Skelton but far more ornate: the same Purbeck marble shafts and the same four-bay arcades with dog-tooth decoration, exactly as at Skelton, and the sculpture is by T .Nicholls, and the *glass* by Frederick Weekes and made by Saunders & Co. It differs in the far greater richness of the chancel with its painted ceilings, brasswork, mosaics, marbles and alabaster. The south aisle has a table-tomb to the Marchioness (d.1907) and the Marquess (d.1909) in white marble, surrounded by a screen of cipollino and verde antico. All very rich.

THORNHILL. 5m SW of Wakefield on B6117. *St Michael.*
A sandstone church mainly of the C15 with an impressive west tower and a nave rebuilt in 1877 by G.E. Street. The main reason for visiting this church is the important Saville north chapel of 1447 filled with superb medieval and Renaissance *monuments.* These include a splendid alabaster *tomb-chest* to Sir George Savile (d.1622) in full armour, by Maximilian Colt, and two oak *effigies.* Note the ten fragments of Saxon crosses of c.850 and the C15 *glass* in the Savile chapel.

TICKHILL. 9m E of Rotherham on A361. *St Mary.*
Rebuilt in white magnesian limestone in the late-C14 and C15 out of wool profits, this church is one of the best in Yorkshire, comprising nave, two aisles, and chancel with chapels. The lower stages of the west tower are C13 but the upper stages are 1429, built from money left in a will by John Sandford. The interior is particularly light, spacious and grand. Over the north door is a painted panel of *Royal Arms,* c.1724; the late-C15 font has a canopy of 1959; the *pulpit* is c.1606; and both the eagle lectern and the high altar are of 1908, while the reredos is 1881. In the south aisle windows is some good late-C15 *glass,* the remaining glass being unremarkable C19, although the window above the chancel arch of 1895 by C.E. Kempe is worth noting. Do not overlook the *monuments* in the north-west corner.

TONG. 4m SE of Bradford off A650. *St James.*
In a surprisingly rural area, trapped between Bradford and Leeds, this ashlar-faced church, built in 1727, has its own surprises. Part of
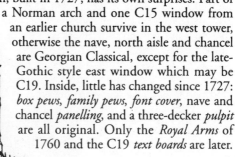
a Norman arch and one C15 window from an earlier church survive in the west tower, otherwise the nave, north aisle and chancel are Georgian Classical, except for the late-Gothic style east window which may be C19. Inside, little has changed since 1727: *box pews, family pews, font cover,* nave and chancel *panelling,* and a three-decker *pulpit* are all original. Only the *Royal Arms* of 1760 and the C19 *text boards* are later.

Tickhill, St Mary. Rebuilt out of 'wool money' in the late C14 and C15.

Note the six *hatchments*. This is an exceptionally undisturbed 'prayer book' interior.

WAKEFIELD. 8m S of Leeds on A61. *St Mary, Bridge Chapel.*
Five bridge chapels remain in Britain and this is the most important. Built c.1350 as a shrine to collect money for the upkeep of the bridge, it was restored in 1847 by Sir George Gilbert Scott who, extraordinarily, removed the west front and re-erected it at Kettlethorpe Hall, Wakefield. The chapel was restored again in 1939. Note the fine carved *reliefs* of the Nativity, Annunciation, Resurrection, Ascension and Pentecost on the parapet. The sacristy is below the east end of the chapel.

Other Churches

ALDFIELD. 3m W of Ripon off B3265. *St Lawrence.*
Small, of three bays with a north chapel, and built in c.1783. The interior preserves an unaltered 'prayer book' layout. *Box pews* face each other across the nave with a three-decker *pulpit*, text *boards*, *font*, Communion *table* and *rail*, all of c.1738.

BRAMHOPE. 5m NW of Leeds A660. *St Giles.*
Built by the lord of the manor in 1649 as a simple stone oblong chapel, it is unusual in that the original Puritan arrangement of the furnishings is undisturbed. *Box pews* face a three-decker *pulpit* set in the centre of the north wall, all contemporary with the building. The *font* is dated 1673.

CLIFFORD. 3m SE of Weatherby off A1. *St Edward.*
Built in 1845-8 by J.A. Hansom in a neo-Norman style, this remarkable Roman Catholic church was paid for out of local and European contributions, including sums from the Pope and the Queen of France. An impressive four-storied west tower was added in 1859-66. A statue of the Virgin in the Lady Chapel was sculpted by K. Hoffman in Rome, a Jew who converted to Catholicism when creating the image. Notable *glass* includes four windows by A.W.N. Pugin.

DONCASTER. 10m NE of Rotherham on A630. *St George.*
Built by Sir George Gilbert Scott in 1854-8 in Gothic style of c.1300, with a C14-style tower; one of his best churches. With a crossing tower of 170ft, aisled nave, transepts and chancel the interior is richly decorated. Note the excellent *glass*, the *reredos* by J.Birnie Philip who did much of the sculpture.

FULNECK. 4m SE of Bradford off B6154. *Moravian Church.*
A Moravian settlement since 1742, the rectangular church dates from 1746-8. The pulpit on the south side is the focus of the interior with galleries on three sides. Over the north entrance is a Snetzler *organ* of 1748. The American architect, Benjamin Latrobe, was baptised here and is commemorated by 1933 *glass*.

GREAT HOUGHTON. 5m E of Barnsley on B6273. *Unitarian Chapel.*

A quaint and slightly forbidding stone building with round-topped battlements, built c.1650. Nave and chancel are one, with a bellcote on the east gable. Inside, the original *box pews* survive, with their knobbed ends. The *pulpit* with tester stands halfway down the south wall opposite the entrance. A modern connection links the chapel to the church hall.

HAREWOOD. 6m N of Leeds on A61. *All Saints.*

An ashlar-faced building in Harewood House Park, almost entirely of the C15 except for the east gable of 1793, restored by Sir George Gilbert Scott in 1862-3. The church is unmemorable, but six C15 alabaster *monuments*, each with two effigies, are well worth a detour.

LEEDS. 40m N of Sheffield on A1. *St Aidan*, Roundhay Road.

Built in an Italian Romanesque style in 1891-4 in red brick with stone dressings, it has an aisled nave, eastern apse and, as yet, no tower. There are outstanding *mosaics* of the life of St Aidan done in 1916 by Frank Brangwyn.

STANNINGTON. 3m W of Sheffield on B6076. *Underbank Chapel.*

Built of stone in 1742, this is a charming and modest Unitarian chapel. The perfectly symmetrical six-bay front comprises two high round-head windows in the centre, flanked by two doors, each with a round window above, the last bays having two windows one above the other. A perfect Classical example of its time.

SCOTLAND

SCOTLAND

There are few medieval churches left in Scotland. Many, in the Lowlands were ruined in the English incursions of 1544 and 1547, others were stripped of lead and fittings after the Reformation when they quickly became ruins. There is also little in the way of medieval fittings. Reformers 'cleansed' churches by throwing out and burning anything pertaining to the old religion. The Civil War (1642-9) completed the despoiling of ancient churches leaving little of any historical value.

From 1581 the Reformed Church of Scotland did not permit burials within the kirk building. This accounts for the number of private family 'aisles' built on to kirks and consisting of a family pew, or 'loft', over a family burial vault. It also explains why there are so few monuments in churches. The fashion for 'aisles' is also responsible for the Scottish post-Reformation T plan where the 'aisle' is built on to the nave midway down the north side. When another family built an 'aisle' on the south side the church became cruciform. Another Scottish feature is the frequence of retiring rooms, with a hearth, off the family 'aisle'. This facility enabled the family to attend the morning service, before fortifying themselves with a meal in the retiring room ready to face the afternoon service.

The Reformed Church also used a long communion table placed down the centre of the aisle with the box pews facing it, as in the Low Countries. This accounts for some of the long narrow naves. Galleries were often taken over by guilds and trades when they became 'lofts', or private guild galleries. These were originally distinguished by being painted with symbols of the tools and cyphers of the tradesmen; some still survive.

It is a common error to regard Scottish church interiors as drab. Many are decorated; Calvinist principles prohibited only the portrayal of the Deity and saints, but other means of 'decorement' were not banned, leaving loft owners free to paint whatever they wished on the panels of their 'aisles'.

An ecclesiastical event, unique to Scotland, was the Disruption of 1843, when something like a third of the congregation of the Church of Scotland left to form the Free Church. In 1840 the United Presbyterian Church was formed out of the Relief Presbytery and the

United Associated Synod. The two events brought about the building of competing churches; the Presbyterians favouring the Gothic Revival style and the Free Church adopting a simple, less ornate, style. Both sects were amalgamated into the United Free Church in 1900, so making half their churches redundant, and many were abandoned.

The influence of the Oxford Movement came late to Scotland and was almost negligible; the Glasgow branch of the Ecclesiological Society was only founded in 1893.

Borders

The region suffered cruelly from warfare and consequently there are many church ruins in the old counties of Roxburgh, and Berwick. The churches that survive are no earlier than the mid-seventeenth century. However, Ladykirk is an exception; it was built in c.1500 and has remained practically unaltered, mainly owing to its lack of any decoration which recommended it to the Reformers. The region also boasts what must be one of the smallest churches in Scotland at Lyne (only 34 feet by eleven inside) and it contains one of only four Scottish canopied pews.

EDROM. 20m SE of Dunbar off A6105. *Parish Kirk.*
The original kirk was built in the late C15 by Bishop Blackadder of which only the aisle remains from a rebuilding carried out in 1732. All was drastically restored in 1886. A strange two-storey belfry dates from the rebuilding. In the churchyard is a gabled early-C19 *hearse-house*, and roofless *stables*.

LADYKIRK. 6m SW of Berwick-on-Tweed on B6470. *St Mary.*
Built in c.1500, ashlar-faced with stone-slab roof, consisting of a tall nave and apsed chancel with apsed north and south transepts, a slender west tower, rebuilt in the upper stages, and cupola, it is complete and practically unaltered. Inside, the nave and chancel are covered with a pointed stone vault marked out by plain ribs. There is no decoration either inside or out except for crocketted finials capping the buttresses.

LAUDER. 25m SE of Edinburgh on A68. *Old Kirk.*
Rebuilt in 1673 by Sir William Bruce with Gothic detail on a Greek cross plan and with a central tower capped by an octagonal steeple. The kirk was restored in 1820 and 1864. The rough-stone finish may have been once harled. Inside, four galleries occupy each of the four arms of the cross and the *pulpit* of 1820 stands by the south-east pier of the crossing.

Lauder, Old Kirk. Rebuilt in 1673 by Sir William Bruce.

Other Churches

BOWDEN, 5m SE of Galashiels off B6359. *Parish Kirk.*
A mid-C17 rebuilding of a kirk founded in 1128, restored and much altered in 1909. The Carver family's north 'aisle' of 1661, above its burial vault, has had its front moved to a new position, and has become the organ loft and choir. The Roxburghe east 'aisle', also with its burial vault beneath, became the chancel in 1909 necessitating a steep flight of steps over the vault below. Note the coloured armorial bearings of the family lofts.

LINTON. 8m NE of Jedburgh on B6436. *Parish Kirk.*
Basically a Norman church of c.1127 but much rebuilt, consisting of a nave and smaller chancel. The south porch, added in 1858, has a carved *tympanum* of a knight slaying a monster, which was previously above the south door. Note the Norman *font*.

LYNE. 4m W of Peebles on A72. *Parish Kirk.*
A tiny kirk measuring only 34ft by 11ft inside, built in c.1645 of ashlar, with windows of c.1645, restored in 1830 and in 1889 when the porch and belfry were added. Inside is a circular *pulpit* of c.1645, rare for Scotland, decorated with fluted pilasters and – another rarity, one of only four in Scotland – a *canopied pew* dated 1644.

Central

This is a region offering only a small selection of churches but of those two in Stirling are outstanding: Holy Rood, one of the best preserved and oldest churches in Scotland, built in the C14 in imitation Norman style; and the Chapel Royal, built in 1594 by James VI (later James I of England), containing extensive wall paintings of the period. Otherwise, it is the sad story of so much of Scotland: roofless

Lecropt. Parish Kirk. Interior, the Kier loft.

and ruined churches left to decay and finally disappear because either new C19 churches were built to take their place or the population has moved away.

LECROPT. 1m NW of Bridge of Allan off A9. *Parish Kirk.*
Built in 1824-6 in Gothic Revival style by William Stirling. The interior has a particularly fine *laird's loft* for the Kier family in the west end looking down into the kirk between slender Gothic columns supporting a Gothic traceried ceiling with seven Kier busts set in Gothic alcoves in the west wall. The pews of the kirk are not original. Note the Kier *hatchments*.

STIRLING. 25m NE of Glasgow off M80. *Holy Rood.*

Stirling Castle, Chapel Royal. Built in 1594 by James VI

One of the best preserved of Scotland's old churches. The aisled nave, notwithstanding the massive piers of the arcades, is early-C14 – it was a Scottish fashion to imitate Norman and pointed architecture in the C14 – with a C16 west tower. The aisled choir, with polygonal apse, is early C16, and it was here that Mary Stuart and James VI (James I of England) were crowned as babies. Both nave and aisles are rib-vaulted and many of the *capitals* both here and in the choir have carved decoration. Attached to the north aisle wall is the chapel of St Andrew of c.1500 where the rib vaults have carved *bosses*; it contains three *graveslabs*, one dated 1584, with the arms of the Durhams of Grange, and another to Forrester of Garden, who built the chapel. Note the *consecration cross*. There is a simple Easter sepulchre in the north wall of the choir. Of particular interest is the restored *wall decoration* including a false window, the cypher of James VI, and swags of fruit, painted in 1628-9 by Valentyne Jenking of Glasgow. *Chapel Royal.*

A simple rectangular building of seven bays with a steep slated roof, crow-stepped gables and an arched south door flanked by Corinthian columns, and built by James VI in 1594. Inside, the C16 *pulpit*, one of only two in Scotland, has been removed and is in the Castle. Extensive wall paintings of 1629 were discovered and restored in 1940.

Other Churches

KILMARNOCK. 8m NE of Dumbarton on A811. *Parish Kirk.*
A handsome rectangular Classical kirk of 1811 with large round-headed sash windows, its harling scraped clean, a pedimented gable over the west door and a cupola bellcote set back over the west end. Only one gallery inside.

KIRKINTILLOCH. 8m NE of Glasgow on A803. *Old Kirk.*
Built in 1644 on a Greek Cross plan, with three windows having typical Gothic-Revival traceries. Once-harled walls were scraped during restorations of 1890. An C18 *pulpit* and fittings survive. Above the C18 rusticated churchyard entrance arch is a small square watch tower with a bird-cage belfry; the bell was tolled as funeral processions approached.

Dumfries and Galloway

Like the Border region, this part of Scotland suffered horribly from border raids and invasions and it is not surprising to find little or nothing in the way of early church buildings. The earliest here is the Parish Kirk of Terregles, with a choir of 1585, unfortunately restored in 1875. Otherwise, there are rebuilt C18 examples in the Classical style – until the Gothic-Revival took hold in the C19 – such as the Kirk at Kirkmahoe. The Parish Kirk at Durisdeer still has some of its double moveable communion pews, a once common feature of C19 Scottish church fittings.

DUMFRIES. 30m NW of Carlisle on A75. *St Michael.*
Rebuilt in local red sandstone in 1744-5 in a plain Classical style by two Dumfries masons, Thomas Twaddell and Alexander Afleck, and James Harley, a wright. A tall, square tower, finished with an octagonal stone spire, dominates a wide rectangular kirk with round-headed windows, which was restored in 1869 and 1881. A spacious interior is divided by arcaded Tuscan columns supporting galleries and a coved plaster ceiling. An original back and *sounding board* forms part of a later pulpit. Note the two C18 turned wood candlesticks, and the painted fragments of *loft panels.* In the kirkyard two elegant stone *gate piers* (c.1750) capped with urn finials are hollow and were used as sentry boxes to guard recent burials from 'resurrectionists' snatching bodies for vivisection.

DURISDEER. 18m N of Dumfries on A702. *Parish Kirk.*
Built in 1699 in the Classical style on a cruciform plan with the north arm formed by the Queensberry *burial 'aisle'.* Attached to the west end is a neatly planned two storey building, formerly the village school. The west tower, ingeniously containing fireplace flues, rises from the centre of the school block. A timber spire was removed in the mid-C19. Moveable, double *communion pews* and a *wrought-iron bracket* to hold a baptismal basin attached to the pulpit, survive from the original fittings. Particularly notice the magnificent Baroque *monument* in black and white marbles to the Duke of Queensberry (d.1711) by John Nost.

Other Churches

KIRKMAHOE. In the parish of Kirkton, 3m N of Dumfries off A701. *The Kirk.*
Built in 1822-3 by Walter Newall in Gothic Revival style, an early example of its use in Scottish churches. Note the early-C18 Greek-revival *memorial tablet* with a draped urn and lengthy epitaph, and the two C18 *Benefaction boards* for the Poor School. In the kirk - yard is a detached gabled *hearse house* once containing the village hearse.

TERREGLES. 2m NW of Dumfries off A75. *Parish Kirk.*
Built in 1799 on to the choir of the old church of 1585 and the mortuary chapel of the 4th Lord Herries (note the date over the south door). Restored in 1875, the window mullions were removed, useless buttresses added, and the roof renewed. Notice particularly

Durisdeer, Parish Kirk. Interior,
Queensberry Monument.

the medieval *painted panel* of the Virgin, two *stalls* from Lincluden
Abbey, and two C16 Maxwell *Tombs*.

Fife

This region is fortunate in having one of the best of the post-
Reformation churches in Scotland in St Columba at Burntisland.
Built in c.1590, it preserves some of the oldest of the original
fittings, and was the first to be built on a central plan with all the
pews centred on the communion table. It preserves an early magistrates' pew dated 1609 and items of seafaring interest. Dunfermline
Abbey built in 1128 was sacked by Reformers in the C16 and left
in ruins, as were so many of Scotland's ecclesiastic buildings,

although this one was happily restored in the 1820s. The Abbey, St Fillan, Aberdour, and St Athernasse at Leuchars, are three of the few surviving Norman churches in Scotland, although only the chancel remains in the latter building, since the nave was rebuilt in the mid-C19.

ANSTRUTHER EASTER. 13m SE of Dundee on A917. *Parish Church.*
Built in 1634-6 on a rudimentary T plan with a north 'aisle' (closed off in c.1830) and a tall west steeple in a Dutch style added in 1644. The south wall facing the town is finished in smart ashlar and the rest is of harled rubble. Entrance is by way of a simple barrel-vaulted passage beneath the tower and one enters the kirk beneath a deep west gallery. The interior was recast in 1908 and nothing remains of original fittings. Note the *armorial* panels in the mural tablets.

BURNTISLAND. 5m SW of Kirkcaldy on A921. *St Columba.*

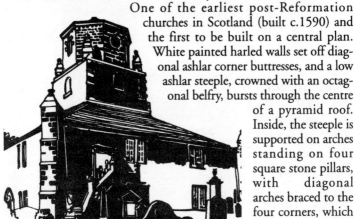

One of the earliest post-Reformation churches in Scotland (built c.1590) and the first to be built on a central plan. White painted harled walls set off diagonal ashlar corner buttresses, and a low ashlar steeple, crowned with an octagonal belfry, bursts through the centre of a pyramid roof. Inside, the steeple is supported on arches standing on four square stone pillars, with diagonal arches braced to the four corners, which explains the necessity for the diagonal exterior buttresses. The interior has some of

Burntisland, St Columba. Built in c.1590 on a central plan.

the oldest original fittings of any Scottish church. The *galleries*, inserted in 1602-30, are supported on fluted Ionic columns. The Sailors' Guild occupied two thirds of the south gallery and their 'loft' is *painted* with decorations of 1618 and 1622. Further decoration was done in 1632 and 1733 showing four ships and a sailor with a cross-staff and compass. In the same gallery is a painting of a C18 *sea battle*. Particularly notice the *magistrate's pew* dated 1606 against the north-east pier and the C18 dated *box pews*. On the east wall is an *inlaid panel* of a ship dated 1609.

CRAIL. 5m SE of St Andrews on A917. *St Mary.*
In 1177 the church belonged to the
Cistercian nuns of Haddington and
Norman masonry is evident in the
north wall of the chancel. The aisled
nave is C13, with an early-C13 west
tower and an octagonal stone spire
added in the early-C16 when the
chancel was lengthened. It became
collegiate in 1517. Finally, it was
heightened and reroofed in 1815 when
the west gallery was constructed. The
interior is painted white with a blue
ceiling and modern chestnut pews
were installed in 1963. In the south
aisle is carved *oak panelling* dated 1598
and 1605. The vestry has a painted
panel of 1765 of a sailor with an astro-

Crail, St Mary. Carved
arms on a pew-back.

labe, the sole survivor of the trade lofts removed from the church in
1815. Note the carved *pew back* dated 1595.

DARSIE. 6m S of Dundee on A91. *Old St Mary's Church.*
Rebuilt by Archbishop Spottiswoode in 1621 in what he claimed
was 'after the English form' and 'one of the beautifullest little pieces of
church work that is left to that unhappy country'. Faced with ashlar
and built on a rectangular plan with what was originally a flat roof,
since replaced with a hipped slate roof, and a strongly corbelled
octagonal belfry on the south-west corner. It is a curiously uncon-
scious mix of Classical and Gothic styles, from the Classicism of the
west end to the Gothic decorated nave. It was restored in 1837 and
refurnished in 1905.

DUNFERMLINE. 14m NW of Edinburgh off M90. *Holy Trinity
Abbey Church.*
A Benedictine priory was founded here in c.1070 on the site of an
earlier Celtic monastery. In 1128 it became an abbey and much
rebuilding took place; the west front and nave of the present church
date from this period. Although the twin west towers are of c.1500,
the south tower was rebuilt in 1811 without a spire to balance that
on the north, so leaving a narrow unbalanced west front. The chancel and transepts were sacked by rioting Reformers in the C16 and
left in ruins until 1818-21 when William Burn built a new east end
incorporating St Margaret's shrine beneath the east window. By the
elaborately carved east processional door is the *Wardlaw vault*, dated
1617, and altered in 1904. Inside, the massive Norman piers of the
aisled nave (those in the east end are carved with a deep chevron

Dunfermline,
The Abbey, Exterior,
mainly mid-C12.

pattern) support a triforium on round arches. Above is a flat roof with simple braces of 1845-8. The aisles are arcaded with decorated cushion capitals. This interior is the best example of the Romanesque style in Scotland. A rare Scottish c.1500 *wall painting* of four apostles is in the east bay of the north aisle, and an early Classical *monument* to William Shaw (d.1602), with another to Robert Pitcairn (d.1584), are in the same aisle. In the C19 choir and transepts the fittings are by R .Anderson of 1890, except for the Royal pew of 1972 and the wood eagle lectern of 1931. Particularly notice the *magistrates' pew* of 1610.

FORDELL. 4M E of Dunfermline off A907. *Chapel.*
A small rectangular, stone-built chapel with a bellcote over the west gable, with heavily traceried windows and, according to the armorial

Fordell, Chapel
A small chapel
built in 1650.

over the south door, built in 1650. The building was restored in c.1855 when a vaulted crypt was created under the west end and the whole reroofed. Note the *judges' arms* from Parliament House, Edinburgh, the C19 *hatchments*, the Flemish and German *glass*, and the many *memorial tablets*.

LEUCHARS. 3m NW of St Andrews on A919. *St Athernase.*
One of the few Norman churches surviving in Scotland, although only the chancel now remains, the nave being rebuilt in 1857-8. The exterior of the apsed chancel is richly decorated with two tiers of blind arcading of the mid-C12. The apse is surmounted, somewhat eccentrically, by an octagonal belfry of c.1700. Inside, the narrow Norman chancel arch leads the eye to the sanctuary arch decorated with billet and chevrons. A tunnel-vault covers the sanctuary, the ribs springing from corbels decorated with carved human and animal heads. Both font and pulpit were introduced in 1914, but note the good 1960s *glass* in the south-east nave. Three *graveslabs* in the church are worth seeking: one of 1565 by the pulpit, and two on the south wall, of 1584 and 1635.

Other Churches

ABERDOUR. 5m E of Dunfermline on A921. *St Fillan.*
A small Norman church built of cubed ashlar and consisting of nave and chancel of c.1140, with south aisle and porch of c.1500. Reroofed in 1588, the stone slabs were renewed in 1925-6 when a restoration was carried out. Inside there is a plain chancel arch of two orders and the furnishings and glass are all C20. Note the two *coffin plates* to the earls of Morton – James, (d.1768) and Sholto (d.1774) – fixed to the north wall.

CUPAR. 7m S of Dundee on A91. *St Michael.*
The tall west tower and three arches date from c.1415 with a 1620 belfry stage and spire; the rest is 1785 with a C19 porch. Inside, the gallery surrounds the pulpit on the east, west and north sides, a common practice in late-C18 Fife. Note the undated *recumbent figure*, in full armour, of a Fernie of Fernie.

Grampian

This region is fortunate in possessing one of the jewels of Scottish ecclesiastical architecture, King's College Chapel, Aberdeen, built in 1495 and which still, unique among Scottish medieval churches, has its original late-C15 screen and fifty-two choir stalls. At Birnie is a tiny Norman chapel of great simplicity and of a type of which there once were many. At Tynet, in a strongly Catholic area on the borders of Banffshire and Morayshire, a Roman Catholic chapel, St Ninian, was built in 1755, a time when Scottish Catholics were persecuted. Although an Act of Relief was strongly supported in the General Assembly of the Church of Scotland in 1779, it was defeated and not passed until 1793, fifteen years after the similar Act in England. Civil disabilities were not removed until 1829 by the Catholic Emancipation Act. St Ninian's is self-effacing. On the other hand, three miles away, the charming St Gregory at Preshome was built only 33 years later, and does not hide the fact that it is a Catholic chapel. Finally, for those who appreciate good architecture the strict Greek-Revival style of St Giles, Elgin (1830), makes it a very satis-factory building, although the interior was unfortunately stripped of all its original fittings in the late-nineteenth century.

ABERDEEN 15m NE of Dundee on A92. *King's College Chapel.*
Founded in 1495 by James IV and Bishop Elphinstone, this late Gothic church has a squat and square west tower surmounted by four flying buttresses carrying a crown. It is also unique among Scottish churches in having its original late-C15 carved *screen*, and fifty-two *choir stalls* with seven carved *misericords*, together with a magnificent oak *ceiling*.
St Nicholas, St Nicholas Street.
Better known as the East and West churches, Scotland's largest parish church was divided into two at the Reformation. Built of granite rubble masonry with sandstone dressings, they date from 1161. Traces of the early building remain in the transepts. The West Church was rebuilt in 1751 to designs by James Gibbs, a native of Aberdeen, who supplied the plans free. The East and West Churches are separated by a 195ft granite steeple built in 1875, and both

Aberdeen, St Nicholas. Interior of the West Church.

churches were restored in 1898 by William Kelly. The West Church has a *Lord Provost's pew* with pedimented baldichino, an imposing *magistrates' loft*, a *pulpit* with sounding board, *chandeliers*, all of 1755, four good C17 *tapestries*, original *galleries*, and C15 and C16 *woodwork* in the medieval crypt.

ARBUTHNOTT. 14m SW of Aberdeen off B967. *St Ternan.*
A simple ashlar-faced collegiate church, with a long C13 aisleless nave and chancel, with C16 doors and windows in the nave and lancet windows in the chancel. A slender three-sided bell tower with a round conical cap rises above the west end. In 1889 a fire burnt some of the nave necessitating a restoration of the whole building. Attached to the south wall of the chancel is the apsed and buttressed, two-storied, late-C15 *Arbuthnott 'aisle'*, a noble building taller than the church. The ground floor is stone vaulted and has a stone sarcophagus with a recumbent figure on the top and Arbuthnott, Douglas and Stewart arms on the sides; a spiral stair leads to a priest's room on the upper floor.

CULLEN. 30m NW of Aberdeen on A98. *Auld Kirk.*
There is more to see here than is usual in Scottish churches. Cruciform in plan, with an aisleless nave, transepts and extended choir, it was rebuilt in 1543 when the church became collegiate. Alexander Ogilvie, who rebuilt the church, has a splendid mid-C16 *monument* in the north wall of the choir. Next to it is a mid-C16 decorated *sacrament house* for church vessels. Facing it is a *laird's loft* supported on four carved pillars, one of which is dated 1608. The whole church was restored in 1863.

ELGIN. 40m NE of Inverness on A96. *St Giles.*
Built in the Greek Revival style by Archibald Simpson in 1830-3. The order is strictly Doric. Above the east end a square tower is crowned by a perfect copy of the monument of Lysicrates and the kirk is entered beneath a pedimented hexastyle portico. Of the original furnishings, nothing is left but a large collection of *benefaction boards*.

Other Churches

BIRNIE. 3m S of Elgin on B9010. *Parish Kirk.*
A small Norman stone-built church comprising nave and a square chancel that is a rare survivor of the many that were destroyed. Its dark interior has a narrow chancel arch of two simple orders with scalloped *capitals*.

CAWDOR. 4m SW of Nairn on B9090. *Parish Kirk.*
Rebuilt in 1839, retaining a south aisle, with typical Gothic-Revival window tracery, with an attached tall tower from a 1616 kirk, refitted in the late-C19.

DYKE. 5m E of Nairn on A96. *Parish Kirk.*
Built in a standard Classical style with round-headed sash-windows in 1781, it keeps its original loft and one of the very few original three-decker *pulpits* in Scotland.

PRESHOME. 8m E of Elgin off A98 (2m SSE of Portgordon). *St Gregory.*
Built in 1788, it was the first post-Reformation Roman Catholic Church to proclaim itself. Consisting of a wide rectangular plan, its white-harled west front, with stone dressings, has a pedimented gable capped with urn finials and the words 'DEO 1788'. This mildly Baroque style might have been seen in the Spanish colonies. A sanctuary was added and the interior refitted in 1896.

TYNET. 8m E of Elgin off A98 (between Portgordon and the mouth of the Spey). *St Ninian.*
A Roman Catholic chapel in a long, low, white-harled, single-storey building, built in 1755. Extended from a cottage, it was intended to look like 'an additione as a cot for ... sheep, but in effect for our use ...', wrote the priest, Goodman, to his bishop in 1754. It was lengthened in 1787 when its thatched roof was replaced by slate, renovated in c.1860 and finally again in 1951. The interior retains the *pulpit* and *sounding board* of 1787.

Highlands and Islands

[Key: Badenoch & Strathspey (B&S), Caithness (C), Inverness (I), Nairn (N), Orkney (O), Ross & Cromarty (R&C), Shetland (Sh), Skye & Lochalsh (S&L), Sutherland (S), and Western Islands (WI)]
Although Christianity was brought to this part of Scotland in the sixth century there is little evidence left today. St Magnus (c.1130) on Egilsay (O) is a ruin in the care of Historic Scotland, thereafter St Magnus' Cathedral (begun c.1140) at Kirkwall (O) is the oldest used ecclesiastical building. Of medieval work, only fragments survive such as those at St Magnus, Birsay (O). So many old kirks in this northern part of Scotland are, like St Magnus, Egilsay, roofless ruins, left when a smart new church was built or simply allowed to decay when the population declined in the nineteenth century.

In Inverness there was an outbreak of church building in the C19 after the Disruption of 1843, but few of these are in use today; one has become a funeral parlour, yet another is a bookshop.

BIRSAY (O). On Mainland 7m NW of Kirkwall on A966. *St Magnus.*
A rectangular harled kirk rebuilt in 1664, renovated and enlarged in 1760, the date of the round-headed windows, and restored in 1867, when the east window was inserted, and again in 1904. There are

traces of medieval work on the north and south walls and a blocked C13 lancet window in the east part of the north wall. Inside, set in the floor is a nameless *graveslab* dated 1645 with arms, probably of Nicol Nisbet. The small sandstone *font* may be late-C15; the glass is of 1904.

CROMARTY (R&C). 15m NE of Inverness on A832. *East Parish Church.*

A long, harled kirk with nave and chancel under one roof and a small bellcote of 1799 over the east gable. Built in the late-C16, its walls were heightened in 1756 when it was reroofed; the north 'aisle' was added seventeen years earlier. Inside, the Cromartie (east) gallery is of 1756, the same date as the Scholars' Loft (west gallery), while the north gallery of 1739, with *original pews*, is painted with the dates 1741 and 1788 with initials. The church was restored in 1981. Note the *hatchment* of George Ross (d.1786) of Pitkerrie and Cromarty painted on the ceiling of the Cromartie Loft. The pews are mainly mid-C19 but a large *pew*, painted with the Mackenzie arms and other devices, has the date 1740.

FORT GEORGE (I). 7m NE of Inverness on B9006. *Chapel.*

Built in 1767 to serve the military establishment of the Fort, the exterior is unremarkable. The interior, however, makes up for this dullness; rectangular with an apsed east end, it has galleries round three sides supported on Roman Doric columns. On the north side of the chancel arch is a C18 three-decker *pulpit*, the only furnishing in the nave. Original *box pews* survive in the galleries. The glass in the apse is all mid-C20. A memorial tablet in the south-west corner to Major Henry Balfowr (d.1776) records that he was 'unfortunately cut off By an Accident much to be regretted'.

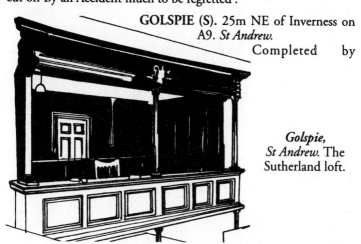

GOLSPIE (S). 25m NE of Inverness on A9. *St Andrew.*

Completed by

Golspie, St Andrew. The Sutherland loft.

1737, this white-harled Georgian T-plan kirk of 1737 was made cruciform in 1750 by the addition of a south 'aisle'. In 1774 a small bellcote was added over the west gable and alterations were carried out in 1849. In appearance it is comfortably domestic with a chimney on the north 'aisle'. However, some fragments of an earlier church of 1616 were incorporated in the rebuilding. Inside, many of the old fittings survive; the apparently C18 pews are of 1954; a vast *pulpit* and sounding board of 1738 stands by the south 'aisle', and the panelled end *galleries* are of 1849. In the north 'aisle', the Sutherland loft of 1738 is Classical with a dark-oak entablature supported on three Corinthian columns. Behind is a retiring room with a blocked fireplace.

GRANTOWN-ON-SPEY (B&S). 15m SE of Inverness on A95. *Inverallan Parish Church.*

A large, ashlar-faced, cruciform church built for the 7th and 8th Earls of Seafield by their estate architect in 1884-6, in a vague Gothic style. The interior has a vast aisleless nave with an elaborate wooden roof. The fittings are of the best quality; the south gallery has a front carrying baroque cartouches. Note the Lord's Prayer and, below, some C17 panelling. The *pulpit* is built-up from C17 Italian panels. On the east and west walls of the chancel are marble *monuments* to the 7th and 8th Earls of Seafield.

INVERNESS (I). 50m NW of Dundee on A9. *Old High Church.*

Rebuilt in rubble-stone in 1769-72 with a C16 west tower and, on the south front, porches and an odd apse in the centre of 1891, when the building was reroofed. Inside, the gallery is of c.1840, the rest of the fittings all of the C19; the glass is all of the 1890s and the C20. Note the *urn monument* to John Inglis who died in 1781 in America 'murdered by a band of ruffians while on a visit at a friend's house'.

KIRKHOUSE (O). On South Ronaldsay off B9044. *St Peter.*

A long rectangular harled kirk built in 1642, with a small bellcote on the west gable end, and reroofed in 1801. The doors and windows probably date from the reroofing. The interior fittings – the end *galleries* with flower-stencilled panelled fronts, three *communion pews*, and the *pulpit* with sounding board and *baptismal bracket* – are mostly of 1801. Note the late-C19 brass and iron *oil lamps*.

LAMB HOLME (O). A small island 7m S of Kirkwall on A961. *Italian Chapel.*

Maintained by the P.O.W. Chapel Preservation Committee. Consisting of two Nissen huts, now covered with felt, this ingenious chapel, designed by Domenico Chiochetti, was created by Italian prisoners of war in 1943-4, when building the Churchill Barriers. The west front, with bellcote, is modelled in cement and decorated with pinnacles, *fleur-de-lis* and crockets. A Classical portico with a relief of Christ in the tympanum leads into the interior tunnel-vault lined with plasterboard and painted in imitation of stone. The chancel, with a painted ceiling symbolising the four Evangelists and the Holy Spirit, is closed off with a wrought-iron screen, and a copy of Nicolo Barabino's (1832-91) Madonna of the Olives covers the east end.

PORTMAHOMACK (R & C). 6m E of Tain on B9165. *Tarbat Old Church.* *(115)

A long harled kirk built in 1756, with nave and chancel under one roof, with a stone cupola bellcote of c.1700 over the west gable. The north 'aisle' was heightened and lengthened in 1780. The interior has a Classical *monument* to William Mackenzie (d.1642) in the north 'aisle', and what furnishings remain are from 1891. In the churchyard, note the MacLeod of Geanies burial enclosure of c.1700.

REAY (C). 7m W of Thurso on A836. *Parish Church.*

A simple T-plan harled kirk built in 1738-9 with a charming, pyramid roofed bell-tower attached to the east end, with additions of 1909. The length of the building is an example of accommodating the long *communion table* which stands in the centre of the kirk. The hexagonal *pulpit,* pilastered back and *sounding board* are original, and the pews are mainly of 1933 when the two south doors were blocked.

RODEL (WI. HARRIS). S point of Isle of Harris on A859. *St Clement.*

In the care of Historic Scotland. An early-C16 church believed to have been built by Alexander MacLeod whose tomb of 1528 is in the chancel. Abandoned after the Reformation until reroofed in the

Portmahomack, Tarbat Old Church.
Exterior, built in 1756.

1780s, it was restored and reroofed again in 1873, and yet again restored in 1913. The rough stone walls were once harled, and with a high square west tower and pyramid roof, it has a chancel and nave under one roof with north and south transepts. Inside are three noteworthy *monuments* to chiefs of the Clan MacLeod: the earliest, and finest, to Alexander in full armour is dated 1528, the others are to William (d.1539) and John of c.1557.

TAIN (R&C). 20m N of Inverness on A9. *St Duthus Memorial Church.*
Unusually, two churches stand in the churchyard, one roofless of c.1300, and the other built for a college of canons in 1487, much altered up to 1814, and heavily restored in 1859-70 and again in 1890. The plan is rectangular, with nave and chancel under one C19 roof. The C19 work was done in yellow sandstone, easily distinguishable from the original C15 pink stone. The walls are supported by tall buttresses with three good C15 traceried windows in each of the north and south walls. The interior is much restored; the *pulpit* is c.1575, heavily restored in the 1890s, and fixed to the west wall is the painted front of the old *trades loft* with the dates 1680 and 1776; the plain *font* is C13. Note the *piscina* and *sedilia* in the chancel south wall.

Other Churches

ARDCLACH (N). 5m SE of Nairn off A939. *Old Parish Church.*
A simple kirk built on the familiar T-plan in 1765 with round-headed windows of 1836 and renovated in 1892 when the gallery was inserted. Its *bell tower* stands on a hill to the north, consisting of a two-storied gabled building with a chimney on one gable and a bellcote on the other, forming the triple purpose of watch tower, prison, and bell tower. A date stone on the west gable gives the year 1655.

DUNNET (C). 4m E of Thurso on A836. *Parish Church.*
An attractive white painted, harled, T-plan church with west bell-tower of c.1700, C16 nave and chancel under one roof, and a north 'aisle' of 1837. The plain interior has a c.1700 *monument* on the south wall and *box pews* of 1837.

Latheron.
Exterior, built
1723-38.

LATHERON (C). 13m SW of Wick on A9. *Clan Gunn Centre.*
Once the parish church, this harled T-plan kirk, with a north 'aisle'
added in 1821, was built in 1723-38. Inside is a large Classical *monument* of 1642 to Lady Sinclair of Dunbeath; all other furnishings
have been removed. Note the burial enclosure to the Sinclairs of
Dunbeath.

Lothian

A new administrative region formed in 1975 but not new in practice
for it was known by this name in the late-sixteenth century. The
main building material is calciferous sandstone from which
Edinburgh is built; the quarries are on the edge of the city. There are
also outcrops of a hard volcanic stone, so hard that it cannot be
dressed but is used for rubble walls which have to be rendered or
'harled'. Like so much of Lowland Scotland, overrun by Vikings,
Normans, various armies and marauding clans, there are many
monastic and church ruins. Those which have survived have little
left of the old fittings, and the nineteenth century saw much restoration and fitting out of parish churches.

St Cuthbert, Dalmeny, built in the mid-twelfth century, is the best
preserved Norman church in Scotland, and in England it would
merit a long detour. There is nothing of note left in the way of thirteenth and fourteenth-century churches except roofless ruins, but for
the fifteenth and sixteenth centuries Lothian is the richest region of
Scotland for churches. St Michael, Linlithgow, and St Mary,
Haddington, are good examples of the period, but their furnishings
are nineteenth-century. St Matthew's Chapel, Roslin, is essentially
Scottish with its exceptional interior, richly carved with late-Gothic
foliage and natural forms – the last of the Gothic before the
Reformation – but, again, nothing survives of early furnishings. St
Mary, Whitekirk, would have had seventeenth-century fittings had
not suffragettes set it ablaze in 1914! Of the nineteenth-century
architects, William Burn and David Bryce, both from Edinburgh,
were among the most competent of church designers; St Mary at
Dalkeith is an example of their work. Dull on the outside (Burn
could be excessively dull as an architect), the interior is something else
and should be seen and enjoyed.

ABERCORN. 3m SW of Queensferry off A904. *Dedication unknown.*
Of the original church built in the C12 only a blocked south door
with tympanum remains and it was almost completely rebuilt in the
1580s. In 1603 the Duddington 'aisle' was added to the chancel, the
Binns 'aisle' was added to the nave in 1618, and the chancel was

Abercorn. Interior, the Hopetoun loft.

made into the Hopetoun 'aisle' in 1708. The building was restored in 1893 when a north aisle was added to the nave. The interior is curious because the *Hopetoun Loft* of 1708, a grand, roofed and panelled gallery, furnished with comfortable chairs, takes up the whole west end and looks down on to the Communion table. Beneath the loft is a room displaying fragments of sculpture including two C12 hogback *burial stones*, the earliest in Scotland.

ABERLADY. 5m NW of Haddington on A198. *Parish Church.*
The whole body of the church was rebuilt with an open timber roof by William Young in 1886, but a C15 rubble-stone tower survives on the west end. The north side has two early post-Reformation burial 'aisles', The complete scheme of *glass* of 1889 is by Edward Frampton. Font and pulpit are of Caen stone, and the Communion table was supplied by Scott Morton & Co in 1961. A replica is shown of an C8 fragment of a cross shaft carved with an angel and pairs of birds; the original is in the National Museum of Antiquities, Edinburgh. Unusually for Scotland, there are *monuments*: a wall monument in the north aisle to Margaretta de Yonge (d.1762), wife of Lord Elibank, is by Antonio Canova, and in the south-east aisle a death-bed effigy to the Countess of Wemyss (d.1882) is by John Rhind.

BANGOUR. 4m SW of Uphall off A89. *Our Lady.*
The best and grandest C20 church in the region, built of coffee-cream rubble sandstone by H.O. Tarbolton in 1924-9 in a simple Romanesque style for the hospital of which it forms part. It was always inter-denominational. The building comprises a long aisleless nave and chancel, with a stumpy south tower, and a war memorial chapel also on the south side. Inside, the walls are faced with smooth ashlar sandstone and the nave roof is constructed of massive hammer-beams with kingposts high above them. The wooden chancel roof is

tunnel-vaulted. All the fittings were designed by Tarbolton, made in the hospital workshop and carved by their woodworkers.

DALKEITH. 6m SE of Edinburgh on A68. *St Mary.*
Built just inside the gate of Dalkeith Palace by William Burn and David Bryce in 1843 in an early-C14 Gothic style as the private chapel to the Palace. It remained so until 1958 when it became an Episcopalian church. The plan consists of an aisleless nave, north transept, and chancel, and a bellcote over the west gable, with a memorial chapel to the 5th Earl of Buccleuch added in 1890. From the outside it looks a dull church but the interior is another matter; with a high double hammer-beam *roof,* stalls of 1846 by William Butterfield, a stone pulpit by Burn and Bryce modelled on that at Beaulieu, Hampshire, and a heraldic *tiled floor* by Minton, it is an impressive interior.

DALMENY. 8m NW of Edinburgh off B924. *St Cuthbert.*
Built in the mid-C12 in grey sandstone, the church consists of a nave, a narrow chancel and small apse, and is rightly famous as the best preserved Norman parish church in Scotland. The north aisle was added in 1671, and it was reroofed in 1766. A recent restoration was undertaken in 1922-37, and a west tower was built in 1937, replacing one which had vanished some time ago. The *south door* of two orders, with an interlaced Norman blind arcade above, is highly decorated with motifs including an Agnus Dei and signs of the zodiac. Inside, notice the rib-vaults of the chancel and apse supported on *corbels* carved with heads of monsters, animals and humans. Two *stools* of 1709 are for collection bowls; the pulpit, in character with the interior, was made in 1928, the *font* in 1950, and the *glass* of 1950 in the apse is by Lalia Lindsay.

Dalmeny, St Cuthbert. Exterior of the best Norman church in Scotland.

DUNGLASS. 27m E of Edinburgh off A1. *St Mary.*
In the care of Historic Scotland. A cruciform collegiate kirk of c.1443 finely built of ashlar with a stone-slab roof and central tower. The nave and a smaller choir were built first, followed shortly afterwards by the transepts and tower, an enlarged choir and a burial vault on the choir north wall. Inside, it is roofed throughout, with the exception of the crossing, with a pointed stone-vault. A fine mid-C15 triple *sedilia* is in the south wall of the choir; two corbels are of angels, one playing a lute and the other holding a shield. Note the *consecration crosses* in the choir and the tomb recess in the north transept with the arms of Sir Thomas and Lady Home, grandparents of the founder of the collegiate church, Sir Alexander Home.

EDINBURGH. 378m N of London. *Canongate Church*, Canongate.
Built from 1649, and opened in 1691, on a Latin Cross plan, unique to C17 churches in Scotland, and comprising an aisled nave, transepts and apsed chancel. The ashlar-faced west front appears more like a Baroque chapel than a church; gables on both aisles curve up to the nave roof which is crowned with a fine curvilinear gable decorated with the arms of William III. Inside, round arched arcades

Edinburgh, Canongate Church.
Exterior, built from 1649.

are carried on Doric columns and the nave ceiling, an arched vault of 1817, hidden by a flat ceiling of acoustic tiles, was revealed in 1961. Restorations in 1946-7 by Ian Lindsay removed the east and west galleries and lowered the south gallery. The organ of 1910 was inserted in 1960, the pulpit is 1847 with tester of 1961, and the gallery clock is 1817. Note the mid-C17 *Benefaction boards* in the vestibule.

Barclay Bruntsfield Church, Barclay Place.
One of the most amazing churches of the C19 and built by F.T. Pilkington in 1862-4 as a result of his winning a competition. Constructed of rough yellow sandstone, a tall slender spire rises from

the north-west corner of a cruciform plan. Thereafter, it is like no other building; turrets, gables, spires and craggy projections give the impression of some Rhineland Gothic castle, converted to a church. Inside, it is equally unusual; a heart-shaped auditorium has two tiers of galleries with spirally carved fronts. In the east apse, the segment-fronted marble *pulpit* is by Pilkington, with an organ case of 1898. Overhead a square roof carried on two columns is an intricate maze of trusses, posts and arch-braces covered with a stencilled design by James Clark.

Magdalen Chapel, Cowgate.

Built from 1537 to 1544 as a chapel for an almshouse, it was taken over in 1553 by the Incorporation of Hammermen, who were metalworkers. Major repairs were undertaken in 1601 and 1613, and in 1620 the Hammermen built a steeple on the north front which became the entrance. Inside, the original C16 *door* still exists, and the chapel is a single space in which the chancel is marked out by a shallow C16 step from the nave. Arcaded *panelling* of c.1615 covers the lower part of the east and north walls, and two semicircular tiers of seats of 1725 fill the chancel. On the back of the lower tier are *painted arms* of the trades incorporated by the Hammermen. A barrel-vaulted plaster ceiling of 1615 was extended over the west end in 1725. Four mid-C16 *glass* heraldic roundels in the south window comprise the only original pre-Reformation *glass* to survive in Scotland.

Old Parish Church, Kirk Loan, Corstorphine.

Sir Adam Forrester built a chapel here before his death in 1405. His chapel survives in the present nave and south chapel; the chancel and west tower are mid-C15. A north aisle was built in 1646 and replaced in 1828. It is built of stone with a stone slab roof and a stumpy west tower capped by a hexagonal squat stone spire. Inside, the stone tunnel-vault of the nave, the chancel arch, and the north aisle are by George Henderson who carried out a drastic restoration in 1903-5. The chancel has good mid-C15 *sedilia* and *piscina,* otherwise the furnishings and glass are all of the C20. Particularly noteworthy are the Forrester *tombs.* Sir Adam's (d.1405) is in the south chapel; Sir John's (d.1440), Master of the Household to James I, is, with his wife, in the north wall of the chancel; Sir John II's (d.1454), with his wife, is also in the north wall of the chancel. All three effigies are in full armour.

Old St Paul, (Episcopal), Jeffrey Street.

This stone-built church in an early-Gothic style is by William Hay, who had worked with Sir George Gilbert Scott. Towering above the busy street, it has a chancel built together with the north half of the nave in 1880-3; the south half followed in 1889-90. The Seabury Chapel was added in 1904-5 by Hay's partner, George Henderson, whose original fittings survive, including a fine Art Nouveau wrought-iron *rood screen* on a coloured marble base, and a high, Gothic-style gilded *triptych* with 40 carved figures. Later work is the War Memorial of 1924-6 in the entrance. Particularly notice the *Warriors' Chapel*.

Tolbooth St John, Castlehill.
Built in 1839-40 by A.W.N. Pugin and Gillespie Graham as a parish church and a meeting house for the General Assembly. It is now secularised. Its exterior is strikingly attractive in a C14 Gothic style and consists of an aisleless nave with a tall, slender spire on the east end. The simple rectangular interior is on two floors with the ground floor given over to church rooms and the church proper on the first floor reached by an Imperial staircase from an inner vestibule. In the auditorium, the raised platform carries a Gothic throne-cum-pulpit, a conversion of 1857, and the U-shaped gallery with the Royal Arms was inserted in 1858-9. The organ is of 1902 and particularly notice the Art Nouveau *electroliers* of 1905.

GIFFORD. 5m S of Haddington on B6355. *Parish Church.*
A T-plan church built of white-harled rubblestone in 1710 by James Smith: T-plan because the square tower is in the middle of the south side. At the back of the church is a *family 'aisle'* with separate entrance, which originally had a fireplace in an attached *retiring room.* Inside, the pew, or loft, has two *hatchments*, and coronetted initials on its panelled front: IHS for Ian Hay and Jean Scott. The C17 *pulpit*, possibly from the earlier church, has a curved front and a sounding board of c.1710. The pierced rail round the Communion table is of 1895.

HADDINGTON. 17m W of Edinburgh on A1. *St Mary.*
A large stone church with a troubled history, built in the mid-C15. Consisting of an aisled nave, transepts, aisled choir, and short stumpy crossing tower, the building was severely damaged in the siege of Haddington in 1548 when the vaults and roofs were destroyed. The nave was restored and the transepts walled off, leaving the choir and transepts ruined until 1971-3, when they too were restored and the church returned to its original form. The interior was always impressive due to the stone vaulting of the nave and choir. It is impressive today, but the nave vaulting is plaster from 1811 restorations – not as originally designed – and the choir vaulting, from the 1970s restoration, is a faithful copy in fibreglass of the original. All the furnishings and glass are late-C19. However, there is good *glass* of the late-1870s by Morris & Co in the south transept, and more in the nave south aisle designed by Sir Edward Burne-Jones. Note the Lauderdale *monuments* in the former sacristy.

LINLITHGOW. 15m W of Edinburgh off M9. *St Michael.*

A large stone-built church blackened with age, it was burned out in 1424, resulting in a partial rebuilding. The aisled nave, with north and south chapels, was completed by 1489, the apsed and aisled choir in c.1532; and the spire of the west tower was added in 1964, replacing an open-work crown lost in the C19. Restorations were carried out in 1812 and in the 1890s. The interior is surprisingly spacious and light, but with no original fittings. In the south chapel is, according to Pevsner, the most 'beautiful late-Gothic window in Scotland', with glass of the 1890s by Clayton & Bell. In the nave south aisle is *glass* by Morris & Co designed in 1899 by Sir Edward Burne-Jones. In the vestry are two late-C15 *carved slabs*, which should not be missed.

NEWBATTLE. ½ m S of Dalkeith off A7. *Parish Church.*
A T-plan church built in 1727-9 by Alexander MacGill with a square tower attached to the centre of the south side. The Lothian family 'aisle', in the stem of the T, was altered in 1859 when the 'aisle' had a retiring room added. In 1895 the Ancram 'aisle' was made out of the second stage of the tower. Inside, the gallery is of 1851, and the Classical *pulpit* of the 1640s is from an earlier church. The *glass* of the windows flanking the pulpit is of 1881 by Mayer of Munich. Note the rose window of 1961 by William Wilson.

PENCAITLAND. 5m SW of Haddington on A6093. *Parish Church.*
One of the earliest post-Reformation rebuilt churches, late C16 or early-C17, although the date 1631 over the west door may only signify the date of the square tower topped by a combined belfry and dovecote. On the north side, the Saltoun 'aisle' was added in the mid-C16. Inside, the front pews of the *Saltoun 'aisle'*, supported on Corinthian pilasters, are, for Scotland, an unusual survival from c.1600. The organ with its colourful pipes was installed in 1889 and the *glass* in the north chapel is by C.E. Kempe of 1883; glass in the east end is of the 1920s.

PRESTONPANS. 10m E of Edinburgh on B1348. *Parish Church.*
One of the earliest post-Reformation churches in Scotland and built in 1592. Of this building only the tower and south door remain; it was enlarged and restored in 1774. Further extensions were made in 1911 which included the white marble font and incongruous, late-C17 style, organ case. The rest of the fittings date from 1891. Note the C18 *painting* of a Royal Navy ship in a storm, and the *monument* outside on the east wall to John Stuart of Phisgul 'barbarously murdered by four Highlanders near the end of the Battle fought in the field of Preston on the 21st Sept. 1745'.

RESTALRIG. 5m E of Edinburgh off A199. *Parish Kirk.*
In the care of Historic Scotland. A small rectangular late-C15 stone-

built church, plain with no 'Idolatrie', for which sin an earlier collegiate church was 'cast down' in 1560. The simple building was correctly restored by William Burn in 1836 who renewed the window tracery. Joined to the south wall is a low hexagonal building, once the lower storey of a two-tier chapel built for James III in 1486-7. The interior has fine *rib-vaulting*, springing from a central column with a decorated capital, and meeting wall shafts with decorated capitals. Six carved *bosses* decorate the vaults.

ROSLIN. 6m S of Edinburgh on D7003. *St Matthew's Chapel.*

By the inscription on the north clerestory cornice, this was built by the 3rd Earl of Orkney in 1450. Only the choir, now the nave with aisles, and sacristry were finished. A restoration was carried out in the 1860s. The decoration inside and out consists of thickly encrusted late-Gothic, carved stone foliage, and the effect is richly spectacular. Although the building is Gothic in appearance, it is Scottish transitional. The tall nave is unusually tunnel-vaulted above the clerestory, an un-Gothic structural feature, yet in the Gothic tradition there are carvings throughout of religious moral intent; for example, the Seven Deadly Sins in the south aisle. An *effigy* of a mid-C15 armoured knight is in the north arcade and a *monument* to the

Roslin, St Matthew. Interior, built from 1649.

3rd Earl of Caithness (d.1582) is in the north aisle. Notice particularly the architectural drawings cut into the stonework of the sacristy. The glass all dates from after the restoration of the 1860s with some good pieces of the 1950s and 1970s in the sacristy.

SETON. 12m W of Edinburgh on A198. *St Mary & Holy Cross.*

In the care of Historic Scotland. Treated by the Seton family as their own chapel, it is in fact the parish church. It consists of an apsed choir of the 1470s, and transepts with broach crossing tower of 1513-45 with an octagonal spire. The aisleless C13 nave has long been ruined and only fragments of walling remain. The church was made collegiate by the second Lord Seton in 1493 who built the sacristy in the north wall of the choir. The interior is completely tunnel-vaulted except for the crossing which is rib-vaulted. Note the *piscina* and *sedilia* of the 1470s, and the *effigy* in full armour lying in a segmental recess in the choir, which may represent the first Lord Seton (d.1478) who built the choir.

UPHALL. 11m W of Edinburgh on A899. *St Nicholas.*
This kirk is an example of the development of the T-plan. The west tower, nave and chancel are C12, restored in 1878 when the Norman details were added, except for the nave south door, which is original, and the Buchanan loft (1644) on the north side, removed to make a north aisle. The Shairp loft, with a tunnel-vault roof, on the south was added c.1620, so making the T-plan. The kirk was restored again in 1937 when the post-Reformation east and west galleries were removed and the walls scraped. Note the Erskine *wall tablets* in the west tower, the burial place of the Earls of Buchanan. In the Shairp loft are more tablets and an *urn* containing the heart of Walter Shairp (d.1787) H.M. Consul General in St Petersburg.

YESTER. 4m S of Haddington on B6369. *The Chapel.*
With the building of a new parish church at Gifford in 1708 this chapel, originally the collegiate church of St Cuthbert founded in 1421, and consisting of only a choir and transepts, became the burial place for the Hay family who became Earls of Tweeddale. The exterior was overlaid with a Gothic gingerbread decoration by the Adam brothers in 1753. The interior is mainly unaltered and stone-vaulted throughout. The chancel arch was rebuilt in 1688 and the east window is dated 1635. In the south transept are two Hay family *tablets* dated 1566 and 1613, and an undated wall monument to William Hay (d.1614) and Helen Cockburn (d.1627). Note the mid-C15 *piscina.*

Other Churches.

CARRINGTON. 6m SE of Edinburgh off A7. *Parish Kirk.*
Built in 1710 of once-harled rubblestone, on a T-plan, with a square tower, crowned by a slate pyramid roof, midway on the south wall, and pointed windows. Internal fittings date from a restoration of 1838. The pulpit and sounding board on the south side form an C18 composite piece; opposite, on the north side marked by a plaque, was the Rosebery loft. Note the detached session house.

COCKPEN. 3m S of Dalkeith off A7. *Parish Church.*
Built in 1818 and designed by Richard Crichton. Cruciform in plan with a west tower above the porch. The interior is Gothic Revival with plaster rib-vaulting, and *galleries* with Gothic fronts. The pulpit is original but built into the less fine organ case of 1884 when the pews were renewed.

CRICHTON. 10m SE of Edinburgh on B6367. *SS Mary & Kentigern.*
Originally a collegiate kirk of 1449, cruciform in plan, with a crossing tower, saddle-back roof and bellcote. The nave is now ruined and the interior of the chancel much altered to accommodate Presbyterian worship. However, a mid-15 *sedilia* and *piscina* remain, and the capitals of the crossing are richly carved, as is much of the remaining C15 decoration.

EDINBURGH. *Greyfriars Church,* Candlemaker Row.
Originally, when opened in 1620 on the site of the old Greyfriars cemetery, this church had a rectangular aisled nave with west tower and no chancel. From 1650-2 it became a barracks when the fittings were destroyed, and in 1718 the tower was demolished and Greyfriars New Church built on to the west end. A fire in 1845 seriously damaged the Old Greyfriars, which was restored, and in 1938 the dividing wall was removed and the two churches became one. The churchyard boasts the finest collection of *gravestones* in Scotland.

St Margaret's Chapel, Edinburgh Castle.
Built in c.1100 on the highest point of the Castle rock on a simple rectangular plan with east apse. The chancel arch is of two orders with zigzag decoration on the arches. Restored in 1851-2 when the nave tunnel-vault and the chancel arch shafts were inserted; the north door is of 1938. Note the good *glass* of 1922 by Douglas Strachan.

LIVINGSTON VILLAGE. 12m SW of Edinburgh on B7015. *Parish Kirk.*
Rebuilt in 1732 on a rectangular plan with four large round-headed windows on the south and a bird-cage belfry. The east end and window were modified in 1837, the date of the Gothic-Revival *pulpit.* The pews are late-C18, and note the well-designed, wrought-iron, baptismal bracket of 1818 with an unusual design of basin, the C17 alms dish, and the early-C19 *mort-safe.*

NEWBATTLE ABBEY. ½ m S of Dalkeith off A68. *Chapel.*
Now an adult education college, the present building dates from the C17 but was considerably rebuilt in the C19. Remains of a once substantial Cistercian abbey of c.1140 are in the cellars. The chapel was created by John Bryce in the medieval crypt in 1900 and is a simple barrel-vaulted space. The *floor,* apparently of Minton tiles, is in fact made of wood blocks, and a Gothic-style reredos has a *tondo* of the Virgin and Child.

WHITEKIRK. 7m NE of Haddington on A198. *St Mary.*
Once a busy medieval place of pilgrimage due to miracles and healing performed at a nearby well, this unassuming C15 church was set alight by suffragettes in 1914 and the C17 fittings, rare in Scotland, were lost. Aisleless and cruciform in plan with a central tower, it was restored in 1830, when much was rebuilt, and again by Sir Robert

Lorimer after the fire. The fine roofs are Lorimer's, as are the *font*, *pulpit* and Communion table. One window with *glass* of the 1880s by C.E. Kempe survived the fire.

Strathclyde

Only fragments of medieval churches survive here. The Abbey Church, Paisley, has remains of the C15 in the nave, and St Bride, Bothwell, has an original choir of 1398. The Parish Kirk of Kilbirnie is exceptional for having so many original fittings, from an 'aisle' of 1597 to an early-eighteenth century canopied pew, and is well worth a detour.

The region is curious in having four churches built during the Commonwealth invasion; one would be a rarity in any county. Of these, the Auld Kirk at Ayr is the least altered. Only one other is found in Scotland; at Mertoun, Borders, built in 1658 but extensively altered in the early nineteenth century. Glasgow proliferates in nineteenth-century churches and there are many good ones. The best is undoubtedly St Vincent Free Church by Alexander 'Greek' Thompson, built in 1857 as a Greek temple on a podium. Charles Rennie Mackintosh built only one church, Queen's Cross; it is not, alas, used as a church, but as the headquarters of the Society devoted to his name. However, since it is a remarkable building it has been included here.

AYR. 10m SW of Kilmanock on A77. *Auld Kirk.*
A rare kirk because built in 1654, during the Commonwealth invasion – Cromwellian troops used the earlier kirk of St John as a fort. Gothic was considered proper for kirks, and the windows and other details are suitably Gothic-Revival. The churchyard is entered by a huge covered *gateway* dated 1656. Inside, note the *mortification board* with a black and gold frame dated 1708 but renewed in 1792. Not unusual for a sea-faring town, there is a suspended model *sailing ship*.

BIGGAR. 25m SW of Edinburgh on A702. *St Nicholas.*
Built from 1545 and one of the last pre-Reformation collegiate churches, it is cruciform in plan, consisting of an aisleless nave and apsed chancel, with a short square crossing tower, and a square C19 vestry on the north side of the chancel. It was restored in the C19. The south door gives into a screened-off space in the west end, with a staircase up to the west gallery. The roofs throughout are C19 and none of the original fittings survive.

FENWICK. 4m N of Kilmarnock off A77. *Parish Church.*
A cruciform church dated 1643, of harled walls, pointed windows and crow-stepped gables with a belfry rebuilt in 1864. Inside, there

are four lofts, three with internal stairs for the east loft has an external forestair. Unfortunately the church was burnt out in 1930 when its wood fittings were destroyed. The jougs (iron shackles and chains worn round the neck) survived and hang by the door; they were used for punishments for crimes such as 'inhuman throwing of Elizabeth White over a brae', or 'cursing ye day that ever ye minister came into this countrie'. Two small hexagonal *'sentry boxes'* of c.1820 stand on guard by the churchyard gate.

GLASGOW. 45m W of Edinburgh on M8. *Queen's Cross Church*, 866 Garscube Road.

Built in 1898-9 for the Church of Scotland by Charles Rennie Mackintosh, and his only church. It is now the home of the Charles Rennie Mackintosh Society. On a restricted site, the red sandstone church is small, with Mackintosh's strong massing pushing up a square stumpy south-west tower with an octagonal stair turret, and with his usual attention to detail. Inside, an elliptical, pointed, timber barrel-vaulted ceiling is spanned by uncovered steel joists. Some of the original fittings survive: the east and south-west *galleries*, *Communion table*, circular and canopied *pulpit* decorated with Art Nouveau carving, and *organ gallery* in the tower (minus the organ). The rood beam is a recent replacement and the glass is of 1960.

St Andrew, St Andrew's Square.

Glasgow's first post-Reformation church, built by A. Dreghorn and M. Naismith in 1739-56. A wide portico supported on Corinthian columns spreads across the west front beneath a tall elegant steeple with an octagonal bell-chamber. The interior is richly finished; an aisled nave has arcades supported on slender Corinthian columns with a barrel-vaulted ceiling decorated with rococo plasterwork. Above the west gallery is a clock in an exuberant rococo setting. Both the mahogany wine-glass *pulpit*, with its serpentine stair, and the *font stand* are original furnishings, but the pews were replaced in 1874 when the present organ was installed. The glass is all of the 1870s and 90s.

Glasgow, St Andrew. The Classical interior of 1739-56.

St Benedict, Drumchapel Road.

A Roman Catholic church built in 1964-70 by Gillespie, Kidd & Coia. The plan is octagonal with harled walls covered by an immense concave copper roof. A dramatic entrance through a porch and narthex leads to the church proper. A timber lined roof, yellow brick walls and lines of open pews draw the eye irresistibly towards the altar. This is a very successful building.

St Vincent Street Free Church, St Vincent Street.

Built in 1857-9 by Alexander (Greek) Thompson, and his masterpiece. Conceived as an Ionic temple designed for the United Presbyterians (and now Free Church), it stands above St Vincent Street looking every bit like a Greek temple, standing on a stylobate, or podium, containing the lower part of the church and the upper portions of the basement rooms. The temple, with porticos at both ends and flanking wings, is the upper part of the church; the wings cover the two aisles. Behind, a slender tower (never a part of Greek temple architecture) looks disconnected. After the excitement of the exterior the interior is no disappointment. The vestibule is a top-lit atrium with wide stone stairs leading to galleries. The church itself is flooded with light from the temple clerestories. Cast-iron columns with anthemion-leaf capitals sprouting extraordinary horns support the galleries and the clerestories. Above is a rich *'antique' roof* coloured, like the columns, with cerulean blue, terracotta and Pompeian red, a scheme not intended by Thompson, but original. Beneath a vast organ in a Greek-style case, stands the platform with a *pulpit* made for thundering sermons. Everything about this church from the gasoliers to the door frames is completely satisfying.

Townhead and Blochan Parish Church, 176 Royston Hill.

One of the few churches by J.J. Stevenson, who had been an assistant to Sir George Gilbert Scott, and built in 1865-6 in grey snecked rubble. Formed of a tall nave and chancel in early-C13 Gothic

Glasgow, St Vincent St Free Church. The Greek temple, exterior.

303

style, with a prodigiously tall north-east tower and spire, it is not to be overlooked. However, the interior is also remarkable; the high narrow nave with galleries on cast-iron columns is lit by round clerestory windows. Fragments of colour on the *gallery fronts* remain from Daniel Cottier's dramatic decorations in red, blue and black. The *east window*, designed by Sir Edward Burne-Jones, William Morris and Ford Madox Brown, of 1866 is one of Morris & Co's earliest in Scotland.

HAMILTON. 6m SE of Glasgow off A72. *Old Kirk.*
Built in 1732 on a Greek Cross plan and the only kirk by William Adam. Internally, the plan is circular with four arms at the points of the compass. Entrance is by the south portico leading to the auditorium by a lobby; the east and west arms are occupied by secondary entrances and pews; while the north arm is filled with the appurtenances of the Hamilton family gallery, with a servants' room on the ground floor and a retiring room above leading on to what was the Hamilton 'loft', now only recognisable by a painted armorial cartouche. A first floor gallery completely surrounds the auditorium. In 1926 a concert organ was installed in the south part of the gallery backing on to the pulpit, of which only the original back and sounding board remain facing the Hamilton 'loft'. Note the contemporary *baptismal basin.*

KILBIRNIE. 20m SW of Glasgow on A760. *Parish Kirk.*
We can ignore the exterior of this kirk; the interior is everything and is filled with a wealth of carved oak and pine. A lone Gothic *Glengarnock 'aisle'* of 1597 remains, overwhelmed by later Classical decoration. The *Crawford loft* is one of the most impressive in

Kilbirnie, Parish Kirk. Interior, Crawford loft of c.1705.

Kilmarnock, Old High. Exterior, built in 1732-40.

Scotland, erected by Viscount Garnock in c.1705 in front of the family 'aisle' of 1642. It is decorated with heavily carved oak; family coats of arms cover the front and two slender Corinthian columns rise from the ground floor to support a grandly carved canopy. The *pulpit*, although it is a made-up piece, is remarkable: over it is a large pediment with the arms of Crawford and Lindsay surrounded by cherubs, birds and serpents, above a carved oak coved cornice; yet the pulpit itself and backboard are in pine and of later date. Note the wrought-iron *baptismal bracket*, and the Ladylands *canopied pew* made up of late-C17 and early-C18 pine and oak pieces.

KILMARNOCK. 17m SW of Glasgow on A77. *Old High.*
Built in 1732-40 by a very competent but unknown architect, the wide kirk is simple with a suggestion of pediments to its gables, but the elegant tower is another matter; finished above a square clock stage, with urn finials, the octagonal belfry is crowned by a cupola. The interior is no less Classical, with galleries correctly supported on Doric columns with entablature blocks. Alterations were carried out in 1858 and its original moveable communion pews have gone.

LARGS. 24m W of Glasgow on A78. *Parish Kirk.*
Of the old church nothing remains but the Skelmore 'aisle' added in 1636. Here, like Grandtully, Tayside, the ceiling is boarded, coved, and painted with elaborate *decorations* simulating a Gothic rib-vault. The decorative scheme includes Adam and Eve, Jacob and Esau, the Seasons and signs of the Zodiac, as well as views of the old kirk and Skelmorlie Castle. Unusually, it is signed 'T. STALKER. FECIT. 1638'. There is also the notable Montgomery *monument* of 1639

consisting of a baldacchino supported on sixteen Classical columns with, for the time, surprisingly advanced Classical decoration comprising cherubs, finials and strapwork. The monument was obviously intended to have a recumbent figure which it lacks.

PAISLEY. 5m W of Glasgow on A726. *Abbey Church.*
A Cluniac priory was founded here in 1163. Burnt by the English in 1307, it was again burnt by accident in 1498 and only rebuilt in time to be destroyed by Reformers. Cruciform in plan, the central tower fell and destroyed the choir. A restoration was begun with the nave in 1859, followed by the transepts in c.1900 and a new choir and cloisters in 1912-28. Notwithstanding all these calamities, there are remains of the mid-C15 church in the nave aisles, triforium and clerestory. The complete west gable and window are also of the same date. St Miram's chapel in the south transept with its stone vaulted roof was built in 1499. It contains an *altar tomb* reassembled in 1812 and believed to be that of the mother of Robert II.

Other Churches

BOTHWELL. 5m SE of Glasgow on A724. *St Bride.*
Founded in 1398, only the original choir with stone-slab roof and large buttresses survived a rebuilding in 1833 by David Hamilton who added a nave and crossing tower. Inside, note the late-C14 *sedilia*, the Norman *capitals* from an earlier church; the *monuments* to two Earls of Forfar (d.1712 & 1715), one of whom was fatally wounded at Sheriffmuir; the *grave-slab* of Walter de Moravia, the builder of Bothwell Castle; the Edward Burne-Jones *east window*, and the C14 *sacristy* next to the elaborate *monument* to the 3rd Duke of Hamilton (d.1694).

GLASGOW.
St Stephen's, Renfield 256½ Bath Street.
Built as an Independent Chapel in early-C14 Gothic style by J.T. Emmett in 1849-52, and consisting of an aisled nave and chancel with a tall south-west tower and an unfortunate addition in 1970 by Munro & Partners. The pulpit of 1915 is from Maxwell church, Pollockshields; all other Gothic fittings are post-1918. Glass of 1905 by N. Macdougall, and of 1980.

Tayside

This region is unusual in having a high proportion of remarkable churches. Tullibardine Chapel built from 1446, an early church by Scottish standards, is practically unaltered. The most exceptional features are the painted ceilings of Fowlis Easter Parish Kirk, Stobhall Chapel, Old St Mary's at Grandtully, and St Mary's, Aberfeldy. All these date from the first half of the seventeenth century and, taken with similar examples at Largs, Strathclyde, by T. Stalker in 1638, and the Chapel Royal, Stirling, by Valentyne Jenking, and of similar date, they point to a school of several Scottish painters working at the same time in an arc-shaped area bounded by Perth, Stirling and Edinburgh, with three other examples in the north-east at Crathes, Aberdeen and Banff. The trend for painted ceilings followed from an earlier fashion for decorative plasterwork in the 1520s, although only one example exists of the two skills combined: Pinkie House, Mussleburgh, dated 1613, discovered in 1963. The fashion for painted ceilings, both domestic and ecclesiastic, had a run of only about fifty years.

FOWLIS EASTER. 5M W of Dundee off A923. *Parish Kirk.*

One of the best preserved and most interesting of the pre-Reformation churches in Scotland. Built in c.1453 by the 2nd Lord Gray, it is a simple oblong structure in fine ashlar with nave and chancel under one roof. The kirk was restored in c.1890 when the small bellcote on the west gable replaced an earlier example. A good four-light, traceried window in the west wall lights the nave, and a three-light window with differing tracery in the south wall lights the chancel. The south-west entrance has a richly carved ogee shaped-label. Inside, marking off the chancel, are the reassembled remains of the original *rood screen* and its door; to either side are stone corbels to support the rood loft. In the chancel east wall is an elaborate and finely carved *aumbry*. Most remarkable are four large pre-Reformation *painted panels*, one showing Christ on the Cross, another with representations of eleven saints. The two remaining panels show fragments of a female saint with a sword, the remains of Christ in Glory. Note the good example of an *alms basin*, the pre-Reformation stone *font* with carved figures, the *jougs* used for punishing misbehaviour and, in the churchyard, the mid-C19 *hearse house.*

GRANDTULLY. 5m (indirectly) SW from Pitlochry on A827. *Old St Mary's.*

The long, low, chapel, about 80ft long and only 24ft wide, stands to the east of Grandtully Castle, high above the Strathtay valley with breathtaking views. The long low exterior of c.1533 is plain in the extreme and might be mistaken for farm buildings with fenestrations and openings in the south wall. The interior is another matter; a wood barrel-vault *ceiling* extending over only half the space from the east end was richly painted in c.1636. Flamboyantly religious and overtly Catholic, the subjects include the Four Evangelists, coats of arms of England and Scotland, the arms of the Earls of Atholl, and of the laird of Grandtully and his wife, and monograms, while the large central panel shows buildings with figures. These are

Grandtully, Old St Mary's. A section of the painted
ceiling of c.1636.

contained in four rows of patterned frames consisting of circles and
other regular shapes.

INNERPEFFRAY. 1m SE of Crieff on B8062. *The Old Kirk.*
In the care of Historic Scotland. A long narrow stone-built kirk, originally collegiate and built by John, Lord Drummond in c.1508.
Rectangular, with a sacristy projecting on the north side, it originally
had a boarded and painted ceiling; two panels were recorded there in
1897. Apart from the west window, all the openings are on the south
side. At the west end an arch marks a vestibule with a spiral stair
into a 'laird's loft'. A simple chancel arch is at the east end and corbels
in the north and south walls once supported a rood loft. Note the
consecration crosses, and the single *hatchment*.

PERTH. 24m N of Edinburgh on M90. *St John the Baptist.*
Rebuilt in 1328 and, although declared 'ruinous' in 1585, not

repaired until 1598, it now consists of an aisled nave and choir, of 1448-9, with north and south transepts and a mid-C15 central tower. Restorations were carried out in 1823, when the north transept gable was rebuilt, and again in the mid-C19. Its past has been turbulent: in 1335 King Edward III slew his brother before the high altar; in 1559 an unruly mob, over-enthused by a sermon from John Knox, stormed out of the church and sacked the many religious houses in Perth, before stripping the interior of St John's. Notwithstanding its troubled past a silver *baptismal basin* of c.1595 and a Flemish early-C16 brass *chandelier* survive. Note the many *hatchments* and the fine pewter *alms dishes* given by Charles II.

TULLIBARDINE. 3m SE of Crief on A823. *Tullibardine Chapel.*
In the care of Historic Scotland. Built from 1446 by Sir David Murray and one of the last pre-Reformation collegiate churches. Originally consisting of an aisleless nave and chancel under the same roof with a low square west tower, two deep transepts were added in c.1500, dated by the window tracery. It is practically unaltered.

Other Churches

ABERFELDY. 7m (indirectly) from Pitlochry on A827. *St Mary.*
A simple white-harled kirk worth visiting for its C16 *painted ceiling* boards showing biblical texts, heraldry, and ornate floral decoration.
DUNDEE. 10m NE of Perth on A85. *St Salvador.*
Built by G.F. Bodley in the Decorated style of the early C14. The aisled nave with clerestory (1865-8) was followed by the choir, only completed in 1874. Its exterior is simple but the spacious interior is gloriously decorated throughout with *stencils* by Burlison and Grylls who also made the *reredos* with its many apostles painted on copper, and the *glass* in the choir

Stobhall, Chapel. The painted ceiling of c.1633.

MONTROSE. 17m NE of Dundee on A92. *Old Kirk.*
Built in 1791 by David Logan, a local architect, with a magnificent west tower and spire of 1834 by Gillespie Graham. It is still known as the 'town steeple'. Inside are the only surviving examples in Scotland of *double-galleries*. Note the 14-branched brass *chandelier* dated 1623 given to the kirk by Richard Clark, a vice-admiral in the Swedish navy.

STOBHALL. 4m N of Perth on A93. *Chapel.*
Built by the Roman Catholic Drummond family on the ground floor of a 1578 tower, and restored in the C19, it is only 27ft by 17ft. The beamed and boarded *ceiling* was painted in c.1633, and the designs show a series of nine horsemen including Prester John, animals and birds and decorative strapwork. The Drummond arms has been cut out and hangs on the west wall.

WALES

Although Wales is mountainous the stone is in the main difficult to work, particularly in the north and east, consequently ashlar is rare and rough stone is the usual finish. There was no shortage of timber and some fine timber roofs of the fifteenth and early-sixteenth centuries have survived, particularly in Clwyd: All Saints, Gresford and St Peter at Ruthin are two good examples.

Wales is a Celtic part of Britain, and the Celtic monastery was responsible for some very grand and large churches. St Illtud, Llantwit Major, Glamorgan, and St Padarn, Llanbadarn Fawr, Dyfed, for example, were both Celtic monastic churches rebuilt by the Benedictines. The Normans went to considerable lengths to Romanise the Celtic church and passed most of their monasteries over to the Benedictines. However, in remote areas the Celtic religious traditions were maintained for a surprisingly long time, mainly because there was no reason for the Normans to penetrate the wilder parts of Wales. Snowdonia, Anglesey, the Cambrian Mountains of mid-Wales, and North Pembroke are rocky, inhospitable and windswept, and were left alone by Vikings and Normans alike; to this day they retain their Welshness. The borders and South Wales – the richer farmlands – built many of the finest medieval churches, such as All Saints, Gresford, Clwyd and St Giles, Wrexham, Clwyd.

Norman work is represented by the nave of St James at Manorbier, Dyfed; the small Norman nave and chancel at St Ishow, Patrishow, Powys; and the late-Norman monastic church of St Mary & All Saints at Penmon, Anglesey.

Medieval Welsh parish churches are of mixed dates; it is unusual to find one all-of-a-date, but St Padarn, Llanbadarn Fawr, Dyfed, is c.1200; St Mary, Carew Cheriton, Dyfed, is c.1400; St Stephen, Old Radnor, Powys, is early-C15; and St Mary, Tenby, Dyfed, was rebuilt in the C15. An amazing survival is the shrine of All Saints at Pennant Melangell, Powys, a small C12 church where the shrine of St Melangell has been painstakingly reconstructed, recoloured, and replaced in the chancel where it once stood.

Churches on the borders were inevitably influenced by English traditions and often built by English masons and joiners. This is most evident in the rood screens: Welsh screens have rectangular tracery heads, while English screens will have arched tracery; this,

WALES

however, is not a hard and fast rule.

A notable feature of Welsh churches is the development of the double nave—two parallel naves of equal size and length. This was a convenient way to double the size of a church, and they mostly date from the late-fifteenth and sixteenth centuries following the founding of the Tudor dynasty.

The industrial south, based on Welsh coal, brought prosperity in the nineteenth century, and some good Victorian churches were built to accommodate the increased population. Two of note are Holy Trinity at Trefnant, Clwyd, by Sir George Gilbert Scott, and St Tisilio at Llandisilio, Powys, by G.E. Street – one of his best.

Clwyd

BODELWYDDAN. 2m W of St Asaph on A55. *St Margaret.*
Known as 'the marble church', it was in fact built of white limestone by John Gibson in 1856-60 for the Dowager Lady Willoughby de Broke in memory of her husband, and its 202ft gleaming white west spire is a landmark for miles. A lack of exterior marble is more than made up for in the lavish interior decorated with alabaster and Caen stone as well as coloured marbles. The *pulpit, stall ends* and *chancel bosses* were richly carved by Thomas Earp. Note the hammer-beam roof over the nave and the good east window *glass* by M.A. O'Connor. The Carrara marble *font* of 1862 by Peter Hollins shows the donor's two daughters holding a shell.

GRESFORD. 3m N of Wrexham on A483. *All Saints.*
Claimed to be the 'perfect Cheshire church in Wales', it was almost entirely rebuilt in the 1490s, leaving some C13 work at the west end. The lower stage of the tower is C14, the upper stages are

Gresford, All Saints. The exterior, almost entirely of the 1490s.

313

C16. The church, consisting of nave, north and south aisles and chancel, was restored in 1867-8 by G.E. Street. The interior is spacious and filled with light and a fine late-C15 roof with painted bosses covers both nave and chancel. A good oak English *rood screen*, *parclose screens*, chapel *screens*, and *stalls* with eleven carved oak *misericords*, are all contemporary. The pulpit by Street and reredos by John Douglas date from the restorations. The C15 glass suffered severe damage in 1966 and was restored; the east window is mainly by Clayton & Bell of 1867. Among the many monuments, notice one by Sir Francis Chantrey of 1829 and another by Sir Richard Westmacott of 1803. Also note the two *hatchments*.

LLANGWYFAN. 4m E of Denbigh off B5429. *St Cwyfan.*
A medieval single cell church with bellcote, in rendered limestone, which happily escaped the Tractarians. The small interior is fitted with C18 *box pews* and a decorated baluster *font*. The east window, dated 1853, is by Alexander Gibbs.

LLANRWST. 10m S of Colwyn Bay on A470. *Seion Welsh Presbyterian Chapel.*
A very large and grand chapel rebuilt in 1881-3 in a neo-Classical style. The interior is equally grand; a curved gallery on three sides focuses on the east end on a raised pulpit beneath a huge organ, installed in 1915 and worthy of the finest cinema. All is furnished in fine shining woodwork.

LLANSILIN. 5m W of Oswestry on B4580. *St Silin.*
A double-nave C13 church remodelled in the C15. The C13 nave west wall is all that remains of the older church whose tower was rebuilt in 1832. All was restored in 1890 by Arthur Baker who exposed the C15 roofs and designed the pews and stalls. The late C17 *Commandment boards,* painted on canvas, are now at the back of the late-C16 west gallery, and the late-C17 canvas *Benefaction board* is in the north nave. Note the *poor box* dated 1664, the medieval dug-out chest, and plaster *Royal Arms* of Queen Anne. A curiosity is the iron box suspended on a chain in the north nave.

LLANYNYS. 4m NW of Ruthin off A525. *SS Mor* & *Saeron.*
A double-nave church, with a double west bellcote, built on the site of a C6 monastery; the old north nave is C13 separated from the C14 south nave by oak Doric columns of c.1768. A C15 *wall painting* of St Christopher faces the south door and the two painted wood *chandeliers* are of 1749. The brass chandelier is C19. Particularly notice the wooden *dog tongs*, the canvas *Royal Arms* dated 1661, and the two *hatchments*. A C14 stone hexagonal *memorial cross* was rescued from the churchyard and brought inside.

MOLD. 10m NW of Wrexham on A541. *St Mary.*

An ambitious rebuilding in limestone, begun by the Countess of Richmond and Derby (d.1509) in c.1500, got no further than the vast aisled nave completed in 1570, leaving the west tower to be added in 1768-71, and the chancel, by Sir George Gilbert Scott, in 1853-6. The wide nave is flanked by highly decorated *arcades* and a roof replaced by Scott in his restorations of the 1850s. The pulpit, stalls and pews are also his, and the alabaster reredos of 1878 is by John Douglas. Most of the *glass* is C19 but there is some of the C16 in the north aisle. The iron gates and screenwork in the north aisle and chancel are c.1762. Note the Art Deco marble floor in the 1921 War Memorial chapel.

Bethesda Welsh Presbyterian Chapel, New Street.

Rebuilt in 1863 with the old dedication stone of 1819 reset, it is a

Mold, St Mary. The nave of 1570.

grand neo-Classical building with, inside, an unchanged standard lay-out of a three-sided gallery facing the organ and raised pulpit.

RUABON. 5m SW of Wrexham on A483. *St Mary.*
Although the west tower is C14, the rest of the church is an unsympathetic restoration of 1870-2 by Benjamin Ferrey and is best overlooked. The principal point of a visit is to see the elegant *font* of 1772 designed by Robert Adam, the 15ft long C15 *wall paintings* of the Works of Mercy, and the many good *monuments* to the Wynn family, one by J.M.Rysbrack of 1751-4, another by Joseph Nollekens of 1773. Note the *Royal Arms* on wood, of 1780.

RUTHIN. 14m W of Wrexham on A494. *St Peter.*
The church, begun in 1310, originally had an aisleless nave, chancel and central tower, with domestic buildings joined to the north wall. Restored early in the C19, and again in 1854-9 when the spire was added, it was once collegiate and a rare example of the Augustinian Bonhommes. A south aisle, added in the C14, gives the familiar double nave plan. The north nave roof is particularly finely carved with badges, arms and inscriptions. Note the *altar table* dated 1621, and the *monuments* in the vestry including a fragment of an early-C14 *effigy* of a priest.

WORTHENBURY. 5m SE of Wrexham on B5069. *St Deiniol.*
Built in brick with limestone dressings in 1736-9 by Richard Trubshaw, this is the finest Georgian church in Wales, consisting of a nave, with a roof oddly flattened at the apex, square west tower, and an apsed chancel. The interior is marked by a covedplaster ceiling with some nice rococo plasterwork in the chancel; the *box pews* and *pulpit* are original and two *squires' pews* in the chancel have *fireplaces*. Made-up fragments of medieval *glass* from the Jesse Window at Winchester College chapel were inserted in the east window in 1822-3. Note the *Royal Arms* painted on canvas, and the three *hatchments*.

WREXHAM. 11m SW of Chester on A483. *St Giles.*
An impressive C14 church consisting of a nave with late-C15 aisles and clerestory, C15 chancel, and an early-C16 west tower; all was sympathetically restored in 1866-7. The interior and glass is now mainly of the C19, and the chancel was refitted in 1914. However, a fine brass eagle *lectern* was given in 1524, and there are fragments of a Last Judgement *painted* over the chancel arch. In the north aisle a particularly fine *monument* of 1751 and another in the nave of 1756 are both by Louis Roubiliac. Another of 1814 in the chancel is by Sir Richard Westmacott. Elihu Yale (d.1721), the founder of Yale University, USA, is buried near the tower.

Derwen, St Mary. Screen and loft of the C15.

Other Churches

BERSE DRELINCOURT. 2m NW of Wrexham on B5101. *Dedication unknown.*
Built in 1742 in now rendered limestone, for the widow of a Dean of Armagh, and extended westward in 1828. Pews are of 1862, and two chandeliers are of 1688 and c.1740 respectively. The late-C17 *Commandment board*, painted on canvas, has Moses and Aaron with the 'Whole Armour of God' in the background; the C17 *creed board* is also painted on canvas. Note the good C17 painting of the Supper at Emmaus.

DERWEN. 4m N of Corwen off A494. *St Mary.*
A small church with nave and chancel under one roof and with a C15 *rood screen* and *loft*. The font is dated 1665. Restored in 1857.

HOLYWELL. 20m NW of Wrexham on A55. *St Winefride.*
Maintained by Welsh Heritage. An early-C16 shrine marks the holy well where the dead St Winefride was miraculously restored to the living world in the early C7. The chapel above is small and richly decorated, with an apsed east end; it was completely restored in 1976. The C16 *roof* has carved bosses.

LLANGOLLEN. 9m SW of Wrexham on A5. *St Collen.*
A double-naved C13 church, chancel and south aisle of 1864-7, with a mid-C18 west tower. Magnificent late-C15 *hammer-beam roofs* in nave and north aisle, heavily carved bosses, animals, masks and filigree work all supported by carved angels.

TREFNANT. 3m S of St Asaph on A525. *Holy Trinity.*
Built regardless of cost in 1853-5 by Sir George Gilbert Scott in C14 Gothic style. The aisled nave, chancel, and double bellcote contain a rich interior with – following John Ruskin's lead – 'every group of leaves' carved on the capitals. Note the elaborate pulpit and font.

Dyfed

CAREW CHERITON. 4m E of Pembroke on A477. *St Mary.*
An interesting church mainly of c.1400, cruciform in plan with long chancel, a nave with two aisles, and a barrel-vaulted C15 west tower with a corner steeple. It was restored by Sir George Gilbert Scott in 1855. In the chancel, heraldic *floor tiles* are c.1500, and notice particularly the interesting *memorials*, including a C14 one of a child holding a heart, and another by J.E. Thomas exhibited at the Great Exhibition of 1851. In the churchyard is a c.1400 *charnel house.*

HAVERFORDWEST. 14m S of Fishguard on A40. *St Mary.*
A fine C13 church, enlarged in c.1500, and with splendid C13 arcades with deeply carved capitals between the nave and aisles, it was restored in 1848. The *roof* of carved and panelled oak dates from when the clerestory was added in the late-C15. Note the carved *mayor's pew*, the C18 organ, and the C15 *effigy* of a pilgrim. Portraits of the Earl and Countess of Pembroke are on the chancel arch.

LLANBADARN FAWR. 1m E of Aberystwith on A44. *St Padarn.*
The fact that this was an early Celtic monastery, eventually given to the Benedictines, accounts for this large, grand, cruciform church, with a low tower over the crossing, built in c.1200. The severe walls are pierced by C12 lancet windows, and the east window was inserted in C15. All was sympathetically restored in 1868 by J.P. Seddon who added the good-quality *fittings*, and the fine boarded chancel roof, marble *reredos* and tiled floor.

MANORBIER. 5m SW of Tenby on B4585. *St James.*
With its impressive Norman nave and transepts, C14 aisles, C13 chancel, and north-east tower unusually sited in the corner between the chancel and the north transept, this church was restored in 1865, when the chancel arch was enlarged. The sculptural element of the vaults of the nave and transepts is memorable. Note the *Royal Arms*, previously over the chancel arch, and the C15 *painting* in the vaulted porch.

TENBY. 10m E of Pembroke on A4139. *St Mary.*
Only the C13 tower, slotted between the chancel and south aisle, remains of an earlier church. The rest is an almost complete rebuild-

ing of the C15, with a chancel extended eastwards in c.1470. The nave arcades are late-C15, and the barrel-vaulted *roof* is notable. The chancel would be dramatic had not the screen been removed. A broad flight of steps leads to the sanctuary, and there is a fine late-C15 waggon-roof with carved *bosses* and standing figures holding shields. Among the monuments with effigies is a C15 carved *skeleton.*

Other Churches

STACKPOLE ELIDOR. 3m S of Pembroke off A4319. *Dedication unknown.*

A delightful church in a charming valley site, sympathetically restored in 1851 by Sir George Gilbert Scott who demolished and rebuilt the nave retaining the original Norman tower and vaulted transepts. Note the *hatchments*, and unusually fine *monuments*.

TALLYLLYCHAU. 6m N of Llandeilo on B4320. *St Michael & All Angels.*

Built in 1773 with, unusually, two west doors leading into the aisles and no central door. Untouched interior with good contemporary, rustic *box pews* and a boarded barrel-vaulted ceiling.

Glamorgan

CARDIFF. 170m W of London off M4. *St John,* Church Street.
The only medieval church remaining in the city. Part C13, but mainly C15, its magnificently carved tower was added in 1473; it was all restored, partly rebuilt and enlarged in 1852. Forty years later the outer aisles were added and further restoration carried out. In the chancel, the east window *glass* is by Sir Ninian Comper who designed the *reredos* in the south aisle. The *reredos* behind the high altar was carved by W.G. John, and there is a splendid window with *glass* by William Morris in the baptistry. Particularly notice the two early-C17 Herbert family *monuments* in the Herbert Chapel.

St German, Star St, Roath.
One of the major churches built by the G.F. Bodley/Thomas Gardner partnership in 1882-4. On a restricted site they constructed a tall, delicate masterpiece in stone. Inside, the delicacy is enhanced by slender clustered columns and a mastery of space. Bodley designed the *rood, pulpit, font, organ case*, and all the *glass* made by Burlison and Grylls in 1900. A carved and painted *reredos* by Cecil Hoare spreads across the width of the sanctuary.

EWENNY. 2m S of Bridgend on B4524. *St Michael.*
The nave of c.1120 is the earliest part of what was once a Benedictine priory and 'a remarkable example of a semi-fortified monastery'. The crossing, tower, chancel, west wall, and north arcade are all late-C12;

the porch and north aisle are C16, rebuilt in 1895. In the chancel, the early barrel-vaulting and decorative ribbons of carved stone give some impression of the original dignity of the building. Note the C16 linenfold *panelling,* the C14 *screen,* and the sepulchral slabs with French inscriptions in the south transept.

LLANTWIT MAJOR. 15m SW of Cardiff on B4265. *St Illtud.*
This church is on the site of a C12 Celtic monastery which became Benedictine and collegiate. This accounts for the unexpected length of the building, comprising nave with aisles, chancel and west tower, all restored in 1888-1905. At one time it was even longer, but the Galilee chapel at the west end is now in ruins. The nave and aisles, with a magnificent timber roof, comprised the original parish church, while the east end was used by the Benedictines. Note the big, restored C14 *reredos;* the C13 carved Tree of Jesse in the south aisle may have been part of an earlier reredos. Notice particularly the Celtic crosses and medieval *tombs* in the nave, and the C13-C15 *wall paintings* including an easily distinguishable late-C14 St Christopher.

Llantwit Major, St Illtud. Mid-C13 carved reredos.

PENARTH. 3m S of Cardiff on A4160. *St Augustine.*
Built in 1865-6 of grey limestone with Bath stone dressings and a low saddle-back tower, this church is one of William Butterfield's best. In contrast to the grey exterior, the interior is riot of geometrical polychrome; red brick walls are diapered with white and black brick, and alternating cream and pink stone arches. Above the splendid *reredos* is the *glass* of an east window by A. Gibbs.

Other Churches

COITY. 2m NE of Bridgend off A4061. *St Mary.*
A large aisleless church with a low crossing tower and a bright, light interior. The glory of the church is the early William Morris *east window* of 1863, made only two years after the firm was founded. Note the C14 *effigies* on either side of the altar.

LLANDEILO TALYBONT. 7m NW of Swansea on A48. *St Teilo.*
Restored by the Friends of the Friendless Churches. A small white-washed C13 church with fine medieval timber *roofs*, restored in 1810 and unchanged since. The *box pews*, two-decker *pulpit*, and other fittings all date from 1810.

OXWICH. 10m W of Swansea off A4118. *St Illtyd.*
A small church of great charm with a huge tower, and well worth a detour. The tiny chancel has a ceiling painted for Dame Lilian Baylis (d.1937) of the Old Vic. Note the beautiful C14 *tomb* also in the chancel. The interior is still lit by oil lamps.

Gwent

ABERGAVENNY. 18m N of Newport on A40. *St Mary.*
A large cruciform church with crossing tower, and once part of a Benedictine priory founded in the C12, the building is mainly C14 and little of the Norman work remains. However, it has some notable contents: carved, canopied, *choir stalls* of the C15 and C16, with sixteen carved *misericords* of c.1500; a large wooden *recumbent Jesse*, probably part of the reredos; a *glass* fragment of a medieval Jesse window; a wooden *effigy* of 1273; and a number of good C15-C16 alabaster *tombs*, perhaps the best of which is that of Sir William Hastings (d.c.1340).

CALDICOT. 5m SW of Chepstow on B4245. *St Mary.*
A good, little altered, medieval church with central tower, restored in 1858 by H.Woodyer, who designed many of the fittings. Recently refurbished by the Friends of the Friendless Churches who also provided a new *candelabrum* and wall brackets.

NASH. 3m S of Newport off B4237. *St Mary.*
A memorable church with a big C15 stone spire on the north-east corner of the nave and a chancel rebuilt in 1861. The large nave is little altered and still retains its C18 *box pews* and three-decker pulpit.

USK. 9m N of Newport on A472. *St Mary.*
Once a Benedictine priory for nuns founded in c.1135. A north aisle, for the use of parishioners, was added to the priory church in the C13 and this is now the parish church with the chancel under what was once the central tower. The two porches are C15. In 1844, the nave was extended to the west when the building was restored. The English medieval *screen* spanning nave and aisle has the oldest surviving Welsh *epitaph* on a brass plate, and the splendid *organ* was made in 1862 for Llandaff Cathedral.

Other Churches

SKENFRITH. 5m NW of Monmouth on B4521. *St Bridget.*
A large square tower with a magnificent, timber, two-tiered, pyramidical belfry dominates the church. Noteworthy for the possession of a splendid C15 embroidered *cope.* An ornate *tomb* of 1557 in the north aisle and an early-C17 *pew* are worth viewing.

Gwynedd

BEAUMARIS, Anglesey. 5m NE of Menai Bridge on B545. *St Mary.*
Built in the C14 with a late-C16 chancel, all restored by G.F. Bodley in 1902. The interior has C18 *pews* and communion rail, and in the chancel are twenty carved *misericords* of c.1500, and early-C16 *bench ends.* There are several good *monuments* including C15 alabaster *effigies* of a knight and his lady. Note the early C19 *watchman's box* in the porch.

CLYNNOG-FAWR. 10m SW of Caernarfon on A499. *St Beuno.*
This mainly C15 church once held the shrine of St Beuno (a C7 Abbot) and was an attraction for pilgrims on their way to Bardsey Island. Traditionally the saint is supposed to be buried beneath the chapel close to the south-west of the church and connected by a C17 passage. Inside, there is a fine C15 timber *roof* and an early-C16 English *screen* restored in the C19. Note the iron *dog-tongs* with spikes, once used to break up dog fights during a service, the simple C.1700 pulpit, and the dug-out *chest* of medieval date in the glass case behind the door.

LLANDDOGED. 2m N of Llanrwst off A470. *St Doged.*
An eccentric double-nave church built in a *cottage orné* style in 1839 by the rector. Left untouched by the Tractarians, the original interior survives. Tall *pews* are centred on a three-decker *pulpit* against the north wall, lit from above by a coloured glass skylight. Directly behind the pulpit is a plaster angel's head with the Commandments and Moses painted on either side, and the *Royal Arms.*

LLANEILLIAN, Anglesey. 15m NW of Menai Bridge off A5025. *St Eilian.*
A church with a C12 west tower, a wide nave and chancel rebuilt in the late-C15, and the C14 *St Eilian's* chapel connected by a passage to the chancel. Notice the wooden fragment of a shrine to St Eilian. The interior is distinguished by the surprising survival of so many C15 furnishings: a fine, rustic *rood screen* with a painting of Death as a skeleton carrying a scythe, chancel *stalls*, and a good late-C15 roof, with carved corbels. Don't overlook the wooden *dog-tongs.*

PENMON. 4m NE of Beaumaris off B5109. *St Mary & All Saints.*
A Celtic monastery was founded here in the C6. Often raided by
Vikings it was as often rebuilt. In 1414 it was given to the Austin
Priors. Today it is a small cruciform church of rough stone with a
nave and transepts of 1140, and a crossing tower with its original
stone pyramid roof of c.1160. The chancel, partly rebuilt, is late-
C13. Above the Norman south door is a *tympanum* carved with a
dragon, then a good omen. The interior has the best-preserved
Norman detail in North Wales; the crossing arches carved with the
Norman chevron decoration, the wall arcades, and a *font* made from
the base of a c.100 AD Celtic cross. To the south stands the prior's
house, now a private dwelling. To the north is a holy well and
remains of an Anchorite's cell.

Other Churches

LLANFAGLAN. 2m S of Caernarvon off A487. *Dedication
unknown.*
In the care of the Friends of Friendless Churches. A small church
built in the C13 with a chancel of c.1800 and still with its C18
fittings: *benches, box pews, pulpit* and *tester,* with *reading desk,* all
intact.

LLANGADWALADR, Anglesey. 10m SW of Menai Bridge on
A4080. *St Cadwaladr.*
A previous church was under the patronage of king Cadfan (d.c.625)
whose graveslab is in the present C12 nave, and named after his
grandson Cadwaladr (d.664). A good C15 east window lights the
C14 chancel and the interior is lit by a series of splendid brass chandeliers. A south chapel was added in the mid-C17 and the north
chapel has a high-Gothic memorial of 1857.

Powys

CAPEL-Y-FFIN. 12m N of Abergavenny off B4423. *Dedication
unknown.*
One of the smallest churches in Wales (only 25ft x 13ft inside), built
c.1762, with a west bellcote, and south porch of 1817. Inside, the
fittings are contemporary: the west *gallery, pulpit,* and *altar rails.* A
settle is dated 1783. The east window eccentrically has coloured
paper glued to it to imitate coloured glass. A headstone in the
churchyard by Eric Gill commemorates a carpenter who died in
1935.

KERRY. 2m E of Newtown on A489. *St Michael.*
Built of rough masonry, the church has a nave with a north aisle, a
chancel, and a massive west *tower* with six-feet thick walls. The two-

Kerry, St Michael. The chunky tower with
two-storied timber belfry.

storied timber belfry with pyramid roof may have replaced a C12
tower. All was restored in 1881-3 by G.E. Street and, after his death
in 1881, by A.W.Blomfield. The interior is marked by three Norman
round, red sandstone *columns* of c.1176 supporting the north arcade.
The screen, lectern and pulpit are of 1883, and chained to the lectern
is a *Welsh Bible* of 1690. The glass of 1871 is by C.E. Kempe. Note
the two Herbert family *hatchments*, and the good C14 *roofs*.

LLANBISTER. 8m NE of Llandrindod Wells on A483. *St Cynllo.*
A church built on a steep hillside with a c.1300 nave and a C16
tower at the east end, all sympathetically restored by W.D. Caroë in
1908. The C15 roof was heavily restored in 1908 and the old box
pews (one dated 1688) reduced in height. The pulpit and tester are
C18. Across the west end is a *gallery* dated 1716 with small parti-
tioned off schoolroom underneath, and lit by windows inserted in
1908. The C15 screen was restored in 1908, and the communion
rails are of 1828. Note the fragments of C18 *wall painting*. Original
oil *lamps* are cleverly adapted to electricity.

LLANFILO. 6m NE of Brecon off A470. *St Bilo.*

An unusual church for Wales because the east part of the nave is Norman and was extended in the C13 when the chancel was built. In 1881 a west tower with shingled spire was added and the whole was restored by W.D. Caroë in 1913 and only completed in 1951. A splendid rood *screen* with rood *loft* is the highlight of the white-painted nave, the figures are restoration replacements as is the rood itself. The stone flagged floor disconcertingly slopes down to the chancel, partly rebuilt in c.1710, with a plaster ceiling of the same date. Additionally, there is a good collection of C17-19 *monuments*. Note the C14 *Angelus bell* with Latin inscription.

MEIFORD. 6m NW of Welshpool on A495. *SS Tysilio & Mary.*
The church once shared its nine acre churchyard with a chapel and another church, both now vanished. The remaining building comprises an aisled nave of which the west end is C12, with an early-C14 south aisle, a north aisle rebuilt in 1871-2 when the church was restored by Benjamin Ferrey, and a C15 west tower. Inside, the nave and south aisle roofs are late-C14 and the font is C16. There are some C17 *pews* and an octagonal Jacobean *pulpit* at the west end. The glass is all C19, as is the heraldic *glass* of 1838 in the aisles. A C10 Celtic cross grave-slab is in the south aisle.

MONTGOMERY. 5m S of Welshpool on B4386. *St Nicholas.*
The long high nave built of rubblestone with sandstone dressings is C13; the transepts are c.1260-70; the C13 chancel was extended in the late-C13 and the west tower was rebuilt in 1816. It was restored once in 1863-8, and again in 1877-8. Inside, the *roofs* are the glory of the building; the nave has a late-C15, open timber, hammer-beam *roof* in the west end, and a ceiled and panelled C16 barrel-vault roof at the east end; the chancel roof is a poor thing of 1868. An unusual double, late-C15 *screen* consists of a west-facing original Welsh screen, with an east-facing English screen from Chirbury Priory, Shropshire put in at the Dissolution, when the nine early-C15 carved *misericords* and stalls, said to be from Chirbury Priory, were also added. Notice particularly the painted *Royal Arms* of 1726, the Herbert *hatchment* of c.1801, and the richly decorated, canopied *tomb* of 1596 in the south transept. In the churchyard is the grave of John Davies, publicly hanged in 1821 for robbing a traveller of a 30s (£1.50) watch.

OLD RADNOR. 3m NW of Kington off B4594. *St Stephen.*
An earlier C12 church was burnt down by Owen Glendower in 1401 and the present church is early-C15. During a skilful restoration in the 1880s the east end was rebuilt leaving the nave, north and south aisles intact. The interior boasts the oldest *organ case* (c.1500) in Britain; the organ itself was replaced in 1872. Nave and south aisles have Tudor roofs with carved bosses; the less-elaborate north aisle

roof is C15; the chancel stalls are also C15. The chancel *screen* is a good late-C15 example; its colour and gilding were stripped off in the C19. There is a fine *Easter Sepulchre* in the north chapel and glorious C15 *glass* in the north aisle east window. Medieval tiles were cleverly copied by E.W. Godwin in the 1880s. Particularly notice the C18 *painting* of Moses and Aaron, the *hatchments* on the west wall, and a monument of 1797 by John Flaxman.

PARTRISHOW. 6m N of Abergavenny off B4423. *St Ishow* or *Issui.*
A small, remote church consisting of a windowless Norman nave and chancel, with a tiny C13 chapel tacked on to the west end with its own entrance and altar. The whole was carefully restored in 1908-9 by W.D. Caroë, when the chancel was rebuilt in C16 Gothic style. The church is famous for its c.1500 *screen* and *rood loft*, restored by Caroë, before which stand two remarkable stone *altars* of indeterminate date, but obviously older than the screen. A large *font* of c.1055 is all that remains of an earlier church. Across the west wall are the remains of a *painted* doom, and there is a decayed painted *Royal Arms* on the north wall. Note the many mid-C17 fittings, and the fourteen *monuments* to the Brute family.

PENNANT MELANGELL. 4m SE of Welshpool off A490. *All Saints.*
A small, remote, and very interesting mid-C12 church, built of rough stonework. In a controversial restoration the building has recently been returned, as far as possible, to its C12 state. With a stumpy C17 west tower (reconstructed in 1877 with a pyramidical roof), nave and chancel in one, and an east apse, the building was badly in need of restoration. Its interest arises from the fact that this was the shrine of St Melangell. Her amazing C12 *shrine*, reconstructed in 1958 from fragments found in the church walls, is now restored almost to its original state, but minus the precious metals and jewels which once decorated it, and replaced in the chancel where it stood before the Reformation. Its attached stone altar serves as the parish altar. The late-C15 chancel *screen*, with carved frieze, has been restored and the space above is now a boarded tympanum with an C18 painted *Benefaction board* mounted on it. Although electricity is installed the church is still lit by hanging oil lamps and a wooden candelabrum dated 1733 in the chancel. The nave roof is C15, and note the C18 *Royal Arms* and C18 pulpit. This church should not be missed.

PRESTEIGNE. 5m S of Knighton on B4362. *St Andrew.*
Rebuilt in the mid-C15 this is basically a late-C14 church with some C10 Saxon masonry at the east end of the north nave. Consisting of an aisled nave, chancel, and a late-C15 south-west tower above the south porch, it was restored by J.L. Pearson in 1889-91. Look for the

Romanesque *sculpture* of St Andrew above the west window. The Tudor *panelled roof* was restored in 1889 and the stone pulpit also dates from the same restoration. Notable are: a splendid early-C16 Flemish *tapestry* of Christ's Entry to Jerusalem; an oak *warden's table* dated 1666; a good early-C16 *painting* of the Holy Family; and beautiful C18 three-tier *candelabra*. There are fragments of wall paintings in the north-west end of the nave.

Pennant Melangell, All Saints. The shrine of St Melangell.

Other Churches

ALLTMAWR. 3m SE of Builth Wells on A470. *St Mauritius.*

Only 35ft long and one of the smallest churches in Wales this was built in the C13 and comprises a single cell with a three-sided apse added in the C19. The pulpit, *box pews* at the back of the nave, and the wooden windows are all C18. The font is C13, and note the charming *monument* by Ernest Gillick to Lord Trevethin (d.1936) and his wife.

COLVA. 7m SW of Kington off B45994. *St David.*

A small single-cell church, probably C13, with a late-C15 porch, and a timber west bell-turret. Inside is a fine open timber roof, a round stone font of c.1200, school benches in place of pews, and a signed *Royal Arms* dated 1733.

LLANANO. 8m N of Llandrindod Wells off A483. *St Anno.*

Completely rebuilt in 1876-7, the interior has one of the best examples in Wales of a late-C15 carved and decorated chancel *screen.* Twenty-five of the *figures* on the loft are c.1880, the rest are original. Note the *churchwarden's box pew* of 1681.

LLANBADARN-Y-GARREG. 5m SE of Builth Wells off B4567. *St Padarn.*

A tiny white painted C13 or C14 church with wooden C18 windows, restored in 1960. The white painted interior has a C15 roof and a simple rood beam with fragments of a Royal Arms painted on it. Pulpit and altar rails are C17.

LLANDYSILIO. 8m N of Welshpool on A483. *St Tysilio.*

Built in 1867-8 in rough stone by G.E. Street and one of his best

Llangasty Talyllyn, St Gastayn. Exterior, wholly rebuilt in 1848-50.

parish churches, it consists of a nave, north aisle, and chancel, with a quaint, slim, circular north-west tower with conical cap. The interior has good fittings, including the east window by Clayton & Bell designed by Street, and a rich south window of 1879 by J. Powell & Sons.

LLANELIEU. 10m NE of Brecon off A479. *St Ellyw.*

A remote, small, charming C13 church and mainly unrestored. The deep *screen* accommodates a large loft big enough for a room with, at the back, a C14 *tympanum*, and remains of the original overall painted decoration of white roses on a red ground.

LLANGASTY TALYLLYN. 13m NW of Abergavenny off A40. *St Gastayn.*

Built to strict Tractarian principles by J.L. Pearson in 1848-50 in C13 Gothic style, and one of his first churches. The austere exterior gives no hint of the incense burners, symbols, painted texts and water stoups of the colourful interior.

LLANSTEPHAN. 7m S of Builth Wells off A470. *St Stephen.*

A church with a C13 nave, a C14 chancel, and a C14 west tower, rebuilt in the C16, with a stable for the parson's horse. Restored in 1867-8 when the nave was reroofed and the chancel arch rebuilt; the chancel waggon-roof is C17.

SUGGESTIONS
FOR FURTHER READING

Blue Guide, Churches and Chapels in Southern England edited by Stephen C. Humphrey; A. & C. Black, 1991.

Blue Guide, Churches and Chapels in Northern England edited by Stephen C. Humphrey; A. & C. Black, 1991.

Church Furnishings: a NADFAS Guide by Patricia Dirsztay; Routledge & Kegan Paul, 1978.

Churches in Retirement; A Gazetteer, Redundant Churches Fund, HMSO.

John Betjeman's Guide to English Parish Churches edited by John Betjeman, revised and updated by Nigel Kerr; HarperCollins, 1993.

English Parish Churches by Edwin Smith & Olive Cook; Thames & Hudson, 1989.

Medieval Wall Paintings by Clive Rouse; Shire Publications Ltd, 1991.

Our Christian Heritage by W. Rodwell & J. Bentley; Guild Publishing, 1984.

Parish Churches by Hugh Braun; Faber & Faber, 1974.

The Architecture of Scottish Post-Reformation Churches by George Hay; OUP, 1957.

The Buildings of England originally by Nikolaus Pevsner and subsequently revised by others. A county by county series covers England in about 50 volumes published by Penguin. This is now supplemented by five volumes of *The Buildings of Scotland* and two of *The Buildings of Wales*.

The Ecclesiastical Architecture of Scotland in three volumes by David MacGibbon & Thomas Ross; David Douglas, Edinburgh, 1897.

The Faber Guide to Victorian Churches edited by Peter Howell & Ian Sutton in conjunction with The Victorian Society; Faber & Faber, 1989.

ORGANISATIONS CONCERNED WITH THE CARE OF CHURCHES

Alexander Thompson Society, 1 Moray Place, Strathbungo, Glasgow G41 2AQ.

English Heritage, Fortress House, Saville Row, London W1X 1AB.

Friends of Friendless Churches, 89 Fleet St, London EC4Y 1DH.

The Georgian Group, 37 Spital Square, London E1 6DY

Historic Buildings & Monuments of Scotland, PO Box 157, Edinburgh EH3 7QD.

The Historic Chapels Fund, 4 Cromwell Place, London SW7 2JJ.

Historic Scotland, 20 Brandon Street, Edinburgh, EH3 5RA.

Heritage in Wales, Brunel House, 2 Fitzalan Road, Cardiff CF2 1UY.

The Redundant Churches Fund, 89 Fleet St, London EC4Y 1DH.

The Society for the Protection of Ancient Buildings (SPAB), 37 Spital Square, London W1R 6AB.

The Victorian Society of Great Britain, 1 Priory Gardens, Bedford Park, London W4 1TT.

GLOSSARY

AISLE: (a) A passage on the north or south sides of a nave, choir or transept separated by columns. (b) In Scotland, the projecting wing of a church reserved for special use by a guild, or a family whose burial vault is beneath.

ALTAR: A raised consecrated slab. After the Reformation this was replaced by the communion table, which is still the case in many Scottish churches. The consecration slab was later re-instated by the Tractarians (see Introduction).

AMBULATORY: Polygonal or semicircular aisle enclosing an apse; originally used for processions.

APSE: Polygonal or semicircular vaulted termination, usually in a chancel or side chapel

ARCADE: A row of columns carrying arches.

ASHLAR: Rectangular, smooth-faced masonry.

AUMBRY: Cupboard or recess to hold sacred vessels for Communion and Mass.

BALDICCHINO: Canopy supported on columns.

BARREL-VAULT: See WAGGON-ROOF.

BEAKHEAD: Norman ornament consisting of mythical birds' and beasts' heads with long pointed beaks. Believed to represent Norman masks.

BENEFACTION BOARD: Boards listing names of charitable benefactors.

BOSSES: Nobs or projections, often carved, positioned over the intersections of rib in a vault to cover the joint.

BOX PEW: An enclosed pew usually with a door, to keep dogs in or out, usually large enough for one family.

BUTTRESS: Projecting brickwork or masonry giving support to a wall.

CAPITAL: Head of a column.

CARTOUCHE: A tablet with an ornate frame usually containing a coat of arms or inscription

CHANCEL: The east end of a church containing the altar.

CHANCEL ARCH: Arch at the east end of the chancel.

CHEVRON: Norman zigzag decoration.

CHOIR: Usually in the chancel where divine service is sung.

CLERESTORY: The upper storey of a nave pierced by windows.

COMMANDMENT BOARD: A board painted with the ten Commandments (often called a Decalogue), and hung in a church. These became a regular feature of church furnishing from the mid-C16.

CONSECRATION CROSS: Crosses cut into the wall of a church marking the places, usually twelve, annointed by the bishop at the time of consecration

CORBEL: A stone bracket projecting from a wall used for supporting a beam.

CRYPT: An underfloor space usually below the chancel.

DALMATIC: A loose, wide-sleeved, long vestment with side slits worn by bishops and deacons, and by emperors and kings at coronations.

DECORATED: Historical division of Gothic architecture from 1300 to 1350.

DRESSINGS: Smooth stones framing doors, windows, the quoins at the corners and stringcourses.

EARLY ENGLISH: Historical division of Gothic architecture from the late-C12 to late-C13.

EASTER SEPULCHRE: A recess with a tomb chest, usually in the chancel wall, to receive the Sacrament from Good Friday to Easter Day.

GOTHIC: The term applied to Western architecture from the C12 to the early-C16. The term 'Gothic Revival' is given to buildings in the Gothic style built from the C18, but in fact Gothic was never dead and was always used.

HAMMER-BEAM ROOF: A medieval type of timber roof supported by two side brackets above each other which avoid the use of a horizontal tie-beam reaching across from wall to wall. They are often highly decorated and carved.

HATCHMENT: A diamond-shaped board painted with a coat of arms. They were carried in funeral processions at the burial of the arms holder, then hung on the house of the deceased before being transferred to the church.

IMPERIAL STAIRCASE: A stair which begins as one flight before splitting to left and right into two returning flights.

KING-POST: An upright timber post resting on the tie-beam of a roof truss and supporting the ridge. See also QUEEN-POST.

LADY CHAPEL: A chapel dedicated to the Virgin Mary.

LECTERN: The reading stand from which the Bible is read in Lessons.

LIERNE-VAULT. Vaulting with a tertiary rib which springs neither from the boss nor any of the main springers.

LINTEL: Horizontal beam over an opening.

LOFT: (a) *Rood loft*: narrow gallery supported by the rood screen. (b) *Organ loft:* holds the organ or only the consol. (c) In Scotland, the reserved gallery in a church for a guild, trade, or family, e.g. guild loft, trade loft.

NAVE: The body of a church from the west door to the chancel, usually separated by columns from the side aisles.

MAIDENS' GARLANDS: Garlands carried at the funeral of a virgin and afterwards hung in the church.

MULLION: Vertical upright of wood or stone in a window.

PALIMPSEST: A re-used monumental brass. They are usually turned over and re-engraved on the reversed side.

PARVISE. In Britain a room over the church porch. The word is borrowed (and wrongly interpreted) from the French term for the open space in front of cathedrals and churches.

PEDIMENT: A Classical, low-pitched, gable.

PERPENDICULAR: Historical division of Gothic architecture from 1350 to 1525.

PISCINA: A basin for washing mass, or communion, vessels, usually set in the south wall of the chancel near the altar.

PRAYER-BOOK INTERIOR. A church interior unaffected by the C19 Tractarians. The emphasis is on the pulpit rather than the altar.

PRESBYTERY: The east end of a church, and the area east of the choir including the altar.

PULPITUM. A stone screen dividing the choir from the nave in larger churches.

PURLIN: A horizontal timber placed longitudinally some way up the roof slope and supported by a roof truss or queen-post.

QUEEN-POST: Upright posts resting on the tie-beam of a roof truss and supporting purlins. Their purpose is to prevent the roof sagging. See also KING-POST.

QUOINS: Dressed stones on the angles of buildings.

REREDOS: The wall or screen behind an altar, often covered with painted carving and statuary.

ROMANESQUE: The style of architecture of the C7 to C12 including Anglo-Saxon and Norman.

ROOD: The Cross of Christ, usually over a *rood screen* at the entrance to a chancel. The screen may have a *rood loft* accessed by a *rood stair*. A *rood beam* is a cross beam supporting the top of the screen and the loft.

ROWEL LIGHT: A lamp hoisted to the rood during Easter services.

SANCTUARY: The most easterly and sacred part of a chancel

SEDILIA: Usually three, but sometimes only two, seats in the south wall of the chancel for officiating priests

SOUNDING BOARD: Also CANOPY: A structure over a pulpit to deflect the sound forward.

SQUINT: Sometimes called hagiograph. A hole cut through a wall or pier to allow sight of the main altar of a church which otherwise would be invisible.

STALLS: Elaborate seats for the choir in the chancel, often with misericords and canopies. Usually found in collegiate churches.

STIFF-LEAF: Early English carved decoration of many-lobed leaves.

STRAPWORK: Late-C15 and early-C16 decoration of interwoven bands resembling straps but, in fact, taken from embroidery designs

STRING COURSE: Intermediate, horizontal, stone course projecting from the surface of a wall.

THREE-DECKER PULPIT: A pulpit with a clerk's stall and reader's desk arranged in descending order.

TIE-BEAM: The cross-beam of a timber roof reaching from wall to wall and tied by its ends to the wall-plates.

TOMB-CHEST: Chest-shaped stone raised above a burial.

TRACERY: Ornamental stonework in the upper part of a window, also used in rood screens and tombs.

TRANSEPT: Transverse arm in a cruciform church.

TRIFORIUM: An arcade above the arches of the nave and below the clerestory.

TUNNEL VAULT: See WAGGON-ROOF.

TYMPANUM: The space above a doorway between the lintel and the arch.

WAGGON-ROOF: A semi-cylindrical roof or vault.

WATER-LEAF: A carved leaf-shape used on late-C12 capitals.